☐ ☐ ☐ ☐ ☐

Communication Assessment and Intervention for Adults with Mental Retardation

Advisory Editor:

Michael Bender, Ed.D.
Vice President of Educational Programs
The Kennedy Institute
Professor of Education
The Johns Hopkins University
Joint Appointment, Department of Pediatrics
The Johns Hopkins School of Medicine
Baltimore, Maryland

Communication Assessment and Intervention for Adults with Mental Retardation

Edited by

Stephen N. Calculator, Ph.D.
Department of Communication Disorders
University of New Hampshire
Durham, New Hamphshire

Jan L. Bedrosian, Ph.D.
The Speech Pathology and Audiology Program
Department of Speech
Kansas State University
Manhattan, Kansas

pro·ed

8700 Shoal Creek Boulevard
Austin, Texas 78758

Printed in the United States of America

Library of Congress Cataloging-in-Publication Data

Communication assessment and intervention for adults with mental
  retardation / edited by Stephen N. Calculator, Jan L. Bedrosian.
        p.   cm.
    Reprint. Originally published: Boston : Little, Brown, c1988.
    Includes bibliographical references.
    Includes indexes.
    ISBN 0-89079-374-3
    1. Mentally handicapped — Language.   2. Communicative disorders.
    I. Calculator, Stephen N., 1952–   . II. Bedrosian, Jan L., 1952–   .
    [DNLM: 1. Communicative Disorders — in adulthood.   2. Language
Disorders — in adulthood.   3. Mental Retardation — in adulthood.   WM
307.C6 C7335 1988a]
RC570.2.C66   1991
616.85'5 — dc20
DNLM/DLC
for Library of Congress   90-9212
                                                                      CIP

pro·ed

8700 Shoal Creek Boulevard
Austin, Texas 78758

1 2 3 4 5 6 7 8 9 10   95 94 93 92 91

To Our Families for Their
Love and Support

Jeanne, B.J., Lauren, Trevor, and Kaitlin
Steve and Michael

CONTENTS

Without doubt the most pervasive problem confronting the person with mental retardation lies in the area of communication. The extent of the communication problem itself, the many ramifications which derive from it, and strategies for dealing with the problem are described in this book. In contrast to the plethora of other books which have addressed the multiple communication problems of persons who are mentally retarded, this book is special in that it focuses on the adult.

For too many years the communication differences and disorders of adults with mental retardation have been misunderstood. This misunderstanding has been due to a variety of factors. A major one relates to a relatively widespread attitude among professionals about whether adults with mental retardation can learn or improve their communication skills.

Providing communication services to adults with mental retardation has not been a widely accepted practice among speech and language pathologists in particular, and is still not one which receives much time or attention in college and university clinical personnel preparation programs. Those speech and language pathologists who do provide services frequently find themselves needing to convince administrators that benefits will be forthcoming for the efforts invested. Physicians are skeptical, relative to the benefits of speech and language services; and, thus, getting support for third party reimbursement remains a struggle. Efficacy studies on intervention procedures and service delivery models are, therefore, extremely important to modify and change these attitudes and practices.

Changing a belief and practice requires one to be challenged and to erase old tapes. I remember the first time I was challenged with the notion that "all persons, regardless of age, are capable of learning and improving their communication skills." I was not ready to agree with this notion. Nor was I able to juxtapose "critical periods of learning in young children" against individuals who were long past those early years, let alone evaluate the concept. I had put into my belief system a notion that adults who were mentally retarded were not capable of learning and improving their speech, language and/or communication skills.

This book will help skeptics put aside past negative attitudes. The information provided in *Communication Assessment and Intervention for Adults with Mental Retardation* is bound to impact on the philosophy of communication services; models of service delivery; personnel preparation programs; and policy formulation and funding support. The challenges and questions raised by chapter authors will also provoke new issues to be handled in research. In addition, the interdisciplinary representation of the authors of this book highlights the issue that changing communication behaviors of adults with mental retardation is larger than any single discipline, and is best done in a team effort within a least restrictive environment.

The challenge that is present for all of us relating to adults with mental retardation is that we must provide them with "functional communication," defined, by an interdisciplinary group of persons at the 1985 OSEP/TADS Symposium in Washington, DC, as:

1. the ability to communicate for a variety of purposes relevant to the individual's life experience
2. the ability to use a variety of means (e.g., verbal and/or nonverbal) to accomplish these purposes effectively
3. the ability to initiate and maintain social interactions as a critical dimension of communication

This definition reflects a strong representation of the pragmatic/function dimension of language and, as such, departs from past perspectives primarily focusing on the linguistic/form dimension of language. Overall, the emphasis is on communication goals as opposed to language goals. The definition's specific reference to various modes of communication, however, indicates that the form component of communication is not completely ignored. Rather, it insists that both the *form* and *function* dimensions of language be well represented in the intervention goals set forth for those adults with communication handicaps associated with mental retardation.

The challenge is to provide functional communication to all persons of the human race regardless of level of cognitive, sensory or physical ability. It is a complex one. There is, however, a healthy evidence in this book that the challenge can be met. We are moving toward a better understanding of the problem of how to provide functional communication and thus can deal better with solutions. Lest we become secure in the solutions we have found thus far, may we keep in mind Robert Frost's admonition, ". . . . the woods are lovely dark and deep, but we've got promises to keep and miles to go before we sleep, and miles to go before we sleep."

David E. Yoder, Ph.D.
Professor & Chair
Department of Medical Allied Health Professions
University of North Carolina at Chapel Hill

☐ ACKNOWLEDGMENTS

We would like to express our sincere appreciation to the following people who helped to make this book an exciting learning experience.

- ☐ To the contributing authors for their time, energy, and enthusiasm
- ☐ To Dolores K. Vetter and David E. Yoder for their continued inspiration and friendship
- ☐ To Gail Nadeau, Rose Bradder, and Ingrid Stephan for their keen clinical insight and encouragement
- ☐ To Harold J. Nichols for his support and encouragement
- ☐ To Marie Linvill for her assistance in the preparation of the manuscript
- ☐ To Elisa Machado and Sharon Rockwell for their library research assistance
- ☐ To Maria Russell, Deb Volesky, Ann Pollock, Monique Scroggins, and Starla Wulf for their secretarial support
- ☐ To Steve Pifer for designing the book cover
- ☐ To those adults who brought us to our current understanding of, and respect for, the population addressed in this book.

☐ CONTRIBUTORS

Kathy Zanella Albright, Ph.D.
Department of Rehabilitation
Psychology and Special
Education, University of
Wisconsin, Madison, Wisconsin

Richard F. Antonak, Ed.D.
Department of Education,
University of New Hampshire,
Durham, New Hampshire

Kathryn B. Bishop, M.A.
School of Education, Division
of Special Education, California
State University, Los Angeles,
California

Lou Brown, Ph.D.
Department of Rehabilitation
Psychology and Special
Education, University of
Wisconsin, Madison, Wisconsin

Jennifer Coots, M.A.
Pasadena Unified School
District, Pasadena, California

Scott Doss, M.A.
Consortium Institute for the
Education of Severely
Handicapped Learners,
University of Minnesota,
Minneapolis, Minnesota

Mary A. Falvey, Ph.D.
School of Education, Division of
Special Education, California State
University, Los Angeles, California

Marquita Grenot-Scheyer, M.A.
School of Education, Division
of Special Education, California
State University, Los Angeles,
California

James Halle, Ph.D.
Department of Special
Education, University of Illinois
at Urbana — Champaign,
Champaign, Illinois

Janell I. Haney, M.A.
Department of Special
Education, University of Illinois
at Urbana — Champaign,
Champaign, Illinois

Ruth Loomis, M.A.
Madison Metropolitan School
District, Madison, Wisconsin

Eileen McCarthy, Ph.D.
Department of Rehabilitation
Psychology and Special
Education, University of
Wisconsin, Madison, Wisconsin

John L. Morse, Ed.D.
Strafford Learning Center,
Somersworth, New Hampshire

Robert E. Owens, Jr., Ph.D.
Department of Speech
Pathology and Audiology, State
University of New York at
Geneseo, Geneseo, New York

Laura Piché-Cragoe, M.A.
Consortium Institute for the
Education of Severely
Handicapped Learners,
University of Minnesota,
Minneapolis, Minnesota

Joe Reichle, Ph.D.
Consortium Institute for the
Education of Severely
Handicapped Learners,
University of Minnesota,
Minneapolis, Minnesota

Patty Rogan, Ph.D.
Department of Rehabilitation
Psychology and Special
Education, University of
Wisconsin, Madison, Wisconsin

Brenda S. Rogerson, M.A.
People Incorporated, Buffalo,
New York

Betsy Shiraga, M.A.
Department of Rehabilitation
Psychology and Special
Education, University of
Wisconsin, Madison, Wisconsin

Jeff Sigafoos, M.A.
Consortium Institute for the
Education of Severely
Handicapped Learners,
University of Minnesota,
Minneapolis, Minnesota

Pat VanDeventer, M.S.
Madison Metropolitan School
District, Madison, Wisconsin

Julio W. Wilson, M.A.
Department of Special
Education, University of Illinois
at Urbana —Champaign,
Champaign, Illinois

David E. Yoder, Ph.D.
Medical Allied Health
Professions, University of North
Carolina, Chapel Hill, North
Carolina

Jennifer York, Ph.D.
Capital View Middle School,
Little Canada, Minnesota

A Misunderstood Population

JAN L. BEDROSIAN
STEPHEN N. CALCULATOR

Adults with mental retardation have traditionally been a misunderstood population in terms of their language and communication needs. Although a great deal of language research conducted in the 1960s and early 1970s focused on communication programming issues and strategies for individuals who are mentally retarded (e.g., Bricker & Bricker, 1974; Graham, 1976; Lackner, 1968; Miller & Yoder, 1974), this research was directed primarily toward children rather than adults. Unfortunately, many practitioners applied these programs to the adult population indiscriminately, and in doing so, routinely ignored the age, social experience, and unique communicative needs of the adult. The results of these earlier attempts were so frustrating to many of us working with these adults in the mid to late 1970s that a concerted effort was made to at least begin to describe the communication skills unique to this population (e.g., Bedrosian & Prutting, 1978; Sabsay, 1975).

Descriptive information about the communication skills of adults with mental retardartion having been provided, there is now a need to focus attempts on meeting the communicative needs of this growing population. Shifts toward community living and employment must be accompanied by efforts to design programs that facilitate the communication skills necessary for these adults to function optimally in these settings. Although clinical researchers have recently begun to design such programs, information about these programs has not been disseminated in such a way as to be generally useful to the practicing communication specialist.

In the discussions that the editors have had during the past 7 years, and in conversations with other colleagues, the idea of compiling a comprehensive review of relevant history, issues, and specific data-supported communicative assessment and intervention strategies for adults with mental retardation was generated. This book represents the materialization of that idea.

The purpose of this book, therefore, is to provide a well-integrated discussion of communication-related information specific to the population of adults with mental retardation. Experts from a variety of disciplines, including speech–language pathology, psychology, special education, vocational rehabilitation, and developmental disabilities, are brought together to present information related to communication instruction for both speaking and nonspeaking adults with varying cognitive abilities.

INTENDED AUDIENCE

This book will provide practitioners (e.g., speech–language pathologists, vocational counselors, teachers, psychologists, case managers) with specific suggestions for meeting the communication needs of their adult clients. Students will also find this book useful in courses dealing with the communication problems of populations with special needs (e.g., mental retardation, autism, emotional disturbances). Finally, the literature reviews and state-of-the-art techniques presented should be of interest to those conducting research about mental retardation in adults.

COMMON THEMES

Two common themes are prevalent throughout this book. First, as a result of their longer social histories (i.e., number of years lived), it is generally agreed that adults with mental retardation are *not* the same as children with mental retardation. This fact alone suggests the need for a different approach to language and communication assessment and intervention, taking into consideration the notion of age-appropriateness and other corollaries of normalization.

The second common theme involves the emphasis on teaching functional communication skills — those skills that are useful to individuals in maximizing their independence in a variety of social contexts. This emphasis requires the educator to focus more on the actual uses of language and less on the form (e.g., sentence structure, sound production) of language. It also requires the incorporation of various participants (e.g., peers, siblings, work supervisors) and settings other than the traditional clinical setting, and the teaching of communicative initiations as opposed to teaching only responses.

PHILOSOPHIC DIFFERENCES

Although common themes are presented, this book also reflects the philosophic differences among the contributors. One such difference involves the extent to which a normal developmental model is applicable in guiding the selection of content and the sequence of goals to be taught in a communication program. Authors also vary in their reliance on cognitive correlates or prerequisites to communication skill instruction, as well as in the degree of structure necessary for teaching communication skills. Together, these differing philosophies provide the reader with a more eclectic understanding of the field.

SUMMARY OF CONTENTS

The chapters that follow are organized according to five major parts. First, an overview of the field of mental retardation is provided. In Chapter 1, Antonak presents a historical account of the field from 500 B.C. to 1970 A.D. In reviewing the philosophies, attitudes, and social practices that pervaded the service delivery system for the mentally retarded during this time period, readers begin to see the roots of present practices directed toward this population.

In Chapter 2, by Falvey, Bishop, Grenot-Scheyer, and Coots, issues and trends in the field of mental retardation are reviewed with specific reference to the adult population. The authors focus on how litigation and legislation have influenced educational, vocational, and residential options for these individuals. The chapter concludes with a discussion of normalization as it relates to communication instruction.

In Part II, characteristics of adults with mental retardation are presented. The primary description and demographic characteristics of the population are provided by Haney, Wilson, and Halle in Chapter 3. Both residential and vocational alternatives are presented, along with corresponding descriptive statistical information. The authors also discuss a variety of issues (e.g., remedial logic, social validation) related to communication expectations and instruction of the population within these settings.

In Chapter 4, Calculator provides the framework for viewing the communicative performance of these adults, along with implications for programming, both of which are expanded on in subsequent chapters. First, cognitive and noncognitive factors influencing the communicative performance of this population are discussed. Communication assessment is then addressed in terms of focusing on functional skills relevant to a variety of communication situations. The problems associated with traditional assessment approaches using language tests standardized on normal language-learning children to describe the communicative performance of adults with mental retardation are highlighted. Finally, Calculator explores trends in communicative intervention for this population.

Part III highlights program considerations related to communication assessment and intervention. Morse, in Chapter 5, outlines various factors obstructing the attainment of valid assessment results. Specific suggestions for modifying standardized test procedures are offered along with a case study illustrating these revisions.

In Chapter 6, Brown and his colleagues outline several dimensions to be considered a priori in the selection of vocational and communication skills for instruction, including the number of environments to which the adult is exposed, functionality, chronological age appropriateness, practice opportunities, requirements in adulthood, individual and parent and guardian preferences, acquisition probability, and enhancement (i.e., physical, social contact, and status).

The rationale for using the natural environment as the primary setting for communication assessment and intervention is presented in Chapter 7 by Halle. Procedures for assessing the communicative repertoire of the adult with mental retardation, aspects of the environment, and communicative requirements in current and future settings are discussed. Several environmental intervention procedures are outlined, concluding with a detailed description of methods by which spontaneous communication can be facilitated.

In Part IV, communication assessment and intervention strategies that are appropriate for adults with varying cognitive abilities are presented. Owens and Rogerson, in Chapter 8, review major issues and strategies associated with communication programming for adults functioning at presymbolic levels. These issues include discussions about the promotion of generalization and the selection of initial intervention goals (i.e., prerequisite skill training versus symbolic communication training). Procedures for assessing the communication skills of presymbolic adults are described, along with considerations of client, context-related, and interactional variables. The authors provide detailed information about their integrated intervention model, focusing on the client–caregiver interaction in the natural environment. Finally, several variables to consider when dismissing such individuals from an intervention program are discussed.

Communication programming issues and strategies related to early symbol usage are discussed in Chapter 9 by Reichle, Piché-Cragoe, Sigafoos, and Doss. The authors outline procedures for optimizing functional communication skills via a variety of communicative modalities (e.g., gesture, communication board, sign). The consideration of cognitive versus noncognitive factors in selecting candidates for intervention in early symbol usage is discussed. Data-based programming suggestions for selecting initial communicative intents as well as the communication mode(s) of these intents are provided. Emphasis is placed on ensuring valid and socially acceptable use of established communicative behaviors in a variety of natural contexts.

Communication-related information pertaining to adults who are mildly to moderately mentally retarded is discussed by Bedrosian in Chapter 10. A review of the literature regarding their communicative strengths and weaknesses is presented in relation to a variety of discourse skills (i.e., communication functions, topic, repair, turn-taking, control, narratives). Data-based procedures for assessing and facilitating discourse skills are provided. A case study is presented that demonstrates the effectiveness of the intervention procedures described.

In Chapter 11, Calculator addresses specific programming issues related to nonspeaking adults who are mentally retarded. The primary emphasis of this chapter involves the role of augmentative communication instruction with these individuals and their listeners. First, Calculator discusses several factors to consider before initiating augmentative training. Procedures for selecting communication modes as well as conducting a needs assessment are presented. Seven training variables influencing the likelihood of augmentative communication programming success with the population are outlined. The focus of this chapter, as well as that of others in this book, is on teaching functional communication skills.

The final chapter in Part V summarizes relevant communication issues addressed throughout the book. Future directions in communication programming and research related to adults with mental retardation are suggested. It is our hope that this book will initiate new levels of interest in and attention to the unique communicative needs of this population.

REFERENCES

Bedrosian, J. L., & Prutting, C. A. (1978). Communicative performance of mentally retarded adults in four conversational settings. *Journal of Speech and Hearing Research, 21,* 79–95.

Bricker, W., & Bricker, D. (1974). An early language training strategy. In R. Schiefelbusch & L. Lloyd (Eds.), *Language perspectives: Acquisition, retardation and intervention* (pp. 431–468). Austin, TX: PRO-ED.

Graham, L. (1976). Language programming and intervention. In L. Lloyd (Ed.), *Communication assessment and intervention strategies* (pp. 371–422). Baltimore, MD: University Park Press.

Lackner, J. (1968). A developmental study of language behavior in retarded children. *Neuropsychologia, 6,* 301–320.

Miller, J. F., & Yoder, D. E. (1974). An ontogenetic language teaching strategy for retarded children. In R. Schiefelbusch & L. Lloyd (Eds.), *Language perspectives: Acquisition, retardation and intervention* (pp. 505–528). Austin, TX: PRO-ED.

Sabsay, S. (1975, December). *Communicative competence among the severely retarded: Some evidence from the conversational interaction of Down's Syndrome (Mongoloid) adults.* Paper presented at the Meeting of the Linguistic Society of America, San Francisco, CA.

PART I

Overview of Mental Retardation

CHAPTER 1

A History of the Provision of Services to People Who Are Mentally Retarded

RICHARD F. ANTONAK

ontemporary services for people who are mentally retarded — and, in general, people who are disabled by any mental, physical, or emotional impairment — are affected by several factors. These include the changing attitudes and values of a society and the society's dominant views of (1) the cause of disability, (2) the nature of disability, and (3) the value associated with the contribution (actual or potential) of the person with a disability. These three views are inextricably linked, and are the outcomes of the dynamic interplay of the social and economic forces, philosophy, and scientific knowledge available to a society (Begab, 1975).

As you will discover in Chapter 2, the most widely accepted contemporary philosophy of disability services is the normalization (social role valorization) philosophy, associated in the United States with the writing of Wolf Wolfensberger (1972). Briefly, *normalization* means making available to people who are disabled patterns and conditions of life that are as close as possible to the patterns and conditions of the lives of people who are not disabled. A number of corollary philosophies have been explicated by scholars, and practices have evolved from the implementation of normalization. Among these philosophies are the following:

☐ People who are disabled are entitled to live in ordinary homes in ordinary communities, to be educated in schools that least restrict their integration with their peers who are not disabled, to work and be economically self-sufficient, and to participate fully in the ordinary social life of the community (Antonak & Mulick, 1987).

☐ All people who are disabled, regardless of the degree of their disability, have the potential to grow, learn, and develop in a predictable sequence; the services that are provided to attain this potential must be individually prescribed and based on a complete, yet humane, assessment of the person's interests and life goals; and, programs and services must change during the person's lifetime as interests and goals change (Flynn & Nitsch, 1980; Lakin & Bruininks, 1985).

☐ Services must be based on a proactive model in which knowledge about a person's past experiences with his or her disability and present situation is used holistically to achieve a future marked by independence, integration, and personal fulfillment (Bernstein, Ziarnik, Rudrud, & Czajkowski, 1981).

☐ People who are disabled are entitled to all the legal and human rights afforded to all citizens, including the rights to vote, own property, marry, procreate, and raise their children (Eisenberg, Griggins, & Duval, 1982).

☐ The services a society provides for people who are disabled must include prenatal prevention, early intervention, education and habilitation, preparation for an adult life of social and economic competence, and programs for the aged disabled (Bruininks & Lakin, 1985).

☐ Society needs a chance to know people who are disabled in everyday life situations, and, in this way, will come to appreciate and respect their uniqueness (Edgerton, 1984).

These philosophies will emerge throughout the remaining chapters of this book. The purpose of this chapter is to present a basis for understanding contemporary normalization philosophy and the related practices by reviewing the philosophies and practices of yesteryear, and the attitudes, values, and discoveries that led to them. This history covers the years from 500 B.C. to 1970 A.D., divided into eight periods. Particular emphasis is placed on the periods covering the years from 1880 to 1925.

Kanner (1964) provided the first of the recent attempts to write "a comprehensive account of developments regarding the care and study of the mentally retarded . . . with the hope that the fascination, the thrill, and the reward will be shared by the readers" (p. vii). Scheerenberger (1983), in the most complete history written to date:

> intended simply to inform, that is to lay before the reader some of the major events and personages that have influenced the development of programs and services for mentally retarded persons. While trends and general social conditions are set forth, there has been no attempt either to prescribe individual motivations or to

render sweeping generalizations concerning society as a whole. (p. xiii)

Lazerson (1975) argued that the histories of mental retardation written up until that time (and I would include Scheerenberger's history as well) were little more than "unfinished morality plays" in which the treatment of people who are mentally retarded is chronicled to show that "it is better today than yesterday" in order to prove that "reforms today will make tomorrow even better" (p. 34). This type of history may fascinate and inspire us, yet it also communicates a sense of the inevitability of past events, as if the leaders of the past had no alternative courses of action available to them. "Historians of mental subnormality make it easy to praise or condemn but difficult to sort out why events occurred" (p. 35).

Lazerson presented his history of the emergence of residential institutions and the establishment of special classes for the mentally retarded as an attempt to rethink the conventional wisdom. This history is presented as my attempt to continue this rethinking.

ERA OF EXTERMINATION (500 B.C.–500 A.D.)

Although the treatment of people who are mentally retarded from prehistory through the time of the Roman civilization is marked by wide variability (Scheerenberger, 1983), it is generally agreed that the prevailing attitude was one that condoned, if not encouraged, the extermination of people who were mentally or physically defective. Plato and Aristotle argued for prevention of the union in marriage of inferior citizens, and for the death of deformed children. The Laws of Lycurgus called for the deliberate abandonment of idiots and fools, and as a result such persons were thrown off mountains, drowned in rivers, or left to the elements to die.

Both the Athenian and Spartan city–states dealt severely with defectives to purify their societies. In Rome, defectives were often kept as fools for amusement at festivals. Newborns of poor families were occasionally purposefully mutilated to increase their value as beggars. In general, defectives were considered nonhuman, incapable of normal feelings, and undeserving of human compassion. Extermination of defectives, to the Greeks and Romans, was not an unreasonable proposal when the value structure of those societies was considered.

The voices of Hippocrates in the fourth century B.C. and Galens in the second century A.D., both of whom would influence medical thinking and practice for centuries, were raised in favor of more humane treatment based on principles of objective study and measurement

(Kanner, 1964). However, it was the rise of the major religions of the world that provided the first real hope for people who were mentally and physically disabled.

ERA OF SUPERSTITION (500 A.D.–1800 A.D.)

The "gentle voices," as Scheerenberger (1983) calls them, of Buddha, Mohammed, Confucius, and Jesus, all taught that humanity was sacred, that generosity and mercy toward the unfortunate contributes to one's salvation, and that both the mentally and physically disabled were innocents and deserving of the compassion and protection of society. It was many centuries, however, before these teachings would provide the foundation for humane treatment of the disabled.

Beginning in the 13th century, the churches of Europe provided places of refuge for abandoned infants and for homeless, ill, and helpless adults. However, these asylums were not designed for treatment or education, but rather to provide a temporary sanctuary and separation from society.

The Protestant Reformation brought with it another view of the mentally ill and the mentally retarded. People of both groups were believed to be impure, without a soul, possessed by evil, and filled with Satan. The strange behavior of some individuals (e.g., epileptic convulsions or the writhing movements common in some forms of cerebral palsy) was interpreted with religious overtones as evidence of possession. As a result, many people with disabilities were tormented and tortured in an attempt to exorcise the demons within them. The victims of the Inquisition in Spain, the lynchings of witches in Medieval Europe, and the stonings in the new American colonies included many people who were mentally and physically disabled.

Less severe (although no more enlightened) treatment included the use of people who were mentally retarded as fools, jesters, clowns, and, in some cases, prophets and seers. The babblings of idiots, the acrobatics of dwarfs, and the antics of hunchbacks and pinheads were welcome additions to courtly banquets and village festivals from the Middle Ages through the Renaissance.

It is possible to point to individual contributions to the care and treatment of people with disabilities before the start of the 19th century, such as Juan Pablo in Spain; Vincent de Paul, Valentin Hauy, and Jacob Pereire in France; and Felix Platter in Switzerland. However, in general, medieval superstition and ancient sorcery would not be replaced until the end of the 18th century, with the gradual acceptance of the philosophies of René Descartes, John Locke, and Jean Jacques Rousseau.

These scholars espoused rational thought in place of dogma, objective evidence in place of faith, and the experimental method in place of the appeal to authority.

CURE THROUGH EDUCATION (1800–1850)

Philipe Pinel

Perhaps the first treatment-oriented approach to mental retardation was the work of Philipe Pinel (1745-1826), director of the Bicêtre and Salpé-trière, mental institutions for men and women, respectively, in Paris (Scheerenberger, 1983). His organization of these institutions and his books on classification and treatment of mental diseases represented a huge improvement over the prevailing practices. Nevertheless, Pinel, an adherent of the nativist (or alienist) philosophy, was convinced of the permanence of idiocy and its irreversibility through education.

Jean Esquirol

Among Pinel's students were two whose views ran counter to their teacher's. Jean Étienne Dominique Esquirol (1772-1840), in his medical text on the treatment of disorders published in 1838, proposed a system of classification in which mental retardation was divided into two levels. Idiots were incapable of being educated and remained throughout their lives in a state of intellectual incapacity. Imbeciles, on the other hand, were able to use their limited intellectual faculties for relatively simple tasks, and these faculties could be improved through training. Esquirol also distinguished between those people who were disabled from birth or an early age (*amentia*) and those who lost their mental faculties in adulthood (*dementia*) — a rough distinction between mental retardation and mental illness.

Jean Itard

Pinel's other gifted student is more widely known, and is considered the father of special education for the mentally retarded (Kanner, 1964). Jean Marc Gaspard Itard (1774–1838) began his medical career at the Institution for Deaf–Mutes in Paris, where he became convinced of the sensationalist philosophy, that is, that man is the product of environmental experiences and not of a predetermined hereditary endowment. An opportunity to verify this theory presented itself when a 12-year-old boy was brought to the institution by the Abbé Bonnaterre from Aveyron,

France. Victor, as he was called, or the "Wild Boy of Aveyron" as he would later be known, was diagnosed by Pinel as an incurable idiot, devoid of redeeming human qualities and impervious to normal sensation, with no language and peculiar motor characteristics. From 1799 to 1804, Itard arranged for a comprehensive five-part training program for Victor under the supervision of Madame Guerin, Itard's housekeeper (Itard, 1962).

The first component, and the one with which Itard had the most success, was to awaken Victor's nervous sensibilities through a program of sense training. Itard considered this to be a prerequisite to speech and cognition. The second component was to interest Victor in a normal social life through pleasurable experiences, such as rides in the country. The third component was to extend the range of Victor's experiences and to develop human needs and wants. Many of the activities Itard designed would be very familiar to contemporary practitioners involved with the development of adaptive behaviors. More than 100 years before E. L. Thorndike's explication of the principle, Itard organized a fourth component of the training program designed to lead Victor to use speech through imitation and the law of necessity. (Victor could not have milk, something he liked very much, until he named it.) Finally, Itard attempted to make Victor use simple mental operations in problem solving, and later to apply these mental processes during instruction on new problems.

Itard terminated the experiment in 1804 because of severe trauma of puberty. Victor continued to live with Madame Guerin on the grounds of the institution until his death in 1828 at approximately age 40. Itard's (1962) report to the French Minister of the Interior on the project was applauded by the French Academy of Science, even though Itard considered his work to be incomplete. He wrote:

> the education of this young man is still incomplete and must always remain so; that by reason of their long inaction the intellectual faculties are developing slowly and painfully, and that this development, which in children growing up in civilized surroundings is the natural fruit of the time and circumstances, is here the slow and laborious result of a very active education in which the most powerful methods are used to obtain the most insignificant results. (p. 100)

In this passage, the invocation of another notion of psychology can be seen, which would remain unexplicated until James proposed the principle of critical periods nearly a century later.

Edouard Seguin

The sense training program developed by Itard was elaborated on by his student, Edouard Onesimus Seguin (1812–1880), and became the basis for most of the training and treatment programs in the United States throughout the 19th century. Seguin trained in medicine under Itard and in psychiatry under Esquirol. His study of Itard's work led him to the conclusion, contrary to the then-prevailing alienist view, that idiocy was not an inherited malformation of the brain, but rather the product of arrested mental development due to various causes. Moreover, mental deficiency could be overcome by careful physiological training of the senses. His Physiological Method, as it became known, was presented in his classic text, published in French in 1846. This work was translated into English with the help of his son Robert, and republished in 1866. Seguin's fame spread and experts from around the world came to Paris to see the work he was doing. Among those from America who visited him were Samuel Gridley Howe (1801–1876) and James B. Richards (1817–1886).

A report concerning Seguin's physiological method written by Dr. Howe and the Honorable George Sumner, Massachusetts Senator, led the Massachusetts legislature to commission a study of "The Condition of the Idiots of the Commonwealth." With Judge Horatio Boyington and Gilman Kimball, Howe spent 2 years completing this report, dated February 26, 1848. As a result, an appropriation of $2,500 was made to permit the creation of an "experimental school" for the care of 10 idiotic children. This program was added to the Perkins Institution for the Blind, a residential school of which Dr. Howe was the director. In fact, Howe gave up his apartments on the first floor of the building on October 1, 1848, to provide a place for the program.

Meanwhile, Seguin, a political organizer and activist who advocated the establishment of a republic, had been forced to leave France following the ascendancy of Louis Napoleon in 1850. He emigrated with his family to Cleveland and later to Portsmith, Ohio, where he had relatives living (Talbot, 1967). For 2 months in early 1852, Seguin served as the nonresident superintendent of the experimental Massachusetts school. During his brief stay, Seguin instructed the teachers in the principles of his physiological method. One of these teachers, having been recommended to Howe by Horace Mann, was James B. Richards, a visitor to Seguin's Paris school in 1845. Richards left Boston for Philadelphia in September 1852, where he founded the Pennsylvania Training School for Idiotic and Feeble-Minded Children with Bishop Alonzo Potter and Dr. Alfred L. Elwyn. Originally located in Philadelphia, this program was moved to a section of Media later to be known as Elwyn, Pennsylvania. This institution continues and is now know as the Elwyn Institute.

Seguin was asked to continue as superintendent of the Massachusetts school, but declined. Samuel Gridely Howe continued as general superintendent of all of the Perkins programs until his death in 1876. In

1887, Dr. Walter Elmore Fernald (1859–1924) become the first resident superintendent of the program for the feebleminded after its move to a new (and present) location in Waltham, Massachusetts.

In 1860, Seguin moved to Mt. Vernon, New York, graduating in 1861 from the University of the City of New York with an M.D. degree. In 1863, he moved his family again, this time to New York City, to enable him to work with children who were mentally retarded in a newly created department of the city's Children's Asylum (later known as the Idiot School) on Randall's Island. This facility, which had been established in 1847 as a Children's Hospital, was run by the City of New York until 1937 specifically for defective newborns and infants up to age 5 years when they would be eligible for transfer to one of the other institutions operated in the state. With his second wife, Elsie M. Mead, Seguin created the Seguin Physiological School for Weak-Minded and Weak-Bodied Children, a private day school, originally in New York City and later moved to Orange, New Jersey.

Idiocy, according to Seguin, was the result of damage to the nervous system. Profound idiots had sustained damage to the central nervous system. Superficial idiots, on the other hand, suffered from damage to the peripheral nervous system. As a result of this damage, a person was isolated from the environment and growth-producing experiences. Seguin argued that the idiot's nervous system must be retrained, but that isolated sense training — such as that proposed by his mentor, Itard — was futile. Rather, a carefully and individually planned program of training was necessary, beginning with the training of the muscles and progressing to the training of the senses of touch, hearing, and vision. Only then could the higher intellectual functions of the mentally retarded student be trained. [It should be noted that Grace Fernald's Visual–Auditory–Kinesthetic–Tactile (VAKT) method (G. Fernald, 1943) bears striking similarity to Seguin's physiological method, as do many of the training methods proposed to educate children with learning disabilities in the 1960s.]

Although he was never the superintendent of a public residential facility, Seguin assisted in establishing many of the first institutions in the United States — in Ohio; in Illinois, with Charles T. Wilbur; in New York City; in Barre, Massachusetts, with Hervey B. Wilbur and later George Brown; in Boston, with Howe; in Albany, and later Syracuse, New York, with Hervey B. Wilbur; in Pennsylvania, with James B. Richards; and in Lakeville (now Mansfield), Connecticut, with Henry M. Knight. Seguin, as did his colleagues in these endeavors, viewed the ideal residential institution as a small educational establishment, located near the community from which its students came and to which they would return after a period of carefully designed treatment and training. In each of these cases, the institution was little more than a tutorial program operated in the home of the founder and serving fewer than six children considered to be suffering from mental deficiency.

In addition to assisting in the establishment of the first institutions, Seguin's legacy was passed on in another important way. On June 6, 1876, a group of seven men, associated with the existing American institutions for the mentally retarded, assembled at the Pennsylvania Training School at the invitation of its superintendent Isaac N. Kerlin (1834–1893). In addition to the host, this group included Hervey B. Wilbur of Syracuse, New York; George A. Doren of Columbus, Ohio; Charles T. Wilbur of Jacksonville, Illinois; Henry M. Knight of Lakeville, Connecticut; George Brown of Barre, Massachusetts; and Edouard Seguin. This meeting, held in conjunction with the Centennial Exposition of the United States taking place in Philadelphia that summer, resulted in the formation of the Association of Medical Officers of American Institutions for Idiots and Feeble-Minded Persons. Seguin was elected the first president, serving from 1876 to 1877, and his image appears in the center of the official seal of the organization, which evolved from that first meeting, the American Association on Mental Deficiency.

EXPANSION OF RESIDENTIAL SCHOOLS (1850–1880)

Treatment Through Education

The residential schools founded by the pioneers during the second half of the 19th century in the United States were the first organized programs for the training of people who were mentally retarded. Lazerson (1975) argues that these institutions were a manifestation of American society's changing response to deviancy. During the colonial period, deviancy was not a critical social issue. The shelter and care provided by the family and local community were considered sufficient for those who were poor, aged, ill, or handicapped. Asylums and hospitals in larger towns and cities were used only when the person's deviance was too severe or when his or her behavior became uncontrollable (Deutsch, 1949).

With the increase in the American population after 1800 — due, in part, to a wave of immigrants in the first two decades of the century and the growth of American cities — local care of people with disabilities became inadequate (Rothman, 1971). Mental retardation, similar to insanity, evolved from being a moral problem in 1700 to being a medical problem in 1800 to being a social problem in 1850. Nevertheless, until 1880, mental retardation was viewed as a problem that could be solved through education and training. Programs for the feebleminded were conceived and designed as schools that would prepare the residents to resume their place in the society.

First Private Residential School

Although the majority of the states had asylums for the insane by 1850, the first private residential school for the mentally retarded was not established until 1848. Hervey Backus Wilbur (1820–1883), although trained as a physician at the Berkshire Medical Institution in Pittsfield, Massachusetts, began his career as a school teacher, a career pursued by both his father and mother. Encouraged by the work of Seguin, which he encountered in an article in *Chamber's Journal* in 1847, Wilbur abandoned the practice of medicine he had established in 1844 in Barre, Massachusetts. Instead, he opened a private school for the feebleminded in his home in July 1848. His first pupil was the 7-year-old son of a distinguished lawyer in town. Wilbur's friends and colleagues considered his work ill-advised, but Hervey persisted, moving with his wife into the larger house next door to their original home in Barre when a second pupil was added. Organized on a family plan, the pupils were constantly supervised and instructed throughout the day and night by Dr. Wilbur, his wife, or a member of their family (Fernald, 1917).

First Public Residential School

Wilbur's success led to inquiries from politicians and civic leaders from several states. In 1850, Wilbur was called on, with his friend and colleague in Massachusetts, Samuel Gridley Howe, to address the New York state legislature. They argued for the founding of a school in New York whose "design and object are not of a custodial character but are to furnish all the means of education to that portion of the youth of the State not provided for in any of its other educational institutions" (Wilbur, 1852, p. 28). Wilbur's and Howe's arguments proved convincing, and on July 10, 1851, the New York legislature passed a bill authorizing a school for idiots aged 7 to 14 years, with Dr. Wilbur appointed the superintendent. To replace him at Barre, Wilbur selected Dr. George Brown (1823–1892) and his wife, Katherine Wood Brown. The Browns greatly expanded the school at Barre in subsequent years, later called the Elm Hill School, and were succeeded as directors by their son, George A. Brown, and then by his son, George P. Brown.

The New York State Asylum for Idiots was opened in October 1851 in rented quarters in Albany, about 2 miles from the state capitol. The school, with an annual budget of $6,000, was designed to serve 20 children from all sections of the state. As noted in the First Annual Report of the Trustees (Wilbur, 1852), "as the enterprise was experimental there seemed great propriety in its being conducted as near the Capitol that members of the Legislature might from time to time examine it and become acquainted with its nature and success" (p. 12). On August 10, 1855, the program was moved to newly constructed quarters in Syracuse "where a group of public-spirited citizens headed by General Leavenworth had offered ten acres of land, free of charge, or $7,500 toward any other site, provided the institution was located in that city" ("Historical Notes," 1940, p. 188). It was renamed the Syracuse State Institution for the Feeble-Minded, the first public facility in the United States built by a state specifically to serve citizens who were mentally retarded. Wilbur presided over the program at Syracuse until his death, when he was succeeded by James C. Carson (1847–1926). Today the Asylum is known as the Syracuse Development Center.

The model of the institution as a school "to awaken dormant faculties to their greatest possible development" was firmly established by 1855 (Wilbur, 1852, p. 17). In 1879, Wilbur was able to report to his colleagues in the association of superintendents, which he helped to found, that "a good proportion of our pupils who have had homes to go to . . . could be dismissed after a proper course of training, capable of a fair degree of useful occupation under intelligent home direction" (Wilbur, 1879, p. 97). Wilbur went on to state that he had "a prejudice against large asylums for any purpose" (p. 97), a view similar to that of both Seguin and Brown.

Other Early Schools

In addition to creating both the first private residential school (at Barre) and the first public residential school (at Albany, then Syracuse) for people who were mentally retarded in the United States, Wilbur was also instrumental in the establishment of many other programs for the mentally retarded throughout the United States. With his brother, Charles T. Wilbur, who had served as Hervey's assistant at Syracuse, he assisted in the establishment of the Connecticut School for Imbeciles. The first director of this program was Henry M. Knight (1827–1880), a member of the Connecticut legislature, who had been appointed by his colleagues to study the care of idiots in other states and to report a census of idiots and their care in Connecticut ("Historical Notes," 1941). A bill to create a school was passed by the Connecticut house, but defeated by one vote in the senate. Abandoning hope of legislative action, Dr. Knight, with the advice of the Wilburs, created a program for 15 children in his home in Lakeville in 1858. The school, incorporated in 1861, joined with the Connecticut Colony for Epileptics in 1918 at the present location in Mansfield, and was known thereafter as the Mansfield Training School.

Charles and Hervey Wilbur also established the Illinois State Institution for the Education of Feeble-Minded Children in 1865, originally at Jackson and later moved to Lincoln, Illinois. Charles T. Wilbur was the first superintendent. Charles had earlier served as assistant superintendent of the State Asylum for the Education of Idiotic and Imbecile Youth at Columbus, Ohio. Henry M. Knight and Hervey Wilbur assisted in the establishment of the Minnesota Institution for the Feeble-Minded at Faribault, at which Henry's son, George Henry Knight, was the first superintendent. Henry's school at Lakeville was later directed, in turn, by his sons, George Henry and Robert P. Knight.

The First School Controversy

One of the enduring controversies in the field of mental retardation is which school was the first for the mentally retarded in the United States (Antonak, 1984). Walter E. Fernald reported in 1917 that the American Asylum for the Deaf and Dumb at Hartford, Connecticut, had enrolled an idiot child for instruction as early as 1818. However, this experiment was terminated shortly thereafter. Howe had also trained a blind idiot at the Perkins Institution in 1839, an experience that led him to urge the Commonwealth to establish a program for their care. As a result, the legislature appointed the committee, chaired by Howe, which led to the founding of the program at Perkins in 1848. However, it is argued that the program at Perkins was a component of a larger school for the education of the deaf. The school established by Wilbur in New York, being founded and built specifically for people who were mentally retarded, is therefore awarded the honor of being the first public residential school for the mentally retarded in the United States.

The program at Perkins was deemed a success and incorporated as the Massachusetts School for Idiotic and Feeble-Minded Youth on April 4, 1850. This program moved to larger facilities in south Boston in 1851 and again in 1856, and then to Dover, Massachusetts, in 1881. Wolfensberger (1972) argued that this last move represented a shift not only in location, but also in the philosophy of care on which the schools for the mentally retarded had been built until that time. A new era was beginning.

INSTITUTIONS AS RETREATS FROM SOCIETY (1880–1910)

Fernald's Waverley Plan

Walter E. Fernald (1859–1924), more than any other leader of his time, embodied the prevailing views of mental retardation during the period from 1880 to 1925. Born February 11, 1859, in Kittery, Maine, Fernald received his M.D. degree from the Medical School of Maine at Bowdoin in 1881. He began his career as an assistant physician (superintendent) at the State Hospital for the Insane at Mendota, Wisconsin, returning to New England in 1887 to marry Kate M. Nolan and assume the superintendency of the Massachusetts school at the age of 28. Under his direction, the school established at Waltham (originally part of Waverley) became the center for mental retardation services and research in the United States, with officials from nearly every state and many of the European nations coming to observe the programs and to study with Fernald. The Waverley Plan, as it became known, was essentially an elaboration of the Physiological Method of Edouard Seguin (Lundberg, 1947).

Beginning in 1890, Fernald established outpatient diagnostic clinics (Fernald, 1920) in association with the common schools to examine children who were backward in their school work and to train psychologists and physicians to make accurate diagnoses. This work led Fernald (1922) to propose his 10 "Zones of Inquiry," which he recommended for an accurate diagnosis of mental retardation: physical examination, family history, personal history, developmental history, school achievement history, social and moral reactions, economic efficiency, school capacity, practical knowledge, and psychological tests. Examination of children 3 or more years behind their classmates became a compulsory school responsibility after a law was passed in 1919. This law also required that if a school district found 10 or more children who met this criterion, they must establish a special education class to provide for them.

A paper published by Fernald in 1892 became the seminal work on the care, treatment, and training of children who were "low-grade" (or severely) mentally handicapped. In this paper, he explained the elements of his program, based on personal experience with more than 100 cases, including diet, clothing, toileting, feeding, exercise, outdoor activities, playthings, music, games, and gymnastic movements.

> I want to emphasize my firm conviction that it is utter nonsense to attempt this training of low grade cases unless it is done in the most painstaking, conscientious and thorough manner by a teacher who thoroughly believes in the real value of this work. (p. 457)

Fernald's Model Spreads

From 1898 to 1908, Fernald employed and trained a series of assistant physicians, each of whom would go on to become influential in the field of mental retardation. George L. Wallace (1872–1930) came to Waverley from Nova Scotia in 1892 as head farmer. He was granted a leave by Fernald to attend medical school in Baltimore, and returned to Massachusetts as assistant physician in 1898. In 1907, Wallace left Waverley to design, build, and be superintendent of the Waverley expansion program on 500 acres in Wrentham, Massachusetts, 20 miles southwest of Boston. In 1917, Wallace designed and directed the construction of the third Massachusetts facility at Belchertown. George E. McPherson (1876–1945) was selected, on Fernald's recommendation, as the first superintendent of that facility. One of the first publicly funded research laboratories devoted to the study of mental retardation was established by Wallace (and bears his name) at Wrentham in 1930.

Dr. Joseph H. Ladd (1876–1974), who joined Fernald as an assistant physician in 1900, left in 1907 to establish and be the first superintendent (until his retirement in 1956) of the Rhode Island School for the Feeble-Minded at Exeter. This facility has been known since 1958 as the Joseph H. Ladd Center. Dr. George S. Bliss (1872–1941) left Waverley in 1908 to build and be the first superintendent of the Maine School for the Feeble-Minded at Pownal, now known as Pineland Center.

In 1901, Dr. Fernald was called on by the Women's Clubs of New Hampshire to speak on his work in Massachusetts and to recommend a plan of care for the feebleminded of New Hampshire. Subsequently, a law entitled "An Act to Provide for the Care and Education of Feeble-Minded Children," passed on March 22, 1901 (New Hampshire Laws of 1901), empowered the state to establish a school for children between 3 and 21 years of age (note the similarity to PL 94-142) *capable of being benefited by school instruction*. These children would be *committed* by a judge and remain *in detention* at the school as *inmates*, where they would be trained and then *discharged* on *parole* to the community. Dr. Fernald not only proposed the model for the school, he also proposed the location, design, and first superintendent.

Dr. Charles Sherman Little (1869–1936) was a graduate of Dartmouth College and the superintendent of the McLean Hospital, a private hospital for the insane in Waverley, across the street from the Massachusetts school that Fernald directed. Dr. Little opened the New Hampshire School for Feeble-Minded Children on February 1, 1903, at Laconia on 247.5 acres of marginal farmland on a hill overlooking two lakes in roughly the geographic center of the state. Dr. Little left Laconia in 1910 to design, build, and be the first superintendent of New York's new facility, located in Rockland County on 2,000 acres of abandoned farmland overlooking the Hudson River at Thiells. This facility was designed predominantly to accommodate children with mental retardation from New York City, and named in honor of William Pryor Letchworth, a prominent philanthropist associated with the New York State Board of Charities for many years. Dr. Fernald also consulted on this facility's physical and educational plans. The facility's name, Letchworth Village, was most appropriate as it was constructed as a separate village — a place of shelter and respite for those unforunate feebleminded citizens of the state who would live there.

A New System of Institutions

When the interconnections with Drs. Fernald and Waverley are plotted, it is not difficult to understand how a group of institutions for people with mental retardation in the six New England states and New York could grow so quickly into a system remarkable for its consistency of purpose, goals, structure, treatment philosophy, and even architecture at the turn of the century. This system is not at all dissimilar to the earlier system of small residential schools established through the efforts of Dr. Wilbur 40 years earlier. When we consider the leadership roles of these two influential men in the American Association on Mental Deficiency (AAMD), which Wilbur helped to found and which Fernald was to lead twice as president, the emerging American system of institutions becomes more understandable.

Yet the institutions that were established under Fernald's direction between 1880 and 1910 were considerably different from the schools established by Wilbur between 1850 and 1880. One obvious difference was their location. No longer were these programs established in neighborhoods in cities and towns. The programs after 1880 were located on large tracts of farmland in isolated sections of their states. Another obvious difference was the size of the programs. The programs at Waverley, Wretham, Exeter, Laconia, and Pownal were started with a dozen or fewer boys, who actually built the first buildings and cleared, or re-cleared, the land for tilling. Yet within a few short years each superintendent would begin a litany of appeals to his state's legislature for more money for continued expansion of dormitories, barns, and school buildings. For example, the program at Letchworth would grow under Little's direction to encompass 75 buildings at a cost of more than $10 million, with a capacity for 3,500 residents.

What prompted this extraordinary expansion? What happened to the educational model of the original programs? What were the goals for these new asylums? To understand the evolution of programs for citizens with mental retardation from 1880 to 1910 as embodied by American institutions, it is necessary to examine the social history of the United States.

Evolving American Society

Three interrelated forces were reshaping American society and values during this period: industrialization, urbanization, and immigration.

The change from an agrarian to an industrial society brought demands for raw materials; improved distribution and transportation systems; and labor to operate the machines, package the products, and move the finished goods to markets in all corners of the country. Coincident with this demand for labor were the political and economic upheavals in Europe, and the consequent tidal wave of immigrants to America seeking freedom, jobs, and prosperity. These immigrants located around the growing industrial centers in the United States — near the factories of Chicago and Detroit, the mines in Pittsburgh, and the shipping and manufacturing centers in Philadelphia, Boston, and, in particular. New York. Where cattle grazed in 1875 in Brooklyn, New York, and Charlestown, Massachusetts, immigrant tenements were teeming with wretched refuse in 1900.

American society was clearly changing, and, in the view of many, not necessarily for the better. Whereas the village and town had been the centers of social support and humane care for the poor, aged, homeless, and disabled, these institutions were no longer adequate to deal with the increased demand after 1880. The residential schools established by the pioneers in the 1850s became the asylums and retreats of the 1880s. Isolated in rural communities, far from the demands of complex urban society, these asylums were proposed as the means to shelter and protect the mentally deficient (Wolfensberger, 1972).

The developmental and educative models of Seguin and Wilbur were replaced by a model in which people who were mentally retarded were viewed as the hapless victims of complex society. The institution, according to Fernald, would provide the higher grade of defectives with the training they needed to make them productive citizens and to return them to society as useful and self-supporting members of the community.

Custodial Departments

There was another group of defectives, however, for whom protection and care was more important than schooling. The failure of many of the lower grade residents to make satisfactory adjustment to the community upon discharge, the lack of a supportive community for many of them to return to, and the lack of financial support from state legislatures necessary to provide the requisite training programs led Fernald and the other superintendents of this time to propose the establishment of custodial departments to complement the school departments. Fernald (1892) proposed that, for those residents who would remain at the institution, training of the senses and the higher mental faculties in the classrooms be replaced by training of the hands for useful occupations on the school's farms and in the school's industrial shops. The institution would become the idyllic and benevolent shelter that this group of the feebleminded needed from the harsh realities and demands of complex industrial society, demands that their limited mental faculties could not hope to meet.

According to Kuhlmann (1940), by 1900 the institution had:

> shops for industrial training and land for farming and dairying. It [had] its own power, light, and heating plant, kitchen, bakery, laundry, as well as hospital, where at time attendants and nurses received special training for their duties in the institution. In its major physical aspects the institution [had] already become of age. Abandonment of the idea of cure was the important factor in the development of the physical plant. (p. 12)

After the first step on the slippery slope of custodial care had been taken, it was not long before the era of pity and retreat changed to a new era typified by resentment, fear, and brutalization (Wolfensberger, 1972).

THE MENACE OF THE MORON (1910–1925)

Threats to Society

The shift from the educational mission of the first residential schools for the mentally retarded to the custodial mission of the institutions during the period from 1910 to 1925 was presaged by Dr. Little in his 1904 report to the trustees of the New Hampshire School at Laconia:

> Such an institution as this must not be considered simply as one of the beneficial charities of the state; its scope is far larger than simply providing for the individual defective; it is one of the safe guards whereby society may protect itself from the vice, corruption, and licentiousness with which it is threatened when anyone of this defective class is left unrestrained and unprotected in the community. (p. 9)

He goes on to make a plea for a custodial department for those over 21 years of age to be added to the school department for those 3 to 21 years of age to protect the communities of New Hampshire from these "irresponsible sources of corruption and debauchery" (p. 10). The original legislation creating the school was amended in 1905 and again in 1909 to allow the courts to commit, and the superintendent and trustees to detain, feebleminded girls of childbearing age, defined to be from 3 to 45 years, if "their segregation seems to be for the best interests of the community" (New Hampshire Laws of 1909, Section 1). A subsequent amendment in 1917 lifted all age restrictions and allowed Dr. Little's successors to detain feebleminded people of all ages.

Social Darwinism

Three forces conjoined around 1910 to support this pessimistic and brutal view of people who were mentally retarded: one is sociological, one is philosophical, and one is psychological. With the increase in immigration and the explosive growth of the cities, there was a concomitant increase in crime, drunkenness, licentiousness, and immorality. The American social fabric was being torn apart during its evolution from a simple agrarian society to a complex industrial one.

The views of Herbert Spencer (1877), a British philosopher popular in Europe in the last half of the 19th century, were discovered in America as a way of understanding this perplexing sociological phenomena. Spencer attempted to apply the Darwinian principles concerning the evolution of species to the evolution of societies. Spencerianism, or Social Darwinism as it was also known, proposed that the health, as measured by the prosperity, of a society depended on the biological fitness of its members. Mendel's laws of inheritance gave neo-Spencerians in America the key to the problems of their evolving society. If society was the product of biology, and biology was the product of heredity, then the fitness of the society was determined by its people's hereditary endowment. The problems of American society were due to the hereditarily determined unfitness of some of its members. The task that remained, however, was to find those who were manifestly unfit to function in the highly organized social structure of industrial America at the turn of the 20th century.

Measurement of Intelligence

Alfred Binet (1857–1911), the preeminent psychologist in Europe during that period, unwittingly provided the solution. The Binet–Simon *Metrical Scale of Intelligence* (Binet & Simon, 1916), published in 1908 in France, was brought to the United States by Henry H. Goddard (1866–1957) and translated by his colleague Elizabeth Kite. Goddard, who was born in Vassalboro, Maine, received his Ph.D. in psychology under the direction of G. Stanley Hall at Clark University, the most important center for the study of psychology in the United States at the time. Among the other students of Hall's during this period who would rise to prominence in later years were Fred Kuhlmann (1876–1941), J. E. Wallace Wallin (1876–1969), and Lewis M. Terman (1877–1956). In 1908, Goddard was the director of research at the Training School at Vineland, New Jersey. He later assumed the directorship of the psychology program at the Ohio State University.

On the other coast, Lewis Terman translated the Binet–Simon scale, standardized it on a large sample of southern California children, and published it in 1916 as the *Stanford Revision and Extension of the Binet–*

Simon Intelligence Scale. Terman was chairman of the psychology faculty at Stanford University from 1910 to 1930. Although they worked on opposite coasts of the country, Goddard and Terman worked closely together for many decades, furthering the science of psychology and, perhaps unwittingly, destroying the lives (figuratively and literally) of many people who they and their students and colleagues determined to be mentally deficient.

Both of these men misconstrued Binet's ideas about the nature of intelligence and the purpose of his scale. Binet warned (Binet & Simon, 1916) that the scale was predictive, not explanatory, of a narrow range of behavior, namely, the ability to succeed in school. Binet doubted that the scale measured anything, and cautioned against the misconception that the scale could be used to rank-order people. Moreover, a person's score on the scale could be raised or lowered by experience. Indeed, Binet had proposed a series of "mental orthopedics" for those students who the scale predicted would have difficulty in school; this series was designed to help them learn how to learn.

While Binet refused to reify the concept of intelligence, Terman, Goddard, and other psychologists in the United States were not so cautious. The Intelligence Quotient (IQ) became not only the person's score on the test but also a measure of intelligence, defined as hereditary potential and biological capacity. Intelligence, as measured by the IQ test, became an unmalleable, predetermined, and fixed characteristic of a person.

Classification of Defectives

Goddard proposed a three-part classification of nine grades of defectives, consisting of three grades each of idiots, imbeciles, and feeble-minded persons, based on the use of the Binet scale. In later publications he expounded his classification system. Idiots and imbeciles were those whose IQs were too low to function in any society. "The idiot is not our greatest problem. He is indeed loathsome . . . . Nevertheless, he lives his life and is done. He does not continue the race with a line of children like himself" (Goddard, 1909, p. 9). The third class Goddard called the morons, from the Greek word *moronia*, meaning foolish. Morons were those whose IQs were only sufficient to function in simple social organizations. As adults, they would have a mental age of between 8 and 12 years, according to Goddard (1915).

> For many generations we have recognized and pitied the idiot. Of late we have recognized a higher type of defective, the moron, and have discovered that he is a burden; that he is a menace of society and of civilization; that he is responsible to a large degree for many, if not all, of our social problems. (p. 307)

The "menace of the moron" was born in that 1915 address, but it had already been mortalized in Goddard's classic research on the inheritance of IQ published in 1912 as *The Kallikak family: A study in the heredity of feeblemindedness.*

The Indictment of Morons

Psychologists, sociologists, and criminologists — guardians of America's moral purity — quickly took up the crusade. Terman (1916) argued that "not all criminals are feeble-minded, but all feeble-minded are at least potential criminals. That every feeble-minded woman is a potential prostitute would hardly be disputed by anyone" (p. 11). Stanley P. Davies wrote eloquently about moral imbeciles as a chronic festering sore on the body politic, likely to threaten the extinction of Western Civilization. Fernald (1904) had earlier proposed that feeblemindedness was the mother of crime, pauperism, and degeneracy. Furthermore,

> Feeble-minded women and girls are very liable to become sources of unspeakable debauchery and licentiousness which pollutes the whole life of the young boys and youth of the community.... The adult males become the town loafers and incapables, the irresponsible pests of the neighborhood, petty thieves, purposeless destroyers of property, incendiaries, and very frequently the violators of women and little girls. (p. 383)

The feebleminded, Fernald argued in 1912, constituted "a parasitic predatory class never capable of self-support or of managing their own affairs.... They cause considerable sorrow at home and are a menace and danger to the community" (p. 90)

Benjamin W. Baker (1912), Little's successor as superintendent at Laconia, claimed that the feebleminded,

> endowed with abnormal desires which are allied with defective judgment and will power, spread abroad in the community the most loathsome and infectious diseases, beget children, often times illegitimate, who are defective and who eventually become public charges .... If provision is not made for these [people] very soon by the state, their children will grow into manhood and womanhood ignorant and untrained, their vicious tendencies unrestrained. (pp. 8–9)

Ending the Menace to Society

Institutional Incarceration

Three solutions to the "menace of the moron" were proposed: institutional incarceration, immigration restriction, and eugenic control. George Knight proposed the first of these solutions — low-cost institutional incarceration and segregation from society — in his challenge to the members attending the AAMD meeting in 1891:

> The sooner you can make the people understand that the most economical thing we can do is to shut up every one of these children, especially the female, the more economical it is going to be for every state in the Union. (p. 218)

The cry went up for more institutions, larger custodial departments, more acreage for farm colonies, and increased scrutiny of backward people in communities. Barr (1904), in one of the few textbooks on mental deficiency published after Seguin's 1864 text, urged that "the safety of society, therefore, demands [the] speedy recognition and separation [of defectives] ... and furthermore [their] permanent detention lest it permeate the whole body socialistic..." (p. 326).

Between 1910 and 1923 the population of U.S. institutions doubled, and most were soon filled to capacity (or overcapacity). Laws providing for the incarceration of defective delinquents (a term defined by Walter Fernald in 1909), who were a menace to the public, were passed in most states throughout the country. People who were mentally retarded were sentenced to an indeterminant period of incarceration in state schools with no court intervention, no trial, no representation, and no chance for parole. These laws would stand, with little public concern, for more than 40 years.

Immigration Restriction

The second solution to the "moron problem" was the restriction of immigration to the United States. As described in the Immigration Act of 1891, restrictions were required to prevent the entry of known idiots, the insane, the diseased, criminals, and those likely to be poor or public charges. Perhaps Mott (1888), director of the Minnesota institution at Faribault, expressed it most eloquently when he said:

> We shall ever welcome the vitality and nobility of the best Celtic, Saxon, Germanic, and Scandinavian blood of Europe, but if the sewage of vice and crime and physical weakness is to pour in upon us from the east, and more nameless abominations to come in like a flood from the west, we are helpless. We cannot build prisons, reformatories, insane retreats, and idiotic asylums fast enough and large enough for our needs. Why not stop this folly? (p. 77)

Once again, Goddard and his colleagues would lead the way. Goddard proudly pointed to the results of his IQ testing (in English) of immigrants arriving at Ellis Island in New York harbor. "The use of mental tests for the detection of feeble-minded aliens has vastly increased the number of aliens deported," he wrote (Goddard, 1917, p. 244). Carl C. Brigham (1923), a colleague of Goddard and the founder and first director of the College Entrance Examination Board, reviewing the data obtained from the army group intelligence tests (the alpha and beta tests) during the period from 1915 to 1918, argued that the deterioration of American intelligence was inevitable unless public action could be aroused. Immigration of aliens should not only be restricted but highly selective, he argued. The Committee on the Scientific Problems of Human Migration — appointed in 1922 by the National Research Council of the Carnegie Foundation and including such scientists as E. L. Thorndike, Stanley P. Davies, Charles B. Davenport, and Henry H. Laughlin — proposed a revision of the U.S. immigration laws to include an assessment of *the economic value* of immigrants in the social order and industrial structure (Yerkes, 1922).

The Immigration Restriction Act of 1924 was considered the greatest success of the period. Harsh quotas established for nations of "inferior stock" were imposed, steamship companies were fined for each feebleminded or insane person they transported to the United States, immigrant families were sometimes divided at Ellis Island when mothers or fathers were sent back to Europe because their IQ scores were found to be too low, and foreign-born residents of American institutions for the feebleminded and insane were deported. Gould (1981) suggests that many of those who perished in the Holocaust were denied entry to the United States during the early years of the Nazi regime, and may have been saved were it not for this law. Some evidence even suggests that more than one of the members of the foundation-supported research centers in the United States at this time actually traveled to Germany and consulted with Nazi politicians on the passage of laws designed to ensure racial purity (Marks, 1981).

Eugenic Control

The third solution to the "menace of the moron" was the eugenic solution. First proposed by Sir Francis Galton (1822–1911) in 1883, eugenics sought the improvement of mankind through selective breeding. This would be accomplished by the regulation of marriage and family size after measuring the hereditary endowment of parents. Again, the IQ test and its proponents offered the solution.

The family pedigrees published by Dugdale (1877), Goddard (1912), and others had proven to their authors that mental retardation was a single-gene defect, and therefore could be eliminated by eugenic control. Based on this evidence, Charles Davenport (1911) was able to state that "two mentally defective parents will produce only mentally defective offspring... [and] probably no imbecile is born except of parents who, if not mentally defective themselves, both carry mental defect in their germ plasm" (p. 66). Terman (1917) argued that "if we are to preserve our state for a class of people who are worthy to possess it we must prevent, as far as possible, the propagation of mental degenerates" (p. 161). Eugenic research so impressed Walter Fernald that, as he told his colleagues in 1915, "we are in possession of knowledge which would enable us to markedly diminish the number of the feebleminded in a few generations if segregation and surgical sterilization of all known defectives were possible" (p. 290).

Sterilization of Defectives

In addition to preventing the transmission of feeblemindedness, sterilization had other presumed benefits. In his AAMD address in 1892, Issac N. Kerlin, superintendent of Pennsylvania's institution, reported that he had permitted the sterilization of some of the residents at Media as early as 1890. He suggested to his colleagues that "life-long salutory results to many of our boys and girls would be realized if before adolescence the procreative organs were removed" (p. 277). Among other presumed benefits of sterilization were the prevention of epilepsy, the reduction of inordinate sexual desires (including the control of masturbation), the induction of tranquility, and the salvation of feebleminded females from vice and corruption. "Whose state," Kerlin asked, "shall be the first to legalize oophorectomy and orchitomia for the relief and cure of radical depravity?" (p. 278).

A bill was introduced in Michigan in 1897 to permit the desexualization of the inmates of the school for the feebleminded, but the bill failed to pass the legislature (Landman, 1932). Such a law was passed in Pennsylvania in 1905, but was vetoed by the governor. Indiana passed the first compulsory eugenic human sterilization law in 1907 to allow institutional physicians to sterilize "confirmed criminals, idiots, imbeciles, and rapists . . . adjudged to be undesirable procreators" (Landman, 1932, p. 54). (The law was found to be unconstitutional by the state's Supreme Court in 1921 because it denied due process guaranteed under the 14th Amendment to the U.S. Constitution. It was replaced by an acceptable law in 1927.) The first compulsory sterilization law in New England was passed by the Connecticut legislature in 1909.

With the war raging in Europe, the need for sterilization and control of defectives became even more important. Benjamin Baker (1918) reasoned that because intelligent young men were fighting and dying in Europe, "an artificial value will be given to the moron man at home, both in the eyes of the opposite sex and in the industrial world" (p. 8). This could only lead to "an increase of defectives through the greatly enlarged opportunities of and even demand on this class" (p. 8). In this plea to the state legislature for more money for an enlarged custodial department at Laconia, Baker made one of the most bizarre assertions of the period:

> It is more than probable that such opportunities, creating a rapid accumulation of the racially ineffectives with a concomitant decrease in the effective and constructive racial values, has been the cause of the downfall of the Grecian, Roman, and previous civilizations. The crying need for labor which has made the people more tolerant of mental defectives should not blind us to their dangerous transmissible hereditary qualities.... Every helplessly feebleminded person is, during his or her life-time, a living first mortgage on the resources of the people of New Hampshire, on which interest must be paid yearly. (p. 8)

Henry H. Laughlin, director of the Eugenical Records Office at Cold Spring Harbor on Long Island, funded by the Carnegie Foundation, prepared model legislation for the sterilization of the feebleminded, insane, criminalistic, inebriate, diseased, blind, deaf, deformed, and dependent (legislation that was reviewed by the leaders of Germany's Nazi party). By 1926, Laughlin was able to report that 26 states had sterilizations laws. By 1950, a grand total of 52,233 sterilizations had been reported, of which 26,858 (51 percent) were performed on mental defectives (Butler, 1951). Clarence J. Gamble (1951), reviewing the results of the sterilization programs of the states, wrote:

> When the results of sterilizations in years of freedom [mentally retarded residents were typically sterilized prior to parole to the community], in the diminution of governmental costs, and in the prevention of mental inadequacy in future generations are considered, it seems fair to conclude that there are few forms of preventive medicine by which so much can be accomplished by so little. (p. 196)

Betsey Scott Johnson reported in 1950 that the sterilization of 264 residents at Laconia had prevented 550 births (rate of 2.5 children per female and 1.25 children per male were based on the fecundity records of previous state school residents), of which 274 would have been borderline or mildly mentally defective. Moreover, without sterilization, these 264 residents would have remained at Laconia for an aggregate of 1,065 years, 8 months, and 9 days, resulting in a cost to the state of at least $388,974. (According to Johnson [1951], this is less than $1.00 per resident per day.)

> From the data collected it is calculated that the sterilization of 264 feebleminded persons will prevent the birth of 550 children of

which 200 would have been mentally deficient and an additional 210 retarded, 250 supported entirely and a further 230 partly by public friends. (pp. 407–408)

Temperate Views

It must be noted that there were voices, if not opposing these hysterical solutions, at least suggesting temperance in the administration of the solutions. Fred Kuhlmann (1915), a fellow student of Goddard and Terman at Clark University and director of research at the Minnesota School at Faribault, argued that IQ alone was not sufficient to diagnose mental deficiency. Some form of *social test* was necessary to show that the person was unable to succeed in the community. (This is perhaps the first reference to the concept of concomitant deficits in adaptive behavior, which is currently required for the definition of mental retardation.)

Edwin G. Boring (1923), in his review of published conclusions from the analyses of the army's alpha and beta test data collected during World War I, suggested that these data could not support C. C. Brigham's gross generalization concerning the imperfection of entire cultures and nationalities. As a psychological examiner at Camp Upton in New York in 1918, Boring had firsthand knowledge of the inadequacy of the tests and the testing situations from which these data were generated. Several of the surviving test protocols, in fact, show blank pages and scores of 0 (Gould, 1981).

Charles Scott Berry (1925), the director of special education for the Detroit public schools and a professor of educational psychology at the University of Michigan, argued that not all children with mental retardation were potential delinquents, that they did not have inordinate sexual urges, and that they were not a menace to society. Most, in his experienced view, could be educated to be self-sufficient, practice birth control, and be contributors to society.

Even Walter E. Fernald, on of the most vocal and forceful leaders of the eugenics movement, began to express a shift in thinking as early as 1920. A series of studies that he directed (Fernald, 1919a, 1919b, 1924) of the *after-careers* of par led defectives demonstrated that (Fernald, 1924): "a very small proportion of the discharged male morons had committed crimes, or had married or become parents, or had failed to support themselves, or had become bad citizens . . . . We have begun to recognize the fact that there are good morons and bad morons." (pp. 119–120)

INSTITUTIONAL EFFICIENCY AND TECHNICAL SPECIALIZATION (1925–1950)

Death of the Eugenics Movement

By 1925, the eugenics movement had peaked, although it was by no means dead. The death knell was sounded by two events. First, the crash of the stock market in 1929 and the subsequent nationwide depression revealed that all people, even those who presumably had been endowed by heredity with considerable intelligence, were subject to changes in the world economy. Those who had advocated the incarceration and sterilization of paupers, vagrants, and criminals from their Wall Street offices and private clubs in 1910 were, in 1930, subject to those same eugenic provisions. The second, and more profound, force ending the eugenics movement was the eugenic solutions perfected by the Nazi regime in Europe.

Institutions for the mentally retarded had evolved from educational programs for fewer than 10 people in the homes of pioneering physicians in 1850, to training schools in 1870, to idyllic rural enclaves in 1890, to the last defense against the demise of civilization in 1920. Wolfensberger (1972) argued that if this evolutionary process had continued, the logical result would have been the gradual demise of the institution as more residents were returned to their communities to be trained for productive, although sheltered, lives. However, this did not happen. According to Wolfensberger (1972), "the large institution, built for the ages, remote from population and teaching centers, was bereft of rationales" (p. 55), but it was not bereft of momentum.

The Institutional Enterprise

Despite increased understanding of the influence of environment on development and the identification of nongenetic determinants of mental retardation (Skeels & Dye, 1939), despite the realization that IQ was not constant and biologically determined, despite the challenges to the claims that mental retardation and criminality co-occured, the institution continued to be the center of programs for adults who were mentally retarded. The institution after 1925 gradually evolved a new structure as a "large and complicated operational and management enterprise" (Roselle, 1952, p. 524), and then slowly slipped from public view as the war in Europe and the Pacific demanded our attention.

Ernest N. Roselle typifies this period of the history of mental retardation just as Walter E. Fernald typifies the preceding period, and Edouard Seguin the one preceding that. In 1936, Roselle was hired to plan and build the second residential institution in Connecticut in order to relieve the overcrowding at Mansfield. After careful study of existing institutions in this country and review of administrative models in other service programs such as hospitals and corporations, Roselle presented his plans to build a $10 million showcase facility. In an article published 10 years after the opening of the training school at Southbury, Roselle (1952) described the facility as one that provided "the highly technical and specialized services required for the deviate and the ill in those of our social structure entrusted to us" (p. 524). These services required

> carefully developed, well-balanced, well-oriented, and efficient administrative organization. This must extend to all levels from top management to department heads and supervisors down to the rank and file, if it is to do a job measuring up to its responsibility and comparable in effectiveness to that being done in business and industry. (p. 524)

Roselle organized eight departments: health and medical services, institutional living (dormitory training and services), training in school and on the job, psychology and classification services, extension services (admission and discharge), finance and business management, plant operations and maintenance, and farms and gardens. A superintendent's cabinet made up of these eight department heads would write major management policy and solve major problems, but the department heads would have the autonomy to run their operations and solve day-to-day problems.

Roselle (1954) later lamented the bad press that institutions had received in previous years because it made them harder for relatives and parents to use. He argued there was a need to make

> these havens for the less fortunate of our brethren inviting and challenging places of attractiveness and efficiency. It is plainly incumbent upon us, as leaders in the field, to do all that lies within our power to plan, to create, and to operate institutions, both in the plants and in the programs of care, of training, and of just living which they house, that they may be so tuned to the needs and so interesting and so inviting that citizens will think of institutions as places they like to know and desire militantly to help. (p. 596)

Roselle (1954) suggested that it was possible to make new institutions and new sections of old institutions more normal and communitylike. Those administrators advocating these institutions must constantly remember that the children with mental retardation who reside there have

> inalienable rights, because they are children, to live in homes and communities which approach as nearly as possible the desirable standards of normal homes and communities. [Compare this to Wolfensberger's definition of normalization.] Society does not possess the moral right to confine these children during this formative period of their lives to institutional plants in conditions so

foreign to the normal needs and interests of childhood as to stunt and warp permanently their growth and development and thereby handicap them still further in taking their rightful place in society. (p. 597)

He saw too much copying of old models for institutions and too little creative planning for new institutions. Roselle wrote that the institution should be close to a city or sizable community to obtain and retain professional personnel. The overall plan for the facility should permit expansion and growth.

Roselle argued that cottages should be built for 24 to 50 children with mild handicaps, and that they should be similar to family homes, arranged as a suburban development, each with its own kitchen, living room, dining room, sleeping quarters, and space for the cottage staff. For residents who were moderately handicapped, units for 60 to 80 should be built, also completely self-contained, with comfort and durability the primary concerns. For the more severely handicapped, an infirmary type of unit for no more than 90 residents was considered appropriate, built around central sanitary and therapeutic service facilities and a nurses' station, with food to be brought in from a central commissary. These units "should be placed in a quiet section of the plant removed as completely as possible from its many activities" (Roselle, 1954, p. 615) (i.e., backwards and hidden from view), yet attractive and not institutionlike. The school should be the community center with gyms, auditorium, bank, stores, and so forth. For the married staff, Roselle suggested Levittown (Long Island) style four-and-a-half room cottages — "$50,000 worth of home for $8,500" (p. 622).

The institution at Southbury was indeed the model of a modern major facility. However, the majority of the residents who were mentally retarded were living in institutions built before 1930, which were enlarged to accommodate more and more residents. Letchworth Village in New York housed nearly 5,000 residents, as did Faribault, Sonoma, Willowbrook, and many others. Little attention was paid to educational programs for school-aged residents or to vocational training for adult residents. To operate large institutions such as these required resident work programs (institutional peonage, as it became known in later court cases), efficient management, and physical plants that could be economically operated. A note in the 1949 issue of the *AAMD News* ("Expansion program at Idaho State School and Colony," 1949) illustrates this concern. The expansion of the program at the Idaho State School and Colony at Nampa included the construction of two new 80-bed dormitories with the novel feature of the central location of the attendant's office to provide a complete view of the sleeping ward, dining area, day room, and bathroom. [Those in New England interested in seeing these marvels of institutional efficiency should visit the so-called star-shaped buildings at Mansfield State School in Connecticut or Pineland Center in Maine before they are torn down.]

FOUNDATIONS OF SPECIAL EDUCATION (1910–1950)

Institutions were not the only programs for people who were mentally retarded in the United States in the beginning of the 20th century. The first special education class for school-aged children with mental retardation was established in Providence, Rhode Island, in 1896. By 1906, 13 school systems were providing classes for such children; by 1922, 23 states reported they had classes serving more than 24,000 children who were mentally retarded. In 1936 this number would increase to 43 states serving nearly 100,000 children in the schools.

Training of special education teachers in Europe had been initiated in Belgium in 1912 by Ovide Decroly (1871–1932) as part of his private school in Brussels. The first comparable teacher training program in the United States was established in 1920; by 1949, 22 colleges offered teachers training in mental retardation, and most state institutions participated in this training by providing internship sites and summer institutes. An example was the summer training institutes created in 1934 at Letchworth Village by Edward J. Humphreys (b. 1903). Among the lecturers at these institutes were Margaret Mead, Gunnar Dybwad, and George Jervis.

Special education programs for children with mental retardation expanded after 1920 when it was realized that the institutions could not hope to provide the segregated environment necessary for people with mild mental retardation who, according to the test distributions, constituted nearly 15 percent of the U.S. population. It should be noted that not even during the peak of the eugenics scare in the 1920s did institutions serve more than 10 percent of citizens with mental retardation. The schools in general were being called on to participate in the maintenance of the social structure by providing the necessary training for citizens to assume their proper economic, vocational, and social roles (Smith, 1973). Special education was one component of this larger mission, albeit the lowest of the tracks. For the 2 to 3 percent of the school's students, it was the last chance before institutionalization.

Of course, the same IQ test that allowed Goddard and Terman to locate and categorize aliens who were mentally retarded allowed them to locate and sort students with mental retardation into the necessary levels of the curriculum that would prepare them for their role in society. Curricula were being designed by Annie Inskeep (1926) in the 1920s, by Christine Ingram (1935) in the 1930s, and by Katherine D.

Lynch in the 1940s. For example, Ingram's classic textbook, published in 1935, contained behaviorally based curricula, organized around units of study, for three levels: primary (chronological age /CA/ 7–11; mental age /MA/ 4–8), intermediate (CA 11–14, MA 6–9), and secondary (CA 14+, MA 8+).

Edgar Doll (1889–1968), director of research at the Vineland Training School, proposed the assessment of social behavior to supplement the assessment of intellect. His *Vineland Social Maturity Scale*, published in 1935, included 117 items on 8 subscales (self-help, dressing, eating, communication, self-direction, socialization, locomotion, and occupations), which could be scored to yield a social quotient (SQ) with the mean of 100 and a standard deviation of 15, similar to the Stanford-Binet scale. Social and occupational education became particularly important during the war years when the needs of industries to provide war materials led to job opportunities for young adults with mild mental retardation, and a reason for many borderline residents to leave institutions. Richard Hungerford (1903–1974) was among the first to promote the technique of job analysis for the development of the necessary training curricula for people who were mentally retarded (Hungerford, 1941).

ERA OF LEGISLATION AND NATIONAL SUPPORT (1950–1970)

The decades of the 1950s and 1960s brought a more enlightened view of human differences, and a more humanitarian — although markedly paternalistic — approach to serving citizens with mental retardation. Increasing interest in the biological sciences led to important insights into the causes and prevention of handicapping conditions. Concern for the rehabilitation of returning veterans after World War II led to the passage of the Vocational Rehabilitation Act Amendments of 1943. Improvements in rehabilitation, medical services, and therapeutic interventions, pioneered in work with adults with disabilities, were soon applied to the habilitation of the mentally retarded. The emerging parent group, the National Association for Retarded Citizens (NARC), founded in Minneapolis in 1950, successfully lobbied for services in public schools for trainable children with (moderate) mental retardation. By 1963, more than 27 percent of these students were being served in public schools.

The parent movement was also successful in awakening the federal government to its role in providing the leadership, coordination, and financial support necessary to provide services to all of America's citizens with mental retardation. The first research programs were funded through grants fron the National Institute on Mental Health in 1956. Legislation passed in 1958 provided funds for colleges and universities to train teachers in special education. Under the inspiring leadership of President John F. Kennedy, the U.S. Congress enacted laws that created centers to study prevention of mental retardation (PL 88-156, 1963), and university-affiliated facilities for research, program development, and professional training (PL 88-164, 1963). By 1970, nearly $5 billion was being spent on services and research in mental retardation and related disabilities, from prenatal prevention to recreation for adults with disabilities.

At the end of the 1960s, the parent movement was responsible for initiating profound change in another area — focusing the attention of the world on the neglect and abuse of residents of the country's mental retardation institutions. For 20 years, from 1940 to 1960, attention had been diverted away from institutions, first, as the country fought World War II, and then, as special education and habilitation programs in the schools and communities grew. Although the "menace of the moron" view was no longer accepted after 1940, the institutions that were spawned by that view were firmly entrenched in the American social system. People who were mentally retarded were put out of sight in these institutions and little more than basic custodial care was provided for them. The lack of scrutiny by the public through their government agencies and the lack of adequate financial support led to the deterioration of the programs and facilities. At the same time, the increased committments of children with mental retardation were necessary because there were no alternatives for parents. In some states, institutions were operating with populations that were double the capacity for which they had been designed and built. Institutional warehousing was the actual service model, despite what administrators may have written about unit systems and community placement.

Studies of mental retardation institutions by the AAMD under the direction of Herschel Nisonger in the 1950s, exposés by prominent national figures (such as Robert Kennedy's tour of Willowbrook State School in 1965), and the photographic essay by Blatt and Kaplan (1966) produced a public demand for improvement in institutional services. Policy statements of the NARC asserting the right of all people who are mentally retarded to live as normally as possible within the community led to court actions supporting their rights to habilitation in the least-restrictive setting. Court cases concerning the programs at institutions in Alabama (*Wyatt v. Stickney*, 1972), New York (*NYARC v. Rockefeller*, 1975), Pennsylvania (*Halderman v. Pennhurst State School and Hospital*, 1977), and New Hampshire (*Garrity v. Gallen*, 1979) pushed reforms of the institutional system across the country and led to the development of services and programs in community settings.

By 1970, the sociopolitical movement to deinstitutionalize people with mental retardation was gathering strength. Some writers have

begun to refer to the current period as the "Era of Normalization." Time must provide the needed perspective and society the context before this part of the history of mental retardation services can be written.

CONCLUSIONS

As Burton Blatt told us many times in many ways, the examination of our history is a means for understanding why it is that we behave as we do, as well as an opportunity to expose our values. To quote from Professor Blatt's autobiographical essay, the history of mental retardation and developmental disabilities "is a puzzle, but not because it can't be put together; more so because it can be put together in so many interesting and logical ways. And however different, each way — each story — can be true" (Blatt, 1984, p. 305). I cannot escape the criticism, applied to all historians that I have selected and interpreted events in this history to match current ideology — my ideology.

My intent in writing this history was to present glimpses of some of the people and the major events of the past, as well as the prevailing attitudes and social condtions that influenced significantly the provision of mental retardation programs and services. It is my hope that by understanding the antecedents of current philosophy and derivative practices we can ensure a future in which our children will wonder why people with mental retardation were ever devalued and segregated.

REFERENCES

Antonak, R. F. (1984). First among equals. In J. A. Mulick & B. L. Mallory (Eds.), *Transitions in mental retardation: Vol. 1. Advocacy, technology, and science* (pp. 275–281). Norwood, NJ: Ablex.

Antonak, R. F., & Mulick, J. A. (1987). *Transitions in mental retardation: Vol. 3. The community imperative revisited.* Norwood, NJ: Ablex.

Baker, B. W. (1912). *Sixth biennial report to the trustees of the New Hampshire School for the Feeble-Minded at Laconia.* Concord, NH.

Baker, B. W. (1918). *Ninth biennial report to the trustees of the New Hampshire School for the Feeble-Minded at Laconia.* Concord, NH.

Barr, M (1904). *Mental defectives: Their history, treatment, and training.* Philadelphia, PA: P. Blakinston's Sons.

Begab, M. J. (1975). The mentally retarded and society: Trends and issues. In M. J. Begab & S. A. Richardson (Eds.), *The mentally retarded and society: A social science perspective* (pp. 3–32). Baltimore, MD: University Park Press.

Bernstein, G. S., Ziarnik, J. P., Rudrud, E. A., & Czajkowski, L. A. (1981). *Behavioral habilitation through proactive programming.* Baltimore, MD: Paul H. Brookes.

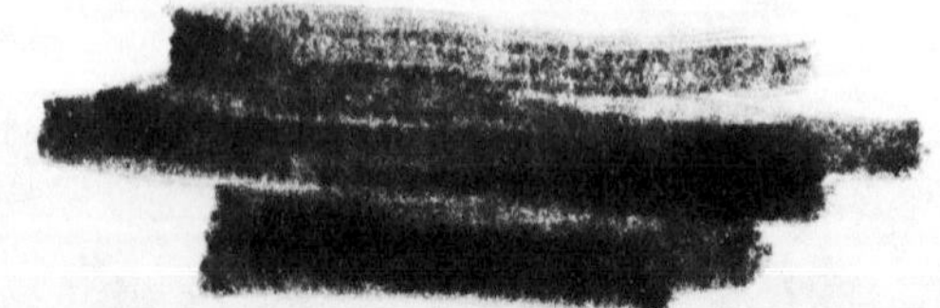

Berry, C. S. (1925). The case for the mentally retarded. *Mental Hygiene, 9,* 725–734.

Binet, A., & Simon, T. (1916). *The development of intelligence in children* (E. Kite, Trans.) Baltimore, MD: Williams and Wilkins (original work published 1908).

Blatt, B. (1984). Biography in autobiography. In B. Blatt & R. J. Morris (Eds.), *Perspective in special education: Personal orientations* (pp. 263–307). Glenview, IL: Scott, Foresman.

Blatt, B., & Kaplan, I. (1966). *Christmas in purgatory.* Boston: Allyn & Bacon.

Boring, E. G. (1923, April). Facts and fancies of immigration. *The New Republic,* 245–246.

Brigham, C. C. (1923). *A study of American intelligence.* Princeton, NJ: Princeton University Press.

Bruininks, R. H., & Lakin, K. C. (Eds.). (1985). *Living and learning in the least restrictive environment.* Baltimore, MD: Paul H. Brookes.

Butler, F. O. (1951). Sterilizations in the United States. *American Journal of Mental Deficiency, 56,* 360–363.

Davenport, C. B. (1911). *Heredity in relation to eugenics.* New York: Henry Holt & Co.

Deutsch, A. (1949). *The mentally ill in America: A history of their care and treatment from colonial times.* (2nd ed.). New York: Columbia University Press.

Doll, E. A. (1935). *The Vineland Social Maturity Scale.* Vineland, NJ: Training School at Vineland.

Dugdale, R. L. (1877). *The Jukes.* New York: Putman.

Edgerton, R. B. (Ed.). (1984). *Lives in process: Mildly retarded adults in a large city.* Washington, DC: American Association on Mental Deficiency.

Eisenberg, M. G., Griggins, C., & Duval, R. J. (Eds). (1982). *Disabled people as second-class citizens.* New York: Springer.

Esquirol, J. E. D. (1838). *Des maladies mentales* (2 volumes). Paris: J. B. Baillière.

Expansion program at Idaho State School and Colony. (1949, October). *AAMD News,* p. 10.

Fernald, G. (1943). *Remedial techniques in basic school subjects.* New York: McGraw-Hill.

Fernald, W. E. (1892). Some of the methods employed in the care and training of feeble-minded children of the lower grades. *Proceedings of the Association of Medical Officers of American Institution for Idiotic and Feeble-Minded Persons, 16,* 450–452.

Fernald, W. E. (1904). Care of the feeble-minded. *Proceedings of the National Conference of Charities and Corrections,* 380–390.

Fernald, W. E. (1909). The imbecile with criminal instincts. *Journal of Psycho-Asthenics, 14,* 16–38.

Fernald, W. E. (1912). The burden of feeblemindedness. *Journal of Psycho-Asthenics, 17,* 89–111.

Fernald, W. E. (1915). What is possible in the way of prevention of mental defect? *Proceedings of the National Conference of Charities and Corrections,* 289–297.

Fernald, W. E. (1917). The growth of provision for the feeble-minded in the United States. *Mental Hygiene, 1,* 34–57.

Fernald, W. E. (1919a). After-care study of the patients discharged from Waverley for a period of twenty-five years. *Ungraded, 5,* 25–31.

Fernald, W. E. (1919b). State programs for the care of the mentally defective. *Journal of Psycho-Asthenics, 24,* 114–122.

Fernald, W. E. (1920). An out-patient clinic in connection with a state institution for the feeble-minded. *Journal of Psycho-Asthenics, 20,* 81–89.

Fernald, W. E. (1922). The diagnosis of the higher grades of mental defect. *Ungraded, 7,* 126–130.

Fernald, W. E. (1924). Thirty years' progress in the care of the feeble-minded. *Journal of Psycho-Asthenics, 29,* 206–219.

Flynn, R. J., & Nitsch, K. E. (Eds.). (1980). *Normalization, social integration, and community services.* Baltimore, MD: Paul H. Brookes.

Galton, F. (1907). *Inquiries into human faculty and its development.* London: J. M. Dent (original work published 1883).

Gamble, C. J. (1951). The prevention of mental deficiency by sterilization, 1949. *American Journal of Mental Deficiency, 56,* 192–197.

Goddard, H. H. (1909). Suggestions for a prognostical classification of mental defectives. *Journal of Psycho-Asthenics, 14,* 48–54.

Goddard, H. H. (1912). *The Kallikak family: A study in the heredity of feeblemindedness.* New York: Macmillian.

Goddard, H. H. (1915). The possibilities of research as applied to the prevention of feeble-mindedness. *Proceeding of the National Conference of Charities and Corrections,* 307–312.

Goddard, H. H. (1917). Mental tests and the immigrant. *Journal of Delinquency, 2,* 243–247.

Gould, S. J. (1981). *The mismeasure of man.* New York: W. W. Norton.

Historical notes on institutions for the mentally defective. (1940). *American Journal of Mental Deficiency, 45,* 187–189.

Historical notes on institutions for the mentally defective. (1941). *American Journal of Mental Deficiency, 45,* 340–341.

Hungerford, R. H. (1941). The Detroit plan for occupational education of the mentally retarded. *American Journal of Mental Deficiency, 46,* 102–106.

Ingram, C. L. (1935). *The education of slow learning children.* Yonkers, NY: World Book.

Inskeep, A. (1926). *Teaching dull and retarded children.* New York: Macmillian.

Itard, J. M. G. (1962). *The wild boy of Aveyron* (G. Humphrey and M. Humphrey, Trans.) New York: Appleton–Century–Crofts (original work published in 1806).

Johnson, B. S. (1950). A study of sterilized persons from the Laconia State School. *American Journal of Mental Deficiency, 54,* 404–408.

Kanner, L. (1964). *A history of the care and study of the mentally retarded.* Springfield, IL: Charles C. Thomas.

Kerlin, I. N. (1892). President's annual address. *Proceedings of the Association of Medical Officers of American Institution for Idiotic and Feeble-Minded Persons, 16,* 274–285.

Kuhlmann, F. (1915). What constitutes feeble-mindedness? *Journal of Psycho-Asthenics, 19,* 214–236.

Kuhlmann, F. (1940). One hundred years of special care and training. *American Journal of Mental Deficiency, 45,* 8–24.

Lakin, K. C., & Bruininks, R. H. (Eds.). (1985). *Strategies for achieving community integration of developmentally disabled citizens.* Baltimore, MD: Paul H. Brookes.

Landman, J. H. (1932). *Human sterilization: The history of the sexual sterilization movement.* New York: Macmillian.

Laughlin, H. H. (1926). *Eugenical sterilization.* New York: American Eugenics Society.

Lazerson, M. (1975). Educational institutions and mental subnormality: Notes on writing a history. In M. J. Begab & S. A. Richardson (Eds.), *The mentally retarded and society: A social science perspective* (pp. 33–52). Baltimore, MD: University Park Press.

Little, C. S. (1904). *Second biennial report to the trustees of the New Hampshire School for the Feeble-Minded at Laconia, for the two years ending September 30, 1904: Vol. I, Part II.* Concord, NH.

Lundberg, E. O. (1947). Pathfinders of the middle years. *Social Science Review, 21,* 1–5.

Marks, R. (1981). *The idea of IQ.* Lanham, MD: University Press of America.

Mott, R. A. (1888). Status of the work — Minnesota. *Proceedings of the Association of Medical Officers of American Institution for Idiotic and Feeble-Minded Persons, 12,* 76–77.

New Hampshire Laws of 1901, Chapter 102, *An Act to Provide for the Care and Education of Feeble-Minded Children.* (Amended Februray 16, 1905, Chapter 23; March 10, 1909, Chapter 47; and April 10, 1917, Chapter 141.)

Roselle, E. N. (1952). Some thoughts on the administrative organization of a training school for mental defectives. *American Journal of Mental Deficiency, 56,* 524–536.

Roselle, E. N. (1954). Some principles and philosophies in the planning and development of institutional plants with particular reference to institutions for the mentally retarded. *American Journal of Mental Deficiency, 58,* 595–624.

Rothman, D. (1971). *Discovery of the asylum: Social order and disorder in the new republic.* Boston: Little, Brown, and Company.

Scheerenberger, R. C. (1983). *A history of mental retardation.* Baltimore, MD: P. H. Brookes.

Seguin, E. O. (1846). *Traitment moral, hygienè et éducation des idiots et des autres enfants arrierés.* Paris: Baillière.

Seguin, E. O. (1866). *Idiocy and its treatment by the physiological method.* New York: W. Wood & Co.

Skeels, H., & Dye, H. (1939). A study of the effects of differential stimulation on mentally retarded children. *Journal of Psycho-Asthenics, 44,* 114–136.

Smith, T. L. (1973). Immigrant social aspirations and American education, 1880–1930. In M. B. Katz (Ed.), *Education in American history: Readings on the social issues* (pp. 236–251). New York: Prager.

Spencer, H. (1877). *Principles of sociology.* New York: Appleton.

Talbot, M. (1967). Edouard Seguin. *American Journal of Mental Deficiency, 72,* 184–189.

Terman, L. M. (1916). *The measurement of intelligence.* Boston: Houghton–Mifflin.

Terman, L. M. (1917). Feeble-minded children in the public schools of California. *School and Society, 5,* 156–187.

Wilbur, H. B. (1852). *First annual report of the Trustees of the New York State Asylum for Idiots to the legislature of the State.* Albany, NY: State Printers.

Wilbur, H. B. (1879). Status of the work — New York. *Proceedings of the Association of Medical Officers of American Institution for Idiotic and Feeble-Minded Persons, 1,* 95–108.

Wolfensberger, W. (1972). *The principle of normalization in human services.* Toronto: National Institute on Mental Retardation.

Yerkes, R. M. (1922). *The Work of the Committee on the Scientific Problems of Human Migration of the National Research Council.* Washington, DC: Carnegie Institution (Circular No. 58).

CHAPTER 2

Issues and Trends in Mental Retardation

*MARY A. FALVEY, KATHRYN B. BISHOP,
MARQUITA GRENOT–SCHEYER,
AND JENNIFER COOTS*

*T*he traditional focus of programming for adults with mental retardation has been on their disabilities rather than on their abilities. This emphasis has, unfortunately, caused more segregation between those with and without an identified disability. In addition, such emphasis has often created a barrier for those attempting to achieve their maximum independence and participation in society. For example, people with behavior disorders and mental retardation are generally grouped together in programs, providing little or no opportunity to learn appropriate social behaviors.

Mental retardation suggests departure from the norm developmentally. Those supporting the continued use of labels have argued that funding and rights are protected and ensured if labeling is used and emphasized. For example, PL 94–142, the Education for All Handicapped Children Act, sets forth the right to a free and appropriate educational program in the least-restrictive environment for school-age children with handicaps, and provides fiscal incentives to states complying with this law.

Definitions of mental retardation (Haney, Wilson, & Halle, Chapter 3 of this volume) provide no direction as to the assistance necessary for persons with mental retardation to live, work, and recreate in their neighborhoods. Nor do they provide hope for remediation or habilitation, implying "once retarded, always retarded." Decisions regarding placement any/or types and amounts of services should be based on the person's strengths, or as Marc Gold (1980) stated, on a person's competencies. Programs and services should identify and build on a person's strengths and abilities, rather than focusing on weaknesses and disabilities.

LITIGATION AND LEGISLATION

Two major sets of actions that have improved the delivery of services to persons with mental retardation and other developmental disabilities are litigation and legislation. These actions have also shaped society's attitudes and commitments toward improving the quality of life for persons with disabilities.

Litigation has had a major impact on the development and expansion of programs and services for persons with disabilities. *Wyatt v. Stickney* was the first landmark case affecting persons with mental retardation being referred to or already placed in institutions. Judge Frank Johnson ruled that persons with mental retardation have the right to the least-restrictive environment for habilitation and intervention. To prevent new referrals to institutions, services must be developed and provided within the community rather than admitting those individuals to institutions. This court case has affected the lives of many people with mental retardation since referrals to state hospitals have diminished, and the quality and appropriateness of programs and services within the community have improved since this case was settled.

In one of the most widely publicized cases in history, *New York Association for Retarded Citizens v. Rockfeller,* the court upheld the rights of the residents of Willowbrook State Institution to a more humane existence. Willowbrook was ordered to reduce its population from 3,000 to 350 within 6 years. This decision has spawned the development of community-based programs and services for persons with mental retardation.

A landmark litigation case affecting and ensuring the residential and educational rights of persons with mental retardation was the Pennsylvania case *Halderman v. Pennhurst State School and Hospital.* Frank Laski (1980) summarized Judge Raymond J. Broderick's orders as:

A series of permanent injunctions to insure that the residents of Pennhurst and those on the waiting list are provided individual program plans and are provided with suitable community living arrangements and services,

Injunctions prohibiting admission or committment of persons to Pennhurst,

Injunctions governing the interim operation of the institution,

Appointment of a Special Master to plan, organize, direct, supervise, and monitor the implementation of the court's order,

A Plan of Implementation consisting of eight discrete plans to be submitted to the court by the Master (p. 169).

Litigation has led to the development of legislation, which in turn has provided statutes that better ensure and protect the rights of persons with mental retardation. Three legislative acts have been particularly influential in ensuring rights and needed services for persons with mental retardation. First, the Rehabilitation Act of 1973, modeled after the Civil Rights Act of 1964, suggested that the United States Congress was committed to the concept of banishing separation and segregation of persons with disabilities. This legislation set forth the following protections:

"No otherwise qualified *handicapped* individual, solely by reason of his handicap, *be exluded* from participation in, *be denied the benefits* of, or *be subjected to discrimination* under any program or activity receiving federal financial assistance." (Sec. 84.4[a])

Senator Humphrey introduced the act with an impressive and poignant speech, stating (118 Cong. Rec. 525, January 20, 1972):

The time has come when we can no longer tolerate the invisibility of the handicapped in America.... I am calling for public attention to three-fourths of the nation's institutionalized mentally retarded, who live in public and private residential facilities which are more than 50 years old, functionally inadequate, and designed simply to isolate these persons from society.... These people have the right to live, to work to the best of their ability — to know the dignity to which every human being is entitled.

The Congress moved quickly after the passage of the Rehabilitation Act of 1973 to enact PL 94–142. Although rights assured under the latter act do not extend to adults with disabilities, the services individuals have received as children and young adults have necessitated changes in existing adult programs and services. The basic guarantees under this legislation are summarized as follows.

□ All handicapped children, adolescents, and young adults shall receive an education, that is, a zero-rejection policy.

□ Children, adolescents, and young adults shall receive an *appropriate* educational program that meets their unique individualized needs.

□ Educational programs shall be provided in the *least restrictive environment,* that is, students must *not* be segregated from non-handicapped peers without documented educationally compelling reasons.

□ Students and parents shall be provided with a *due process* procedure.

The Developmentally Disabled Assistance Act (PL 95–602), signed by President Carter in 1978, made it possible to coordinate and deliver services for persons with mental retardation and other developmental disabilities. This act ensures persons with developmental disabilities the right to "a combination sequence of special, interdisciplinary, or generic care, treatment, or other services that are of lifelong or extended duration and are individually planned and coordinated" (Breen & Richman, 1979, p. 5). This act, often referred to as the "Bill of Rights" for persons with developmental disabilities, guarantees and ensures the development of appropriate and needed programs and services for all ages of persons with developmental disabilities.

NORMALIZATION

In addition to litigation and legislation, another dynamic influence that has continued to shape the quality of life for persons with mental retardation has been an ideology: the *normalization principle.* Bank–Mikkelsen, head of the Danish Mental Retardation Services in 1969, defined normalization as a facilitative process by which persons with mental retardation can obtain an existence as close to "normal" as possible (Bank–Mikkelsen, 1969).

Normalization was further defined by Wolfensberger (1980) as:

□ The use of culturally valued means, in order to enable people to live culturally valued lives

□ Use of culturally normative means to offer persons life conditions at least as good as that of average citizens, and to as much as possible enhance or support their behavior, appearances, experiences, status and reputation

□ Utilization of means which are as culturally normative as possible, in order to establish, enable or support behaviors, appearances, experiences and interpretations which are as culturally normative as possible. (p. 8)

The normalization principle has continued to guide and direct professionals and parents to develop and provide integrated services and programs for persons with mental retardation. The remainder of the chapter will address the characteristics of quality services and support necessary for persons with mental retardation to participate to the maximum extent possible in normalized and integrated communities.

EDUCATION PROGRAMS

The successfulness of special education programs can best be determined by evaluating the lifestyles, opportunities, and activities of their graduates. Van Deventer, Yelnick, Brown, Schroeder, Loomis, and Gruenewald (1981) conducted such a review of former students with mental retardation who attended the Madison (Wisconsin) School District from 1971 to 1978. Characteristics evaluated in this study included the following: (1) whether a person worked; (2) whether the work environment afforded opportunities to interact with nonhandicapped peers; (3) average income per month; (4) amount and type of community integration; (5) nature and type of recreation activities and opportunities; and (6) amount and type of interaction with nonhandicapped peers in their living environment. Results from this study and informal observations of other educational programs across the United States suggest inadequacies of these programs in preparing children who are mentally retarded for adulthood. Graduates are frequently unprepared to participate in the general work force, having had minimal opportunities to live, work, and recreate in integrated environments with their nonhandicapped peers. Because the ultimate goal of such programs is to prepare people to participate in a variety of heterogeneous, integrated environments, these results have had significant effect on educational services and programs (Brown, Nietupski, & Hamre–Nietupski, 1976).

The concept of normalization is clearly reflected in the establishment and development of integrated educational programs for students with mental retardation. The segregation of students with mental retardation is currently being rejected as parents, educators, administrators, and resource personnel realize that when such students attend segregated schools, ultimately their adult lives will be spent in segregated environments (Brown, 1986). This does not, however, imply that all school-age individuals will be mainstreamed into regular educational programs without the support of special education. Instead, the movement to integrated educational settings requires that the services and resources, previously only provided in segregated settings, be provided in integrated settings. By using resources earlier expended in segregated programs, school districts all across the country have developed and implemented exemplary, specialized, and individualized educational programs for students with the most significant and complex disabilities in regular neighborhood public schools (Taylor, 1982).

As educational settings have changed from segregated to integrated, so too have the educational curricula for students with mental retardation. Early educational programs were based on a developmental approach. The predominant view during this time was that because these students were developing very slowly, intervention should be directed at replicating in them the growth patterns of nonhandicapped individuals, regardless of the students' ages (Certo, 1983). Unfortunately, this led to the teaching of chronologically age-inappropriate and non-functional skills, which resulted in maintaining their segregation from nonhandicapped peers.

As a result of the inadequacy of a developmental approach, Lou Brown and his colleagues presented an alternative curriculum development strategy based on three major assumptions:

1. Students with mental retardation should be prepared to function as independently as possible across as many integrated, heterogeneous environments as possible, i.e., criterion of ultimate functioning (Brown, Nietupski, & Hamre-Nietupski, 1976).
2. Students with mental retardation have substantial difficulties generalizing skills taught in one environment to other environments. Therefore, activities must be taught in the environment that requires the activity, according to the natural cues and corrections particular to that environment (Falvey, Brown, Lyon, Paumgart, & Schroeder, 1980).
3. Instructional strategies should be sufficiently flexible and individualized to meet the diverse needs of students with mental retardation (Falvey, 1986).

One assessment strategy, ensuring the teaching of chronologically age-appropriate and functional skills, involves the use of Ecological and Student Repertoire Inventories (Brown, Branston, Hamre–Nietupski, Pumpian, Certo, & Gruenewald, 1979). First, those skills performed by nonhandicapped age-matched peers in the natural environment of interest are identified. Next, the student's abilities to perform these same skills are assessed. Table 2–1 provides an example of how such an inventory can be applied.

These inventories and subsequent instruction should occur in natural environments (i.e, those frequented by nonhandicapped peers who live, work, and recreate in the same community as the student with a handicap. The adult is taught to perform skills in response to natural cues and correction procedures (Falvey et al., 1980), natural consequences

Ecological and Student Repertoire Inventory

Domain: Vocational	Name: Nathan
Environment: Vons Grocery Store	Date: September 3, 1986
Sub-Environment: Canned Fruit & Vegetable Aisle	Age: 36

Ecological Inventory	**Student Repertoire Inventory**	**Recommendations**
Activity 1: Stacking Shelves		
Skill 1: Locate shelf for items to be stacked	Unable to locate shelves	Provide extensive practice: use picture cues
Skill 2: Arrange existing cans on shelf	No problem	
Skill 3: Take cans out of box and place on shelf	No problem	
Skill 4: Arrange cans on shelf	Not arranged straight enough	Provide extensive practice
Skill 5: Returns cans that do not fit on shelf to storeroom	Does not initiate this activity	Use picture cues for sequence
Skill 6: Break up empty boxes	No problem	
Skill 7: Put empty, broken-up boxes in garbage dumpster	Does not initiate this activity	Use picture cards for sequence
Activity 2: Interacting with Customers		
Skill 1: Look in direction of customer requesting assistance	Looks at floor when someone approaches	Provide extensive experiences at interacting with others
Skill 2: Answer customer's question(s), if possible.	No verbal skills	Develop augmentative aid and teach student to use
Skill 3: If not possible, direct customer to manager's desk at front of store	Will not direct customer	Augmentative aid should be of assistance

(LaVigna & Donnellan, 1986), and natural materials (Falvey, 1986). Haney et al., in Chapter 3 of this volume, provide additional discussion of ecological analysis and the use of social validation as means of identifying program content.

PARTIAL PARTICIPATION

To ensure that *all* individuals with mental retardation, even those with a limited number of skills in their repertoire, have the opportunity to become as independent as possible, the principle of *partial participation* has been adopted (Baumgart et al., 1982). This principle is based on the assumption that it is better for a person to at least partially participate than to be denied access to or participation in an activity or environment because of incomplete or absent skills. For example, a nonspeaking person who is not familiar with labels of particular items on the shelves of a grocery store should *not* be expected to develop oral communication abilities and vocabulary specific to the grocery store as a prerequisite to participating in that environment. On the contrary, the individual should be provided with an augmentative communication aid and then be systematically instructed within the natural context of the grocery store. This aid might take the form of a communication booklet consisting of pictures connoting a grocery shopping list and other concepts he/she would like or need to express.

TRANSITION PROGRAMS

As individuals make the transition into adulthood, the challenge to educators and clinicians to provide them with the opportunities to develop the skills necessary to participate in integrated, heterogeneous, adult environments becomes even more critical. Transition programs specifically designed to prepare individuals for adult life must be developed and provided. Integrated community-based training relies on the skills of the individual with mental retardation and the interdependence and reliance of nonhandicapped peers (Voeltz, 1983). Nonhandicapped adults who live, work, and recreate in integrated environments are to some degree dependent on other members of their community for various forms of support at different times. Adults with mental retardation, similar to nonhandicapped peers, must be provided with the skills necessary to interact with community members and the opportunity to do so. Instead of offering a "handicapped recreation" program on Wednesday nights and Saturdays, normalized recreation should be available and accessed, for example, the local YMCA, movie theaters, and local parks. The fostering of this interdependence, that is, mutual care and respect for one another, is greatly enhanced and can only be accomplished effectively if opportunities to grow together and establish relationships and friendships are provided (Strully & Strully, 1986). Systematic and longitudinal planning and coordination between school and post-school programs, services, and agencies must be conducted to facilitate the maintenance of functional skills already acquired and the continued acquisition of skills leading to increased integration of the individuals into the community.

INSTRUCTIONAL PROCEDURES

The majority of instructional programs for adults with mental retardation share certain principles and techniques. Applied behavioral analysis is evident in most quality programs for individuals with mental retardation. This analysis includes

- □ Direct and frequent measurement of behaviors,
- □ Individual task analysis of target behavior, and
- □ Use of reinforcement principles.

Systematic and individualized application of applied behavior analysis techniques and strategies have proven successful in skill acquisition and maintenance (Premack, 1959; Skinner, 1974; Sulzer–Azaroff & Mayer, 1977).

Generalization is an essential component of training programs and must be systematically planned for and taught in all instructional activities (Zeaman & House, 1963). General case programming (Horner, Sprague, & Wilcox, 1982) is one strategy for teaching generalization by identifying all possible stimulus dimensions (e.g., people present, cues provided) present in the person's natural environments. The person is then provided with direct instruction involving all those naturally occurring stimulus dimensions. For example, street-crossing skills vary across street corners in that sometimes it is necessary to respond to street lights, whereas at other times a person is directing traffic. Also, the absence of cars traveling in the direction of the corner being crossed needs to be considered. To teach a person to respond to just one of these cues would not provide him/her with the opportunity to generalize the skill to safely cross the street with different cues present.

In addition to teaching persons to respond to relevant stimulus dimensions, some attention must be devoted to reducing inappropriate behaviors. In the past, aversive procedures and physical punishment have been used for instructional purposes and/or in response to socially inappropriate, self-injurious, or dangerous behaviors. The instructional technology to manage such behaviors has been analyzed, scrutinized, and refined such that these practices are now regarded as both unethical and unnecessary (LaVigna & Donnellan, 1986).

Positive programming, an alternative to the use of aversive procedures, can be effective in establishing functional behaviors while reducing problems (LaVigna & Donnellan, 1986). The major goal of positive programming is to replace the behavioral deficits with functional skills. For example, an adult with mental retardation who is unable to verbalize, yells and shouts to indicate the completion of a task after placing two dirty towels in the hamper at a beauty parlor, his job training site. Instead of using punishment procedures and ignoring this inappropriate attempt at communicating, the job coach physically prompts the adult to put one towel in the hamper while positively reinforcing him using a soft voice as a model of acceptable sounds in that environment. Over time, the physical prompts are faded as the adult exhibits an increase in the number of towels placed in the hamper without yelling or shouting. When this behavior becomes a part of the adult's repertoire, there is no longer a need for artificial reinforcement.

WORK PROGRAMS

An adult's status in the United States is often measured by issues related to his/her employment or lack of employment. As indicated by Haney, et al. (see Chapter 3 of this volume), adults with mental retardation are experiencing increasing opportunities to participate in meaningful work situations. Historically, adults with significant disabilities were restricted to involvement in segregated activity center programs, sheltered workshops, or no day program at all. These options were developed as a continuum of sheltered training programs, which an individual would "flow through" before moving in to competitive employment (Bellamy, Rhodes, Bourbeam, & Mank, 1987).

Sheltered workshops are segregated facilities that subcontract work from outside industries and train employees to perform the necessary tasks. Unfortunately, these programs have not generally prepared people with mental retardation to work in nonsheltered environments. According to federal statistics, less than 2 percent of these individuals enrolled in sheltered environments ever made it out into the "real" world of work (Bellamy, Rhodes, Bourbeam, & Mank, 1987).

An alternative to sheltered, traditional day programs for adults is supported employment. The reader is referred to Haney et al. (Chapter 3 of this volume) for a comprehensive discussion of features characterizing these respective vocational settings. *Supported employment* is a concept that focuses on a set of outcomes rather than functioning as a vehicle of service delivery (McDaniel & Flippo, 1986). The outcomes for supported employment are:

- □ The individual requires and will receive ongoing support (not time limited);
- □ The individual must have paid employment;
- □ Work is performed in integrated settings: and
- □ A place and train model is used, eliminating time-consuming and generally ineffective prevocational training programs.

Individuals targeted for supported employment are those who are either ineligible for, or have been unsuccessfully served by, traditional vocational rehabilitation programs because of the infeasibility of competitive employment. Supported employment targets individuals who will most likely be in need of ongoing assistance to maintain employment. It is a "zero-reject" model in that there are no minimum requirements to be placed (Barker, Kogen, & Youngdahl, 1986). Brown, Albright, Solner, Shiraga, Rogan, York, and VanDeventer (in preparation) maintain that successful placement is possible as long as an individual has one consistent motor movement. For example, a 23-year-old female with only one consistent motor response was taught to operate a computer through the use of a pointer, and a 43-year-old male with only one consistent motor response operated a trash masher at a hospital through the use of an adapted switch. According to Brown and his colleagues, if an individual does not have a consistent motor movement necessary for performing a particular job, then intervention would focus on teaching such a movement.

In 1985, the Office of Special Education and Rehabilitation Services (OSERS) issued a supported employment initiative indicating that it should be the primary service option for adults with mental retardation. To accommodate the demand for supported employment, adult service agencies have made use of different strategies in developing a supported employment program. Some existing facilities have chosen to continue to operate an activity center and/or sheltered workshop while adding a supported employment component and gradually phasing out their segregated programs. Others are new agencies created for the sole purpose of facilitating supported employment (McDaniel & Flippo, 1986).

In providing supported employment to individuals, agencies have utilized a variety of placement methods. Some placements are individual sites in which an adult with mental retardation is employed by a business and supported by the agency. Agency support can include direct job task training at the site, providing adaptations (e.g., augmentative communication system, long-handled brooms, shorter file cabinets), teaching lunch or break-time behaviors, providing or teaching skills for transportation, and so forth. Following are some specific examples of individual placements the authors have observed utilizing supported employment.

Matt was a 56-year-old man who was severely retarded. He had no school programs nor was he involved in any day programs. He lived with his mother in an apartment and spent most of his time "hanging out" on the streets. He was an alcoholic and was on probation with the police department for frequent exhibitionism. When he was initially referred for supported employment, he was placed and trained to work in the kitchen of a restaurant and taught to ride the public bus to and from work. Matt earned an hourly salary above minimum wage. He was supported by the agency when new equipment was installed, adaptations were needed, or new managers arrived and needed to understand Matt's communication modes. Matt no longer drinks, nor have there been any incidents with the police.

Chip, a 25-year-old man with mental retardation and autism, was very intolerant of other people and was unable to cope with changes in his routine easily. He worked at a local college as part of the groundskeeping crew. His job was to check the sprinkler system and water areas not covered by sprinklers. He worked alone but was able to eat lunch and take breaks with the rest of the crew without exhibiting significant behavior problems. Chip received support related to his behavior when new staff were added to the crew or if his job changed that day due to employer needs. He was receiving minimum wage and was paid directly by the employer.

Tracy was 32 years old and diagnosed as multihandicapped, including severe cerebral palsy, blindness, and profound mental retardation. Tracy worked as a recycler. Her gurney was positioned to the right of a bin full of metal and aluminum cans. With a large magnet attached to her hand, Tracy was able to move her hand over the bin containing aluminum and metal cans. The metal cans were attached to the magnet and she placed them in the bin on the left of her gurney by scraping the can off the magnet using the side of the bin. Tracy worked in a large room with 25 nonhandicapped co-workers and one other worker with a significant disability. She received support for transportation to and from work, assistance in beginning and ending the sorting task, assistance in eating her lunch, and assistance periodically throughout the day for other personal needs. She was paid by the employer with a U.S. Department of Labor subminimum wage certification for the work she performed.

Group placements are also possible through practices such as work stations in industry, affirmative action, or mobile crews. The main concern with group placements is the difficulty of developing integrated sites where interactions with nonhandicapped individuals will occur, and maintaining natural proportions of workers with and without disabilities (Brown et al., 1985). Examples of group placements from the authors' experiences that also reflect interaction opportunities are provided below.

Work stations in industry: Four adults and one job coach work at a linen supply house that employs more than 150 people. The clients do specific tasks alongside nondisabled co-workers, with the job coach intervening when behavior problems are exhibited, new tasks are assigned, and/or rate or quality of work needs improvement.

Affirmative action: In a rural town, an agency opened a factory that employed eight adults with severe disabilities throughout different shifts. The agency employed a total of 35 nondisabled workers who worked alongside the workers with severe disabilities.

Mobile crew: Five adults were employed by a construction company to serve as the finishing crew for their construction sites. With the help of an agency van and a job coach, the clients were sent to completed sites to sort through usable and unusable materials, do general cleaning, and any specific finishing touches, such as tightening fixtures, and watering the grounds. This work was performed while the construction company staff were still on the job to allow opportunities for interaction.

Supported employment is a concept that is necessary if people with the most significant disabilities are ever to be integrated into the work place. However, integrating people into employment is not the only area that needs attention. Bellamy, Rhodes, Wilcox, Albin, Mank, Boles, Horner, Collins, and Turner (1984) suggested that such supports should prevail 24 hours a day.

It is important to consider that after an individual is employed, he/she should not lose needed instruction and/or assistance in the other domains of adult life. Domestic, community and mobility, consumer, and recreation and leisure skills are also deserving of direct instruction and ongoing support for these adults to participate in community-integrated environments. Support in all domains should include the integration of basic skills such as communication (e.g., using augmentative aids) and motor skills. Only when the "whole" individual is being positively supported and encouraged to become as independent in the community as possible will adult service providers be effective.

LIVING OPTIONS AND ARRANGEMENTS

Most people in our society have the opportunity to live in a neighborhood with people of their choice (i.e., with family or friends, or alone). Unfortunately, people with mental retardation have often been denied this basic opportunity in the name of treatment or intervention. Assumptions have been made with regard to the necessary habilitative characteristics of living environments. Historically, the need for specialized living environments has been considered more important than the need for interacting with "typical" neighbors and other community members. As a result, insitutions warehousing large numbers of persons with mental retardation were built, and these so-called "specialized habilitation services" were provided. Studies have found that institutions have not been able to provide the services and resources necessary to habilitate a person with mental retardation (Aanes & Moen, 1976; Goroff, 1967; Nihira & Nihira, 1975; & Wolfensberger, 1976). Comparative studies between institutional and community-based living have found that community-based living arrangements are more habilitative in terms of acquiring skills as well as interacting with neighbors and the community, and in general provide for a better quality of life (Browder, Ellis, & Neal, 1974; Krishef, Reynolds, & Stunkard, 1959).

Numerous efforts have been made to establish and maintain community-based living arrangements. Perske (1980) relayed several scenarios he discovered when conducting research on persons with mental retardation in neighborhoods. One such scenario follows (p. 24).

> Peter Graves was sent to an institution in 1949 after a diagnosis of "mental retardation: encephalopathy due to postnatal cerebral infection." Since he was not expected to develop normally, he stayed at the institution for 25 years, with government paying a total of $432,600 for his keep. Of course the later years were the most expensive: The government paid $21,624 for 1974, his last year. However, by 1979, Peter Graves had been living in his hometown for five years, and he
> - ☐ was working full-time in the auto body shop;
> - ☐ had moved from a small-group home into his own apartment;
> - ☐ no longer received supplementary income checks from the government;
> - ☐ recorded a taxable income of $11,752.85 for 1978;
> - ☐ paid $1,620 in income to the government;
> - ☐ received only periodic follow-up counseling from a regional caseworker (average cost to the government: $17 per month)

Not all persons with mental retardation leaving institutions will be able to live independently or earn as much as Peter Graves. However, the possibilities and probabilities significantly increase when people are provided with integrated living options and necessary interventions and support. In summarizing his research, Perske (1980) indicated that persons with mental retardation added "zest and rejuvenation" to neighborhoods because when people in the same community had common goals, they supported one another. The advantages of such a movement to community-based living arrangements appear to be reciprocal in nature.

In recommending living arrangements for persons with mental retardation, service providers have often considered existing living options and attempted to determine the closest fit, for example, if a large residential facility and an unsupervised apartment are the only two living arrangements available within a particular community. If the individual who requires support 24 hours a day to assist in daily life activities, the only option available would be to place this person in the large residential facility. What that person needs is not the large residential facility but rather the resources to hire an attendant to live in a more normalized living environment. These limited options considerably inhibit and restrict the development of new arrangements that would be appropriate for and preferred by an individual. A person's home and neighborhood living needs should be considered first so that necessary resources can be identified to match these needs in an effective and efficient manner. This concept, referred to as *supported life,* involves people living, working, and recreating within an integrated community setting while being provided with the support services or other resources necessary for them to participate to the greatest extent possible within that community.

Ten characteristics of integrated community-based living options have been delineated by Falvey (1986, p. 10):

1. The homes must be located within existing normalized communities.
2. The number of people living in one home should reflect the same number of people living in other homes within that community (i.e., generally one to six people).
3. Specialized staff and resources should be provided when necessary.
4. Homelike atmospheres should be present.
5. Access to neighborhood and community recreational facilities and activities with nonhandicapped peers must be present.
6. Access to neighborhood and community work opportunities with nonhandicapped peers must be present.
7. Socialization opportunities both within and outside the home must be provided.
8. Residents of homes must be provided the right to choose whom they socialize with, both within and outside the home.
9. Residents of homes must have opportunities to make decisions for themselves and, if necessary, must be provided with the

> opportunity to acquire the skills necessary to make deci-
> sions.
> **10.** Residents of homes must be treated with dignity and respect.

Once again the normalization principle has had a significant effect on the development and creation of integrated living options and arrangements for persons with mental retardation. A great deal of work, attention, and advocacy is needed to continue to promote integrated living options and arrangements.

IMPLICATIONS FOR COMMUNICATION

Communication is a skill that must be performed across all domains of life Therefore, a discussion specific to the implications of communication intervention across all the domains is appropriate. The trend in communication training has been to view the development of communication and speech abilities as an active process. Persons with mental retardation must be taught more than isolated forms and words; rather, they must be taught the overall functions of language and communication and strategies to learn new language and communication skills. The development of more efficient and effective communicative behaviors and strategies can then assist the individual to function more independently in his/her community and workplace and at home.

A critical aspect of functioning as a full member of any community is the ability to interact and communicate with co-workers, employers, family members, friends, community service providers, and other persons with whom adults come into contact during daily functioning in their communities. To become active participants in communication, persons with mental retardation must be taught to assume an initiating role in interactions rather than just a responding role (Bedrosian, Chapter 10 of this volume; Coots, 1985; Falvey, 1986; Halle, Chapter 7 of this volume; MacDonald, 1985; Reichle, Piche–Cragoe, Sigafoos, & Doss, Chapter 9 of this volume).

Communicative behaviors are more likely to be functional and generalizable if they are taught in the environment or setting in which they will be used (Halle, 1982; MacDonald, 1985; Warren & Rogers–Warren, 1985). Instruction in isolated, structured, and distraction-free settings (i.e., therapy rooms) will not assist an individual in acquiring the ability to be involved in the interchanges in the real world. These settings do not provide the opportunity for observing more advanced models or exhibiting spontaneous initiations.

Training in natural settings also assists in identifying critical communicative content. Language differs between workplaces and homes;

therefore the individual must be taught the forms and words that are needed in those work, home, and community settings. Job coaches, speech–language specialists, teachers, parents, and clients must work together as a team in identifying the important communicative content and relevant training environments.

The location of communicative training will have a significant effect on the results of that training. In addition, it is necessary to determine which communication skills to teach. The research on the function of communicative behaviors has resulted in reclassifying behaviors previously considered noncommunicative (Hurtig, Ensurd, & Tomblin, 1982; Prizant & Duchan, 1981; Rein, 1984). The fact that most behaviors have a communicative function implies that everyone should be taught to communicate (Donnellan, Mirenda, Mesaros, & Fassbender, 1984; Gaylord–Ross, Stremel–Campbell, & Storey, 1986: MacDonald, 1985; Musselwhite & St. Louis, 1982). For those clients classified as noncommunicative, behaviors such as temper tantrums, ignoring, and other similar behaviors should be evaluated in terms of their communicative value and possible function.

Although vocal and verbal communication should be stressed because it is used most frequently in our society, nonspeech modes such as signing, gestures, eye gazes, pictures, and objects may be more appropriate in order to teach persons with significant communication disabilities to communicate with others. Decisions about which mode of communication to teach are often viewed as an "either–or choice"; however, researchers and practitioners suggest implementing a mixed-mode approach (MacDonald, 1985; Musselwhite & St. Louis, 1982; Reichle & Keogh, 1986). This means that each individual and environment must be fully assessed to determine individual preference, discreteness of mode, physical ability of the client, adaptability of modes and all other features that would affect the functionality of the mode for each individual. Individuals must be taught to use efficient modes to more effectively communicate. All options must be carefully studied to determine which modes will most effectively meet the person's individual needs within the environments frequented by that person. Calculator (Chapter 11 of this volume) and Reichle et al. (Chapter 9 of this volume) provide a lengthy description of mixed–mode approaches relative to functional augmentative communication training.

SUMMARY

In reviewing the history or service delivery for adults with mental retardation (see Antonak, Chapter 1 of this volume), it is evident that great advances have been made with regard to the development of quality programs and services for these individuals over the past several decades. As these advances become incorporated in local community programs and services, a need to look ahead is inevitable.

In the future, the focus on programs and services should be secondary so that primary attention can be directed toward individuals who are in need of support. Without regard for qualifying labels or diagnoses, persons in our society requiring support to live, work, and recreate in integrated environments should be provided with such support. The human service worker should no longer be asking the question: "In which program should a person be placed?" but rather, "What support systems are necessary for a person to be integrated into his/her community?" Although advances have been made, there is much more to be done to eliminate prejudices toward, barriers against, and lack of resources available for persons with mental retardation.

REFERENCES

Aanes, D., & Moen, M. (1976). Adaptive behavior changes of group home residents. *Mental Retardation, 14(4),* 36–40.

Bank–Mikkelsen, N. E. (1969). A metropolitan area in Denmark: Copenhagen. In R. Kugel & W. Wolfensberger (Eds.), *Changing patterns in residential services for the mentally retarded* (pp. 227–254). Washington, DC: U.S. Government Printing Office.

Barker, L., Kogen, D., & Youngdahl, A. (1986). *Development of performance measures for supported employment programs* (draft report). Berkeley, CA: Berkeley Planning Associates.

Baumgart, D., Brown, L., Pumpian, I., Nesbit, J., Ford, A., Sweet, M., Messina, R., & Schroeder, J. (1982). Principle of partial participation and individualized adaptations in educational programs for severely handicapped students. *Journal of the Association for the Severely Handicapped, 7* (2), 17–27.

Bellamy, G. T., Rhodes, L., Bourbeam, P., & Mank, D. (1987). Mental retardation tion services in sheltered workshops and day activity programs: Consumer benefits and policy alternatives. In F. R. Rusch (Ed.), *Competitive employment: Delivery models, methods and issues.* Baltimore, MD: Paul H. Brookes.

Bellamy, G. T., Rhodes, L., Wilcox, B., Albin, J., Mank, D., Boles, S., Horner, R., Collins, M., & Turner, J. (1984). Quality and equality in employment services for adults with severe disabilities. *Journal of the Association for Persons with Severe Handicaps, 9,* 270–277.

Breen, P., & Richman, G. (1979). Evolution of developmental disabilities concept. In R. Wiegernick & J. W. Pelosi (Eds.), *Developmental disabilities: The DD movement* (pp. 3–6). Baltimore, MD: Paul H. Brookes.

Browder, J., Ellis, L., & Neal, J. (1974). Foster homes: Alternatives to institutions. *Mental Retardation, 12(6),* 33–36.

Brown, L. (1986). Foreword: Then and now. In R. H. Horner, L. H. Meyer, & H. D. B. Fredericks (Eds.), *Education of learners with severe handicaps: Exemplary service strategies* (pp. xi–xiii). Baltimore, MD: Paul H. Brookes.

Brown, L., Albright, K., Solner, A., Shiraga, B., Rogan, P., York, J., & VanDeventer, P. (1985). *The Madison strategy for evaluating the vocational milieu of a worker with severe intellectual disabilities.* In L. Brown, B. Shiraga, J. York, A. Euvairi, P. Soner, K. Zanella, M. Albright, P. Rogan, E. McCarthy, & R. Loomis (Eds.) *Educational programs for students with severe intellectual disabilities Vol. 15* (pp. 113–228). Madison, WI: Madison Metropolitan School District.

Brown, L., Branston, M. B., Hamre–Nietupski, S., Pumpian, I., Certo, N., & Gruenewald, L. (1979). A strategy for developing chronological age appropriate and functional curricular content for severely handicapped adolescents and young adults. *Journal of Special Education, 13(1),* 81–90.

Brown, L., Nietupski, J., & Hamre–Nietupski, S. (1976). The criterion of ultimate functioning and public school services for severely handicapped students. In M. A. Thomas (Ed.), *Hey, don't forget about me! Education's investment in the severely, profoundly and multiply handicapped* (pp. 2–15). Reston, VA: Council for Exceptional Children.

Certo, N. (1983). Characteristics of educational services. In M. E. Snell (Ed.), *Systematic instruction of the moderately and severely handicapped* (2nd ed., pp. 2–15). Columbis, OH: Charles E. Merrill Publishing Co.

Coots, J. J. (1985). *The effects of integration on the functional nature of the communicative/interactive attempts of students with severe handicaps.* Unpublished master's thesis, California State University, Los Angeles.

Donnellan, A. M., Mirenda, P. L., Mesaros, R. A., & Fassbender, L. A. (1984). Analyzing the communicative functions of aberrant behavior. *Journal of the Association for Persons with Severe Handicaps, 9,* 201–212.

Falvey, M. A. (1986). *Community-based curriculum: Instructional strategies for students with severe handicaps.* Baltimore, MD: Paul H. Brookes.

Falvey, M. A., Brown, L., Lyon, S., Baumgart, D., & Schroeder, J. (1980). Strategies for using cues and correction procedures. In W. Sailor, B. Wilcox, & L. Brown (Eds.), *Methods of instruction for severely handicapped students* (pp. 109–134). Baltimore, MD: Paul H. Brookes.

Gaylord–Ross, R., Stremel–Campbell, K., & Storey, K. (1986). Social skill training in natural contexts. In R. H. Horner, L. M. Meyer, & H. D. Fredericks (Eds.), *Education of learners with severe handicaps: Exemplary service strategies* (pp. 161–188). Baltimore, MD: Paul H. Brookes.

Gold, M. W. (1980). *Try another way training manual.* Champaign, IL: Research Press.

Goroff, N. N. (1967). Research on community placement: An exploratory approach. *Mental Retardation, 5,* 17–19.

Halle, J. W. (1982). Teaching functional language to the handicapped: An integrative model of natural environment teaching techniques. *Journal of the Association for Persons with Severe Handicaps, 7,* 29–37.

Horner, R. H., Sprague, J., & Wilcox, B. (1982). General case programming for community activities. In B. Wilcox & G. T. Bellamy (Eds.), *Design of high school programs for severely handicapped students* (pp. 61–98). Baltimore, MD: Paul H. Brookes.

Hurtig, R., Ensrud, S., & Tomblin, J. B. (1982). The communicative function of question production in autistic children. *Journal of Autism and Developmental Disorders, 12,* 57–69.

Krishef, C. H., Reynolds, M. C., & Stunkard, C. L. (1959). A study of factors related to rating post-institutional adjustment. *Minnesota Welfare, 11,* 5–15.

Laski, F. (1980). Right to services in the community. In R. J. Flynn & K. E. Nitsch (Eds.), *Normalization, social integration and community services* (pp. 167–176). Austin, TX: PRO-ED.

LaVigna, G. W., & Donnellan, A. M. (1986). *Alternatives to punishment: Solving behavior problems with non-aversive strategies.* New York: Irvington Publishing Co.

MacDonald, J. M. (1985). Language through conversation: A model for intervention with language-delayed persons. In S. F. Warren & A. K. Rogers-Warren (Eds.), *Teaching functional language* (pp. 89–122). Austin, TX: PRO-ED.

McDaniel, R., & Flippo, K. (1986). *Telesis: Supported employment resource manuals* (draft report). San Francisco, CA: University of San Francisco, Rehabilitation Administration.

Musselwhite, C. R., & St. Louis, K. W. (1982). *Communication programming for the severely handicapped: Vocal and nonvocal strategies:* Austin, TX: PRO-ED.

Nihira, L., & Nihira, K. (1975). Normalization: Behavior in community placement. *Mental Retardation, 13(2),* 9–13.

Perske, R. (1980). *New life in the neighborhood: How persons with retardation of other disabilities can make a good community better.* Nashville, TN: Abingdon Press.

Premack, D. (1959). Toward empirical behavioral laws: I. positive reinforcement. *Psychological Review, 66,* 219–233.

Prizant, B. M., & Duchan, J. F. (1981). The functions of immediate echolalia in autistic children. *Journal of Speech and Hearing Disorders, 46,* 241–249.

Reichle, J., & Keogh, W. J. (1986). Communication instruction for learners with severe handicaps: Some unresolved issues. In R. H. Horner, L. H. Meyer, & H. D. Fredericks (Eds.), *Education of learners with severe handicaps: Exemplary service strategies* (pp. 189–220). Baltimore, MD: Paul H. Brookes.

Rein, R. P. (1984). *Observational study of the use of verbal perseverations by persons with autism.* Unpublished doctoral dissertation, University of California, Los Angeles.

Skinner, B. F. (1974). *About behaviorism.* New York: Random House.

Strully, J., & Strully, C. (1986). Friendship and our children. *Journal of the Association for Persons with Severe Handicaps, 10,* 224–227.

Sulzer-Azaroff, B., & Mayer, G. R. (1977). *Applying behavior-analysis procedures with children and youth.* New York: Holt, Rinehart and Winston.

Taylor, S. (1982). From segregation to integration: Strategies for integrating severely handicapped students in normal school and community settings. *Journal of the Association for Persons with Severe Handicaps, 7,* 42–49.

Van Deventer, P., Yelnick, N., Brown, L., Schroeder, J., Loomis, R., & Gruenewald, L. (1981). A follow-up examination of severely handicapped graduates of the Madison Metropolitan School District from 1971–1978. In L. Brown, D. Baumgart, I. Pumpian, J. Nesbit, A. Ford, R. Loomis, & J. Schroeder (Eds.), *Curricular strategies that can be used to transition severely handicapped students from school to nonschool and postschool environments* (Vol. II. pp. 1–177). Madison, WI: Madison Metropolitan School District.

Voeltz, L. M. (1983). *Why integration.* Unpublished manuscript, University of Minnesota Consortium Institute, Minneapolis, MN.

Warren, S. F., & Rogers-Warren, A. K. (1985). Teaching functional language: An introduction. In S. F. Warren & A. K. Rogers-Warren (Eds.), *Teaching functional language* (pp. 3–23). Austin, TX: PRO-ED.

Wolfensberger, W. (1976). The origin and nature of our institutional models. In R. B. Kugel and A. Shearer (Eds.), *Changing patterns in residential services for the mentally retarded* (revised edition) (President's Committee on Mental Retardation Report No. 040-000-00365-7) (pp. 59–171). Washington, DC: U.S. Government Printing Office.

Wolfensberger, W. (1980). The definition of normalization: Update, problems, disagreements and misunderstandings. In R. J. Flynn & K. E. Nitsch (Eds.), *Normalization, social integration and community services* (pp. 71–116). Baltimore, MD: University Park Press.

Zeaman, D., & House, B. J. (1963). The role of attention in retardate discrimination learning. In N. R. Ellis (Ed.), *Handbook of mental deficiency* (pp. 159–223). New York: McGraw-Hill.

PART II

Characteristics of Adults With Mental Retardation

Adults with Mental Retardation: Who They Are, Where They Are, and How Their Communicative Needs Can Be Met

JANELL I. HANEY
JULIO W. WILSON
JAMES HALLE

Two keys to a clear understanding of communicative assessment and intervention for adults with mental retardation are knowledge of the types of individuals included in this population, and an accurate understanding of the various residential and vocational settings in which these individuals find themselves. The purposes of the present chapter are to provide this foundation and to clarify the linkage between the communication expectations within various settings and the training to be undertaken in those settings. To this end, three sections have been included. In the first section, the population is described in terms of disability and age. Next, residential and vocational placements as well as their relationship to communication training are described. In the final section, placement trends and their implications are discussed.

DESCRIPTION OF THE POPULATION

As indicated by the title of this book, the population of interest is that of adults with mental retardation. However, a brief discussion of developmental disabilities, of which mental retardation is a part, is warranted. This discussion focuses on two dimensions: disability and age.

Disability

The definition of developmental disabilities that is currently in use is based on the Developmental Disabilities Assistance and Bill of Rights Act of 1978 (PL 95-602):

> A severe chronic disability of a person which (a) is attributable to a mental or physical impairment or combination of mental or physical impairment; (b) is manifested before the person attains age twenty-two; (c) is likely to continue indefinitely, (d) results in substantial functional limitations in three or more of the following areas of major life activity (self-care, receptive and expressive language, learning, mobility, self-direction, capacity for independent living, economic self-sufficiency); and (e) reflects the person's need for a combination and sequence of special, interdisciplinary, or generic care, treatment, or other services which are of lifelong or extended duration and are individually planned and coordinated.

The population of individuals with developmental disabilities is characterized by much diversity. Kiernan, Smith, and Ostrowski (1986) report the following prevalence figures for categorical disabilities that are traditionally associated with developmental disabilities:

☐ Mental retardation — 1.0 percent of the population (Bruininks, Rotegar, & Lakin, 1982).

☐ Cerebral palsy — .35 percent of the population (National Cerebral Palsy Medical Directory, 1983).

☐ Epilepsy — 0.75 percent of the population (Meighan, Queener, & Weitman, 1976).

☐ Autism — 0.09 percent of the population (National Society for Autistic Children, 1983).

It is important to note that mental retardation and the other categories frequently overlap. Other possible disabilities that often coexist with mental retardation and that may be included under the rubric of developmental disabilities include sensory handicaps and emotional disturbance other than autism. Because mental retardation is the primary focus of this book, this area will be discussed in detail, followed by a brief description of some major disabilities that may occur concurrently with mental retardation.

The most frequently used definition of mental retardation is that of the American Association on Mental Deficiency (AAMD) (Grossman, 1983). According to this definition, mental retardation is defined as "significantly subaverage general intellectual functioning existing concurrently with deficits in adaptive behavior and manifested during the developmental period." It is important to note that "the developmental period" refers to the time period between conception and the 18th birthday. In addition, the remainder of the definition describes the population in terms of two dimensions: intellectual functioning and adaptive behavior.

General intellectual functioning is to be measured by individual administration of one or more standardized general intelligence tests. "Significantly subaverage" performance on such a test refers to an IQ of 70 or below (although this figure is intended as a guideline rather than a dictate).

Adaptive behavior is to be measured by clinical assessment, which is usually undertaken in conjunction with the administration of standardized scales. *Deficits in adaptive behavior* refers to substantial limitations in effectiveness in meeting age and cultural standards for maturation, learning, personal independence, and/or social responsibility.

The AAMD (Grossman, 1983) defines four levels of retardation: *mild,* with an IQ in the range of from about 50 to 70; *moderate,* with an IQ in the range of about 35 to 50; *severe,* with an IQ in the range of about 20 to 40; and *profound,* with an IQ below about 20. Descriptions of adaptive behavior at each of these levels and at various ages are presented in detail in Appendix A of the AAMD manual. The descriptions pertaining to adults are highlighted in Table 3-1. Disabilities associated with mental retardation include areas such as sensory handicaps, cerebral palsy, epilepsy, and emotional handicaps:

I. *Sensory handicaps* include vision and hearing impairments (Haring, 1986).
2. *Cerebral palsy* is defined as "any disorder of movement and posture that results from a nonprogressive abnormality of the immature brain" (Batshaw & Perret, 1981, p. 191). Thus, cerebral palsy occurs as a result of damage that takes place prior to full maturation of the brain (generally described as occurring at age 16) and that does not progress.
3. *Epilepsy* consists of repeated seizures caused by abnormal, excessive electrical brain function (Bigge & Sirvis, 1986).
4. *Emotional handicap or psychological disorder* is defined as "behavior that deviates from an arbitrary and relative social norm in that it occurs with a frequency or intensity that authoritative adults in the child's environment judge, under the circumstances, to be either too high or too low" (Ross, 1980, p. 9).

Age

Regarding age, this book specifically focuses on adults. Intervention among post-school-age individuals is becoming increasingly important as the size of this population grows. Projections for the future suggest

TABLE 3–1.

Examples of Maximum Levels of Adaptive Behavior for Individuals 15 Years of Age and Older

Area	Mild	Moderate	Severe	Profound
Independent Functioning	Takes care of feeding, bathing, toileting, and grooming; may need help in areas such as personal care reminders or purchase of clothing	Feeds, bathes, and dresses independently; may select clothes; prepares simple foods; combs and brushes hair, may shampoo hair; may wash and/or iron clothes	Feeds self but may need help cutting meat; dresses, including buttons & zipper, may tie shoes, bathes with supervision; uses toilet	Feeds self with spoon and fork; dresses with help on small buttons and zippers; bathes with help; uses toilet but may have accidents or need to be reminded
Social	Interacts both cooperatively and competitively; initiates some group activities; belongs to social groups and enjoys recreation not requiring great skill (e.g., not photography clubs, chess, or tennis)	Interacts both cooperatively and competitively	Participates in group activities spontaneously; chooses friends and maintains friendships for weeks or months	Participates in group activities; interacts in simple play
Communication	Carries on every day but not abstract conversation; uses telephone and writes simple letters	Carries on simple conversation; reads and understands simple prose	May use and understand complex sentences; usually speaks clearly and distinctly; recognizes signs and words, but does not read prose with understanding	Has 300– to 400–word vocabulary; if nonverbal, uses many gestures; understands simple directions and questions; may recognize some words; may have some articulation problems

Note: Data are summarized from the 1983 AAMD manual (Grossman, 1983).

that the average age of the population with mental retardation will continue to increase as the average age of the general population increases (Nanus, 1980). In 1970, there were an estimated 2,049,000 adults with mental retardation in the United States; by 1990 there are expected to be 2,587,000 (McHale, 1980). Accompanying this trend toward increased age is a growth in the number of individuals with retardation who live to old age (Puccio, Janicki, Otis, & Rettig, 1983). Although prevalence estimates vary wildly (see Tarjan, Wright, Eyman, & Keeran, 1973, for a discussion of this issue), the existence of such a trend is well documented.

PLACEMENT

A number of residential and vocational placements are currently available for individuals with mental retardation. These placements and the types of clients typically served in each will be described in this section. Two points are important. First, the descriptions represent only current placement practice and do not necessarily reflect optimal placements for the clients served. Complete reliance on the widely advocated ideology of normalization (see Falvey, et al., Chapter 2 of this volume and Wolfensberger, 1980, for a discussion of normalization) would result in increased placement in community-based settings and integration with nonhandicapped peers to the maximum extent possible. Second, no attempt will be made to describe residential services for specific developmental disabilities other than mental retardation. The prevalence of these other disabilities is relatively small, and these individuals are often placed within the mental retardation service system.

Residential Alternatives

Several typologies of residential facilities for individuals with mental retardation have been proposed (e.g., Baker, Seltzer, & Seltzer, 1977; Bruininks, Hauber, & Kidla, 1979; Butler & Bjaanes, 1977; Eastern Nebraska Community Office of Retardation, 1977; Scheerenberger, 1978, 1983). Issues surroundings the development of these residential typologies (e.g., the diversity of classification systems across states) are discussed in recent reviews (e.g., Heal, Novak, Sigelman, & Switzky, 1980; Hill & Lakin, 1986; Landesman–Dwyer, 1985). The use of the classification system reported by Hill and Lakin (1986) will be discussed here because of its inclusion of most types of facilities of interest, its accompaniment by national prevalence data (from 1982), and its exhibition of high test–retest reliability (i.e., 85% agreement in classification of facilities).

The following residential living arrangements (and typical resident populations for each) will be described:

1. Large public group residences,
2. Large private group residences,
3. Specialized nursing homes,
4. Personal care homes,
5. Board and supervision facilities,
6. Foster homes,
7. Small group residences,
8. Semi-independent living programs,
9. Generic residential services,
10. Natural homes,
11. Independent living programs, and
12. Independent living.

The first eight residential settings are included in Hill and Lakin's (1986) taxonomy. (Numbers 1, 2, and 7 are combined in their discussion as "group residences".) Hill and Lakin's definitions and prevalence figures are specified below. The prevalence figures are for the entire population with mental retardation, rather than for adults only. Although the last four settings were excluded from Hill and Lakin's taxonomy, they are needed to provide a comprehensive overview of all residential facilities for individuals with mental retardation.

Large Public and Private Group Residences

Both large public and large private facilities were defined as providing supervision, care, and training. The mean number of residents in large public facilities was reported to be 365.7 (S.D.= 383.9); while the mean number of residents in large private facilities was reported to be 52.0 (S.D. = 55.7). Of the 122,971 residents with retardation in large public facilities, 7.0 percent were in the mild to borderline range of mental retardation, 12.9 percent were in the moderate range, 24.3 percent were in the severe range, and 55.8 percent were in the profound range. Of the 40,347 residents with mental retardation in the large private facilities, 26.8 percent were in the mild-to-borderline range of mental retardation, 29.9 percent were in the moderate range, 24.0 percent were in the severe range, and 19.3 percent were in the profound range.

Specialized Nursing Homes

Specialized nursing homes were defined as facilities offering daily personal care and nursing care for individuals with mental retardation, with an emphasis on nursing care. The mean number of residents in specialized nursing homes was reported to be 81.8 (S.D. = 61.8). Of the 12, 982 residents with retardation in specialized nursing homes, 9.2 percent were in the borderline-to-mild range of mental retardation, 16.2 percent were in the moderate range, 26.2 percent were in the severe range, and 48.5 percent were in the profound range.

Personal Care Homes

Unlike nursing homes, personal care facilities were not defined as offering nursing care. However, the definition did include provision of personal care such as assistance with eating and dressing and possibly aid with toileting and bathing (homes that do not provide toileting and bathing were sometimes referred to as "domiciliary care homes"). The mean number of residents in personal care homes was reported to be 13.6 (S.D. = 19.8). Of the 4,070 residents with retardation in personal care homes, 31.2 percent were in the borderline-to-mild range of retardation, 39.8 percent were in the moderate range, 20.6 percent were in the severe range, and 8.4 percent were in the profound range.

Board and Supervision Facilities

Although board and supervision facilities were defined as not providing any personal care or formal training, their definition did include provision of bedrooms, meals, and some housekeeping. Residents were supervised but given no formal training. The mean number of residents in board and supervision facilities was reported to be 13.8 (S.D. = 20.3). Of the 1,264 residents with retardation in these facilities, 47.1 percent were in the borderline-to-mild range of retardation, 33.6 percent were in the moderate range, 17.6 percent were in the severe range, and 1.7 percent were in the profound range.

Foster Homes

Foster homes were defined as residences where one or more individuals with mental retardation reside as members of an unrelated family. The mean number of residents in foster homes was reported to be 2.8 (S.D. = 1.9). Of the 17,147 residents with retardation in these facilities, 25.9 percent were in the borderline-to-mild range of retardation, 37.7 percent were in the moderate range, 26.0 percent were in the severe range, and 10.4 percent were in the profound range.

Small Group Residences

Small group facilities were defined as those providing not only care and supervision but also training, and having 15 or fewer residents. The mean number of residents in small group residences was reported to be 6.8 (S.D. = 3.2). Of the 42,018 residents with retardation in these facilities, 29.3 percent were in the mild-to-borderline range of retardation, 37.9 percent were in the moderate range, 23.3 percent were in the severe range, and 9.5 percent were in the profound range.

Semi-independent Living Programs

Semi-independent living programs were defined as units or apartments where staff live in a separate unit in the same building. Supervision in independent living was provided for areas such as meal preparation and banking, although such assistance was not available on a 24-hour basis. The mean number of residents in semi-independent living programs was reported to be 10.3 (S.D. = 8.8). Of the 2,870 residents with retardation in semi-independent living settings, 61.8 percent were in the borderline-to-mild range of retardation, 32.5 percent were in the moderate range, 5.3 percent were in the severe range, and 0.49 percent were in the profound range.

Generic Residential Services, Natural Homes, Independent Living Programs, Independent Living, and Other Settings

Generic residential services are defined as residential programs that are not formally licensed to serve individuals with mental retardation (i.e., services that are available to the general population). Natural homes are residences in which the individual with mental retardation lives with his or her own family. Independent living programs are defined as programs where staff are present but do not reside in the same facility as the residents. Independent living residences are those in which the individual is totally responsible for his or her own welfare (i.e., is independent of the mental retardation service system).

Statistics regarding individuals in these types of settings are understandably unavailable. Reports indicate that roughly 1 percent of the U.S. population use developmental disabilities services (Lindberg, 1976; Mercer, 1973). Meanwhile, only about 0.1 percent of the U.S. population resided in residential facilities that were part of the mental retardation service system, based on information obtained in 1977 and 1982 surveys (Hill, Bruininks, & Lakin, in press). Calculations from Hill and Lakin's (1986) figures suggest that in 1982 about 183,000 adults with mental retardation resided in residential facilities that were part of the mental retardation service system. Therefore, about 1,647,000 resided in other settings: nursing homes, boarding homes, and foster homes not formally licensed to provide services for individuals with mental retardation ("generic" residential services); natural homes; independent living situations; and facilities with less than 24-hour, 7-day-a-week responsibility for individuals with mental retardation ("other" settings).

Expectations

Resident responsibilities and leisure activities often vary more *within* rather than *between* residential settings (see, for example, Bjaanes & Butler, 1974). However, some general characteristics across residential settings may be described with respect to these factors as well as the types of services provided. These characteristics are summarized in Table 3-2, based on a report by Baker et al. (1977) of a nationwide survey and other sources.

In addition to presenting descriptive information, Baker et al. (1977) analyzed residents' autonomy and responsibility across residential settings. Their study included (but was not limited to) small-sized group homes (10 or fewer adults), medium-sized group homes (11 to 20), large-sized group homes (21 to 40), mini-institutions (programs similar to group homes but serving 41 to 80), group homes for older adults (could be group homes or rest homes), foster family care, and semi-independent living (less than 24-hour supervision).

The autonomy scale was based on facility policies regarding curfew, bedtime, alcohol use, and entertainment of the opposite sex. They found the highest degree of autonomy within semi-independent living settings and the least autonomy within mini-institutions. Residents in homes for the elderly had the next lowest degree of autonomy. In the group homes, autonomy decreased as size increased. Autonomy in foster homes was about the same as autonomy in medium- and large-sized group homes.

The responsibility scale was based on household responsibilities: cleaning (bedrooms, living and dining rooms, kitchen), setting the table, preparing and serving meals, doing the dishes, doing the laundry, maintaining the grounds, and shopping (for supplies, food). The greatest responsibility was found in semi-independent living settings; the least was found in homes for the elderly. Within group homes, responsibility decreased somewhat as size increased. However, residents of mini-institutions had roughly the same degree of responsibility as residents of medium-sized group homes, and foster home residents had the next-to-the-lowest degree of responsibility. Thus, size was not as clearly related to responsibility as it was to autonomy.

Summary

In summary, a number of residential alternatives is currently available. These settings vary widely in terms of service provision, resident

TABLE 3–2.
Description of Service Provision, Resident Responsibilities, and Resident Leisure in the Various Residential Settings

Setting Type	Services Provided by Setting (see Lakin et al., 1986)	Typical Resident Responsibilities (see reference given for setting)	Examples of Leisure (see reference given for setting)
Large public and private group residences (MacMillan, 1982)	Supervision; training; personal care	Some self-help tasks; higher IQ residents assist lower IQ residents	Sitting, napping, watching TV, and occasionally playing catch
Specialized nursing homes	Supervision; personal and nursing care	(Baker, et al., 1977, describes homes for those above 50 years of age, which may be similar.)	
Personal care homes	Supervision; personal care	Some self-help tasks and cleaning room	Watching TV, playing cards, sewing, conversing, and sitting outside
Board and supervision facilities (Bjaanes & Butler, 1974)	Supervision; sleeping room, meals, and some housekeeping	Self-help tasks; domestic tasks in some placements	Passive leisure such as watching TV and napping as well as active leisure such as playing games, doing crafts, and dancing; little supervision; able to go out on own
Foster homes (Baker et al., 1977)	Treated as a family member	Self-help tasks and chores such as drying dishes; riding bus to day program	Participating in family activities
Small group residences (Baker et al., 1977)	Supervision; training; personal care	Self-help and domestic tasks such as assisting in meal preparation; taking public transportation	Taking walks, conversing with other residents, playing records, and watching TV

Semi-independent living programs (Baker et al., 1977)	Supervision only for tasks such as meal preparation and banking	Self-help tasks, meal preparation, and use of public transportation	Determining own activities as well as how late to remain out
Generic residential services	Treated as other residents	Varies	Varies
Natural homes (Willer & Intagliata, 1980)	Treated as family member	Self-help tasks and routine chores	Participating in family activities, bowling, and dancing
Independent living programs	Supervision where needed (e.g., budgeting)	All except where supervision is needed	Determine own activities as well as how late to remain out
Independent living	None	Total responsibility for self	Determine own activities as well as how late to remain out

responsibility, and resident leisure activity. In the study by Baker et al. (1971), autonomy increased as facility size decreased. In addition, examination of the data in Table 3-2 shows an increase in both autonomy and responsibility in more integrated settings. For example, the lowest degree of autonomy and responsibility is present in large group residences, medium amounts of autonomy and responsibility are present in settings such as foster and small group residences, and the highest degree of autonomy and responsibility is present in independent settings.

Vocational Alternatives

As for most adults, one of the crucial life activities for those with mental retardation is employment (see Kiernan et al., 1986). Certainly, much of adult life is spent in work or work-related activities. As Flexer (1983) writes, employment provides the means by which an individual can engage in other activities through the use of earnings to purchase living and social options.

For persons with mental retardation, employment opportunities can vary from programs involving specially designed activities with no pay to competitive employment (i.e., adult activity centers, sheltered workshops, industrial enclaves, mobile work crews, supported employment, and competitive employment). These settings involve a continuum of training opportunities that focus on increasing the individual's independence and range of potential activity (Horejsi, 1975). The goal of this continuum is the last setting: competitive employment. Table 3-3 presents an overview of program and work conditions across these vocational settings.

Adult Activity Centers

"The adult activity center emphasizes the concept of readiness: that is, the need for the individual to develop skills and overcome disabilities so he or she can enter vocational rehabilitation or enter competitive employment at some future time" (Wehman, Moon, & McCarthy, 1984, p. 7). A variety of activities is provided as a means of job preparation within activity centers, including recreational activity and adaptive, academic, and vocational skill training.

As the number of students graduating from school and in need of continuing service has increased, some have argued for expansion of day activity centers (Wehman et al., 1984). However, at least two major disadvantages of these centers have prompted the development of other options. The first is the segregation of people with severe handicaps from the community. The second is that, in reality, the emphasis of such centers is not on client movement into the community (Wehman et al.,

TABLE 3–3.

Program and Work Conditions By Setting

Setting	Pay	Activity	Supervision	Contact with Nonhandicapped
Adult activity center	No pay	Focus is on learning activities of daily living, functional	Ongoing supervision	Segregated; all workers disabled physically or mentally
Sheltered workshop	$1 to $3/day [a]	Contract work under sheltered conditions	Ongoing supervision	Segregated; all workers disabled physically or mentally
Industrial enclave	Paid; no minimum wage established	Contract work	Ongoing supervision	Segregated group works on a special set of tasks within a normal work setting; breaks and lunch may provide for some integration
Mobile work crew	Paid; no minimum wage established	Contract work; work performed in different parts of the building or in different locales	Ongoing supervision	Breaks and lunch may provide for integration, but otherwise work is in a segregated group within "normal" work settings
Supported work	Paid; no minimum wage established	Involves many different work arrangements and staffing patterns	Ongoing supervision	Usually integrated
Competitive employment	Wage appropriate for position	"Normal" expectations	No special supervision	Integrated with nondisabled peers

Note: Based on Wehman, Moon, and McCarthy (1984).

[a] Wages in regular workshops must be no less than one-half of the current federal minimum wage, with few exceptions (Elder, Conley, & Noble, 1986).

1984). Instead, underlying assumptions that clients are not "ready" and need more training appear to prevail.

Sheltered Workshops

The purpose of the sheltered workshop is to provide contract bench work under supervised conditions in a segregated atmosphere (Wehman et al., 1984). This vocational setting is also designed to foster work readiness and adjustment through the provision of training, evaluation, and counseling services. Theoretically, individuals remain at the workshop until their performance is judged to indicate readiness for the next step in the continuum.

In 1938, amendments to the Vocational Rehabilitation Act permitted workshops to pay subminimum wage (typically must be at least 50 percent of minimum wage) to workers with handicaps. This allowed workshops to compete with other businesses for work contracts. In recent years, the number of persons with mental handicaps who are placed in workshops has grown tremendously. According to the U.S. Department of Labor (1979), 34 percent (13,772) of workshop participants in 1965 had mental handicaps. Participants with mental handicaps in 1973 accounted for 46.5 percent (38,671) of the total population, and by 1976, 61 percent (88,000) of the entire number of persons placed in sheltered workshops were mentally handicapped. [However, from 1963 to 1976 the actual number of persons with mental retardation increased 545 percent (Bellamy et al., 1986)].

Industrial Enclaves

"An enclave in its broadest application describes a group of individuals with handicaps who are working with special training or job support within a normal business or industry" (Rhodes & Valenta, 1985, p. 13). Participants within this vocational setting are assumed to require long-term assistance to meet the social and production requirements of a competitive employment placement. They are physically present in an environment with nondisabled individuals. However, the range of opportunity for social and physical integration depends on the constraints dictated by the employer. The working conditions may not be typical and fringe benefits are usually not an option. However, the industrial enclave may eventually provide the opportunity for persons to be hired as full-time workers in a competitive employment setting.

Mobile Work Crew

The mobile work crew, discussed by Bellamy, Rhodes, Bourbeam, and Mank (1986) is very similar to the industrial enclave model in that it also consists of a very small group of disabled employees working under a permanent supervisor. However, the workers do not remain stationary. Some examples of mobile work crews are paint crews, janitorial staff, and grounds maintenance crews. Usually work contracts are made available to the agency or nonprofit organization administering the programs. The funds serve as a source of revenue to pay workers who are handicapped and also to subsidize staff support. Mobile work crews are an attractive method of providing wages and vocational integration for persons who may require more substantial supervision and structure than work enclaves.

Supported Employment

> Supported employment is defined as paid work in a variety of settings, particularly regular work sites, especially designed for handicapped individuals (i) for whom competitive employment at or above the minimum wage is unlikely; and (ii) who, because of their disability, need intensive, ongoing support to perform in a work setting. (Rhodes & Valenta, 1985, p. 1)

According to Wehman et al. (1984), four characteristics are common to all supported employment alternatives: (1) paid employment, (2) community integration, (3) on-going support, and (4) severely disabled service recipients. A minimum wage or productivity level is not established.

Supported employment is intended for persons usually served in day activity and sheltered work centers. This vocational setting could be provided in many environments with varying degrees of integration with nonhandicapped co-workers. An important aspect of supported employment is that it challenges service planners and providers to develop alternative service models that fit different disabling groups, industries, and communities (Rhodes & Valenta, 1985).

Competitive Employment

"Competitive employment is work done for at least minimum wage with non-handicapped co-workers at a job that provides room for advancement in settings that produce valued goods or services" (Rusch, 1983, p. 504). During the late 1970s and early 1980s, two factors improved the competitive employment prospects of individuals who were mentally handicapped. First, the Education for all Handicapped Act (PL 94-142), Section 504 of the Rehabilitation Act and the Educational Amendments of 1976 (PL 94-482), mandated that functional school programs be offered to handicapped individuals to ensure that they become self-sufficient, productive members of society. Second, several demonstration projects have developed competitive employment options that successfully placed individuals in the community (e.g., Bates & Pancsofar, 1983; Rusch & Mithaug, 1980; Vogelsberg, 1984; Wehman, 1981). Competitive employment is an option that may not be suitable for all persons with handicaps; yet it should be available so that they can, if possible, engage in and enjoy work options that are available to their nondisabled peers.

Summary and Status of Settings

Vocational settings may be placed on a continuum from little to total independence. The least independence is experienced by individuals in day activity centers, which focus on readiness. Somewhat more independence is found in sheltered workshops, where individuals engage in vocational activity. Further independence is experienced in industrial enclaves, mobile work crews, and supported work settings — all of which involve work at regular integrated job sites. Although industrial enclaves and mobile work crews may sometimes actually be supported work, these two types of settings are also sometimes distinguishable from supported work in that individuals with moderate and mild levels of disability (rather than only individuals with severe disabilities) are also served in these settings and support may be less extensive. Total independence is experienced in competitive settings.

Although consumers of the vocational service system display diverse needs, the overwhelming majority of individuals who are mentally handicapped are currently served in the two bottom levels of the vocational service continuum, day activity and sheltered workshops, where the probability of progression toward competitive employment is virtually nonexistent. For example, even if each person with a mental handicap had a realistic probability of movement through the system, initial placement in a day activity program currently requires an average of 58 years to progress through program levels before graduation to competitive employment (Bellamy et al., 1986). Still, handicapped individuals who are graduating from school today are better prepared now than previously, with both superior training and improved placement practices made available to them.

Overview of Settings and Expectations

In both residential and vocational settings, a wide variety of placements is available. These settings vary greatly in terms of both the amount of independence permitted and the degree of integration into the community. At one end of the spectrum are the highly segregated large group residences and day activity centers; at the other end are independent living and competitive employment. A consequence of this wide range of settings is a wide range of communication needs and expectations. In the next section, an approach to meeting the varying needs of individuals residing and working in these different settings is discussed.

Developmental Versus Remedial Logic (Which Approach?)

Regardless of the setting in which training occurs, a decision regarding an approach to determining the curriculum or content of language programming must be made. Guess, Sailor, and Baer (1978) divided the many approaches to curriculum development into two major categories: developmental and remedial.

Developmental logic is based on the assumption that the best way, and maybe the only way, to teach language is to follow the normal developmental sequence. This logic presupposes that language development is characterized by a continuum of ever-increasing complexity such that most structures have prerequisites and the sequence of language learning must be preserved to produce the desired outcome. Certainly the normal developmental sequence must be one effective strategy (as evidenced by the fact that most fluent language users followed such a sequence), if not the only effective strategy.

Remedial logic is based on an assumption that some learners will acquire language later in life than normally developing infants and toddlers. As a result, these learners may not follow the same sequence as the normally developing child: they have had different experiences and thus possess a unique complement of abilities and disabilities. This argument may be particularly true for adults with mental retardation. Because of the differences inherent in the learners and their varying experiences with the environment, advocates of remedial logic emphasize a language training sequence that optimizes the rapid acquisition of *functional* communication. Language is functional to the extent that it enables learners to exercise control over their environment. Through language, they can gain the attention and assistance of others as well as access preferred materials and desired activities that are mediated by others. As Guess et al. (1978) conclude, a learner "must find that language . . . is useful in accomplishing better reinforcement . . . than was possible without the language. Thus, a program based on remedial logic will try to establish first the most useful elements of language that the 'learner' might need" (p. 106).

In the evolution of special education philosophy, a current trend appears to be the use of remedial logic as the approach to communication training for learners with moderate and severe developmental disabilities. Other recent trends — such as placing individuals in the least-restrictive environment, using age-appropriate tasks and materials, and teaching functional, community-referenced skill — mesh comfortably with a remedial logic for the development of communication curricula.

A key issue that arises from the choice of remedial logic is how to identify "the most useful elements of language that a learner might need." In the remaining pages of this section, recent trends in communication curriculum development based on ecological analyses of settings and social validation of "needed" language skills will be discussed. Two cases that illustrate the implementation of such state-of-the-art procedures will be presented.

Ecological Analysis Using Social Validation (What To Teach?)

Our premise is that a determination of what constitutes useful and functional language skills must include an analysis of the environment in which those skills are to be displayed. Thus, the content of a language-training curriculum is relative and varies depending on both the communicative repertoire of the individual and factors related to his/her residential and vocational settings. Consideration of these factors, and thus determination of curriculum content, may be undertaken within the framework of a relatively new methodology referred to as "social validation" (cf. Kazdin, 1977; Wolf, 1978). A recent trend in communication training with learners who are mentally retarded entails the application of social validation methodology in residential and employment settings to determine the skills that are required to survive (minimal standard) or to thrive (optimal standard) within each unique setting.

Social validation refers to a process for assessing the social acceptability of training programs. At least three facets are distinguishable (Kazdin, 1977):

1. The acceptability of the focus of training;
2. The acceptability of the training procedures used; and
3. The acceptability or clinical importance of the behavior change achieved through training.

In this chapter, we are concerned only with the acceptability of the training focus (content).

Currently, social validation methodology consists of two procedures; subjective evaluation and social comparison. *Subjective evaluation* is a means of validating curriculum content by asking those who interact with the learner or those with expertise in a given area to determine potential targets for training. *Social comparison* enables validation of curriculum content by assessing the performance of individuals who are similar demographically to the learner but differ in their performance of the target behavior (i.e., communication skills).

The primary difference between these two validation procedures pertains to the manner in which the data are collected (Rusch, Schutz, & Agran, 1982). In subjective evaluation, verbal interviews or written surveys are used and result in ratings or rankings; in social comparison, direct and repeated observations of selected peers engaged in the target behavior are gathered and the resulting data provide an indication of functional content.

Although the combination of the two procedures may provide an optimal validation methology, each is expensive in terms of time and resources. Kazdin (1977) pointed out some of the potential drawbacks when either is used alone. Disadvantages of the subjective-evaluation methodology include a reliance on face validity as the sole criterion for evaluating the validity of the assessment device and a reliance on the opinions of untrained individuals (untrained in terms of the task requested) for determining the content of training. Perhaps these untrained individuals (e.g., employers) would identify specific training targets that, after acquired, would not have tapped the original concern. That is, a question may always remain about the agreement between what employers identify as important communication skills and what they really accept and expect.

One limitation of social comparison is the reliance on normative standards. Normative standards may represent an inadequate or inappropriate criterion for goal setting. In the workplace, for example, nonhandicapped employees (norm group) may interact verbally with other workers at high rates. These interactions may be unrelated to work and may even interfere with work production. To use these norm-referenced rates as training targets would be inappropriate and, if accomplished, could lead to dismissal.

A second consideration when using social comparison is determination of the "appropriate" norm group. Currently, this determination is made arbitrarily: there are no empirical rules or guidelines, and, depending on the variables used to select the norm group, the resulting standards will vary immensely. Again in an employment-related example, very different training targets might be generated if workers with mental retardation and other developmental disabilities who communicate effectively are chosen as our comparison group instead of nonhandicapped workers. The major point is that normative standards are relative and depend on the variables used to choose the norm group.

A method of avoiding the disadvantages of the procedures singly is to combine the approaches (e.g., Mankin, Braukmann, Minkin, Timbers,

Timbers, Fixsen, Phillips, & Wolf, 1976). This represents a most power-ful strategy for validation of curriculum content.

Examples of Implementation

To elucidate each of the validation procedures, two studies will be sum-marized. The first illustrates subjective evaluation; the second is an example of social comparison.

Rusch et al. (1982) used subjective evaluation to validate what they referred to as "entry-level survival skills" for food service and janitorial and maid service occupations. The assessment areas included commun-ication and social skills as well as a number of other vocation-relevant categories. An expert panel, representing members from the service occupations surveyed, was formed to assess the content validity of all questionnaire items. Survey questionnaires were mailed to 120 employ-ers in food and janitorial and maid service occupations in six Illinois communities. The yellow pages of the local phone directories were con-sulted in the selection of respondents.

Table 3-4 gives a summary of the survey results. It represents a com-pilation of the social survival skills that 90 percent or more of the re-sponding employers selected as entry-level skills.

Although social behavior relevant to the workplace has frequently been identified using subjective evaluation procedures, few attempts have been made to validate this behavior with direct observation. Therefore, Chadsey–Rusch (1986) used direct observation to assess social behavior in the workplace and compared her findings with those obtained when employers were asked to identify behavior important for employment (i.e., subjective evaluation). Sixteen individuals were se-lected for participation: seven clients with developmental disabilities working in food service, one working in a printing shop, and eight non-handicapped co-workers working at the same job sites. Of the clients with developmental disabilities, four were selected because they were judged to have poor or "at-risk" social skills and four were selected because they were judged to have "good" social skills.

Data were collected on all 16 individuals using narrative recording procedures (Cooper, 1981). Information was also gathered on additional ecological variables believed to influence social behavior, such as job task and number of co-workers/customers in the vicinity. A completed sample data sheet is shown in Figure 3-1.

Each of the 16 participants was observed during four time periods for five working days. The four time periods — including two work periods, arrival to work, and break — were selected because they sampled the varying conditions that existed and they were thought to have the greatest potential for social interaction and thus the display of social skills.

Social Survival Skills Selected for Entry by 90 percent or More of the Respondents. (Rusch, 1982)

1. Follow one instruction provided at a time (100%).

2. Recite verbally upon request:
   a. Full name (100%),
   b. Home address (98%),
   c. Home telephone number (98%),
   d. Previous employer (91%).

3. Maintain proper grooming by:
   a. Dressing appropriately for work (98%),
   b. Cleaning self before coming to work (96%).

4. Maintain personal hygiene by:
   a. Keeping hair combed (100%),
   b. Shaving regularly (98%),
   c. Keeping teeth clean (96%),
   d. Using deodorant (96%),
   e. Keeping nails clean (93%).

5. Communicate such basic needs as:
   a. Sickness (98%),
   b. Toileting necessities (94%),
   c. Pain (92%).

6. Speak clearly enough to be understood by anyone on the second transmission (97%).

7. Respond appropriately and immediately after receiving one out of every two instructions (96%).

8. Remember to respond to an instruction that requires compliance after a specific time interval with one reminder (95%).

9. Respond appropriately to safety signals when given verbally (94%).

10. Initiate contact with supervisor when cannot do job (94%).

11. Initiate contact with co-worker when needing help on task (94%).

12. Work without displaying or engaging in major disruptive behaviors (e.g., arguments) more frequently than one to two times per month (94%).

13. Initiate and/or respond verbally in 3- to 5- word sentences (92%).

14. Work without initiating unnecessary contact with strangers more frequently than three to five times per day (92%).

15. Reach places of work by means of own arrangements (e.g., walking, taxi, personal car) (92%).

16. Follow instructions with words such as "in" and "on" (90%).

Note: From Rusch, 1982.

Observer   Pat G.

Employer   PAR   Date   4/28/86

Type of observation (circle)   Arrival/Work 1/**Break**/Work 2

Start Time   10:34   **a.m.**/p.m.   Stop Time   11:49   **a.m.**/p.m.

Codes

CU = customer JT = job trainer S = supervisor C = coworker P = participant	**Context** dock area, delivery coming in dock door all other happenings are as usual - lunch prep

Participant #   03

Time, Context, Other Notes	Observations
10:23 enters by dock and turns	P enters dock hall at 10:34 greets (initiates) S/ she
left to dressing room past FC	responds and adds "how are you?" / he answers "fine"
w/no comment	S says "I see you shaved this am" / he says "yeah" and
	punches in / P goes toward locker past MC, who says
	"hello, my Friend" / P does not respond / P dresses in
11:37	apron and hat and goes to food line past 04 w/no
	comment from either / P comes into dining room approx.
	2 min / later past approx. 5 emp with no comment from
Sits alone at table with back to	either / sits down at usual table and begins eating
table of MC's behind including	at 11:39 / looks around while eating but eats rapidly /
01 and 04 (they talk sports the	one MC scrapes chair on floor getting up, P turns to look
whole time)	then turns away / S passes behind to look over salad bar,
	P glances her direction but neither speak / P eats
	steadily till end of obs. 11:49 a.m.

Figure 3–1. *A sample data sheet for the Chadsey-Rusch (1986) study.*

Although the results at this time are preliminary at best, they corroborate the findings determined by subjective evaluation. That is, a number of the social skill categories identified by employers when surveyed corresponded to those skills that were displayed and observed in actual work settings. Some of these skills included initiating and engaging in conversations, interacting when the opportunity arises (e.g., a greeting), and responding appropriately to supervisor criticism.

In summary, these two studies are of heuristic value in demonstrating a process for identification and validation of communication curriculum content. Although the examples were limited to vocational settings, the demonstrated process used has wide applicability to a multitude of environments, including the variety of residential settings discussed earlier.

PLACEMENT TRENDS AND THEIR IMPLICATIONS

In conclusion, it should be noted that the residential and vocational systems described are by no means static. For example, within the residential service system, four major trends have been noted over the past two decades: shifts to small (rather than large) facilities, to private (rather than public) operation, to integrated (rather than segregated) locations, and to the use of generic (rather than specialized) resources and services (Lakin, Hill, Bruininks, & White, 1986). Moreover, the belief has been expressed that by the year 2000 a noninstitutionalization policy may be essentially in effect in most states in this country (Hill & Lakin, 1984).

A major result of these placement trends is increased contact with nonhandicapped peers: that is, integration. Karlan (1980) discussed implications of integration for communication needs of individuals with developmental disabilities: increased demands on communicative skills, increased opportunity to use language socially, and increased exposure to language as an instructional tool. Individuals in more integrated settings, which provide a greater degree of autonomy, need to be able to order a meal, ask directions, and interact with others in a variety of ways that are not required in segregated settings. These individuals will also find increased opportunity to communicate socially as they gain access to a telephone and make a greater number of social contacts.

Finally, they will more often need communicative skills to comprehend instructions used during training of the numerous skills needed to adapt to the integrated settings. Clearly, greater integration has the effect of increasing the importance of communication training for the individual with mental retardation. On a broader (societal) level, the relevance of communication to the attainment of needs and desires, to the establishment of friendships, and to the learning of other skills makes it one of the more critical skills to promotion of the currently socially valued ideology of normalization.

REFERENCES

Baker, B. L., Seltzer, G. B., & Seltzer, M. M. (1977). *As close as possible: Community residences for retarded adults.* Boston: Little, Brown, and Company.

Bates, P., & Pancsofar, E. (1983). Project EARN. *British Journal of Mental Subnormality,* XXIX Part 2, No. 57, 97–103.

Batshaw, M. L., & Perret, Y. M. (1981). *Children with handicaps: A medical primer.* Baltimore, MD: Paul H. Brookes.

Bellamy, G. T., Rhodes, L. F., Bourbeam, P. E., & Mank, D. E. (1986). Mental retardation services in workshops and day activity programs: Consumer benefits and policy alternatives. In F. R. Rusch (Ed.), *Competitive employment: Service delivery, models, methods, and issues.* Baltimore, MD: Paul H. Brookes.

Bigge, J., & Sirvis, B. (1986). Physical and health impairments. In N. G. Haring & L. McCormick (Eds.), *Exceptional children and youth* (4th Ed.) (pp. 313–354). Columbus, OH: Charles E. Merrill Publishing Company.

Bjaanes, A. T., & Butler, E. W. (1974). Environmental variation in community care facilities for mental retarded persons. *American Journal of Mental Deficiency, 78,* 429–439.

Bruininks, R. H., Hauber, F. A., & Kidla, M. J. (1979). National survey of community residential facilities: A profile of facilities and residents in 1977. *American Journal of Mental Deficiency, 84,* 470–478.

Bruininks, R. H., Rotegard, L., & Lakin, K. (1982, August). *Epidemiology of mental retardation and trends in residential services in the United States.* Paper presented at the NICHD conference concerning research on the impact of residential settings on mentally retarded persons, Lake Wilderness, WA.

Butler, E. W., & Bjaanes, A. T. (1977). A typology of community care facilities and differential normalization outcomes. In P. Mittler (Ed.), *Research to practice in mental retardation: Vol. I. Care and intervention.* Baltimore, MD: University Park Press.

Chadsey-Rusch, J. (1986). The relationship between social behaviors and supported employment. Presented at The Rehabilitation Research and Training Center Third Annual Symposium, Virginia Beach, VA.

Cooper, J. O. (1981). *Measuring behavior* (2nd Ed.). Columbus, OH: Charles E. Merrill Publishing Company.

Elder, J. K., Conley, R. W., & Noble, J. H. (1986). The service system. In W. E. Kiernan & J. A. Stark (Eds.), *Pathways to employment for adults with developmental disabilities.* Baltimore, MD: Paul H. Brookes.

ENCOR (Eastern Nebraska Community Office of Retardation). (1977). *Residential specific training.* Omaha: Author.

Flexer, R. (1983). Habilitation services for developmentally disabled persons. *Journal of Applied Rehab Counseling, 14* (3), 6–9.

Grossman, H. J. (Ed). (1983). *Classification in mental retardation.* Washington, DC: American Association on Mental Deficiency.

Guess, D., Sailor, W., & Baer, D. M. (1978). Children with limited language. In R. L. Schiefelbusch (Ed.), *Language intervention strategies* (pp. 101–143). Baltimore, MD: University Park Press.

Haring, N. G. (1986). Introduction. In N. G. Haring & L. McCormick (Eds.), *Exceptional children and youth* (4th ed.). Columbus, OH: Charles E. Merrill Publishing Company.

Heal, L. W., Novak, A. R., Sigelman, C. K., & Switzky, H. N. (1980). Characteristics of community residential facilities. In A. R. Novak & L. W. Heal (Eds.), *Integration of developmentally disabled individuals into the community.* Baltimore, MD: Paul H. Brookes.

Hill, B. K., Bruininks, R. H., & Lakin, K. C. (in press). Characteristics of residential facilities for individuals with mental retardation. In L. W. Heal, J. I. Haney, & A. R. Novak (Eds.), *The integration of developmentally disabled individuals into the community.* Baltimore, MD: Paul H. Brookes.

Hill, B. K., & Lakin, K. C. (1984). *Trends in residential services for mentally retarded people: 1977–1982* (Brief No. 23). Minneapolis: Center for Residential and Community Services, University of Minnesota, Department of Educational Psychology.

Hill, B. K., & Lakin, K. C. (1986). Classification of residential facilities for individuals with mental retardation. *Mental Retardation, 24,* 107–115.

Horejsi, C. (1975). *Deinstitutionalization and the development of community-based services for the mentally retarded: An overview of concepts and issues.* Missoula: University of Montana, Project on Community Resources and Deinstitutionalization.

Karlan, G. R. (1980). Issues in communication research related to integration of developmentally disabled individuals. In A. R. Novak & L. W. Heal (Eds.), *Integration of developmentally disabled individuals into the community.* Baltimore, MD: Paul H. Brookes.

Kazdin, A. E. (1977). Assessing the clinical or applied importance of behavior change through social validation. *Behavior Modification, 1,* 427–452.

Kiernan, W. P., Smith, B. C., & Ostrowsky, M. B. (1986). Developmental disabilities, definitional issues. In W. E. Kiernan & J. A. Stark (Eds.), *Pathways to employment for adults with developmental disabilities.* Baltimore, MD: Paul H. Brookes.

Lakin, K. C., Hill, B. K., Bruininks, R. H., & White, C. C. (1986). Residential options and future implications. In W. E. Kiernan & J. A. Stark (Eds.), *Pathways to employment for adults with developmental disabilities.* Baltimore, MD: Paul H. Brookes.

Landesman–Dwyer, S. (1985). Describing and evaluating residential environments. In R. H. Bruininks & K. C. Lakin (Eds.), *Living and learning in the least restrictive environment.* Baltimore, MD: Paul H. Brookes.

Lindberg, D. (1976). *Prevalence of developmental disabilities in West Virginia.* Elkins, WV: Davis and Elkins College.

Macmillan, D. L. (1982). *Mental retardation in school and society.* Boston: Little, Brown, and Company.

McHale, J. (1980). Mental retardation and the future: A conceptual approach. In S. C. Plog & M. B. Santamour (Eds.), *The year 2000 and mental retardation* (pp. 19–69). New York: Plenum Press.

Meighan, S., Queener, L., & Weitman, M. (1976). Prevalence of epilepsy in children of Murnomon County, Oregon. *Epilepsia, 17,* 245–256.

Mercer, J. (1973). The myth of the 3% prevalence. In R. K. Eyman, C. E. Meyers, & G. Tarjan (Eds.), *Sociobehavioral studies in mental retardation.* Washington, DC: American Association on Mental Retardation.

Minkin, N., Braukmann, C. J., Minkin, B. L., Timbers, G. D., Timbers, B. J., Fixsen, D. L., Phillips, E. L., & Wolf, M. M. (1976). The social validation and training of conversational skills. *Journal of Applied Behavior Analysis, 9*(2), 127–139.

Nanus, B. (1980). Living and working in the year 2000: Some implications for mental retardation policy. In S. C. Plog & M. B. Santamour (Eds.), *The year*

2000 and mental retardation (pp. 71–96). New York: Plenum Press.

Puccio, P. S., Janicki, M. P., Otis, J. P., & Rettig, J. (1983). *Report of the committee on aging and developmental disabilities.* New York: New York State Office of Mental Retardation and Developmental Disabilities.

Rhodes, L. E., & Valenta, L. (1985). Industry-based supported employment: An enclave approach. *Journal of the Association for Persons with Severe Handicaps, 10*(1), 12–20.

Ross, A. O. (1980). *Psychological disorders of children* (2nd ed.). New York: McGraw–Hill.

Rusch, F. R. (1983). Competitive vocational training. In M. E. Snell (Ed.), *Systematic instruction of the moderately and severely handicapped* (2nd ed.), Columbus, OH: Charles E Merrill Publishing Co.

Rusch, F. R., & Mithaug, D. E. (1980). *Vocational training for mentally retarded adults: A behavior-analytic approach.* Champaign, IL: Research Press.

Rusch, F. R., Schutz, R. P., & Agran, M. (1982). Validating entry-level survival skills for service occupations: Implications for curriculum development. *The Journal of the Association for the Severely Handicapped. 7*(3), 32–41.

Scheerenberger, R. C. (1978). *Public residential services for the mentally retarded: 1977.* Madison, WI: National Association of Superintendents of Public Residential Facilities for the Mentally Retarded.

Scheerenberger, R. C. (1983). *Public residential services for the mentally retarded: 1982.* Madison, WI: National Association of Superintendents of Public Residential Facilities for the Mentally Retarded.

Tarjan, G., Wright, S. W., Eyman, R. K., Keeran, C. V. (1973). Natural history of mental retardation: Some aspects of epidemiology. *American Journal of Mental Deficiency, 77,* 369–379.

U. S. Department of Labor. (1979). *Study of handicapped clients in sheltered workshops* Vol. II. Washington, DC: U.S. Department of Labor.

Vogelsberg, R. T. (1984). Competitive employment programs for individuals with mental retardation in rural areas. In P. Wehman (Ed.), *Proceedings from the National Symposium on Employment of Citizens with Mental Retardation.* Richmond, VA: Virginia Commonwealth University.

Wehman, P. (1981). Competitive employment. *New Horizons for Severely Disabled Individuals.* Baltimore, MD: Paul H. Brookes.

Wehman, P., Moon, S. M., & McCarthy, P. (1984). Transition from school to adulthood for youth with severe handicaps. Manuscript invited for publication in *Focus on Exceptional Children.*

Willer, B., & Intagliata, J. (1980). *Deinstitutionalization of mentally retarded persons in New York State.* Buffalo: State University of New York at Buffalo.

Wolf, M. M. (1978). Social validity: The case for subjective measurement or how applied behavior analysis is finding its heart. *Journal of Applied Behavior Analysis, 11,* 203–214.

Wolfensberger, W. (1980). The definition of normalization: Update, problems disagreements, and misunderstandings. In R. J. Flynn & K. E. Nitsch (Eds.), *Normalization, social integration, and community services.* Austin, TX: PRO-ED.

CHAPTER 4

Exploring the Language of Adults With Mental Retardation

STEPHEN N. CALCULATOR

*T*he literature regarding language problems associated with mental retardation contains a plethora of information describing the communicative skills of children. Several comprehensive summaries of this information are now available (e.g., Calculator, 1985; Macchelo, 1986; Miller & Chapman, 1984). General consensus has been reached that although children who are mentally retarded display several communication characteristics that appear peculiar to this population, further investigation generally reveals similar behaviors in the younger, normal language-learning population. This finding has been summarized repeatedly by stating that the language of children who are mentally retarded is developmentally delayed relative to normal language-learning children. They appear to follow the same sequences in acquiring language, yet proceed through this process at significantly slower rates. The degree of disparity between their performances and those of their normal language-learning counterparts appears to be strongly correlated with their respective levels of intellectual functioning (i.e., at higher levels of intellectual ability there is increased similarity in the communication performances of those who are mentally retarded and age-matched normal language-learning individuals). Further discrepancies are associated with the effects of institutionalization, experiential deprivation, lack of opportunities to communicate, and so forth.

Turning from children who are mentally retarded to adults, we find a paucity of descriptive data regarding the communicative competencies and idiosyncracies of this population. Although investigators have begun looking at the performances of adults with mental retardation on specific linguistic tasks (comparing the results obtained with those reported for normal language-learning *children*), there are simply not enough data at this time to present a lucid summary of these findings. It might be more appropriate to instead note directions in which such research and subsequent programming efforts have proceeded. This is the tack that will be taken throughout this chapter, avoiding summaries of literature reviewed elsewhere in this book. The chapters by Reichle, Piché-Cragoe, Sigafoos, and Doss (Chapter 9); Bedrosian (Chapter 10); and Owens and Rogerson (Chapter 8) include descriptive information about individuals at early, advanced, and presymbolic levels of communicative functioning, respectively.

First the role cognition plays in influencing the communication skills of these individuals will be examined. There is a lack of direct correspondence between intellectual and communicative abilities, particularly with respect to these individuals' use (i.e., pragmatics) of language.

Next, the efficacy of applying our knowledge about normal language-learning children to assess and treat adults with mental retardation will be evaluated. It remains a common practice to summarize the communication skills of these individuals on the basis of instruments standardized on normal language-learning children. Similarly, the linguistic skills of adults who are mentally retarded are frequently summarized in the form of language ages (syntactic, semantic, and morphologic), which are also derived from large samples of normal language-learning children. It will be seen that these individuals demonstrate communication characteristics that differentiate them from both younger children who are mentally retarded and normal speaking persons. Implications of the above discussions related to the lack of empirical data to substantiate current practices with this adult population, will then be discussed relative to the assessment process. What role should formal testing occupy with these individuals when such instruments lack any normative data on the population of adults with mental retardation? What clinical implications can be drawn from such assessment devices? Is there evidence to support the ecologic validity of these devices (i.e., are they measuring skills that are truly relevant to these individuals and persons they are interacting with in their respective social and vocational settings?)?

Finally, a discussion of issues pertinent to the intervention process will be presented. How do we identify those adults who might benefit from communication intervention? What should be the foci, or overriding objectives, of intervention? How do we know whether what we are doing is going to make a difference with respect to the adaptive skills of our clients?

COGNITION AND COMMUNICATIVE PERFORMANCE

Cognitive Levels and Expected Language Skills

Although cognitive deficits may constrain the levels of language functioning that children who are mentally retarded can be expected to attain (Chapman & Nation, 1981; Kamhi & Johnston, 1982; Miller & Chapman, 1984; Miller, Chapman, & Bedrosian, 1978; Yoder & Calculator, 1981), their uses and understanding of language have been described to be commensurate with that expected of younger normal language-learning children. The results of investigations (e.g., Chapman & Miller, 1980; Finch–Williams, 1984; Karlan, 1980; Macchelo, 1986) that have examined changes in communicative functioning relative to advancing levels of cognitive ability in *children* are summarized below. Because of the absence of empirical data examining the relationship between cognition and language in adults with mental retardation, we can only speculate as to the implications these findings for children will have on the adult population.

Sensorimotor Stage IV

Language comprehension is limited to references to objects, persons, and events in the immediate environment. An adult operating at this level may respond to verbal cues that are embedded in highly routine action sequences. When handed a mop and instructed to "finish waxing the floor," the individual may respond appropriately not because the command was understood but because he or she knows what to do with a mop in this particular context. Similar confusion regarding what has truly been understood arises when a client is instructed to do something he or she would normally do without the accompanying verbal cue. Karlan (1980) referred to this as a "preference strategy." A client who has been confined indoors on a rainy day might successfully comply with the direction to "stay inside" upon the caregiver's opening the door not because he/she has understood the request but because he/she would prefer not to get wet.

Sensorimotor Stage V

Comprehension remains tied to events occurring in the immediate context. An increasing number of action words are understood. The client's communication is primarily nonverbal, consisting of giving and showing objects, pointing, physically manipulating listeners, and so forth.

Sensorimotor Stage VI

Comprehension is now freed from the immediate context and includes an understanding of two-term semantic relational meanings. The client now uses words to express a variety of one- and two-term relational meanings.

Preoperational

Relational meanings continue to expand, along with utterance lengths and complexity. The client can now respond (in context) to Wh Questions, uses various tense markers, and relates past and future events.

Concrete Operations

More complex forms of language (passives and comparatives) are understood and produced.

Discussion

In reviewing data just presented it would appear that knowledge of individuals' levels of cognitive functioning would be sufficient to predict corresponding communicative skills. Further examination of these data reveals that this is not the case. To the contrary, a comprehensive review of the literature exploring the cognitive–linguistic relationship led Reichle and Karlan (1985) to conclude that there is a lack of empirical support for such prognostic uses of cognitive data. Although cognitive and linguistic behavior appear to follow similar courses of development, the actual nature of the influence of one upon the other has yet to be demonstrated.

In summary, there appears to be sufficient justification for using data obtained on normal language-learning children to describe the language of children who are mentally retarded. Drew, Logan, and Hardman (1984) noted that such applications of normative data permit an analysis of the extent to which childrens' language performances deviate from normal age expectations. We can expect to see the degree of difference in the uses and understanding of language between speakers who are mentally retarded and those who are not to diminish with increased levels of cognitive ability.

Noncognitive Factors Influencing Language Performance

The lack of an exact fit between children's cognitive and corresponding language skills suggests that noncognitive factors also play a role in determining their communicative competencies. Kamhi and Johnston (1982) posited that although mental age appears to determine the pace at which children acquire the propositional complexities of their language, noncognitive factors such as motivation and experience influence the frequency with which these children actually use these same structures.

The residential environments of children and adults who are mentally retarded have frequently been described as highly regimented settings in which routines preclude the need and opportunity for these individuals to communicate (Calculator, 1985; Halle, Baer, & Spradlin, 1981; Mittler & Berry, 1977). There may be little concern for the quality of social interactions on the part of these individuals and/or their listeners, with the majority of verbal exchanges motivated by clients' immediate desires for objects and events. Experiences with the interpersonal nature of conversation are minimal in these settings (Graham, 1976; Owings & Guyette, 1982).

FACTORS CONTRIBUTING TO VARIABLE COMMUNICATIVE PERFORMANCE IN ADULTS

The role of the environment and previous experiences in the communicative performances of adults with mental retardation was summarized by Karlan (1980), who noted that the greater the mismatch between individuals' old and new environments, the greater the probability that conversation will be inhibited. Some individuals' previous experiences with communication have been limited to highly structured settings in which communication was neither rewarded nor responded to. The resulting dictionaries of experience they draw on might result in communicative behaviors that are qualitatively different from those observed in the population of normal speakers.

Chapter 11 provides examples of clients who rely on ambiguous behaviors to convey their messages. We find that the successfulness of these behaviors often depends on listeners' interpretational skills. Entering a new environment in which the meanings corresponding to these behaviors are lost, the client may be mistakenly viewed as *noncommunicative.*

Other adults are viewed as passive communicators in need of instruction to become more assertive conversational partners who initiate conversations, request actions of others, and so forth. The adult without an experiential basis for such communicative acts (e.g., one whose peers in previous residences did not comprehend his uses of verbal language or consistently failed to comply with such requests) might, in time, cease attempting these behaviors.

A recent investigation of the abilities of four adults with mental retardation to request clarification following their clinicians' purposeful uses of ambiguous utterances revealed an absence of this communicative function despite the individuals' abilities to issue such requests (Calculator, 1985). Previous investigators have suggested that adults with mental retardation vary the frequency with which they use the various functions of communication, depending on the age and status of their listener and the particular speaking situation (Bedrosian & Prutting, 1978; Owings & McManus, 1980). Thus, the lack of clarification requests directed at the clinicians in the Calculator investigation might have been an artifact of the clinician's status rather than the adult's language deficiencies.

A similar hypothesis is supported by Abbeduto and Rosenberg's (1980) finding that adults who were mildly mentally retarded used this same communicative function frequently and spontaneously during natural conversations with peers. These investigators also reported the adults in their study to be adept at observing the rules of conversational turn-taking, maintaining topics, requesting information, and so forth. It would thus appear that at least some of the conversational deficiencies demonstrated by particular adults with mental retardation might be associated with specific contextual events.

A third commonly seen discourse behavior in adults who are mentally retarded involves their meaningless repetition of old information throughout the day. Karlan (1980) attributed this to a lack of exposure to novel events, which they could then relate to others. Calculator (1985) suggested that for many of these individuals, the act of conversing was strong enough to override any concerns about whether they had anything meaningful to say. This has been borne out repeatedly in situations in which such individuals have suddenly shifted toward more informative uses of language concurrent with their instructors' efforts to provide them with a broader range of experiences.

EVALUATING COMMUNICATION SKILLS

Assessment protocols that are particularly useful for evaluating the communication abilities of adults with mental retardation across the various ranges of functioning are presented throughout this book. I will thus limit my discussion here to general considerations that should guide the assessment process regardless of these individuals' social, intellectual, and vocational abilities.

Adaptive Behavior

It is important that all assessment activities directed at adults who are mentally retarded look beyond the mere presence and absence of specific communication skills to instead evaluate the role that such competencies and deficiencies play in the individuals' overall levels of adaptive behavior. In the case of adults, communication skills evaluated should be ones required in adulthood (see Brown, Shiraga, Rogan, York, Albright, McCarthy, Loomis, and VanDeventer, Chapter 6 of this volume). Such a protocol assures a logical progression from evaluation to intervention. Instruction addresses those communication skills that, if acquired, will have an immediate impact on the adults' abilities to function more independently across a variety of conversational settings and listeners.

A recent example of this approach was provided by Karen, Austin-Smith, and Creasy (1985). These investigators developed a protocol for evaluating telephone skills deemed important to facilitating the social and vocational independence (e.g., calling others to the phone, dealing with wrong numbers, referring callers to the correct number, and taking messages) of adults with mental retardation. Subsequent intervention efforts followed a task analysis of those skills just cited that were found to be missing from their six subjects' repertoires. These behaviors were evaluated and then taught as chains of vocal and motor responses through a variety of prompting, reinforcement, and rehearsal strategies.

The relative importance of specific communicative attainments is judged in relation to how their acquisition might influence individual clients' capabilities of living and working as independently as possible. Grossman (1983) noted that changes in the language abilities of individuals who are mentally retarded can precipitate changes in other aspects of their functioning as well (i.e., adaptive behavior), resulting in their progressing along the severity continuum toward progressively milder levels of mental retardation.

The reader is referred to Grossman for a description of the *typical* as well as the *highest* degrees of communicative performance associated with each level of mental retardation in adults, as they relate to these individuals' adaptive behaviors. For example, individuals who are mildly and moderately mentally retarded typically develop functional (although limited) communication skills, which include uses and understanding of spoken language. However, Grossman stated that some adults who are mildly mentally retarded can carry on everyday conversations, have no difficulty using the telephone, and are also able to communicate through writing. Also atypical, although present, are those individuals labeled moderately mentally retarded who are able to carry on simple conversations and read advertisements, signs, and simple prose.

Grossman noted that adults who are severely and profoundly mentally retarded typically develop minimal communication skills of any type despite intensive training. However, Grossman reported that at the highest level of communicative performance in this range of mental retardation are adults who engage in complex verbal exchanges and recognize signs and words. Finally, some adults labeled profoundly mentally retarded are able to use grammatically correct utterances to relate their experiences to others, and recognize advertising words and survival signs (e.g., "stop," "exit," "danger," "ladies").

Role of Formal Testing

Falvey, Bishop, Grenot–Scheyer, and Coots (Chapter 2 of this volume) indicated that intervention efforts with adults who are mentally retarded are paying increasing attention to the selection of functional skills that, after acquired, will result in these adults displaying increased levels of independence. This theme is operationalized further in a later chapter, by Brown et al. (Chapter 6), which presents a set of criteria that can be used to evaluate whether a skill should be taught.

Unfortunately, our growing committment to teaching functional skills has not been paralleled by the use of instruments designed to uncover individuals' uses of such behaviors. A national survey of 46 residential and nonresidential facilities serving adults with mental retardation revealed that the majority of speech–language pathologists in these settings continued to rely primarily on tests standardized on normal language-learning children (Pickett & Flynn, 1983). The six most frequently used tests (all of which were cited by a minimum of 20 percent of the respondents), listed from most to least often used were:

1. Peabody Picture Vocabulary Test,
2. Test for Auditory Comprehension of Language,
3. Goldman–Fristoe Test of Articulation,
4. Utah Test of Language Development,
5. Illinois Test of Psycholinguistic Abilities, and,
6. The Preschool Language Scale.

Many of the respondents indicated that they routinely supplemented these tests with locally developed instruments. However, as the investigators noted, the latter devices remain unpublished and generally unavailable sources for acquiring additional information.

Yoder and Villarruel (1985) noted several problems that arise when attempting to administer formal tests to children and youths who are severely handicapped. As the severity of their handicaps increases, the number of valid and reliable assessment tools decrease. Also, these individuals frequently display low rates of responding to stimuli, and diminished levels of attention and interest in the tasks presented. Finally, those exhibiting accompanying motoric and sensory problems might require modifications in test administration and expected modes of responding. Morse (in Chapter 5 of this volume) provides a comprehensive discussion of factors that may influence adults' test performances, ways of controlling these potentially confounding variables, and uses of information regarding these factors (as they relate to facilitating or inhibiting adults' performances in other instructional tasks).

CONCLUSIONS

If the bulk of descriptive data on which we are basing our instructional programs are derived from tests normed on normal language-learning children whose language experiences and communicative needs bear little or no relation to those of adults with mental retardation, the practical value of any information derived from these same instruments must be questioned. Such tests should be drastically modified and/or replaced by alternate instruments that evaluate adults' abilities to meet current and projected communicative demands across listeners and settings. Bedrosian's assessment and teaching protocol (Chapter 10 of this volume), designed to facilitate the interactional skills of adults who are mentally retarded with peers in small group settings, represents one example of a more ecologically valid approach. Similarly, Calculator (Chapter 11) discusses how needs assessments can be used to identify adults who would benefit from augmentative instruction, and to help determine the content of such instruction.

DIRECTIONS IN INTERVENTION

This topic has been touched on throughout this chapter, and will be emphasized throughout the remaining chapters. I will thus again limit my discussion to a consideration of factors influencing the content of intervention.

Gullo and Gullo (1984) contrasted the growing emphases on teaching appropriate and functional communication skills that will prepare clients to assume more independent positions in the community with traditional approaches that focus on isolated linguistic skills without considering the relationships these skills have to one another. Programming with adults who are mentally retarded — regardless of their residential placements, levels of functioning, prior history, and so forth — should focus on skills that are developmentally and chronologically age appropriate and meaningful. Contextually appropriate settings should be used, whenever possible, to promote clients' functional uses of language with various listeners in a variety of natural settings. Instructional content should be derived from the needs assessment, with all content directed toward a common goal of maximizing clients' levels of adaptive behavior.

Spiegel (1983) provided evidence suggesting that adults with severe mental retardation who were trained to produce 2- and 3-word utterances that conveyed various semantic relations learned more rapidly, produced lengthier utterances, and generalized these skills into natural settings more readily when instruction employed active manipulation (versus picture pointing) of stimuli. Spiegel recommended using real objects and events in intervention, and employing natural cues (i.e., environmentally realistic behavioral events) to promote the clients' acquiring and then using functional communication skills.

If we are to accept the notion that communication instruction must interface with clients' specific social, vocational, and residential needs, every attempt must be made to move toward increasingly integrated methods of service delivery. There is little justification for conducting communication intervention as an isolated activity because communication is neither any more nor less than a tool that facilitates individuals' abilities to function in the various activities of daily living. It would seem prudent, then, to enlist the assistance of those persons with whom these clients interact, in the settings in which these same interactions occur, to carry out the majority of communication instruction with appropriate consultation. It would also seem appropriate to evaluate changes in clients' communicative abilities and base decisions regarding program dismissal on their actual performances in these same settings.

REFERENCES

Abbeduto, L., & Rosenberg, S. (1980). The communicative competence of mildly retarded adults. *Applied Psycholinguistics, 1,* 405–426.

Bedrosian, J., & Prutting, C. (1978). Communicative performance of mentally retarded adults in four conversational settings. *Journal of Speech and Hearing Research, 21,* 79–95.

Calculator, S. (1985). Describing and treating discourse problems in mentally retarded children. The myth of mental retardese. In D. Ripich and F. Spinelli (Eds.), *School discourse problems* (pp. 125–147). San Diego, CA: College-Hill Press.

Calculator, S. (1985, November). *Training adult mentally retarded persons to request clarification.* Paper presented at the annual meeting of the American Speech-Language-Hearing Association, Washington, DC.

Chapman, D., & Nation, J. (1981). Patterns of language performance in educable mentally retarded children. *Journal of Communication Disorders, 14,* 245–254.

Chapman, R., & Miller, J. (1980). Analyzing language and communication in the child. In R. Schiefelbusch (Ed.), *Nonspeech language and communication:*

Analysis and intervention (pp. 159–196). Baltimore, MD: University Park Press.

Drew, C., Logan, D., & Hardman, M. (1984). *Mental retardation: A life cycle approach* (3rd ed.). St. Louis, MO: Times Mirror/Mosby.

Finch–Williams, A. (1984). The developmental relationship between cognition and communication: Implications for assessment. *Topics in Language Disorders, 5*(1), 1–13.

Graham, L. (1976). Language programming and intervention. In L. Lloyd (Ed.), *Communication assessment and intervention strategies* (pp. 371–422). Baltimore, MD: University Park Press.

Grossman, H. (Ed). (1983). *Classification in mental retardation.* Washington, DC: American Association on Mental Deficiency.

Gullo, D., & Gullo, J. (1984). An ecological language intervention approach with mentally retarded adolescents. *Language, Speech, and Hearing Services in Schools, 15*(3), 182–191.

Halle, J., Baer, D., & Spradlin, J. (1981). Teachers' generalized use of delay as a stimulus control procedure to increase language use in handicapped children. *Journal of Applied Behavior Analysis, 14,* 389–409.

Kamhi, A., & Johnston, J. (1982). Towards an understanding of retarded childrens' linguistic deficiencies. *Journal of Speech and Hearing Research, 25,* 435–445.

Karen, R., Astin–Smith, S., & Creasy, D. (1985). Teaching telephone–answering skills to mentally retarded adults. *American Journal of Mental Deficiency, 89*(6), 595–609.

Karlan, G. (1980). Issues in communication research related to the intergration of developmentally disabled individuals. In A. Novak and L. Heal (Eds.), *Integration of developmentally disabled individuals into the community* (pp. 121–137). Baltimore, MD: Brookes.

Macchelo, R. (1986). Language and mentally retarded children. In V. Reed (Ed.), *An introduction to children with language disorders* (pp. 80–104). New York: Macmillan Publishing Company.

Miller, J., & Chapman, R. (1984). Disorders of communication: Investigating the development of language of mentally retarded children. *American Journal of Mental Deficiency, 88*(5), 536–545.

Miller, J., Chapman, R., & Bedrosian, J. (1978). Defining developmentally disabled subjects for research: The relationship between etiology, cognitive development and language and communicative performance. *New Zealand Speech Therapists Journal, 33,* 2–19.

Mittler, P., & Berry, P. (1977). Demanding language. In P. Mittler (Ed.), *Research to practice in mental retardation: Vol. II, Education and training.* Baltimore, MD: University Park Press.

Owings, N., & Guyette, T. (1982). Communication behavior assessment and treatment with the adult: An approach. In N. Lass (Ed.), *Speech and language advances in basic research and practice* (Vol. 7) (pp. 185–216). New York: Academic Press.

Owings, N., & McManus, M. (1980). An analysis of communicative functions in the speech of a deinstitutionalized mentally retarded client. *Mental Retardation, 18,* 309–314.

Pickett, J., & Flynn, P. (1983). Language assessment tools for mentally retarded adults: Survey and recommendations. *Mental Retardation, 21*(6), 244–247.

Reichle, J., & Karlan, G. (1985). The selection of an augmentative system in communication intervention: A critique of decision rules. *The Journal of the Association for Persons With Severe Handicaps, 10*(3), 146–156.

Spiegel, B. (1983). The effect of context on language learning by severely retarded young adults. *Language, Speech and Hearing Services in Schools, 14*(4), 252–259.

Yoder, D., & Villarruel, F. (1985). Toward a system for developing communicative competence for severely handicapped children and youth. *Proceedings of the Symposium. Children and Youth with Severe Handicaps: Effective Communication. Section II.* (pp. 1–56). Washington, DC: U.S. Department of Education.

Yoder, D., & Calculator, S. (1981). Some perspectives on intervention strategies for persons with developmental disorders. *Journal of Autism and Developmental Disorders, 11,* 107–123.

PART III

Program Considerations

Assessment Procedures for People with Mental Retardation: The Dilemma and Suggested Adaptive Procedures

JOHN L. MORSE

It is customary to emphasize three conditions which are essential to securing valid test results: (1) standard procedures must be followed; (2) the subject's best efforts must be enlisted by the establishment and maintenance of adequate rapport; and (3) the responses must be correctly scored. Unless the tests are given in strict accordance with the procedures by which they were standardized, the examiner can never be sure of what his results mean. (Terman, 1973, p. 46)

THE ASSESSOR'S DILEMMA

As clinicians and service providers, we are requested, and in some cases required, to assess levels of functioning of adults with mental retardation for diagnostic, placement, and remedial purposes. Subsequent programming efforts and perceptions of the individual's capacities are greatly influenced by assessment results, coupled with other sources of valuable information that are available and must be utilized. Assessors must be aware of their responsibility to carefully provide accurate, descriptive, and thorough evaluations in accordance with the ethical practices of their professions and the procedures outlined in test manuals.

It is encouraging and reassuring to have available continuous information from test publishers describing their efforts to ensure that users have the latest information relative to revised editions, statistical analyses of items, and measures of reliablity and validity. In addition, discussions in professional journals and among users often relate to the application of specific instruments for varying populations in a variety of settings.

Nevertheless, the sensitive and conscientious assessor is in a legitimate quandry when faced with the questions, How does one adhere to standardized procedures as explicitly required by the authors of the instruments utilized, knowing that the adult with mental retardation to be assessed has receptive or expressive difficulties that are atypical of the established norms? On the other hand, if one modifies administration procedures or materials, have not the tests lost their significance? The dilemma is especially pertinent when attempting to use standardized instruments to assess adults with mental retardation with severely restricted language, lengthy histories of institutionalization, experiential deprivation, and varying degrees of sensory and motor handicaps.

Breaking Standardization

Many assessors respond to the dilemma of using standardized instruments by modifying standard procedures. These modifications include allowing credit for pantomimed responses, offering multiple-choice responses, assisting motor responses, crediting pointed responses, enlarging test materials, and offering manipulatives in place of pictorial stimuli. The modifications may represent major errors, considering the purpose for which standardized tests are administered — namely, a representative sample of a client's behaviors to be compared with a reference group. On the other hand, when modifications are not made, the response requirements may not be fair and consequently the test may not reflect the client's ability, but rather the influence of the client's impaired motor or verbal skills (Cruickshank, 1980). If this statement is even partially accurate, consider how many clients with significant motor impairments (e.g., cerebral palsy) have been misdiagnosed as mentally retarded on the basis of standardized tests with rigid administrative procedures. Heilman (1952) reported a summary of early research studies, all employing the 1937 Stanford revision of the Binet Intelligence Scale. This scale is a traditional, reliable, and valid measure of cognitive functioning. Standardized procedures are described in detail to allow direct comparisons between clients studied and the established norms. The instrument assesses cognitive functioning by measuring motor output (expressive language and visual–motor manipulations) in response to visual and auditory input. Heilman's review suggested that of all the cerebral palsied clients combined, 25 percent had average or above average intelligence, 30 percent had borderline to dull intelligence, and 45 percent were in the mentally defective range. The results of these studies of cerebral palsied clients imply cognitive functioning is skewed downward compared with the standardized norms of a nonhandicapped population. Worse yet, if these results are accepted at face value, would it not be logical to assume that impaired expressive functioning implies the presence of reduced cognitive functioning? These results and subsequent faulty assumptions are a result of the misuse of the instrument and not a reflection of the instrument itself.

Zelazo (1979) found that many traditional test items are bound to the motor facility and do not assess cognitive functioning. Sensorimotor instruments predict cognitive development by assessing neuromotor development and functioning. He stated that speech requires a specific motor facility and that a review of the existing scales reveals that the preponderance of items is bound to motor facility. He postulated that cognitive and neuromotor development may progress independently and that the independence between cognitive and neuromotor growth is neither acknowledged in existing measures nor in their underlying theory. This argument has been supported by findings of normal intelligence among children damaged by thalidomide exposure, as reported by Kearsley (1981), and the inability of sensorimotor instruments to be accurate predictors of later intellectual competence (Kearsley, 1979).

Assessment Assumptions

Three basic assumptions are inferred from the assessment of client functioning. First, central processing skills must be inferred because they cannot be measured directly. Second, because these skills are measured in terms of an individual's performance, visual and auditory sensory modalities must be intact. Third, the presence or absence of central processing skills is inferred from a client's verbal and motor responses.

The first assumption is certainly accurate. At this point in time, no methods are available for determining the efficiency and effectiveness of cortical operations as information is received, compared and contrasted, stored and retrieved, and acted on. Both Kearsley (1981) and Zelazo (1979) have utilized eye fixations and changes in heart rate and respiration as indicators of cognitive functioning (anticipatory responses) in children with motor handicaps. However, no technique is available that directly measures central processing as it takes place within the brain.

The second assumption cited appears obvious, yet is not directly addressed in test manuals. Instructions are frequently offered regarding the need to secure the individual's attention to test directions and stimuli. In addition, it is suggested that a testing session be discontinued should attention or cooperativeness wane. Caution is urged to ensure that records are reviewed that may indicate a vision or hearing deficit. However, the author has never seen a reference made within a test manual relative to determining or observing visual and auditory dysfunctioning as they may affect a client's performance.

Regarding the third assumption, disturbances in peripheral systems, illustrated by limited motor and verbal responses, do not automatically imply defective central processing, as mentioned earlier. Alternative modes or augmentative communication systems have enabled nonverbal individuals to express their thoughts. Eye fixations and head movements are means by which choices may be made and a yes/no response indicated.

Figure 5–1 conceptualizes the task of assessing central processing skills. As indicated, intervening factors may affect the efficiency with which information is received and the ability to express the decision that is made.

These intervening factors are environmentally imposed, organically based, and reflect peripheral system difficulties. It is postulated that these factors are not constituents of central processing, yet exist whether central processing is intact or limited. The continuum suggests that what is processed will be limited, and expressive responses will be further affected by the presence of intervening factors.

Table 5–1 gives a list of possible organic and environmental factors that will intervene with an efficient reception of information. Many clients have visual and auditory acuities sufficent to see and hear information presented, yet experience difficulty when attempting to use these senses functionally. They may be unable to smoothly, quickly, or efficiently track and scan information or shift visual focal points with ease from one part of a work space to another. They may be unable to systematically view or attend to multiple visual and/or auditory stimuli and respond only to selected portions of information. They may prefer to attend only to gross characteristics rather than specifics or details even though they possess sufficient acuity to discriminate details. They may be confused by the available ground when attempting to attend to a particular figure. Kinesthetic difficulties may prevent them from obtaining valuable sensory information when attempting to manipulate and discern properties of objects presented. They may become confused, not understand what is required, and be unable to attend to salient

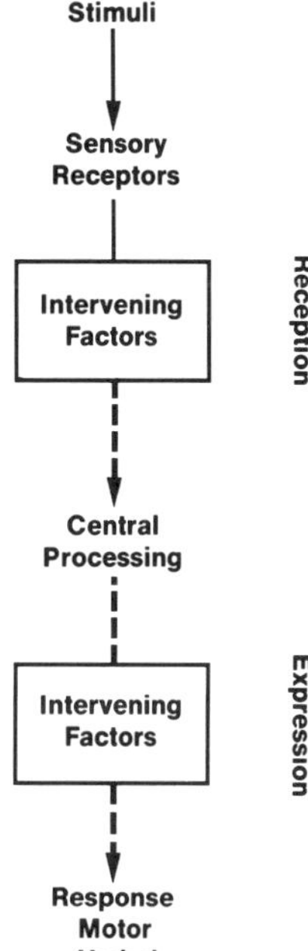

Figure 5–1. *Assessing central processing skills.*

information when presented with multiple or lengthy information. The problem is exacerbated for many clients when faced with a requirement to attend to visual and auditory information presented simultaneously.

Environmental factors may distort stimulus characteristics. It is difficult for many clients to attend to information presented in the presence of multiple and extraneous sights and sounds. Information that is

TABLE 5–1.
Receptive Intervening Factors

Within Organism	**Environmental**
Occular motor control difficulties 　Alignment and fixation 　Tracking and scanning	Poor contrast of stimuli presented
	Limited lighting or glare
Auditory and/or visual figure-ground difficulties	Extraneous sights and sounds
	Limited provision of repetitions/exposure
Kinesthetic and/or proprioceptive difficulties	
Overloading	

not succinct and blends with the background, visually and auditorily, will not be clearly received. In addition, many clients require frequent repetitions and increased exposure to presented stimuli to ensure that they understand what is presented and required.

For illustrative purposes, many clients, when presented with tests employing multiple line drawings, (Dunn & Dunn, 1981), become confused with extraneous marks within pictures depicting dimension or action, are unable to perceive four distinct stimuli, and are not able to systematically scan all possibilities — because they have limited experience with line drawings. Recognizing these possibilities, would a poor performance indicate limited vocabulary recognition or a measure of the degree to which these interfering factors exist?

Table 5–2 gives a list of possible organic and environmental factors that will intervene with expressive responses. Although many instruments are designed to measure gross and/or fine motor skills, the assessment of other skills often requires graphic reproductions and object manipulations, especially under timed conditions. Assembling parts to a whole, placing objects within containers, stacking and sorting, and performing paper and pencil tasks are frequently response requirements that are required to demonstrate the presence or absence of a particular skill or concept. Fine and gross motor difficulties as well as motor accuracy or planning difficulties may interfere with the client's ability to express what is known. Expressive language difficulties may pose problems for those individuals who know an answer yet are unable to respond with few contextual clues; those who can show or demonstrate what is asked for, but cannot recall or express the label; and those who are unable to be understood. Many skills are assessed not only by what is known but also the speed with which they are demonstrated. Speed, rather than power, requirements place the slow-to-respond individual at a severe disadvantage.

TABLE 5–2.
Expressive Intervening Factors

Within Organism	Environmental
Gross and/or fine motor difficulties	Poor posturing
Motor accuracy and planning difficulties	Temperature
Absent or affected expressive language	Work space undefined
Decreased response speed	Limited familiarity with objects

Environmental factors greatly influence the quality of responding. A physically involved client will experience poor visual attending and limited expressive abilities if not positioned properly. When clients are in a flexed position, it is difficult for them to keep their heads erect to view information and respond by eye gaze or pointing. As an illustration, the author attempted to assess a client with spastic cerebral palsy, who was seated in a wheelchair, by offering visual information and requiring her to respond with an eye gaze. Her performance was sporadic and it was observed that she did not scan all possible response choices. During a moment of respite while lying on her stomach on the floor, she assumed an extension position, which brought her head up. While in this position, she visually attended to her environment for a longer period of time than had been the case while seated in her wheelchair. Although this position increased spasticity, it suggested that her visual attending skills were dependent upon positioning.

The temperature of the environment and materials presented directly affect the ability and or willingness of a handicapped client to respond. Several years ago, the author was a member of an on-site evaluation team assigned to evaluate a special education facility for physically handicapped clients. The author observed wheelchair-bound clients propelling themselves along an unheated, underground tunnel in the winter from various buildings to the area used for classrooms and remedial therapies. The quality of their responses to interventions was influenced by their reactions to the cold temperature. In addition, assessors should consider the temperature of testing equipment and materials presented to clients, especially when carrying them while traveling out-of-doors from one location to another. Many clients react adversely to materials and objects that are cold to the touch. These reactions may not be obvious or verbally expressed. Clients may be noncompliant and avoid directions to examine or manipulate objects. They may prefer to attend to stimuli external to task requirements.

It has been the author's experience that many clients, especially the visually handicapped, are assessed without first orienting them to the work space. The client may miss or be unaware of the objects and materials to be examined and manipulated as well as the position of one object relative to another, including recepticles and other response locations. Misplacements, slowed response speed, and unexamined materials may reflect work-space confusion rather than being indicative of skill deficiencies.

Finally, clients' performances may vary depending on how familiar they are with objects and materials presented. A hesitancy to examine or manipulate unfamiliar objects should not be confused with the assumption that a particular skill being assessed is absent.

OBSERVATIONS OF BEHAVIOR

An assessment attempts to determine a client's strengths and weaknesses as a prelude to remediation. What is often unknown and requires documentation is how best to instruct or remediate according to how a client learns best (learning style). A determination of learning style utilizes observations of behavior to document the set of conditions necessary for maximum learning to take place, as well as what is responsible for difficulties in the acquisition of skills or knowledge.

Typically, observations are made at one point in time as a component of an assessment or to answer a concern about a specific issue (e. g., level of activity or frequency of a specific behavior). Additional behaviors may be descriptively recorded or only those related to the specific concern. Unfortunately, and all too frequently, narrative descriptions of behavior are often limited to what is wrong, are expressed negatively and do not include what has been accomplished. Occasionally, nothing is recorded. When questioned, the observers will comment that nothing negative happened. The problem, however, is that positive behaviors are omitted as well.

Various test publishers have attempted to assist assessors by offering guidelines or a framework by which observations may become more organized. Whereas they assist the assessor regarding the diversity of behaviors to be observed, they do not address the influence of setting or task requirements on demonstrated behaviors. The influence of these variables must be understood to understand the client's learning style.

The cube presented in Figure 5–2 suggests a conceptual framework that, when utilized, will ensure that behaviors are recorded as influenced by the variables of task and setting. Behaviors recorded will vary depending on whether the adult is engaged in a self-initiated or caregiver-imposed task involving listen–speak or look–do sensory modalities. Moreover, it is critical to document the influence of the setting, with or without the presence of a caregiver. Of paramount importance, behavioral observations must occur over the passage of time to refute or consolidate earlier observations.

The usefulness of the cube is illustrated by the example of attempting to record a client's attending behaviors. Traditional devices involve rating behaviors on a multi-point scale without considering how these behaviors are influenced by the task or setting. The author was requested to assist a teacher in conjunction with a physician in documenting a handicapped client's attending behaviors before and after pharmaceutical intervention. A form was developed, shown in Figure 5–3, which described attending behavior depending on the setting involved.

The teacher was instructed to observe and record attending behavior for brief time intervals at the same time each day in each of the

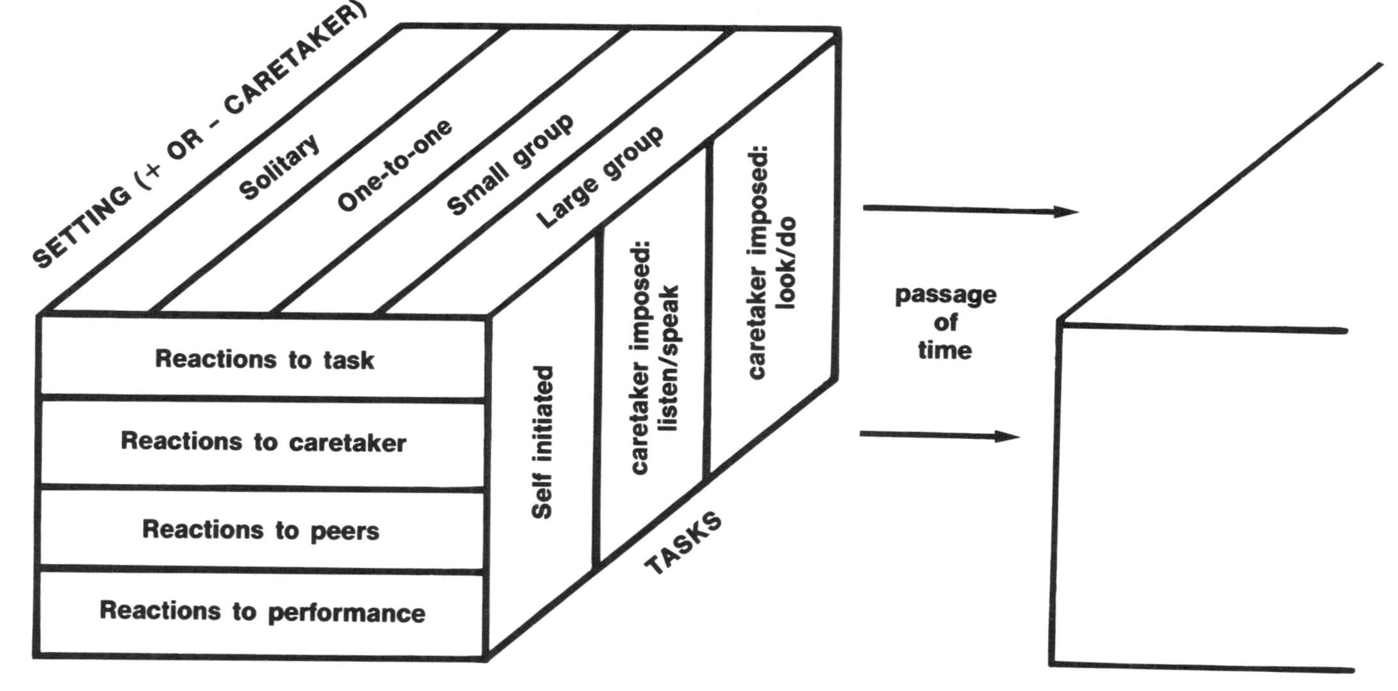

Figure 5-2. Observations of learning style.

117

ATTENDING BEHAVIORS

Solitary Play
1. Is not distracted by extraneous stimuli.
2. Returns to play following disruption.
3. Play is purposeful.

One-to-One Instruction
1. Is not distracted by extraneous stimuli.
2. Body movements are task related.
3. Attends during directions and demonstrations.

Small Group Instruction
Is not distracted by environmental stimuli.
2. Is not distracted by behaviors of others.
3. Attends during directions and demonstrations.
4. Individual work is task related.

Large Group Instruction
1. Is not distracted by environmental stimuli.
2. Is not distracted by behaviors of others.
3. Attends during directions and demonstrations.
4. Individual work is task related.

Intermissions
1. Attends to directions to resume activities.
2. Movements are goal directed.

OBSERVATIONS

Figure 5–3. Sample form for recording attending behaviors.

settings. Particular attention was paid to the sensory modality required for each task, and information was recorded in a narrative format. The advantage of the form was that through its use the teacher was able to note variations in clients' attending behaviors across settings. The listing of behaviors shown was descriptive of a particular client and could be modified for others. In addition, an opportunity was available on a single form to record behaviors over time.

The form was used by the teacher to establish baseline data prior to the beginning of medication. She was not informed until later when medication was begun. A review of the data was useful to the physician in determining whether medication was appropriate and at what level.

It is understood that a determination of a client's learning style, as proposed by the author, is time consuming. However, which is more tedious: spending time observing a client in a variety of settings longitudinally to determine how variations of behavior relate to task and setting variables, or instructing or remediating without knowing the reasons why variations in behavior occur? It is possible that the likelihood of a client benefitting from instructional or remedial efforts will depend heavily on whether listen–speak or look–do tasks are stressed, whether such efforts take place in a group or one-to-one setting, and the relative familiarity of that setting.

MODIFIED ASSESSMENT PROCEDURES

> Neither a conscientious desire to see a child perform to the limit of his abilities nor a blind faith in a kind of clinical omniscience leads him to alter the standard conditions of the test to suit the requirements of the individual case. (Terman, 1973, p. 47)

This caution, expressed by the publishers of the Stanford–Binet Intelligence Scale, represents the concerns expressed by publishers of other instruments measuring a variety of aspects of functioning regardless of age, especially to ensure uniformity of practice and adherence to standardized procedures. The caution is valid whenever an assessment is conducted by using a norm-referenced instrument to compare a client's performance with that of a standardized group. However, strict adherence to standardized procedures when assessing adults with mental retardation will more than likely measure receptive and expressive limitations rather than the presence or absence of the skill to be assessed. The concern becomes greater as receptive and expressive difficulties increase in complexity and extensiveness.

Rather than adopting a position that all standardized and norm-referenced instruments should be avoided with this population, with observations representing the only viable alternative, it is suggested that assessment procedures be modified to minimize the adverse influences of receptive and expressive difficulties. The suggestion is made in full recognition that such modifications will invalidate a reporting of norm-referenced scores. The exception would be those modifications that ensure that information is more adequately received (e.g., namely, increasing visual and auditory attending, ensuring proper positioning, ensuring adequate lighting, eliminating glare, and minimizing extraneous sights and sounds). These modificaitons will not preclude the reporting of norm-referenced scores. They do not modify test directions. However, any modification that does it a different way, unless specified as an acceptable alternative within the test manual, should be viewed as breaking standardization procedures and must be thoroughly documented and explained in the report. These modifications include the use of alternative response modes, using alternative sensory modalities, modifying test stimuli, enlarging materials, and substituting manipulatives for pictures.

General Considerations

Assessors of adults with mental retardation must be aware of changes in their levels of performance over time, depending on location and task requirements. It is the assessor's obligation to document those conditions that optimize higher levels of functioning as well as clients' performances. To ensure representative behaviors and levels of functioning are obtained, it is suggested that the assessment consist of multiple sessions conducted in an environment that is familiar to the individual, in spite of the traveling time necessitated by such an approach. The presence of a familiar person during the assessment should be considered for those clients who are unfamiliar with the assessor and experience difficulty in establishing rapport. The familiar person would assist in recording behaviors as well as helping, in some cases, in the assessment process itself. It is intriguing to note those clients who will only respond to a familiar person and refuse to answer questions or perform actions when requested by a stranger. A refusal may lead the assessor to assume that the skill being measured is absent rather than reflecting a behavioral manifestation. The author has documented variable performances by adults with mental retardation when assesed within a variety of settings with and without a familiar persons being present. These observations are useful for diagnostic and programming purposes.

The performance of an adult with mental retardation will be further enhanced by eliminating the factor of fatigue. The session should be brief and terminate before the individual becomes fatigued, as expressed behaviorally. Fatigue is often demonstrated by diminished attentiveness, an increase in off-task behaviors, and an increase in response randomness or perseveration. An offering of respite may suffice to counter fatigue and allow the client to resume assessment activities.

Power, rather than speed, requirements should be considered when assessing adults with mental retardation. It is more important to document the presence or absence of a skill than whether a task is completed within a time frame, usually established for nonhandicapped individuals. Adults with mental retardation should be allowed to work toward completion even though a time limit has expired and their success or failure noted within the report. Moreover, when test manuals specify the point at which a task should terminate following a prescribed number of failures (items arranged according to increasing difficulty), it is suggested that clients be encouraged to attempt items after the cut-off point, with their successes and failures duly recorded. Adults with mental retardation possess varying levels of experience and developmental gaps that may lead to a false ceiling should their performance be terminated according to the prescribed number of failures.

It is recommended that assessors consider teaching to the skill being assessed. Although subsequent use of an instrument may be invalidated if this is done, information related to clients' abilities to benefit from modeling and correction may help the assessor draw conclusions on how to better instruct or train the client.

Reception of Information Considerations

Acknowledging the presence of intervening factors, none of which are constituents of central processing that interfere with the ability of an adult with mental retardation to receive information to be processed, the following modified assessment procedures are proposed.

Positioning of Client

Adults with head and trunk control difficulties will demonstrate increased visual attending to information presented, provided that their heads are stabilized. Reflexive movements are minimized when prone standers are used or the client is positioned in a sideline position. Certain clients may demonstrate an asymmetrical tonic neck reflex and experience difficulty when required to look directly in front. These clients have been observed to attend better when stimuli are placed in their extended hand.

It is important to allow the client to determine the distance from which information is presented. Should he/she not possess sufficent motor control to regulate how close or far information should be presented for ease of viewing, the assessor should vary the distance and observe reactions.

It is advisable to present stimuli on an inclined plane, horizontal to the client's gaze. Information presented on table tops frequently requires a downward gaze, which may encourage a reflexive posture.

Temperature of Room, Materials, and Equipment

Care must be instituted to ensure that the environment and stimuli to be presented for manipulation are not of a temperature that will initiate spasms, especially for those clients with cerebral palsy or those relying on the tactile sense for information. The itinerant assessor who travels from one location to another with materials must ensure that these materials are not too cold to the touch. The assessment room and materials must both be of a comfortable temperature. Time constraints should never be an excuse for not waiting for a comfortable temperature to be obtained.

Orientation to Work Space and Materials

To avoid confusion about what is to be examined, it is suggested that a raised border be utilized within which materials are presented. The client should be instructed to examine the defined work space before materials are presented. Clients, especially those who possess questionable vision, should be instructed to tactually examine all information presented before receiving task directions to be sure that they are aware of what is to be manipulated. These procedures do not offer clues as to how to perform the task and will not artificially inflate individual's performances.

Lighting and Contrast of Materials

Sufficient lighting should be available to ensure that information is clearly seen and succinctly viewed. However, lighting is often diffused and may result in glare. It is suggested that directional lighting be offered at a position that is slightly behind and off to the least-preferred side of the client. Shadows and glare will be eliminated by using this procedure.

Sharp contrasts between information presented and the background should be offered to increase receptivity of information. Line drawings and paper materials should present black information on a white or yellow background. Colored materials should be presented against a work-space background that is of sufficient contrast.

Visual Attending

Adults with mental retardation may experience difficulty when required to visually attend to information presented. Difficulties in visual attending may not reflect diminished central processing. If the difficulty is not countered, the information to be processed and acted on will be diluted or diminished. Modified procedures are available to increase visual attending in a manner such that the task to be performed is not compromised.

Clients can be encouraged to be more visually attentive by the assessor using a penlight to illuminate each stimulus or a pointer to differentiate which stimulus is to be viewed. The author has observed clients to be more attentive as they are encouraged to touch each stimulus to be viewed. Occasionally, an encouragement to verbalize stimulus characteristics while looking will increase attentiveness.

Many adults demonstrate poor visual searching and scanning skills. They look in a cursory and unsystematic manner. Before being allowed to indicate a response choice, these clients should be required to follow a prescribed sequence when presented with multiple information to be viewed. Occasionally, it will be beneficial to occlude multiple information to ensure that each stimulus is carefully attended to singularly. Clients who experience difficulty viewing information presented horizontally because of a difficulty in tracking across the midline may demonstrate greater visual attending when information is presented vertically. In addition, individuals who become confused when presented with multiple materials may experience greater attending to specifics when each object is presented singularly and is slowly brought into view. Many clients look more carefully when attempting to obtain objects presented.

Adults with mental retardation, especially those with questionable vision, may experience difficulty distinguishing essential from non-essential visual information. Extraneous visual information may be present within pictures or drawings to reflect dimension, movement, or other qualitative information. Many drawings or pictures to be viewed contain multiple information, whereas the client is required to attend to only selected details. All too frequently, clients with limited vision are assisted during an assessment by enlarging information presented. The procedure increases the size of the information to be viewed, yet does not eliminate the problem of extraneous details. Accordingly, it is suggested that information to be viewed be simplified and not merely enlarged to ensure that essential details are illuminated.

Central Processing Considerations

Procedures to assist adults with mental retardation in processing information received visually and auditorily represent significant departures from standardized assessment procedures and must be carefully documented. Although it is acknowledged that these modifications will invalidate test scores, the information obtained relative to a client's performance will have significant instructional and programming value.

Proactive Inhibition

Adults with mental retardation may demonstrate a tendency to repeat a previous answer when presented with a task involving a sequence of similar questions using the same sensory modality. For example, when presented with a series of questions involving the labeling of pictures, the client may continue to offer the label of a picture previously presented. The previous learning interferes with his/her ability to respond to the current question. Proactive inhibition may be minimized by the assessor offering fewer repetitions or alternating between tasks requiring different sensory modalities. The expressive task should be changed (pointing instead of speaking), or a different task involving other sensory modalities should be offered (alternating a listen–speak task with a look–do task).

Perseveration of Response Location

Adults with mental retardation have been observed to perseverate on a response choice location when presented with a choice of four possibilities. It is suggested that the assessor attempt to intervene by explaining that the response location will vary (verbal intrusion) or by alternating the response presentation mode. Circular presentations should be alternated with vertical and horizontal orientations. The procedure will require the assessor to cut response presentations containing multiple choices into individual parts.

Looking, Listening, and Performing Simultaneously

Adults with mental retardation have been observed to look, listen, and perform simultaneously, a behavior that results in no single operation being performed efficiently. These clients attempt to look at information and perform actions while directions are being offered. It is suggested that assessors counter this tendency by ensuring that their clients visually attend to their face while directions are offered, before presenting information to be viewed. A response should not be allowed until it has been ensured that they have carefully attended to all information presented.

Latency of Response

Adults with mental retardation may experience a delay in responding to a question or stimulus. The assessor should acknowledge the delay and allow time for a response. Repeating the question may be beneficial, yet not before the individual has had an opportunity to respond. A bombardment of repeated questions or stimuli may be confusing and should be avoided.

Auditory Processing

The author has found it helpful to avoid offering multistepped or prolonged directions to those clients who experience difficulty with processing auditory directions. These clients signify their difficulty by responding to portions within directions or offering significant pauses before responding. It is suggested that the directions be "chunked" to include only salient points or that they be offered in segments. It is helpful to ask the client to restate the direction to ensure what has and has not been understood.

Off-Task Behaviors

Clients may demonstrate a tendency to emit off-task verbal and behavioral expressions and may not respond to the question asked. They may begin to offer associations or attend to peripheral information. A client asked to state the days of the week responded by saying, "Monday, Tuesday, 18th, 19th, and tomorrow." It may be helpful to verbally intrude by asking the client to repeat the question.

Off-task behaviors arising when clients attempt look–do tasks may include attending to peripheral stimuli, becoming distracted by extraneous auditory or visual information, or engaging in non-task-related manipulations. It may be helpful to ask the client what he/she is doing or what he/she is supposed to perform. The behavior may represent fatigue and should be responded to by offering a respite or a change in the nature of the task to involve a different sensory modality.

Expression of Response Considerations

Expressive language difficulties and motor involvements place the adult with mental retardation 'at risk' when using norm-referenced instruments and strictly adhering to standardized procedures. These instruments and procedures use sensorimotor functioning to infer the presence or absence of central processing. Accordingly, the assessor should use instruments that minimize expressive difficulties by relying on alternative modes — usually pointing, eye fixations, and head or eye movements — to express affirmation and negation.

Alternative Responses to Nonverbal Tasks

Assuming that the client is motorically involved and is unable to physically manipulate objects, it is suggested that the assessor manipulate materials and require him/her to indicate affirmation or negation by head or eye movements. Allen (1955) and Arnold (1951) reported on these adaptations when administering the Leiter International Performance Scale and Porteus Mazes to physically handicapped clients.

An alternative to pointing to a response choice might include eye fixations or a head or eye movement to indicate affirmation or negation. French (1964) stated in the *Pictorial Test of Intelligence Manual* that no significant differences were obtained when comparing a pointing response with eye fixations.

Alternative Responses to Verbal Tasks

Verbal directions usually require a verbal answer. Adults with mental retardation with expressive language difficulties may be unable to adequately respond verbally to directions. It is suggested that assessors consider offering visual choices to be responded to as a substitute for verbal expressions. Auditory memory tasks, for example, require the client to verbally repeat information presented. The author has utilized visual information that requires the client to visually fixate on the answer of his/her choice. A strip containing the numbers one through nine may be used for clients to fixate on to indicate what numbers they remember hearing. Pictorial choices replicating situations may be used for clients to visually fixate on when asked questions probing their comprehension skills.

SUMMARY

Assessing the adult with mental retardation is a most arduous task, considering that most standardized instruments (1) are not designed for adminstration to this population, (2) assess sensorimotor functioning as indicators of central processing, and (3) require intact motor and verbal expressions. Occasionally, these instruments are appropriate and should be administered strictly according to standardized procedures. It is inappropriate, however, to use these instruments without modifications when assessing clients with motor and verbal impairments. Without modifying testing procedures, the results obtained may be more descriptive of the degree of peripheral system involvement than the presence or absence of the skills assessed. Accordingly, assessments of adults with mental retardation often necessitate breaking standardization.

The author has attempted to (1) describe intervening factors necessitating adminstration modifications, (2) offer suggestions for documenting a client's observable learning style, and to (3) illustrate previous research about modified procedures. Suggestions for controlling environmental influences while maximizing receptive and expressive skills have been described. It was explicitly stated that all modifications must be clearly documented and reported. The resulting invalidation of test scores, when appropriate, is of secondary importance, considering the information that will be obtained for diagnostic and programming purposes.

The author offers a case study for illustrative purposes (see Chapter 5 Appendix, page 129). This case involves a previously diagnosed adult with mental retardation with severely limited communication skills who had attended a state institution for years. Behavioral considerations were believed to be the reason for his limited verbal expressions. A thorough review of existing documents, repeated observations of behaviors, modified procedures to increase attending behaviors, and information offered by caregivers is reported. Multiple instruments were administered in multiple sessions to ensure obtaining a representative sample of behaviors.

The assessment process revealed that his level of interactive and social behaviors depended on the setting. He was more attentive and verbally and socially interactive when assessed in his home environment. He demonstrated a slight increase in visual attending subsequent to receiving procedures designed to evoke higher levels of visual functioning. These procedures were documented and offered for other service providers to emulate. Names and locations have been deliberately disguised to ensure confidentiality.

The procedures and approaches utilized in assessing this adult reflect issues, concerns, and suggested approaches discussed throughout this chapter. They will assist the assessor in answering the question that must be asked, namely, Do the results reflect what is believed to be measured? Adults with mental retardation deserve and require an affirmative answer to this question.

REFERENCES

Allen, R. M., & Collins, M. G. (1955). Suggestions for the adaptive administration of intelligence tests for those with cerebral palsy. *Cerebral Palsy Review, 16,* 11–14.

Arnold, G. F. (1951). A technique for measuring the mental ability of the cerebral palsied. *Psychological Services Center Journal, 3,* 171–180.

Cruickshank, W. M. (Ed.). (1980). *Psychology of exceptional children and youth* (4th ed.). Englewood Cliffs, NJ: Prentice–Hall, Inc.

Dunn, L. M., & Dunn, L. M. (1981). *Peabody Picture Vocabulary Test—Revised.* Circle Pines, NM: American Guidance Service, 1–4.

French, J. L. (1964). *Pictorial Test of Intelligence.* Boston, MA: Houghton Mifflin Co., 29–30.

Heilman, A. (1952). Intelligence in cerebral palsy. *The Crippled Child, 30,* 12.

Kearsley, R. B. (1979). Iatrogenic retardation: A syndrome of learned incompetence. Infants at risk (pp. 154–177). Hillsdale, NJ: Lawrence Erlbaum Associates.

Kearsley, R. B. (1981). Cognitive assessment of the handicapped infant: The need for an alternative approach. *American Journal of Orthopsychiatry, 51*(1), 46–54.

Terman, L. M., & Merrill, M. A. (1973). Stanford–Binet Intelligence Scale — 1972 edition. Boston, MA: Houghton Mifflin Co.

Zelazo, P.R. (1979). Reactivity to perceptual–cognitive events: Application for infant assessment. In R. Kearsley and I. Sigel (Eds.), *Infants at risk* (pp. 49–83). Hillsdale, NJ: Lawrence Erlbaum Associates.

☐ *Case Study*

PSYCHOLOGICAL EVALUATION: February 28, 1987
Name: David Rowe
Date of Birth: 5/4/56
Place of Residence: Able Community Residence, New Hampshire
Referred by: Evan Table, Administrator
Dates of Evaluation: 12/31/85, 2/12/86, 2/18/86
Tests Administered: Leiter International Performance Scale, Pictorial Test of Intelligence (Immediate Recall), Developmental Activities Screening Inventory, VMI, Vineland Adaptive Behavior Scales, and Observations.

A psychological evaluation was administered to David Rowe on multiple testing dates. David, age 29 years and 8 months, was referred for an evalution to determine his current level of cognitive functioning, assess his learning style, and assist his mother and the agency personnel involved with programming considerations.

BACKGROUND

David's medical, developmental, educational, and psychological histories are extensive and reported in other documents. He resided at the State School and Training Center from September 1967 until recently. He now resides in a group home and attends the workshop. A review of his records indicated that David was the first born to a 32-year-old mother. The pregnancy was considered normal. Eating and respiratory problems were noted 2 days after birth. Developmental milestones were reportedly delayed. He was able to roll over at 1 year of age and spoke words at 3 years of age. Cranial asymmetry and severe mental retardation were noted at 22 months of age. A report by the Medical Center Neurological Institute in April 1958 indicated diffuse cerebral damage.

A psychological evaluation performed in April 1982, using the Slosson Intelligence Scale, indicated a mental age of 2 years and 2 months. Strengths were noted in the areas of sociability, feeding skills, and ability to orient himself to his living environment.

An annual psychological review performed at the State School in March 1984 indicated that David was able to comprehend simple requests and instructions but will hesitate, on occasion, before complying. He has been known to stamp his feet and strike out at objects when frustrated or in response to performance requests. Much of David's leisure time was described as being spent by himself, engaged in relatively nonpurposeful activities. It was noted that participation in group activities must be encouraged. David reportedly displays little initiative to engage others in interactive play. Expressive skills were limited to manual gestures and vocalizations with appropriate displays of emotional affect. He was reported to have uttered single words. He was characterized as a rather passive and unmotivated individual. Nevertheless, he was described as being generally cooperative with occasions of resistive behaviors. Idiosyncratic behaviors were limited to pulling thread from clothing.

David was seen by Ernest Hall, M.D., on June 6, 1985. An abnormal waking EEG was obtained. Brain stem auditory evoked potentials were obtained bilaterally. All results were within normal range. It was concluded that David can indeed hear and that there was no evidence for delay in the central auditory conduction.

PARENT INTERVIEW

Mrs. Rowe was interviewed on December 31, 1985. She indicated that David had had a few tantrums and bedwetting lately. She was unsure as to the etiology. She indicated that these behaviors are usually a reaction to frustration in not being allowed to do what he wanted. David had been home for approximately one week. Mrs. Rowe stated that she handled the behavior by being very firm and indicating that is was unacceptable. The behaviors were noted at his group home. Mrs. Rowe questioned whether a change in physical structure within his workshop may have been responsible. Mrs. Rowe indicated that David will express himself clearly and appropriately when motivated and interested. He answers the telephone with a barely audible "hello."

Mrs. Rowe impressed me as a very caring mother who desires the very best for her son. She is actively involved in his case management.

CONSULTATION WITH GROUP HOME ADMINISTRATOR

Mr. Table spoke of David's history of behaviors and poor expressive language skills. He commented on David's reluctance to perform chores independently without an adult's involvement. He was of the opinion that David's lack of expressive language reflected not an inability to speak, but rather was the result of his learned passivity and history of being attended to without a requirement for language as a means of affecting one's environment. He spoke highly of and appreciated the involvement of Mrs. Rowe.

OBSERVATIONS

David was observed in his workshop setting on February 12, 1986. During a work activity, David sat at a table with four other clients. The area had several tables and workbench areas. The task involved snapping together plastic hangers. A radio was playing loudly in the background.

David noticed the examiner's arrival but showed no sign of recognition. He occasionally glanced at a client adjacent to him as she was spoken to by a staff member. He occasionally reached down and pulled at his socks. His movements were noted to be very slow and he occasionally forgot to press all snaps together or lay the hangers on the table in their correct position.

A male client next to David leaned over and patted his hand. David smiled and leaned over to the client to touch foreheads. They clasped hands.

During break time, David put sugar in his cup. A staff member came over and asked if he was making tea. David said nothing and got another cup out on the table. He took the kettle off the burner and poured water. He was given a tea bag. He took the bag out of the cup and squeezed it with his fingers. Some tea spilled on the table. He showed no reaction to squeezing the hot tea bag. David sat at a table with other clients, glanced around occasionally, stared off, and drank his tea. There was no interaction between David and the other clients at the table. After the break, he got up from the table, put his cup in the barrel, and went back to the work table.

Receptively, David appeared to understand directions and commands from staff members, but made no attempt to communicate.

TEST BEHAVIORS

David met the examiner at the door to his home at the beginning of the initial testing session. As his mother was greeting the examiner, David reached to take his coat. He was dressed in a jacket, shirt, and tie. He smiled warmly and helped carry test materials. He poured coffee for everyone, receiving directions from his mother not to fill the cup too full. His mother carried the cups to the table. During the examiner's conversation with Mrs. Rowe, David was noticed to smile warmly each time the examiner glanced in his direction.

David was assessed in his home environment with his mother present for information and supportive purposes. The session consisted of a 1-hour work period. As novel materials were presented to be manipulated and scanned, David became immediately involved and attempted to assist in task preparation. He was noticed to attend briefly to presented visual stimuli. Accordingly, modified administration procedures were employed to increase his visual attending. Each block was brought slowly into his visual gaze and oriented to his field of vision only as he demonstrated curiosity. Multiple arrays were avoided. Whenever possible, visual stimuli were presented singularly. He was required to touch each stimulus to be viewed. David was required to verify each placement by touching each stimulus and response choice. He was continually reminded verbally to "look".

These procedures resulted in more frequent visual attending. As David fatigued, after 30 minutes of work, his span of attending decreased, he stared off or glanced repeatedly at his watch, or attended to lint on his jacket. He was easily brought back to task.

David occasionally expressed one-word utterances spontaneously and repeated words of salutation subsequent to his mother's prompting. He sighed when first meeting the examiner. He gave no recognition of a need to suppress his burps when in the presence of a stranger.

David's hand movements, when manipulating and placing 1-inch cubes, were slow and deliberate. He preferred his right hand and demonstrated a pincer grasp.

David showed no resistance to reminders to look, verify his performance, or correct his mistakes. No unusual or inapproprite behaviors were observed. His only reaction to fatigue or indication of disinterest was to disengage himself by looking away and getting up to get a drink of water. His mother reinforced and supported his performance verbally.

The second testing session occurred at the workshop after a period of observation. David made no response and continued his assembly task as the examiner approached him and invited him to a table in the kitchen area. He finally stood up and accompanied the examiner after several invitations. He did not look at the examiner or give any sign of recognition or that he heard the examiner's request. After being seated, he immediately reached for test materials and appartus presented. As noted earlier, no visual attending to pictorial stimuli presented was noted. Similar procedures were used to increase his visual attending. Constant reminders were necessary. The session was terminated after 15 minutes of work, at which time the room was used by the other clients for their break. During the break, David occasionally looked over to the examiner, smiled, and waved.

The third testing session occurred in his group home setting. He was seated in the living room watching television when the examiner arrived. Although he gave no immediate sign of recognition, he began to establish eye contact, waved, and hid his face as the examiner consulted with the director of the home. David's face lost all expression as the examiner approached him to invite him into the next room to begin testing. He complied subsequent to fiddling with the television set and gazing out the window. He immediately reached for manipulatives presented.

David's interactions, behaviors, and social responses more closely resembled what was observed during the initial assessment session in his home. Although visually inattentive regardless of assessment location, his interactive skills were qualitatively of a higher level than when assessed in the workshop setting.

David allowed a hand-over-hand involvement in an attempt to teach to the skill being assessed. It was encouraging to notice his ability to benefit from instruction.

TEST RESULTS

Acknowledging David's language difficulties, the Leiter International Performance Scale was administered to determine his current level of cognitive functioning. The results were as follows:

	Years	*Months*	
III	3	6	(basal age)
IV	-	0	
V	-	3	
VI	-	0	(ceiling age)

C.A.: 29–8
M.A.: 3–9
I.Q.: Severe to profound mental retardation

A review of David's performance revealed all cognitive skills to be demonstrated at age levels considerably below his chronological age. Relative cognitive strengths were noted in his ability to match pictures of objects and people by genus, directly match forms, complete a picture completion task, and match by one and two variables. Analogous progression, parts to whole, and seriation tasks were not successfully performed.

The Immediate Recall subtest of the Pictorial Test of Intelligence was administered to document his short-term visual memory skills.

David obtained a Mental Age of 2 years, 6 months. He remembered gross visual differences but was unable to discriminate small, subtle visual differences when attempting to recall what had been seen.

The Developmental Activities Screening Inventory was administered for comparison. The DASI involves manipulatives rather than stressing pictorial representations and requires no expressive language. David obtained a Basal Month score of 31. His overall developmental level was determined to be 40 months. Considerable scatter was observed with an observation made of his ability to perform developmental skills between the 48- and 53-month age level. Developmental strengths were noted in the area of his stacking five rings according to size, following two-step commands, matching six pairs of pictures to indicate functional associations, and classifying pictures into three groups. He imitated a two-step vertical paper fold. Developmental weaknesses were noted in his inability to demonstrate an understanding of the concept of "one," copy designs on paper, and other developmental skills involving language.

The VMI was administered to determine his ability to express motorically what he had perceived visually. David successfully made circular strokes. When presented with single-line drawings, David preferred making circular strokes. When allowed to immediately replicate the drawing, David initially began to make a line stroke and then reverted to circular lines.

The Vineland Adaptive Behavior Scales was administered using Mrs. Rowe as the informant. The results are indicated in Table 5A–1. Compared with ambulatory adults with mental retardation in residential facilities, David's daily living skills and socialization behaviors are considered to be strengths. Specifically, his domestic daily living skills and play and leisure time behaviors are above average compared with those of the supplementary norm group. His communication skills are of significant concern.

SUMMARY AND RECOMMENDATIONS

David has an extensive history of central nervous system dysfunction, resulting in mental retardation. He now attends a group home after an extended day in a facility for the mentally retarded. Concerns centered on his lack of expressive language, passivity, and occasional mild behavioral expressions when required to perform an activity that is not preferred or desired. A recent EEG was abnormal. His hearing was described as adequate with no delay in the central auditory conduction being noted. An interpretation of the evoked potentials suggested that

TABLE 5A–1.
Results of Administering Vineland Adaptive Behavior Scales to David

Subdomain	Raw Score	Standard Score	Supplementary Norm-Group Percentile Rank	Supplementary Norm-Group Adaptive Level	Age Equivalent
Communication domain	34	<20	SP 45		1–6
Receptive	22			SP avg.	2–6
Expressive	12			SP avg.	1–4
Written	0			SP below avg.	1–6
Daily living skills domain	76	<20	SP 65		3–11
Personal	55			SP avg.	4–0
Domestics	11			SP above avg.	4–5
Community	10			SP avg.	3–6
Socialization domain	50	<20	SP 65		2–5
Interpersonal relationships	26			SP avg.	1–11
Play/leisure time	20			SP above avg.	3–5
Coping skills	4			SP avg.	2–7

SP=Supplemental population.

there was a slowing of central conduction. Results were within the normal range.

The results of the current evaluation revealed David's level of interactive and social skills to be qualitatively better when assessed in his home setting. An attempt was made to document his current level of cognitive functioning excluding expressive language requirements and fine motor manipulative skills. All levels of cognitive, developmental and adaptive functioning were considerably below expectations for his chronological age. It is acknowledged that his poor visual attending skills were contributing factors to the levels of functioning obtained. Modified administration procedures were used to increase visual attending, an effort that resulted in a slight increase in visual attending.

Accordingly, the following eight recommendations were offered:

1. The results of this evalution will be conveyed to Mrs. Rowe and agency personnel involved.
2. David's current placement in the group home and attendance at the workshop is considered justified and warranted. David was perceived as a passive participant at times and independently performs activities of his choice, his degree of independent functioning reflecting whether he has had previous experience in the activity as well as reflecting his desire to perform preferred and familiar activities. Accordingly, it is suggested that the personnel involved convey to David that task attempts or involvements are not negotiable by passivity or other behavioral manifestations. If necessary, involved personnel should provide a hand-over-hand approach and offer demonstrations of the performance desired. It may be necessary for adults involved to be physically present and perform the activity with David prior to expecting him to perform independently.

   It will be helpful for the personnel involved to establish a list of activities that are enjoyable to be offered as a reinforcement for attempting tasks or being involved in activities that are unfamiliar or not preferred. These reinforcements should be verbally explained to David as being offered immediately following involvement with unpreferred or unfamiliar tasks.
3. The results of the current evaluation should be considered a minimal estimate of his current level of cognitive functioning. It was impossible to document higher levels of cognitive functioning that are implied in David's functioning when performing familiar and preferred tasks. It is suggested that the adults involved not use a developmental approach, according to the results obtained in this evaluation. To the contrary, it is suggested that the adults involved present activities and tasks appropriate for a man of David's age with regard to

independent functioning and workshop activities and, subsequently, to teach to these skills required for a successful performance. David learns by imitation and benefits from a hand-over-hand approach. Certain developmental skills expected at younger age levels may never be accomplished, namely, developing an understanding of the concept of "one," or making marks on paper according to a developmental sequence. However, it is conjectured that David is capable of performing assembling and disassembling tasks involving multiple parts. Developmental skills not in evidence should be directly taught.

4. David is perceived as a man who has learned that passivity results in few demands for independent functioning. The observation is particularly noted with regard to expressive language. It is encouraging to note that he spoke as a young child and that his hearing is within normal limits. The examiner is of the opinion that expressive language is possible. It is acknowledged, however, that attempts by all personnel involved to encourage expressive language may result in an increase in maladaptive or mild aggressive behavior. Any attempt to demand expressive language should be made only subsequent to Mrs. Rowe's approval and subsequent to informing David of the approach to be utilized. Should such a course of action be considered, it is considered imperative that a psychologist or specialist in behavior management be available for consultation on a regular basis to the personnel involved.

5. David's behaviors are not considered to be indicative of serious emotionality. His behaviors appear to reflect his resistance to change, and arise when he is placed in a demand situation. A behavior-management approach is considered more beneficial and constructive than an attempt to offer formal psychotherapy.

6. It is considered imperative that the personnel involved and Mrs. Rowe communicate frequently and exchange concerns as well as indications of progress (descriptively) in an effort to ensure that the approach is consistent.

7. David was observed to become immediately involved and attempted to assist in task preparation as novel materials were presented to be scanned and manipulated. However, he attends very briefly to visual stimuli presented. Accordingly, it is recommended that the adults involved use techniques to increase his visual attending. The following suggestions are offered:

   a. It will be necessary for the personnel involved to continually insist that David "look" at presented information.

   b. All visual information should be brought slowly into his visual gaze and oriented to his gaze subsequent to his demonstrating curiosity. He should not be allowed to obtain materials without carefully observing during the process.

c. Multiple arrays of information should be avoided. Whenever possible, visual stimuli should be presented singularly.

d. David should be required to verify each placement by touching each stimulus and response choice.

David demonstrates fatigue as noticed by decreased attending, staring off, glancing at his watch, or attending to lint on his jacket. These moments of fatigue will best be countered by providing frequent rest intervals and alternating known and familiar tasks with those that are unfamiliar or difficult. It is encouraging to note that David is easily brought back to task.

8. The examiner will be available, upon request, for information and support.

John L. Morse, Ed.D.
Psychologist

The "Why" Question in Programs for People Who Are Severely Intellectually Disabled

LOU BROWN, BETSY SHIRAGA, PATTY ROGAN,
JENNIFER YORK, KATHY ZANELLA ALBRIGHT,
EILEEN McCARTHY, RUTH LOOMIS,
AND PAT VanDEVENTER

Special education for the lowest intellectually functioning 1 percent of our population can never be viewed as an end, only a means — a means to a decent chance to function with proficiency, individuality, and responsibility in small, warm, and individually responsive family-style homes; to perform meaningful jobs in the integrated world of work; to realize personal joy and fulfillment in recreational and leisure environments and activities utilized by people who are not disabled; and to utilize an expanded array of rich and varied environments in the general community.

This paper was supported in part by *Grant Nos. G008302977 and G008630388* to the University of Wisconsin and the Madison Metropolitan School District from the U.S. Department of Education, Office of Special Education and Rehabilitation Services, Division of Innovation and Development; and by *Grant No. G008400669* to the University of Wisconsin from the U.S. Department of Education, Office of Special Education and Rehabilitation Services, Division of Personnel Preparation.

An earlier version of this paper is contained in Brown, L., Shiraga, B., Rogan, P., York, J., Zanella Albright, K., McCarthy, E., & Loomis, R. (1985). The "why question" in educational programs for students who are severely intellectually disabled. In L. Brown, B., Shiraga, J., York, A. Udvari Solner, K., Zanella Albright, P. Rogan, E. McCarthy, & R. Loomis (Eds.), *Educational Programs For Students with Severe Intellectual Disabilities Vol. XV* (pp. 17–42). Madison, WI: Madison Metropolitan School District.

If the effectiveness of educational and other instructional services offered to people with severe intellectual disabilities historically is examined, it appears that integrated post-school life spaces have been arranged and realized for only a meager few. Most pass through adulthood experiencing only constricted, antihabilitative, devalued, and unnecessarily costly segregated environments and activities (Buckley & Bellamy, 1986; Hasazi, Gordon, & Roe, 1985; Mithaugh, Horiuchi, & Fanning, 1985; VanDeventer, Yelinek, Brown, Schroeder, Loomis & Gruenewald, 1981; Wehman, Kregel, & Seyfarth, 1985; Wheller, Brankin, Hihill, Smith, McDannel, Costello, Peters, & Freagon, 1953).

There are many reasons why people are labeled severely intellectually disabled by practicing professionals.[1] One of the most basic is that they acquire substantially fewer vocational, domestic, community, and recreation and leisure skills than 99 percent of the rest of the population (Brown, Nisbet, Ford, Sweet, Shiraga, York, & Loomis, 1983). If an individual is projected to acquire fewer skills than virtually everyone else, it is critical that the skills selected for instruction be the most important ones. The problem, of course, is the process used to determine whether a particular skill is important and valuable, as opposed to unnecessary and wasteful.

One process that can be used when selecting specific skills for instructional purposes is offered here, that is, the systematic use of the "why question." The "why question" requires professionals to clearly articulate the reasons why one particular skill is selected over all others, *before* instruction begins. Specifically, when a skill is being considered for instruction, a series of important questions must be answered in professionally defensible ways. Some, but certainly not all, of these questions are as follows:

1. Given a population of skills that might be taught, can those selected be deemed the most important both now and in the future?
2. Will the skills selected yield the best possible instructional gains for the resources invested?
3. If selected, will the skills be those most likely to enhance the individual's quality of life?

---

[1] The label "severely intellectually disabled" refers to approximately the lowest intellectually functioning 1 percent of a naturally distributed population. This 1 percent range includes people who also have been ascribed such labels as psychotic, autistic, moderately/severely/profoundly retarded, trainable level retarded, physically handicapped, multihandicapped, and deaf/blind. A person can be ascribed one or more of the labels and still not be just referred to as severely intellectually disabled for purposes here because he/she may not be currently functioning intellectually within the lowest 1 percent of the population.

4. Does the skill have potential for being useful to the community at large?

Other strategies for selecting particular skills for instructional purposes are presented by Sailor and Guess (1983), Savage (1983), and Snell (1983).

WHY A SKILL SHOULD BE SELECTED

A dimension refers to a characteristic that can vary. Height, skin color, running speed, and spelling ability are but a few examples. In this section, 11 dimensions and related phenomena will be delineated, defined, and discussed in relation to the *a priori* selection of a skill for instructional purposes. The reader is asked to realize that

- ☐ The dimensions delineated are neither mutually exclusive nor exhaustive;
- ☐ Each dimension must be viewed in relation to all others;
- ☐ Synergistic relationships between dimensions should be assumed;
- ☐ Acceptable ideological positions on these dimensions must be realized *before* a skill is selected for instruction; and
- ☐ If extreme positions are taken in relation to one dimension, reasonable positions in relation to others are virtually impossible.

The dimensions to be considered in the selection of skills for instructional purposes are as follows:

- ☐ Increasing the number of environments
- ☐ Functionality
- ☐ Chronological age appropriateness
- ☐ Practice
- ☐ Required as an adult
- ☐ Individual preference
- ☐ Parent and guardian preference
- ☐ Physical enhancement
- ☐ Social contact enhancement
- ☐ Acquisition probability
- ☐ Status enhancement

Increasing the Number of Environments

Increasing the number of environments refers to expanding the actual number of discrete places one enters and leaves each day, week, and year.

Almost all individuals with severe intellectual disabilities frequent fewer environments per unit of time than nondisabled people of the same chronological age or older (VanDeventer et al., 1981). One way to interpret this relative paucity of environments experienced is that such individuals have unnecessarily constricted life spaces. An important instructional objective must be to increase the number of environments in which a person functions until that number is in reasonable accordance with those frequented by people without disabilities. This objective is necessary if an individual is to have the most normalized life style possible.

Historically, the strategy of *increasing the number of skills* has been used as a vehicle to increase the number of environments experienced. That is, an individual is confined to a few instructional settings per week. Attempts are then made to teach many skills. It is presumed that if many skills are taught, the number of environments to which a person is allowed access will then increase. Such a strategy has not yielded meaningful instructional returns for resources invested (Buckley & Bellamy, 1986). For example, imagine two 21-year-old people who have just completed their public school careers. One has a repertoire of over 10,000 skills and the other has one of fewer than 200. The historic assumption has been that the individual with the larger repertoire will have access to more environments than the other. No longer can this assumption be considered empirically tenable (Biklen, in press). If you are an adult who is severely intellectually disabled, chances are overwhelming that a special vehicle picks you up at your house in the morning, takes you to an activity center or a sheltered workshop, and returns you to your house in the evening. There you will stay until the vehicle comes the next day. Your skill repertiore can be limited or remarkably varied, but it will not affect the number of environments you experience. Conversely, a few people with severe intellectual disabilities have relatively limited skill repertoires, but experience remarkably stimulating lives and frequent a variety of enhancing environments (Brown, Rogan, Shiraga, Zanella Albright, Kessler, VanDeventer, & Loomis, 1986).

An alternative strategy is offered here. The number of environments in which a person with severe intellectual disabilities actually functions is increased immediately so that differences in relation to nondisabled people of similar chronological age are minimized. The number of environments having been increased, all instructional services designed to engender meaningful skill repertoires or to otherwise enhance functioning in each environment are provided.

In summary, a critical question that must be asked in the skill selection process is, will acquisition of the skill enhance functioning in an increased number and range of environments? If the acquisition of a skill will not directly lead to or enhance functioning in an increased number and array of environments, it is viewed as less valuable or less important than others that will. Therefore, it is extremely important to identify environments that will enhance the life space of the individual and to teach the skills essential for success therein [2] (Brown, Sweet, Shiraga, York, Zanella, & Rogan, 1984).

Functionality

Functionality refers to an action that will be performed by a nondisabled person, if it is not performed by an individual with severe intellectual disabilities. For example, Sue is being taught to put stamps on envelopes. Is this action functional? In this instance it is because if she did not do so, her group home manager would have to because the envelopes contain checks assigned to pay bills. Putting stamps on the envelopes would not be considered functional if another person would not be required to perform the same task.

As another example, John is being taught to put pegs in a peg board and vacuum a rug in a simulated work environment. Are these actions functional in accordance with the definition offered? No, because if he did not put pegs in the peg board, they would not be so placed by a nondisabled person, and if he did not vacuum the rug, it would not be necessary for a nondisabled person to do so.

Instructional programs for people with severe intellectual disabilities should be committed to teaching individually determined and developmentally defensible functional skills. Which, how many, how often, and so forth can only be determined on an individual basis. An instructional program that does not attempt to teach the performance of functional skills is inherently unacceptable. In contrast, an instructional program that teaches only functional skills, although perhaps slightly better, is also unacceptable. Although there may not be much to the quality of a life if a person cannot perform functional skills, there is probably not much more to the quality of life if a person only performs functional skills. Watching a sunset, listening to music, fishing, and strolling in a park are but a few examples of skills that would be considered other than functional under the definition offered. The reader interested in a supplementary discussion of functionality is referred to Brown et al. (1984).

---

[2] In this context "life space" refers to factors and experiences that impinge on a person 24 hours per day, 7 days per week, 365 days per year.

Chronological Age Appropriateness

Chronological age appropriateness refers to skills, attitudes, instructional materials, environments, and activities that are associated in affirmative, culturally sanctioned, and respected ways with particular age groups. Jim is severely intellectually disabled and 23 years old. At his last birthday party, his father gave him records by Bruce Springsteen, Madonna, and Billy Ocean. Paul is also severely intellectually disabled and 23 years of age. His uncle gave him three records for his birthday. One was the story of Peter and the Wolf and the others contained nursery rhymes. In accordance with the definition offered, Jim received chronologically age appropriate gifts and Paul did not. Chances are great that 23 years olds who are nondisabled would receive the music of Springsteen, Madonna, and Ocean, not the music typically ascribed to nondisabled children under the age of 5.

The instructional assumption here is that all education, communication, and other service needs can be met in chronologically age-appropriate ways. Specifically, phenomena of a chronologically age-appropriate nature can and should be expected, preferred, and enjoyed by someone who is severely intellectually disabled. Denying access to such phenomena is unacceptable in that a normalized and dignified lifestyle will forever be unattainable.

Practice

Practice refers to the performance of a skill under noninstructional conditions after it has been acquired. Kevin was taught to make toast using a toaster in his supported apartment by his nondisabled housemate. After this skill was taught under instructional conditions, arrangements were made for him to make his toast every morning unsupervised.

Two of the criteria for labeling people severely intellectually disabled are that they manifest more long- and short-term memory difficulties than 99 percent of the general population. Further, after they forget that which has been learned, they are likely to take longer and need more instructional trials to relearn or recoup than all nondisabled peers (Brown et al., 1983). In general, if it is known that an individual is highly likely to forget and that recoupment will require almost as many resources as original learning, such a skill should not be selected for instruction without a prior commitment for practice opportunities under noninstructional conditions. However, there are exceptions.

Dave, age 20, is a nonambulatory severely intellectually disabled individual who lives on a ward of a local institutions for people who are retarded. He attends a chronologically age-appropriate regular public school. His teacher has decided to teach him to use a picture communication booklet to assist him in ordering food in a public restaurant, planning meals, and performing household chores. Unfortunately, opportunities for the practice of these skills in the noninstructional environments (the institution) in which he currently functions are nonexistent. Nevertheless, the skills were selected because the instructor judged that acquisition would enhance probabilities of him being placed in a normalized community living environment.

In summary, it is extremely difficult to justify the selection of a skill for instructional purposes without prior commitments from noninstructional personnel that opportunities for practice will be arranged consistently. A priori practice commitments from noninstructional personnel also require the support and systematic involvement of parents, guardians, brothers, sisters, and significant others in the instructional process.

Required as an Adult

Required as an adult refers to whether a skill being considered for instruction is a required, needed, respected, or allowed expression in adulthood. Judy is 24 years old and severely intellectually disabled. She is being taught to clap her hands, touch her nose, shake her head, and wiggle her toes when she is happy and she realizes it. Carol is 24 years old and severely intellectually disabled. She is being taught to alert group home parents when her television needs adjustment, to express preferences for music, and to request bait from fishing companions.

When the *required as an adult* factor is considered, the more appropriate skills would be those being taught to Carol. That is, even though acquisition may take longer, the skills she is being taught will be important and respected throughout her adult life. Generally, if a skill is appropriate for performance in adulthood, it is considered more acceptable than others that are not.

Individual Preference

Individual preference refers to arranging for and allowing a degree of choice in the selection of skills that will be learned. Allowing an individual to choose all the skills that will be addressed instructionally is inherently unacceptable because only those that are enjoyable might be selected and those that might be critical for maximal productivity in important environments and activities might be neglected. Conversely, not allowing participation in the choice-making process in relation to at least some of the skills selected for instruction is equally unacceptable (Shevin, 1983).

There are four important reasons why individuals with severe intellectual disabilities should be allowed to influence skill selection through expressions of personal preferences:

1. Most nondisabled individuals are responsible for deciding many of the skills they will learn.
2. Participation in the skill selection process increases the likelihood of extended effort in the associated instructional activities.
3. All training programs should provide practice in decision making.
4. Participation in decisions that affect an individual is a basic right that humans should extend to other humans.

If people with severe intellectual disabilities are to have the most fulfilling and normalized life-styles possible, they must have opportunities for making choices. Only when these opportunities are given can maximum societal acceptance and self-worth be realized.

Parent and Guardian Preference

Parent and guardian preference refers to securing the extremely important contributions parents and guardians can make to instructional programs. In the past, when parents and guardians banded together to establish and operate much-needed day services for their children because public school personnel would not, many actually determined the nature of the entire experience. Teachers and other direct service personnel were allowed limited, if any, professional input. Conversely, there have been professionals who have systematically and effectively excluded parents and guardians from even minimal involvement in the design and implementation of instructional services. Educators and adult service providers now realize that parent and guardian involvement in the instructional process is critical. They also realize that a constructive balance between parent and professional decision making is appropriate and educationally sound (Shevin, 1983).

All reasonable attempts should be made to ensure the informed and consistent input of parents and guardians into the design and implementation of instructional programs. The delicate professional issues seem that of balance and proportion. Specifically, such issues concern the following: how much decision-making authority and what decisions should be ascribed to parents; how much decision-making authority and what decisions should be ascribed to professionals; and what decisions should be rotated, compromised, or made jointly must be determined individually (Sweet, Shriaga, York, Zanella, Rogan, & VanDeventer, 1984; Turbull, Strickland, & Brantley, 1982).

Physical Enhancement

Physical enhancement refers to selecting a particular skill for instruction because its performance will enhance the physical well-being of the individual. Conversely, it refers to avoiding the instruction of skills that may have negative and, in many instances, neutral effects on physical well-being. Almost all people with severe intellectual disabilities function with impaired bodies and/or are in substantially less-than-acceptable physical condition. These impairments often have long-term deleterious effects on employment, recreation and leisure, and a wide variety of other life-space opportunities. Thus, it is extremely important that many skills likely to enhance physical well-being be selected for inclusion in instructional programs. Assume that an instructor was deciding whether to teach a client to indicate that he wanted to bake a cake or to go swimming. With consideration given to many other dimensions and related factors, it was decided to teach the swimming-related skills because they offered better chances of realizing improvements in physical well-being.

Social Contact Enhancement

Social contact enhancement refers to selecting a skill because it is likely to increase the probability of appropriate interactions with nondisabled people in integrated environments. Rex, who is severely intellectually and physically disabled, was taught to present pictures of food items to clerks at fast food restaurants. This skill allows him to establish contact, to exchange information, and enjoy pleasant social interactions with anonymous nondisabled people. It is extremely important that a substantial proportion of all instruction offered individuals with severe intellectual disabilities be oriented toward teaching skills that facilitate social interactions with nondisabled people in integrated environments.

Acquisition Probability

Acquisition probability refers to the relative likelihood that a skill will be acquired, if reasonable resources are devoted to its instruction. Obviously, skills that have from 0 to 100 percent probability of acquisition can be selected. However, unless other dimensions are considered, acquisition may be meaningless. For example, 25-year-old Sara can easily learn to assemble a three-piece Donald Duck puzzle. Unfortunately, the skills required are not functional, chronologically age appropriate, status enhancing, and so forth.

Selecting a skill for instruction just because it is highly likely to be acquired is unacceptable. Selecting a skill that is highly unlikely to be acquired, however potentially valuable, is equally unacceptable. The decision of choice is to select a skill that is valuable and that can be acquired given reasonable instructional resources. Jim will require intensive instruction over a relatively long period of time to operate an electric wheelchair safely and efficiently. Nevertheless, this skill has been selected because it will increase the number of environments to which he will have access; it will increase opportunities for social interactions with people who are not disabled; and it will enhance his status.

Status Enhancement

Status enhancement refers to the relative effects performance of a skill is likely to have on the positive social status of a person who is disabled. Given two or more skills, the one more likely to enhance social status should be chosen.

Tim is severely intellectually disabled and has no arms or legs. At his work site he was taught to stamp envelopes using a prosthetic arm. After doing quite well at this, additional work tasks were considered. From a list of possible options, Tim, the employer, and his job coach selected a typing task because it would enhance his status in the work environment.

Why A Skill Should Not Be Selected

In the previous section, attempts were made to articulate a list of factors, concepts, and values that can be used to select skills for instruction. The assumption is that there are a large number of skills that can be taught and that there should be many good reasons for selecting a particular one. Conversely, there are many skills that should not be selected because there are few good reasons to justify their instruction.

Several unacceptable justifications for the selection of skills for instructional purposes will be addressed. The four primary reasons for referring to these justifications as unacceptable are that

1. They rarely represent credible positions on the dimensions delineated,
2. They rarely lead to the instruction of real skills in the real world,
3. Meaningful individualization is extremely unlikely, and
4. The creativity and ingenuity so important to adequate instruction are minimized.

The Kit Makers Say To Do It

One of the authors visited an instructional session offered by a speech and language pathologist. She was sitting behind a semicircular table and four individuals with severe intellectual disabilities were distributed around the outside rim and facing her. She said, "Make this sound," and she made an "S" sound. Unfortunately, these individuals were unable to respond appropriately. When asked why she was attempting to teach the skills necessary to imitate the "S" sound she replied, "It says to do so on page 12 of the QRAB-PLOCK-RXTZ-DIPPYDO KIT."

Many professionals attempting to develop the skill repertoires of individuals with severe intellectual disabilities obtain their instructional objectives and materials from commercially available "kits." The contents of these kits are usually based on one or more theories of normal human development, hypotheses related to prerequisites of mature intellectual functioning, and popular interpretations of prevailing or emerging language development systems. Professionals using such programs often assume that the producers have sufficient justification for the instructional sequences therein.

Prepackaged sequences, clusters of core skills, standardized instructional activities and materials, and other such phenomena are generally inapplicable and substantially inappropriate for use in instructional programs for individuals with severe intellectual disabilities. Deciding what a person should learn without having spent considerable time with him or her, without basic knowledge of current assets and liabilities, and without comprehensive information about the current and most likely subsequent environments and activities in which he/she will function is a less-than-acceptable instructional practice. Certainly, limited use of some commercially prepackaged information may be appropriate. However, it must be scrutinized carefully and rejected whenever it is in conflict with acceptable positions on at least some of the 11 dimensions delineated.

I Was Trained To Do It

Several years ago, one of the authors visited a classroom operated by a teacher with a master's degree in special education. She was instructing a 19-year-old young man with severe intellectual and physical disabilities, including limited use and control of his arms and hands, to pick up a plastic egg and place it in a plastic refrigerator door container. When asked why this skill was selected for instruction, the teacher replied, "I was trained to do it."

At face value this justification seems neutral, but it is usually negative. That is, many special education teachers, administrators, psychologists, physical therapists, speech and language pathologists, and others have been trained to teach skills that would now be considered unacceptable in relation to some or all of the 11 affirmative dimensions and related factors delineated earlier in this chapter. Indeed, considering how rapidly special education and other services for people with severe intellectual disabilities are evolving, training offered only a few short years ago in many instances is hopelessly outdated and in some cases even harmful. In short, "I was trained to do it" is not a sufficient justification for skill selection. The effects of what someone was trained to do must be compared with at least the 11 dimensions presented. If it is not, risks of offering inadequate instruction are too high.

That Is Where She Is Developmentally

Sally is 20 years old, still in school, and severely intellectually disabled. At her group home she is being taught to visually track a ball as it rolls across a table. When her instructors were asked why she was being taught this skill, they replied that she was given tests that compared her performance to that of normally developing two-year-old children and the level at which she scored dictated that she should be taught skills such as this.

Certainly all people should be given opportunities to progress through prevailing views of normal human development stages and phases. The problem for individuals with severe intellectual disabilities, of course, is that they require many more instructional trials and longer periods of time to acquire almost any skill. Thus, they begin life substantially behind normally developing children and, through the long-term use of normal human-development strategies, their differences actually increase over time.

Perhaps normal human-development hypotheses can be combined with other dimensions and used to justify skill selection when students with severe intellectual disabilities are very young. However, with increases in chronological age, such theories must be viewed with cumulative professional skepticism and replaced with more appropriate curriculum-development strategies. The second major problem for those who answer the "why question" with normal human development hypotheses is that developmentally based curricular strategies rarely, if ever, result in the skills, attitudes, and values necessary for reasonable functioning in integrated work, play, and living environments and activities at age 21.

SUMMARY AND CONCLUSIONS

A basic goal of instructional programs for individuals with severe intellectual disabilities is preparation for meaningful functioning in integrated work, play, domestic, and general community environments. Being able to generate professionally responsible answers to the "why question" is an integral part of providing the instructional experiences so important to a decent quality of life.

When a professional is asked why he/she has decided that a person with severe intellectual disabilities should be taught a particular skill, he/she should be able to respond with a series of specific, enhancing, and affirmative reasons. For example, the reasons that Joe will be taught to perform a particular skill are that:

1. It will increase the number of environments in which Joe can operate.
2. If he does not do it, a nondisabled person will have to.
3. It is chronologically age-appropriate.
4. It will enhance his status in the eyes of many nondisabled people.
5. His parents clearly prefer that he learn it.
6. He will enjoy being able to perform it.
7. He should be able to acquire this skill in a reasonable period of time.
8. Opportunities for post-acquisition practice have been arranged.
9. It will enhance his physical well-being.
10. It is required of him in adulthood.
11. It will increase his chances for positive social interactions, particularly with nondisabled people.

The basic reason for utilizing these 11 dimensions is that they are considered inherently more acceptable than others that are often used. "I picked this skill because it says to teach it in lesson seven of the PRE-PAC PLASTIC FRUIT KIT," or "because normal infants with the same mental, social, sensorimotor, language, and cognitive ages learn it" are but a few examples.

Finally, the reader should be cautioned that although the "why question" is the focus here, other important phenomena must be factored into the instructional equation and treated with at least as much intellectual scrutiny. *Where* instruction should be provided, what are the natural *performance criteria, who* can best provide the instruction, what are the most realistic and appropriate *instructional materials, how* is the individual going to be taught the skill selected, and what are the *measurement strategies* that will be used to empirically verify progress or lack thereof are but a few.

REFERENCES

Biklen, D. (in press). The myth of clinical judgment. *The Journal of Social Issues.*

Brown, L., Nisbet, J., Ford, A., Sweet, M., Shiraga, B., York, J., & Loomis, R. (1983). The critical need for nonschool instruction in educational programs for severely handicapped students. *Journal of The Association for the Severely Handicapped, 8*(3), 71–77.

Brown, L., Rogan, P., Shiraga, B., Zanella Albright, K., Kessler, K., VanDeventer, P., & Loomis, R. (1986). A vocational follow-up evaluation of the 1984–1985 Madison metropolitan school district graduates who were severely intellectually disabled. In L. Brown, R. Loomis, K. Zanella Albright, P. Rogan, J. York, B. Shiraga, & E. Long (Eds.), *Educational programs for students with severe intellectual disabilities, Vol. 16* Madison, WI: Madison Metropolitan School District.

Brown, L., Shiraga, B., Rogan, P., York, J., Zanella Albright, K., McCarthy, E., & Loomis, R. (1985). The "why question" in educational programs for students who are severely intellectually disabled. In L. Brown, B. Shiraga, J. York, A. Udvari Solner, K. Zanella Albright, P. Rogan, E. McCarthy, & R. Loomis (Eds.), *Educational Programs For Students with Severe Intellectual Disabilities, Vol. XV* (pp. 17–42). Madison, WI: Madison Metropolitan School District.

Brown, L., Sweet, M., Shiraga, B., York, J., Zanella, K., & Rogan, P. (1984). Functional skills in programs for students with severe handicaps. In L. Brown, M. Sweet, B. Shiraga, J. York, K. Zanella, P. Rogan, & R. Loomis (Eds.), *Educational programs for students with severe handicaps, Vol. XIV* (pp. 55–60). Madison, WI: Madison Metropolitan School District.

Buckley, J., & Bellamy, G. T. (1986). Day and vocational programs for adults with severe disabilities: A national survey. In P. Ferguson, *Issues in Transition Research,* (pp. 1–12). Eugene, OR: University of Oregon Specialized Training Program.

Hasazi, S. B., Gordon, L. R., & Roe, C. A. (1985). Factors associated with the employment status of handicapped youth exiting high school from 1979 to 1983. *Exceptional Children, 51*(6), 455–469.

Mithaug, D. E., Horiuchi, C. N., & Fanning, P. N. (1985). A report on the Colorado statewide follow-up survey of special education students. *Exceptional Children, 51*(5), 397–404.

Sailor, W., & Guess, D. (1983). *Severely handicapped students: An instructional design.* Boston, MA: Houghton–Mifflin.

Savage, S. (1983). *Individualized critical skills model.* Training Resource Group, California State University–Hayward, Department of Education.

Shevin, M. (1983). Meaningful parental involvement in long range educational planning for disabled children. *Education and Training of the Mentally Retarded, 18,* 17–21.

Snell, M. E. (1983). *Systematic instruction of the moderately and severely handicapped.* (3rd Ed.), Columbus, OH: Charles E. Merrill.

Sweet, M., Shiraga, B., York, J., Zanella, K., Rogan, P., & VanDeventer, P. (1984). Continuity in educational programs for students with moderate or severe mental retardation: IEP development. In L. Brown, B. Shiraga, J. York, M.

Sweet, K. Zanella, P. Rogan, & P. VanDeventer (Eds.), *Educational programs for students with severe intellectual disabilities, Vol. XIV* (pp. 61–78). Madison, WI: Madison Metropolitan School District.

Turnbull, A., P., Strickland, B. B., & Brantley, J. C. (1982). *Developing and implementing individualized education programs.* Columbus, OH: Charles E. Merrill.

VanDeventer, P., Yelinek, N., Brown, L., Schroeder, J., Loomis, R., & Gruenewald, L. (1981). A follow-up examination of severely handicapped graduates of the Madison Metropolitan School District from 1971–1978. In L. Brown, D. Baumgart, I. Pumpian, J. Nisbet, A. Ford, A. Donnellan, M. Sweet, R., Loomis, & J. Schroeder (Eds.), *Educational programs for severely handicapped students, Vol. XI* (pp. 1–177). Madison, WI: Madison Metropolitan School District.

Wehman, P., Kegel, J., & Seyfarth, J. (1985). Transition from school to work for individuals with severe handicaps: A follow-up study. *Journal of The Association for Persons with Severe Handicaps, 10,* 132–136.

Wheeler, J., Brankin, G., Nihill, R., Smith, B., McDannel, K., Costello, D., Peters, W., & Freagon, S. (1983). *A follow-up examination of severely handicapped graduates of the DeKalb County Special Education Association from 1978–1982.* Unpublished manuscript, Northern Illinois and DeKalb County Special Education Association.

CHAPTER 7

Adopting the Natural Environment as the Context of Training

JAMES HALLE

For most adults, communication intervention is unnecessary; they have learned to use language appropriately simply by interacting with other language users in ordinary, everyday settings. However, for many adults with mental retardation, this naturally occurring process has not provided sufficient instructional opportunities and support for the acquisition of language at normal rates. It is difficult to determine whether the problem rests with the settings where the learners resided (settings that were deficient in terms of stimulation and support), with the learners themselves (deficits that contributed to the label "mentally retarded") or some combination of the two. In any case, it is clear that a large proportion of this group requires systematic communication intervention.

The language intervention literature related to these adults is not nearly as large nor as well-developed as that for children with mental retardation. Therefore, I would like to invoke the experience gained from the intervention literature with children in an effort to provide some guidelines and recommendations for environmental approaches to communication assessment and intervention with adults who are mentally retarded. In the decade of the 1970s, language training programs proliferated (Bricker & Dennison, 1978; Guess, Sailor, & Baer, 1978; Gray & Ryan, 1973; Kent, 1974; MacDonald, 1978; Miller & Yoder, 1974).

The context for training in most of these programs was a laboratory or a therapy room. Although language intervention in highly structured, one-to-one training settings demonstrated its efficacy in teaching new language forms and structures, corresponding display of skills in ordinary, everyday settings was very disappointing (Guess, Keogh, & Sailor, 1978; Harris, 1975; Rincover & Koegel, 1975; Warren, Rogers–Warren, Baer, & Guess, 1980).

Researchers (e.g., Hart, 1985; Hart & Rogers–Warren, 1978) analyzing this phenomenon have suggested that environmental conditions such as distracting stimuli, opportunities and consequences for language use, language directed to the individual, and available materials and events play an important role in language acquisition and use. While learners' language skills do not change when they move from one setting to another, environmental conditions may vary considerably and may occasion very different repertoires.

Consider the following anecdote. Jenny, a 26-year-old woman with mental retardation, is standing on a city street corner waiting for the traffic light to change. A stranger approaches and asks her a number of questions such as, "What's your name?" and "Where do you live?". Jenny does not respond to the stranger's questions. Later that evening, Jenny attends a dance sponsored by the local recreation department. Beau, a young man that Jenny had wanted to meet for two months, approaches and asks her to dance. While dancing, Beau asks Jenny her name, address, and phone number. Jenny quickly and enthusiastically replies to each of Beau's questions. Jenny's language repertoire had not changed in the hours that elapsed between the stranger's questions and Beau's questions; rather, the environment had changed (i.e., the conditions under which the responses were to occur changed).

Because language production is necessarily the result of an interaction between the skills of the speaker and events in the environment and because of the overwhelming emphasis in the literature on skill acquisition and a corresponding neglect of the role of the environment, I am advocating an increased emphasis on environmental factors related to language assessment and intervention. By attending to environmental issues, language goals may become more functional and the problem of generalization to natural settings (alluded to above) may be ameliorated. A strategy for promoting an emphasis on environmental factors entails a major shift in the way assessment and intervention occur: this shift consists of changing the context of assessment and intervention from an isolated therapy room to the natural environment (e.g., residence, job, store, restaurant, bus, park), where language ought to occur.

There are several reasons for adopting the natural environment as the setting for language assessment and intervention (Halle, 1982).

1. The problem of transferring stimulus control of language from the therapy setting to the natural environment is circumvented. When a response is taught, multiple components inherent in the setting may assume control of responding (influence the probability of responding) (Halle, 1987). If training is conducted in a therapy setting, then control of newly acquired skills must be transferred to conditions that exist in ordinary, everyday settings. In contrast, if training is conducted in these ordinary everyday settings, this transfer step is unnecessary.

2. Persons indigenous to the learners' environment are exposed to, and thus more likely to be involved in, the training and facilitation of language. They can assess learners' skills and gain experience prompting and reinforcing language, thus increasing the likelihood of facilitative interactions in the absence of formal training. This is in contrast to the traditional model in which language-delayed learners may spend at most 30 to 60 minutes a day with a communication specialist, whereas they spend the remaining 23 hours in nontraining settings with caregivers who are unfamiliar with language training procedures and where opportunities and support for language are not emphasized (Rogers–Warren, 1975). When training occurs in a therapy setting, significant others are often excluded from the process and are thereby never given the opportunity to witness or learn about language-promotion procedures. Historically when they have been included, the training they receive is so context-specific that learned skills do not generalize from the structured therapy format to naturally occurring opportunities (Miller & Sloane, 1976).

3. Maintenance of newly trained skills may be improved by assuring functional consequences for communication. If language displayed in ordinary, everyday settings results in natural (unprogrammed) consequences, the transfer from artificial reinforcers used in therapy settings to natural consequences available in everyday settings would be unnecessary. If this advantage is to be realized, it is important to assure that the natural consequences are reinforcing to the learner. In a sense, this defines what is *functional*: the communication must influence the environment in ways that produce reinforcement for the communicator.

The just presented rationale argues strongly for assessing and intervening directly in the natural environment. This shift in context, however, produces new problems that did not exist in the therapy setting. Probably, researchers and clinicians had selected small, distraction-free, one-to-one settings because of the degree of control they were able to exercise. For learners with attentional problems, they engineered the environment to minimize irrelevant stimuli and to maximize the salience of relevant stimuli; they chose known potent reinforcers as consequences. This control produced positive results in terms of efficient training of targeted language structures. However, as mentioned earlier, the function of language was sacrificed; thus, generalization to ordinary, everyday settings of newly trained structures was lacking. A tradeoff exists: when moving from a structured to a natural setting, some control of antecedent and consequent variables is lost but the function of language (i.e., effecting a change in the environment) is preserved.

ASSESSMENT

When language training is moved from a structured therapy setting to the natural environment, concomitant changes must be made in the procedures used to assess current performance. Assessment of the learner's communicative repertoire needs to occur, but rather than confining this process to the therapy room, it should reflect learner performance in everyday settings. Form, function, and context need to be considered when conducting the assessment. In addition to the learner's communicative repertoire, the assessment must include a survey of the environmental support of and demands for communication. Thus, the identification of opportunities available for language use in current natural settings and of the language requirements in current and future natural settings is a key to thorough and functional assessment.

Assessment of the Learner's Communicative Repertoire

All learners possess a communicative repertoire. To assess this repertoire, three components must be considered: the function, form, and context of the communicative behavior. These three components will vary substantially depending on the individual's level of functioning.

Communicative function for adult learners with mental retardation may vary from the most basic display of pleasure and displeasure to rather sophisticated displays of elaboration to maintain an ongoing conversation. To assess communicative repertoires at the most basic level, Mount and Shea (1982) suggest presenting an array of sensory stimuli and noting any differential and reliable responding. The senses assessed include sight, sound, touch, and smell.

In their *Comprehensive Communicative Curriculum,* Klein, Wulz, Hall, Waldo, Carpenter, Rathan, Myers, Fox, and Marshall (1981) suggest caregiver (teacher, parent, supervisor) interviews to assess the function of their clients' communicative behavior. They sample very basic functions such as those associated with hunger, thirst, sickness/pain, wetness/soiled, happiness, sadness and anger. This assessment process produces ratings of the frequency with which these functions are communicated as well as the form of the communication. To assess more elaborate communicative functions — such as comments, protests, requests, greetings, and imitation — observational codes (e.g., Rogers–Warren, 1983) can be developed. Parents, caregivers, and supervisors could help assess these more sophisticated functions using checklists such as those provided elsewhere in this volume by Owens and Rogerson (Chapter 8), and Calculator (Chapter 11).

Communicative form (behavioral topography) represents the second component of a communicative repertoire. Communicative forms can be categorized in many different ways. For example, Mount and Shea (1982) grouped responses to sensory stimuli into positive and negative categories. Examples of forms that are positive include stops movement, looks at caregiver or object, points, turns head toward sound or object, moves a limb, vocalizes, smiles, and cries when stimulation is removed. Examples of negative forms include cries when object is presented, pushes caregiver's hand or object away, turns head away, throws object, bites, and kicks.

Klein et al. (1981) recommend assessing learners' communicative response forms with caregiver or supervisor interviews. A checklist containing items such as laughs, cries, screams, throws tantrums, smiles, frowns, looks at people and/or objects, moves body, gestures, points to or reaches for objects or people, and makes sounds — is presented and the respondent is required to check the frequency of each on a scale from often to rarely or never. The respondent also determines the learner's use of particular response modes, which are characterized by more general response categories such as gestures, vocalizations, speech, manual signs, and communication boards or books.

Rogers–Warren (1983) uses a nonverbal–verbal dichotomy to represent communicative response forms. For example, gesture, visual focus, grabbing, and head nods are nonverbal responses; vocalization, one-word utterances, and sentences are verbal responses. MacDonald (1985) categorizes communicative response forms into three modes: nonlinguistic (without words), vocal (with sounds), and linguistic (with words). These three modes serve as a continuum of objectives for a communicative repertoire. For example, if an adult with mental retardation communicates frequently but nonlinguistically, one goal of training would be to translate nonlinguistic responses into vocal or linguistic productions. MacDonald refers to this process of translating from less to more sophisticated response forms as "second-language" training.

Determining the current forms of one's communicative repertoire does not complete the assessment process. Identification of those forms that will serve as training objectives is also required. Mount and Shea (1982) advocate the use of three criteria for selecting training targets. They must (1) be easily understood by caregivers and supervisors; (2) be easily produced by the learner; and (3) offer potential for future conversion to more complex and sophisticated forms. MacDonald's second-language training is an example of this conversion.

The third component of a communicative repertoire is the *context* of the conditions under which the repertoire is displayed. Halle (1987) developed a continuum that includes six levels of conditions that set the occasion for language use. These levels range from occasions in which manual guidance is used to mold a learner's hands to form a sign (highly artificial and contrived) to occasions in which naturally available events or materials serve as functional cues for learner communicative initiations. (This aspect of spontaneity of language is discussed at length later in the chapter). Assessors using this continuum might indicate the relative frequency on a five-point scale from "never" to "always" with which each level of condition occasions a communicative response. Alternatively, one might gather frequency data on relevant contextual levels defined by the continuum.

Assessment of the Environment

Opportunities Available in Natural Settings

Four strategies have been developed to facilitate the identification of these opportunities:
1. Preempting,
2. Analyzing routines,
3. Recognizing alternative forms of communication, and
4. Selection of materials and activities.

PREEMPTING. The social and physical environment must set the occasion for communicative performances (i.e., increase their probability of occurrence) and reinforce them when they occur. To assess whether this prerequisite is satisfied requires consideration of both the social and physical environments because the two act in concert to facilitate or inhibit communicative interactions. Several investigators have reported that caregivers or significant others may interact with handicapped children in ways that occasion behavior that is incompatible with language use (Halle, Baer, & Spradlin, 1981; Hart, 1985; McDonald, 1985; Mittler & Berry, 1977). For example, Mittler and Berry (1977) speculate that underfunctioning in individuals who are retarded may be due to "the failure on the part of those working with retarded people to provide appropriate settings of demand, expectation, and opportunity for effective language performance" (p. 245). MacDonald (1985) suggests that parents and teachers of children with handicaps often lack appropriate expectations for communication and thus "talk for the child" or engage in rhetorical interactions that unintentionally teach the child *not* to communicate. Even when caregivers have expectations for communicative improvement, they are often unaware of the individual's current behavioral repertoire or they are unskilled in training procedures. Thus, they may attempt to evoke communicative behavior that is inappropriate or impossible in light of the individual's skill level, and they may not systematically model, prompt, elaborate, and reinforce appropriate communicative performance.

Halle et al. (1981) observed classroom activities and routines to identify naturally occurring language opportunities and found that caregivers (i.e., teachers) often unintentionally preeempted natural occasions for language. The authors described a continuum of three levels of preempting. The most basic level is *environmental preempting,* which is characterized by arrangements of the physical environment that negate the need for language use. For example, when needed or desired materials, events, or activities are readily accessible to learners who are mentally retarded, they have no reason to communicate.

Nonverbal preempting, the second level, refers to occasions when materials, events, or activities are not readily available and caregivers provide access to them without requiring any communicative interchange. The third and final level, *verbal preempting,* refers to situations in which the learners are already communicating, and caregivers inhibit language initiation by asking questions and providing prompts *before* the adults have the chance to initiate communication. In their efforts to encourage more communicative interactions, those working with mentally retarded adults often unintentionally teach them to communicate only in response to caregivers' initiations, that is, the learners become prompt-dependent (cf. Hubbell, 1977; Kaczmarek, 1983; Sosne, Handleman, & Harris, 1979; Woods, 1984).

ANALYZING ROUTINES. Conceptualizing behavior in natural settings (home, community, work) as part of a routine or link in a behavioral chain may be of value when assessing the support these settings provide for language or when determining how to intervene in these settings to facilitate and teach functional language use. Mount and Shea (1982) distinguished between two qualitatively different routines: the daily schedule of activities (including rising in the morning, dressing, "bathrooming," and preparing and eating breakfast), and the procedure followed in completing each daily activity (for example, "bathrooming" involves washing face, brushing teeth, combing hair, toileting, etc.). Each of these activities can be broken down still further. For example, brushing teeth involves accessing toothbrush and toothpaste, removing cap from toothpaste, squeezing paste on brush, screwing cap on tube, wetting bristles, placing brush in mouth, and so on [see Horner and Keilitz (1975) for a 15-step toothbrushing program]. The same process of identifying routines can be applied to employment settings. Natural language opportunities may arise during the *beginning* and *ending* of each activity that occurs within the daily schedule, and potentially during each step required to complete the activities.

To establish routines as a context for language facilitation, two conditions must be met: first, routines should occur every day in the same order so that adults with mental retardation will expect or anticipate what happens next and, second, clear and consistent cues must signal the beginning and ending of each step of the routine so that these cues can become discriminative for adults' requesting or labeling (Klein et al., 1981). At least two different procedures, delay and interruption, have been used in the context of routines to create language opportunities. Two recent studies (Goetz, Gee, & Sailor, 1985; Hunt, Goetz, Alwell, & Sailor, 1986) have validated a procedure that the authors have labeled "chain interruption" (it capitalizes on the use of routines or behavioral chains) to facilitate communicative display.

RECOGNIZING ALTERNATIVE FORMS OF COMMUNICATION. Clear opportunities for language exist on those occasions when other forms of communication are currently used. Extended eye gaze, pointing, gesturing, and tapping caregivers are examples. Consider a language-delayed adult with mental retardation who taps a supervisor on the shoulder, leads her to a window, and then points to the falling snow outside. This form of communication may be reinforced by the supervisor who responds enthusiastically, "Wow, it's snowing out there!" and offers a broad smile. Thus, a rudimentary form of communication becomes functional. This form ought to be accepted and reinforced until such time that the learner has acquired the prerequisites for a more sophisticated form (e.g., "Look here"). At such time, acceptability or reinforcement contingencies ought to change to require the form that is more flexible and normalized. Otherwise, the learner may not be encouraged to learn new, maybe more difficult-to-produce, forms of communication because he/she is able to influence his/her environment sufficiently with current forms.

In addition to the typical examples of alternative forms of communication already mentioned, other examples can be exploited to create new language opportunities. Carr (1983) and Schuler and Goetz (1981) have hypothesized that socially inappropriate behavior, such as self-injury, aggression, and tantrums, may serve a communicative function and therefore their presence may signal an opportunity for socially appropriate language. Carr, Newsom, and Binkoff (1980) demonstrated that, under controlled conditions, the aggressive behavior of two retarded children was negatively reinforced by the withdrawal of a "demand" condition (the trainer continuously instructed the children to perform specific behavior). Under "nondemand" conditions (the trainer talked to the children, but placed no demands on them), aggressive behavior occurred at very low rates. A possible interpretation of these results is that the children were communicating their displeasure with the demand condition by being aggressive, which in turn functioned as an escape response, terminating the demand condition. In the nondemand condition, little aggression occurred because they had no message to communicate. To test this interpretation, one child was taught a socially appropriate language form (a sign for displeasure) that terminated the demands, thus allowing him to escape from the unpleasant situation. In sessions in which the sign resulted in termination of demands, and aggression had no effect on the continued presentation of demands, the frequency of sign use increased and aggression decreased. If the occurrence of socially inappropriate behavior is indeed communicative, then these occurrences represent ideal teaching opportunities for more socially appropriate behavior.

SELECTION OF MATERIALS AND ACTIVITIES. Learners must have something about which to communicate and must have the "desire" to communicate (Mount & Shea, 1982). Hart and Rogers–Warren (1978) recommend that a variety of materials and activities be available in ordinary, everyday settings to provide occasions or subject matter for language use. Simply providing materials and activities, however, does not guarantee an adequate level of engagement nor a reason to communicate (Horner, 1980). Thus, specific criteria (Halle, 1984) have been developed to facilitate the determination of whether appropriate materials and activities are available. Their potency as reinforcers is the primary criterion. If a learner does not enjoy the material or activity, little motivation is generated to promote communication. To operationalize "enjoyment" (and "desire") and thus determine the reinforcement value of a particular item, the frequency and/or duration of learner engagement (Cataldo & Risley, 1974) can be assessed. According to Hart and Rogers–Warren (1978), a high rate of engagement is a prerequisite for teaching language in natural settings. Therefore, if it does not exist, trainers must prompt and reinforce engagement (to obtain acceptable levels) prior to introducing facilitation and intervention strategies.

Other means of identifying reinforcers for prospective learners include the following: interviews (Klein et al., 1981) with significant others, in the learners' lives who are queried about learners' probable responses to different materials and events; direct observation, whereby learners are left on their own under various conditions and information is gathered on what they choose and their engagement with chosen materials and events; reinforcement menus (Daley, 1969) that enable higher functioning learners to select their own reinforcers where the items are represented by line drawings or pictures; and systematic preference testing (Striefel, 1974). The latter is accomplished by conducting multiple trials in which three to five objects or symbols of events (i.e., potential reinforcers) are displayed and the learner selects one to manipulate, engage in, or consume until a prioritized, ordered list is generated.

A second criterion that may be invoked in choosing appropriate materials and activities pertains to the amount of time required to complete the activity (Anderson, 1982). For a learner with limited language skills (such as gestures or object labels), after an item has been requested, few additional opportunities arise during the activity for teaching functional communication. However, if such learners complete activities quickly, new occasions or reasons for language use are established (e.g., informing the trainer that the activity is completed and then making a request for another item). Activities that may be completed quickly differ from one learner to another; variables that should be considered in the assessment are the reinforcing value of the activity and mastery of the skills required to engage in the activity.

Identifying materials and activities that contain multiple components represents a third criterion. Each component constitutes a new opportunity for a request or a label. For example, when preparing a meal, each of the ingredients and each of the utensils required provide potential opportunities to communicate. Other multiple-component activities are assembly tasks, home-living chores (clean bathroom, vacuum carpet, make bed), and community-based activities (e.g., riding a bus, ordering food in a restaurant). Multiple-component materials and activities will be discussed further in relation to routines.

A fourth criterion used to select materials and activities is repetitive action. Assuming that the material or activity is reinforcing and a caregiver can regulate continued engagement, repeated opportunities exist for language use. Examples include leisure activities such as board games ("my turn") or playing catch with a ball or frisbee ("throw it").

Novelty is a fifth criterion. According to Alpert (1984), language-delayed individuals are more likely to request information when unfamiliar objects are available, and they are more likely to share information when novel things are presented. Thus novelty of the materials and activities chosen may occasion language use.

Activities that are a part of daily living constitute a sixth criterion. Eating, dressing, bathing, toileting, home-cleaning, meal preparation, and other domestic routines are examples of daily-living activities that are functional in the natural environment and may include many of the criteria previously mentioned. Eating, for example, could be structured to capitalize on each of the five preceding criteria.

None of the six criteria should be used in isolation. Materials or activities that successfully combine two or more criteria are likely to provide clearer reasons for the individual to communicate. That the materials or activity contain reinforcers for the learner is the critical criterion because without it, the reason or motivation to communicate is lacking. If learners do not like to brush their teeth (often the taste of toothpaste is a reinforcer), they are not likely to respond to the multiple opportunities to communicate generated by the many components inherent in a toothbrushing routine (Hamer & Keilitz, 1975).

Language Requirements in Current and Future Settings

To conduct an assessment of the language of learners who have mental retardation, it is necessary to consider not only the learner's repertoire and the opportunities available in natural settings, but also the language requirements inherent in these settings. That is, for individuals to succeed in particular contexts, they must possess the corresponding language repertoire required in those contexts. After learners have begun to use language functionally to satisfy needs and wants, they in a sense graduate to a higher level of analysis. At this new level, we no longer ask, "Do they have an appropriate form or mode of language?" Nor do we ask, "Do language opportunities exist in their everyday settings?" Rather, we ask, "Do learners have the language skills necessary to succeed in these settings?"

To answer this question, the language requirements of the setting need to be assessed. Social validation (Kazdin, 1977; Wolf, 1978) methodology may be invoked to determine the language skills that are required to survive (minimal standard) or to thrive (optimal standard) within each unique natural setting. Social validation was defined previously (see Chapter 2) and its methodology described. Both subjective evaluation and social comparison can be used as a means of determining the language skills needed. In the former procedure, others who inhabit the target setting might be surveyed to assess their opinion about skills required pertaining to language. In the latter procedure, others who were succeeding in the setting might be observed to determine their use of language — its form, function, and specific context.

ENVIRONMENTAL INTERVENTION

The first objective of environmental intervention is to increase the number of opportunities for learners to communicate functionally in naturally occurring situations. This objective may be accomplished by arranging the environment in ways that require learners to communicate with others to gain access to reinforcers (i.e., materials, activities, assistance, attention). To preserve the "naturalness" of natural environment intervention, significant others should survey current settings to identify naturally occurring occasions that could be altered only slightly to afford communicative opportunities.

The slight alteration or change in the natural environment will consist of the caregiver or supervisor delaying or interrupting ongoing events at "critical"moments. Critical moments are those occasions when the learner is about to receive help, a desired item, or access to a preferred event. The interventionist simply delays or interrupts the receipt of assistance, the item, or engagement in the event, thus creating a reason for the learner to communicate. Please note that delay and interruption procedures by themselves do not teach language, rather they only provide opportunities to practice existing language. Specific teaching strategies will be discussed in the next section of the chapter. A few examples may be helpful. I will draw on the naturally available opportunities already described.

In an employment setting, if a job coach notices that a worker has just packaged the last utensil and will now require more to continue working, rather than immediately asking "What do you need?" (verbal preempting), the coach could wait to determine whether the worker will attempt to communicate that he needs more utensils. Using the same scenario just described, let's assume that the worker had communicated his plight in the past by bringing the empty container (of utensils) to the job coach, who responded by getting more and bringing them to the worker. Let's assume further that the word "more" is in the worker's repertoire. The coach now recognizes that approaching with an empty container is a form of communication; thus, rather than immediately getting additional utensils, the coach attends to the worker and waits for a verbal request. Attending to the worker and waiting do not constitute ignoring; rather, they may function as a mild form of reinforcement. Greater reinforcement is available if the worker were to say "more."

Delays might also be applied at mealtime. If learners are receiving cafeteria-style meals and food is provided with no communicative requirement, delays can be used to provide reasons to communicate (Halle, Marshall, & Spradlin, 1979). VanBiervliet, Marshall, and Spangler (1981) found that by simply changing from cafeteria-style to family-style meals, the communicative rate of adolescents with severe developmental disabilities increased substantially.

Goetz et al. (1985) provide an example of the use of chain interruption in a toast-preparation routine that consisted of getting bread from a bag, putting it in toaster, pushing down, taking toast out, and putting it on the plate. Chuck, an adolescent with a severe disability, was "interrupted" after he put the toast in the toaster. That is, the trainer said, "Wait," passively blocked the next action (pushing down the handle), and asked, "What do you want?"

Although many naturally occurring opportunities may exist, it may be helpful to manipulate the current ecology to provide additional communicative occasions that are somewhat contrived but whose probability of provocation is especially high. These strategies are placed under environmental intervention (and distinguished from naturally occurring opportunities just described) because they require manipulation or change of the natural environment, and include the following:

- □ Place preferred materials out of reach, but in clear view.
- □ Present engaging materials that require assistance.
- □ Provide small or inadequate amounts or portions of desired edibles or materials.
- □ Do something that the learner does not like.
- □ Establish a blatantly "unfair" situation.
- □ Violate an expectation by doing something absurd.

Validated Procedures for Training Language in the Natural Environment

During its relatively brief history in the language intervention literature, training that occurs in the natural environment has been referred to as *milieu training, incidental language teaching,* and *natural environment language training.* Although the labels differ, they all refer to language training procedures that are (a) brief and positive, (b) conducted in the natural environment where opportunities for teaching functional language occur naturally, (c) occasioned by learner interest in the topic to which training will relate, and (d) applied in a context of reinforcing people, materials, and activities (Halle, Alpert, & Anderson, 1984).

This section of the chapter will concentrate on three natural environment language-training procedures that have been used by teachers, caregivers, and parents to improve the functional communication skills of learners with language deficits. The procedures will be described in terms of their objectives or what they attempt to accomplish; the steps involved in each; the manner in which they complement one another; and examples of how each might be used. Empirical studies that document the effectiveness of each procedure are cited. However, a discussion of their findings is beyond the scope of this chapter. (Please refer to the references for further information.)

Mand-Model Procedure

The mand-model procedure was developed by Rogers–Warren and Warren (1980) as a means of actively programming for generalization of language skills from one-to-one training sessions to a preschool classroom. Alpert and Rogers–Warren (1983) and Warren, McQuarter, and Rogers–Warren (1984) have also employed the mand-model procedure as a direct language-training technique. The specific objectives sought by the application of the procedure include (a) establishing joint attention (topic selection) as a cue for communication (Hart, 1985), (b) training turn-taking, (c) training the learner to provide information when requested or instructed, and (d) training the learner to respond to a variety of adult-presented verbal cues (Alpert & Rogers–Warren, 1983).

Prior to implementing the mand-model procedure, caregivers must arrange the physical environment to ensure that a variety of attractive materials is available to the learner. Interaction generated by this procedure is initiated by caregivers, who establish joint attention and then mand (instruct) the learner to describe or label the material or event that constitutes the focus of the interaction. Caregivers accomplish these steps by directing attention to a particular material, thereby establishing joint attention, or by following the learner's lead (e.g., learner approaches material or watches ongoing event). If the learner's response is appropriate, then the caregiver provides praise (and expansion of the response) and the material or access to the activity. If the learner's response is inappropriate, a corrective mand or corrective model is provided. Ideally, caregivers should be responsive to learners' interests and present mands related to those topics. A flowchart of the specific steps included in the implementation of the mand-model procedure is presented in Figure 7–1.

An example of the application of the mand-model procedure might entail the provision of a variety of materials related to a preferred recreational activity such as softball. Bats, balls, and mits could be readily accessible to the participating learners. As they are approaching a ball, just before they reach for it, the caregiver mands ("Tell me what you want") the learners to label the object ("ball"), or after it is in hand, to label the action ("throw"). As the mand-model procedure is used more frequently, it becomes a routine indistinguishable from other routine events that occur throughout the day. Labeling and requesting, using language, are an integral part of *every* activity.

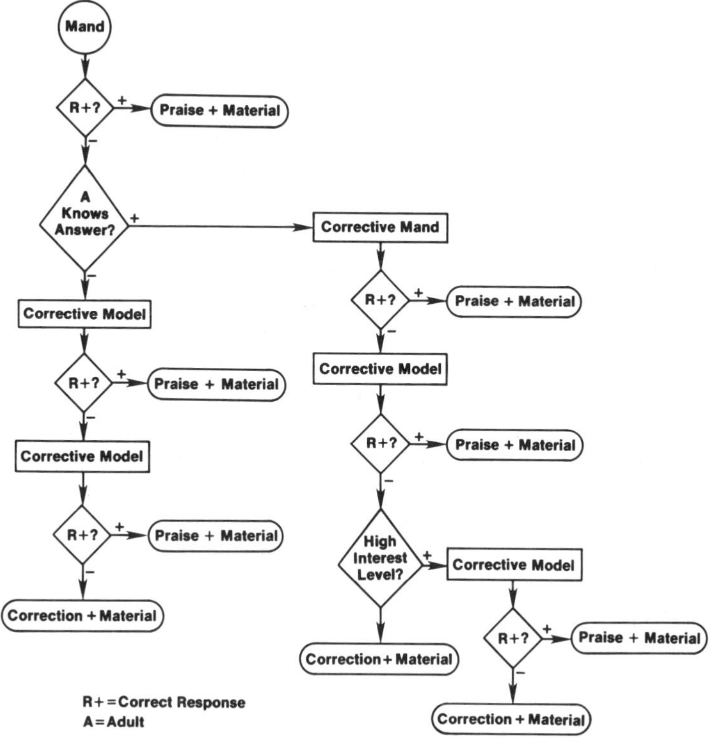

Figure 7–1. *The mand-model procedure.*

- Instructor presents mand
- If adult responds appropriately, instructor offers praise (expansion) plus material
- If adult responds inappropriately, instructor has option of:
  - (A) • presenting corrective mand
    - if adult responds appropriately to corrective mand, instructor offers praise (expansion) plus material
    - if adult responds appropriately to corrective model, instructor offers praise (expansion) plus material
    - if adult responds inappropriately to corrective model, instructor has option of:
    - (1) offering corrective feedback plus material or
    - (2) presenting another corrective model
      - if adult responds appropriately to corrective model, instructor offers praise (expansion) plus material
      - if adult responds inappropriately to corrective model, instructor offers corrective feedback plus material, or
  - (B) • presenting corrective model
    - if adult responds appropriately to corrective model, instructor offers praise (expansion) plus material
    - if adult responds inappropriately to corrective model, instructor presents another corrective model
    - if adult responds appropriately to corrective model, instructor offers praise (expansion) plus material
    - if adult responds inappropriately to corrective model, instructor offers corrective feedback plus material

With increased use, learners become more responsive and caregivers establish themselves as facilitators: people who help learners gain access to valued materials and events. To obtain the joint focus of attention, caregivers may look or gesture alternately from learner to ball while delivering the mand. If the learner says or signs "ball," the caregiver allows access to the ball and praises the learner. If, however, learners respond incorrectly or not at all, the caregiver models "ball." An imitation produces praise and the ball; no response or an incorrect response produces a correction and then the ball.

A shortcoming of the mand-model procedure is that it teaches learners to respond to verbal cues of others. Although this may be an appropriate objective for learners who are noncompliant or for those who are not under the verbal control of others, it may foster their dependence on others' verbal cues. That is, learners may not initiate communication under conditions other than when they are asked a question or instructed to respond. To overcome this potential shortcoming, caregivers may employ the time–delay procedure (more accurately referred to as delayed prompting).

Time Delay

The delayed-prompting procedure was developed as a means of establishing environmental stimuli other than verbal prompts as cues for language. Its effectiveness has been empirically validated in two studies (Halle et al., 1979; 1981). In addition to teaching learners to respond to an expanded variety of environmental stimuli, a second objective of delayed prompting is to provide learners with opportunities or reasons to use communication skills that may already be in their repertoire.

Prerequisite components of delayed prompting include (1) arranging the environment to increase the probability that learners will require assistance (see previous subsection on environmental assessment and intervention) and (2) others attending to learners' actions and introducing delays on occasions when the learners need assistance or want an inaccessible material. The delay itself requires listeners to (1) position themselves near and orient toward the learner; (2) wait silently for an established period of time (e.g., 3 to 10 seconds); (3) look at the learner and assume an expectant facial expression; (4) offer praise and the material or assistance when the learner communicates appropriately; and (5) provide models of appropriate responses (i.e., the Model Procedure) when the learner responds inappropriately or not at all (see Figure 7–2).

To facilitate the distinction between the mand-model and delay procedures, softball will be used as the context for this example. Balls, bats,

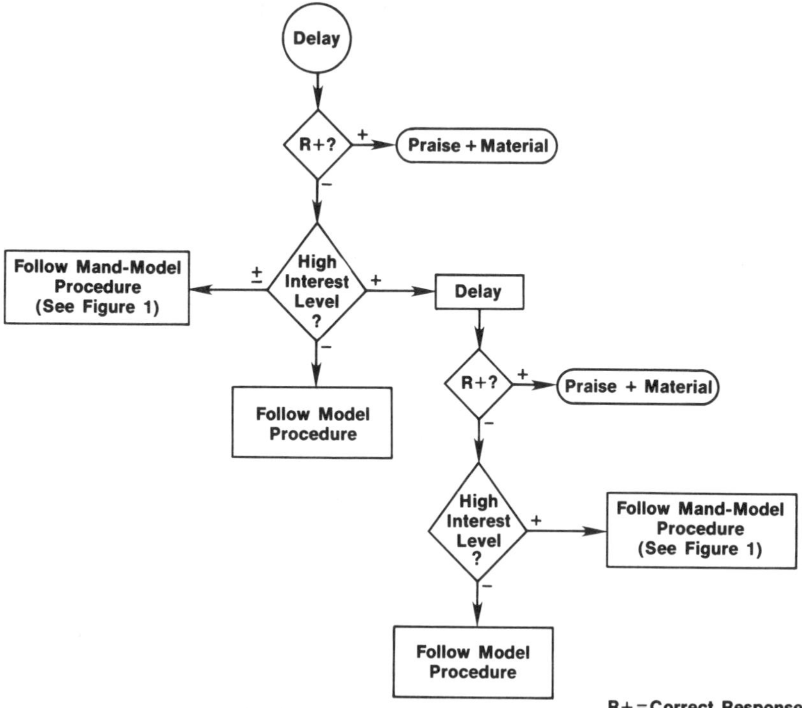

Figure 7–2. *The time-delay procedure.*

- Instructor presents time delay
- If adult responds appropriately, instructor offers praise (expansion) plus material
- If adult responds inappropriately, instructor has option of:
    - (A) • presenting time delay again
        - if adult responds appropriately, instructor offers praise (expansion) plus material
        - if adult responds inappropriately, instructor has option of:
            - (1) • following steps of Mand-Model Procedure or
            - (2) • following steps of Model Procedure
    - (B) • following steps of Mand-Model Procedure or
    - (C) • following steps of Model Procedure

and mits are available in the setting. Mand-models have been used routinely so learners are now waiting for mands before picking up these objects and before performing appropriate actions with them. Thus mands are controlling requests and labels, that is, these responses occur in response to mands. To transfer control from mands to the objects themselves, two changes are required. Access to the items must be controlled by the listeners (if readily available, the request function is eliminated) and mand-models are delayed (listeners simply wait, allowing learners an opportunity to scan the environment to determine the appropriate response).

To accomplish these two changes, listeners might have the materials available on a shelf located behind them and access will be provided contingent on an appropriate request. Rather than manding when a learner gazes or points to a ball, listeners will focus attention on the learner, assume an expectant look, and wait for a request. If learners say or sign "ball" during the delay period, they will receive it immediately along with praise. If, however, they fail to make an appropriate response during the delay period, a model of an appropriate response will be provided. Imitation produces praise and the item.

Although the use of delayed prompting may broaden the control of events that provoke communication by learners with mental retardation, previous applications have lacked the appropriate technology to further advance learners' language skills. Incidental teaching contains an elegant teaching technology that individualizes every language interaction with the objective of approximating "normal" language usage.

Incidental Teaching

Incidental language-teaching procedures were developed by Hart and Risley (1968; 1974; 1975; 1980) in a series of studies with culturally disadvantaged preschoolers. Incidental teaching is used to evoke language related to reinforcers specified by the learner. It may be appropriate before describing incidental teaching to note that all three of the procedures reviewed were initially validated with young children (the delay procedure was used with adolescents also). Intuitively, there is no reason to believe that chronological age of the learner would influence the effectiveness of the procedure (developmental age would appear to be more relevant); however, only future replication research will provide an empirical answer to this issue.

The first step in the incidental teaching process is to arrange the environment in ways that will encourage requests for materials and assistance. When learners request materials or assistance, they are identifying what is of pre-potent interest (i.e., a reinforcer) at that moment. The caregiver responds by manding or delaying for a more complex response or for additional information about the reinforcer. When learners respond appropriately, they receive the reinforcer, praise, and repetition of the response in expanded form (they are presented with a model of more complex language for future responses). If learners do not respond appropriately to caregiver prompts, corrective feedback is provided (i.e., a desired response is modeled) and the requested item is presented. Because the caregiver capitalizes on the motivation derived from the reinforcer, teaching can occur only as long as it remains a reinforcer. As more response output is requested, the value of the reinforcer diminishes in comparison. Thus, teaching episodes should be brief and positive. The specific steps involved in the incidental-teaching procedure are displayed in the flowchart in Figure 7–3.

Invoking the same example may provide a clearer basis for comparisons and contrasts. With incidental teaching, the listener waits for learners to initiate. If the delay procedure has been successful, learners will be initiating for help, attention, and desired materials and events. Learner initiations may assume many forms, for example, focused attention, pointing, vocalizing, verbalizing, and gesturing. Invoking the

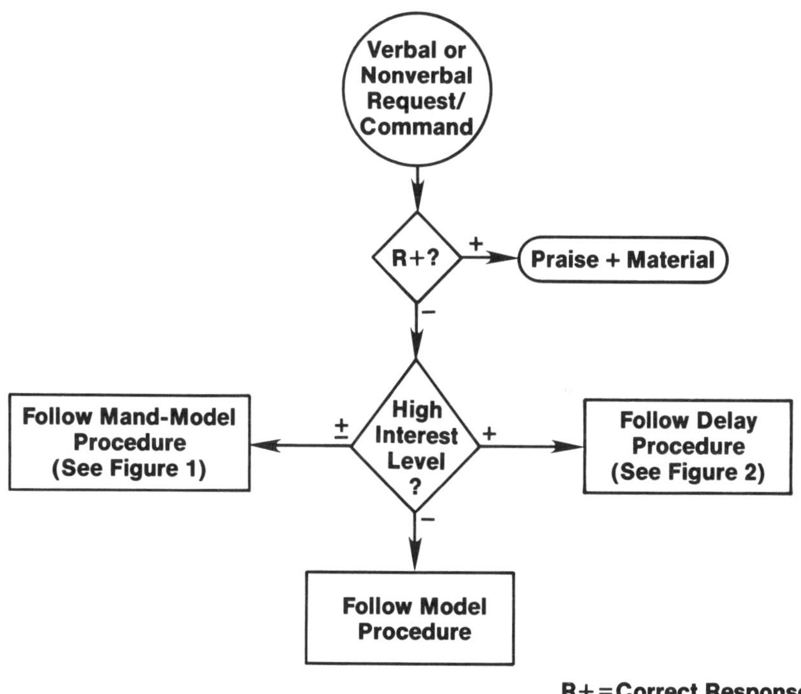

Figure 7–3. The incidental teaching procedure.

- Adult makes verbal or nonverbal request/command
- If request/command is appropriate, instructor offers praise (expansion) plus material
- If request/command is inappropriate, instructor has option of:
  - (A) • following steps of Delay Procedure
  - (B) • following steps of Mand-Model Procedure or
  - (C) • following steps of Model Procedure

same example, if a learner approaches the shelf where the materials are on display and initiates by saying "ball," the listener may focus attention on the learner and wait (delay) for an elaboration. This would only occur if the learner was consistently using one-word requests and a new objective was two-word (action–object) requests. A requirement of this procedure is that the listener possesses knowledge of current and future language objectives for each learner.

Returning to the example, if the learner produces an elaboration, descriptive praise and the ball are delivered immediately. If, however, no response or an inappropriate response occurs, the listener mands (asks) for a more complex or elaborate response. If an incorrect response occurs again, a model is provided. Increased complexity or expansion may constitute longer utterances or more description of the item or event desired (e.g., "Tell me the color'" or "Give me a full sentence"). A hallmark of this procedure occurs when listeners provide feedback after the learner's response; they not only praise, they also repeat the answer in expanded form, foreshadowing what will be expected in future learning interactions.

None of the three procedures reviewed has the capacity currently to make adult learners who are developmentally delayed and possess few communication skills into fluent communicators (able to use elaborated language as a means of controlling their environment). The mand-model procedure contains no mechanisms for ensuring or building initiated language. The delay procedure cannot build rate of responding quickly because opportunities for language depend on environmental events; nor does this procedure include an efficient technology for teaching new, more complex language. Incidental teaching requires a learner initiation as a prerequisite to any incidental-teaching interaction; thus adults who rarely initiate language would almost never come in contact with incidental teaching practices. Although none of the procedures by themselves may meet the needs of learners at different developmental levels, taken together they comprise an integrated model (cf. Halle, 1982) that possesses great potential for language training in natural settings.

Developing Spontaneous Communication

This entire chapter has been dedicated to communication assessment and intervention in ordinary, everyday settings with adults who are mentally retarded. A major problem with current practice is that after intervention, learners do not communicate spontaneously. If one invokes incidental teaching, then learners are indeed communicating spontaneously. The difficulty has been teaching learners with more severe disabilities the prerequisite skill of initiating communication. If environmental approaches to assessment and intervention are to be effective, learners who are involved in such an approach must acquire communicative spontaneity. Before broaching the subject of how to teach spontaneity, a practical and precise definition must be established.

Definition

The task of defining spontaneity is not a simple one and, perhaps, contributes to much of the confusion related to spontaneity (Halle, 1987). The definition cited most often, similar to the dictionary definition, refers to spontaneous language as language that is uncued; it emanates from within an individual; its display does not depend on cues in the physical environment. Such a definition may present problems. If language emanates from within an individual and has no apparent relationship with the context in which it occurs, such language might be considered bizarre.

To resolve this difficulty, let's assume that all language is, at least in part, environmentaly cued. This assumption does not eliminate the possibility, even probability, that many communicative responses are also evoked by interoceptive stimuli (e.g., hunger, thirst, bladder tension, deprivation states associated with a variety of wants and needs). However, even at those times when stimuli "beneath the skin" produce responses, other stimuli in the external environment may influence the probability of the response. For example, if learners are visiting a new park and they do not know where the bathrooms are, they are more likely to communicate spontaneously (inquire about the location of the bathroom) in the presence of other people than in their absence.

Rather than conceptualizing spontaneous communication as uncued, perhaps a more accurate definition might be communication for which the antecedent cues are not readily identifiable. Spontaneity, then, may be a label used for communicative responses when we do not know the variables that influence their occurrence. This perspective sheds new light on the term "spontaneity" and its definition.

By conceptualizing stimuli that influence the occurrence of responding on a continuum of discriminability, we may make a contribution to the definition of spontaneous communication. In general, the more discernible the cues, the less spontaneous the response is believed to be; and the less discernible the cues, the more spontaneous the response, (see Figure 7–4).

Categories of Influential Cues

Invoking the continuum as a guide, examples of selecting categories may illuminate the definition of spontaneous communication offered.

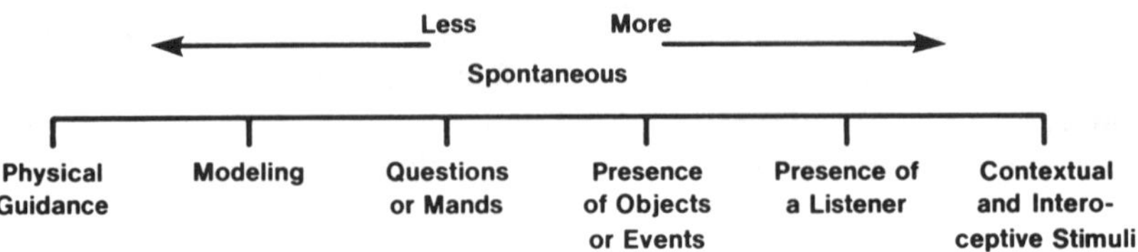

Figure 7–4. *Continuum of controlling or discriminative stimuli in whose presence responses appear more or less spontaneous.*

Bill, a learner who is mentally retarded, is beginning to do his own laundry for the first time. He has never used a coin-operated washing machine. An early step in the training program requires him to obtain quarters from the laundry operator. Bill communicates by pointing to a picture book. On the first occasion, the trainer accompanies Bill to the operator's desk and instructs (*mands*) him to take out his picture book and point to quarters. Bill complies by taking his picture book out of his pocket, but he fails to point to the picture of a quarter. The trainer points to the picture of the quarter (*model*) and waits for Bill to imitate the response. After 5 seconds the trainer *physically guides* Bill's finger to establish the correct point response.

This sequence of events might be interpreted in terms of stimulus control as follows: neither the mand nor the model was successful at evoking Bill's pointing response, so the trainer used physical guidance, which did produce the correct response. Only the latter cue controlled Bill's response. On the continuum, physical guidance is the cue associated with the least-spontaneous response, but communication in response to models and mands (or questions) would not be considered "spontaneous" by most people.

Later in the training program, Bill approaches the operator by himself, gives her a dollar, and points to the picture of the quarter in his book. In this situation, the operator's availability constitutes *the presence of a listener* in the laundry context who functions as a cue for the request for quarters. Although Bill's request appears spontaneous, identification of the functional cue requires only the knowledge of what occurred on earlier occasions in the laundry setting.

To provide an example of what may be referred to as the "ultimate" in spontaneity according to the definition offered, let's see how Bill manages still later in training. He now comes to the laundromat by himself; after placing the "whites" in the washing machine, he reaches in his pocket and picks out the quarters. He has only one and the machine requires two, so he puts the one in the slot and then proceeds to the operator's desk, gives her a dollar, and points to the picture of the quarter in his book. The cue for what appears to be a "spontaneous" response is the "deprivation" of quarters required to complete the task of washing clothes. However, this is not the only cue. This spontaneous response depends on the history of training in the laundromat context (e.g., the availability of the operator, reinforcement history of having received quarters in the past when he gave a dollar and pointed to the picture of quarter).

Transferring Stimulus Control to Achieve Spontaneity

Delayed prompting or time delay (Halle & Touchette, 1987; Halle et al., 1979; 1981; Touchette, 1971; Touchette & Howard, 1984) is a strategy that may be employed to transfer control of a communicative response from one category on the continuum to another. Inserting a delay prior to a prompt encourages transfer. In delayed prompting, controlling and target cues are paired on the first occasion or two, then controlling cues are delayed gradually such that the time elapsed between the two cues increases across occasions. The delay provides an opportunity on every occasion for the learner to respond appropriately prior to the presentation of the controlling cue. When correct responses occur consistently prior to the delivery of the controlling cue, stimulus control has transferred and the controlling cue is no longer necessary.

For example, in the anecdote above, Bill was learning how to use the laudromat. The trainer needed to manually guide (controlling cue) Bill to point to the picture of a quarter in his language book. To transfer control from physical guidance to a mand (target cue), the trainer would say, "Point to the picture of the quarter" while simultaneously guiding Bill's hand to make the point response. On the next occasion at the laundromat when change is needed, the trainer would deliver the mand, wait (approximately 3 seconds), and if no response occurs, provide manual guidance. On the next such occasion, the trainer would wait 6 seconds after the mand and before delivering the guidance. The objective, of course, is for Bill to anticipate the guidance and respond to the mand alone.

Let's focus on a different example to illustrate the transfer process. Dana is a young woman with developmental disabilities that are manifested by physical and cognitive deficits. She recently moved to a group home, where a routine procedure for all residents when they return home from work includes eating a snack and drinking juice. Dana had always been served her meals and snacks in the past; thus when she was asked "What do you want to drink?", she did not know how to respond. The group home supervisor decided to use delayed prompting to encourage more spontaneous requesting. Because Dana was imitative, the supervisor paired the question "What do you want to drink?" with a model "Juice, please" (the modeled phrase occurred immediately after the question). The supervisor presented these two cues together on three occasions, on each of which Dana imitated "Juice, please" and received the juice and descriptive praise (e.g., "Nice asking") for the request.

On the fourth occasion, the supervisor asked the question as before; however, instead of providing the model immediately, the supervisor waited 2 seconds (one one-thousand, two one-thousand) and then presented the model. After three such occasions in which Dana waited for the model and then imitated correctly, the supervisor increased the delay to four seconds. On the third 4-second delay occasion, Dana requested "Juice, please" before the model (i.e., an anticipation). Anticipated requests occurred on almost every subsequent occasion. Control of Dana's request had transferred from model to the question. Although this transfer was successful, responding to a question does not constitute a spontaneous request. Therefore, further intervention is required.

To wean Dana from dependence on the question, the supervisor decided to pair a visual cue, holding the glass of juice in front of Dana, with the question. As in the procedure above, first the visual cue is presented, followed immediately by the question. After success on these occasions, delays are introduced such that the glass of juice is held in front of Dana for 2 or 3 seconds before the question is asked. The objective is to teach Dana to anticipate the questions, thereby responding in the presence of the juice glass alone. Assuming success with this transfer, Dana's request "Juice, please" is now controlled by a visual cue — glass of juice held by the supervisor. Dana is no longer relying on a verbal cue, but the request remains under the control of an unnatural, contrived cue.

Thus a final step employed by the supervisor is transferring control from one visual cue (holding up glass) to another (pouring juice into glasses). The supervisor determined by informal social comparison (see Chapter 3, section on social validity) that other group home residents whose requesting was spontaneous and appropriate made their requests for juice when it was being poured from the pitcher into the glasses. Therefore, the supervisor wanted this cue to control Dana's request. As before, the two cues were paired: the juice was poured from the pitcher into Dana's glass and immediately afterward the glass was held up in front of her. After successful occasions, delays were introduced by pouring the juice into others' glasses after Dana's to assess whether Dana would request her juice in anticipation of it being held in front of her.

Assessing the Cues That Control Communicative Responses

In our efforts to teach new skills to adults with mental retardation, we often refer to *the* cue for a response. This phrasing implies that there is a single, unitary cue that controls the response (Halle, 1987). However, human behavior may not be so easily explained. A concrete example may illustrate this point as well as offer hints about the assessment of controlling cues. In preparation for teaching a community skill, street-crossing, the objective is the acquisition of a receptive label. Specifically, the learner is to select the red object in a two-choice discrimination task in which the choices are red and green. The community trainer conducts the training in a one-to-one session in the living room of a group home. The objects are placed on a table and the trainer says, "Touch red." The trainer refers to the instruction (or mand) "Touch red" as *the* cue; that is, the goal is to obtain correct responding in the presence of the instruction.

When the learner responds correctly, does the trainer really know what cues are controlling the response? For example, if the trainer were to substitute a blue object for the green one and suddenly the learner began responding at chance levels, it would appear that the color of the distractor cue was partially controlling the response. This phenomenon could be explained by exclusion (Dixon, 1977): that is, the learner could identify the color green but not blue; thus when the trainer said, "Touch red" the learner *excluded* green and touched the *other* choice. The word "red" never achieved control.

To assess other cues that may be controlling the response, the trainer might ask another staff member at the group home to conduct a session. If the learner again responded at chance levels, it would appear that the person who did the training may have become a controlling cue. An additional cue that may exercise control of responding is the setting in which training was conducted. Another probe of stimulus control may include assessing the instruction "Touch red" that was believed to be *the* controlling cue. If the community-trainer were to say "Sunny skies" instead of "Touch red" and the learner performed flawlessly over a number of trials, one would have to conclude that the words "Touch red" were not controlling the response; rather in this situation, any words uttered by the trainer may have functioned as a "go" signal, informing the learner of the time to initiate the response.

Conditional discrimination is another aspect of "multiple control" of communicative responses (Halle, 1987). A simple example of a conditional discrimination occurs when a person greets another by saying "Hi + *a name*." This response requires a learner first to discriminate an appropriate greeting situation and after it is identified, to determine the name of the person to be greeted. Attaching a name to the person is conditional on first identifying an appropriate context for greeting. To establish initiated requests, Halle et al. (1981) used delays that appeared to function as an "orienting" cue for participants: when they identified a delay occasion, they surveyed the local environment to determine a request that was appropriate in that context. It appears that even the simplest of responses may be controlled by more than a single, unitary cue. Therefore, we need to expand our model of conditions that occasion communicative responding to encompass the phenomenon of multiple control.

It is clear from the analysis just presented that "spontaneous" communication is a complex event. We have not yet identified the plethora of factors influencing the spontaneous use of language among non-disabled individuals; thus the successful training of those with disabilities may have to await further analysis.

SUMMARY

The acquisition of communicative skills by persons with mental retardation does not occur at typical rates. In fact, communicative performance is often a diagnostic indicator of developmental delay. After such a label has been applied, the traditional focus of intervention has been the labeled individual. An assumption is made tht the problem lies solely within the individual. In this chapter, I have attempted to shift the focus to an ecological perspective wherein the individual is assessed and instructed in everyday, ordinary settings. Furthermore, this perspective requires assessment and manipulation of the contexts within which the individual behaves: it is an interactive perspective that assumes that the delay in communicative performance is caused by factors inherent in everyday settings as well as disabilities exhibited by the individual.

Performing the operations of assessment and intervention within natural contexts exacts a price in terms of the amount of control that an interventionist may exercise. Thus, fewer learning trials are conducted, more distracting stimuli are impinging, cues are inconsistent, and as a result of these and many other factors, acquisition rates are reduced. The accompanying benefits, however, may outweigh the price. Learners acquire communication that is functional and is generalizable to natural occasions because it is learned within the context of functional and natural occasions.

The task of assessment was divided into five steps, three (i.e., form, function, and context) that focused on the communicative repertoire of the learner and two (i.e., opportunities and requirements for language in current and future settings) that focused on the social and physical environment with which the learner interacts. Specific methods for assessing the learner and the context were offered.

After the assessment task has been completed, manipulation of environmental contingencies may allow an interventionist to provide more "natural" learning opportunities than existed previously. By slightly modifying naturally occurring occasions (e.g., placing desired materials out of reach or intentionally skipping one's turn in a favorite activity) and delaying at critical moments, such an objective may be accomplished. Three additional procedures, the focus of which is the learner's communicative repertoire as well as the context in which it occurs, were discussed. Each was described in terms of its objective, the steps required for its implementation, its relation to the other two procedures, and an example of its application.

Finally the issue of spontaneous communication use was broached. A major problem with current practice is that even when intervention strategies are successful, learners often are responding to spoken cues of others or to contrived, nonverbal cues. As a first step to rectify this problem, an analysis of spontaneous language use was conducted. First, a definition was offered; then procedures for training spontaneity were outlined; and finally, a means for assessing functional cues that occasion "spontaneous" responding was provided.

I hope that two major themes are apparent to the reader of this chapter. First, communication assessment and intervention cannot focus only on the individual with the communicative disability. The context in which the communication occurs or fails to occur must be part of the analysis. Secondly, although we have learned how to teach specific language forms or structures effectively and efficiently, when communicative function, generalization, and spontaneity are sought, the analysis becomes very complex very quickly, encompassing sophisticated operations such as multiple stimulus control and conditional discrimination. Although work in this area will be difficult, the potential benefits are overwhelming.

REFERENCES

Alpert, C. (1984). *Training parents to use incidental teaching as a means of improving the communication skills of their language-delayed children.* Unpublished doctoral dissertation. Lawrence: University of Kansas.

Alpert, C. L., & Rogers–Warren, A. K. (1983, March). *Mothers as incidental trainers of their language disordered children.* Paper presented at the 16th annual meeting of the Gatlinburg Conference on Mental Retardation, Gatlinburg, TN.

Anderson, S. R. (1982, May). *Developing and maintaining language teaching opportunities in the natural environment.* Presented at the Annual Convention of the Association for Behavior Analysis, Milwaukee, WI.

Bricker, D. D., & Dennison, L. (1978). Training prerequisites to verbal behavior. In M. Snell (Ed.), *Systematic instruction of the moderately and severely handicapped* (pp. 157–178). Columbus, OH: Charles E. Merrill.

Carr, E. G. (1983, August). *Application of pragmatics to the conceptualization and treatment of severe behavior problems in children.* Presented at the Annual Convention of the American Psychological Association, Anaheim, CA.

Carr, E. G., Newsom, C. D., & Binkoff, J. A. (1980). Escape as a factor in the aggressive behavior of two retarded children. *Journal of Applied Behavior Analysis, 13,* 101–117.

Cataldo, M. F., & Risley, T. R. (1974). Evaluation of living environments: The MANIFEST description of ward activities. In P. O. Davidson, F. W. Clark, and L. A. Hammerlynck (Eds.), *Evaluation of behavioral programs in community, residential and school settings* (pp. 201–222). Champaign, IL: Research Press.

Daley, M. F. (1969). The "reinforcement menu": Finding effective reinforcers. In J. D. Krumboltz and C. E. Thorenson (Eds.), *Behavioral counseling: Cases and techniques* (pp. 42–45). New York: Holt, Rinehart & Winston.

Dixon, L. S. (1977). The nature of control by spoken words over visual stimulus selection. *Journal of the Experimental Analysis of Behavior, 27,* 433–442.

Goetz, L., Gee, K., & Sailor, W. (1985). Using a behavior chain interruption strategy to teach communication skills to students with severe disabilities. *Journal of the Association for Persons with Severe Handicaps, 10,* 21–31.

Gray, B., & Ryan, B. (1973). *A language program for the nonlanguage child:* Champaign, IL: Research Press.

Guess, D., Keogh, W., & Sailor, W. (1978). Generalization of speech and language behavior: Measurement and training tactics. In R. L. Schiefelbusch, (Ed.), *Bases of language intervention,* (pp. 373–395). Baltimore, MD: University Park Press.

Guess, D., Sailor, W., & Baer, D. M. (1978). Children with limited language. In R. L. Schiefelbusch (Ed.), *Language intervention strategies* (pp. 101–143). Baltimore, MD: University Park Press.

Halle, J. W. (1982). Teaching functional language to the handicapped: An integrative model of natural environment teaching techniques. *Journal of the Association for the Severely Handicapped, 7,* 29–37.

Halle, J. W. (1984). Arranging the natural environment to occasion language: Giving severely language-delayed children reasons to communicate. *Speech and Language Seminars, 5,* 185–197.

Halle, J. W. (1987). Teaching language in the natural environment: An analysis of spontaneity. *The Journal of the Association for Persons with Severe Handicaps, 12,* 28–37.

Halle, J. W., Alpert, C. L., & Anderson, S. R. (1984). Natural environment language assessment and intervention with severely impaired preschoolers. *Topics in Early Childhood Special Education, 4* 36–56.

Halle, J. W., Baer, D. M., & Spradlin, J. E. (1981). An analysis of teachers' generalized use of delay in helping children: A stimulus control procedure to increase language use in handicapped children. *Journal of Applied Behavior Analysis, 14,* 389–409.

Halle, J., & Touchette, P. (1987). Delayed prompting: A method for instructing children with severe language handicaps. In J. Hogg, & P. Mittler (Eds.),

Staff training in mental handicap (pp. 125–167). Cambridge: Brookline Books.

Halle, J. W., Marshall, A., & Spradlin, J. E. (1979). Time delay: A technique to increase language use and facilitate generalization in retarded children. *Journal of Applied Behavior Analysis, 12,* 431–439.

Harris, S. (1975). Teaching language to non-verbal children: With emphasis on problems of generalization. *Psychological Bulletin, 82,* 565–580.

Hart, B. (1985). Environmental techniques that may facilitate generalization and acquisition. In S. F. Warren & A. K. Rogers-Warren (Eds.), *Teaching functional language* (pp. 63–88). Baltimore, MD: University Park Press.

Hart, B., & Risley, T. R. (1968). Establishing use of descriptive adjectives in the spontaneous speech of disadvantaged preschool children. *Journal of Applied Behavior Analysis, 1,* 109–120.

Hart, B., & Risley, T. R. (1974). Using preschool materials to modify the language of disadvantaged children. *Journal of Applied Behavior Analysis, 7,* 243–256.

Hart, B., & Risley, T. R. (1975). Incidental teaching of language in the preschool. *Journal of Applied Behavior Analysis, 8,* 411–420.

Hart, B., & Risley, T. R. (1980). In vivo language intervention: Unanticipated general effects. *Journal of Applied Behavior Analysis, 13,* 407–432.

Hart, B., & Rogers-Warren, A. K. (1978). A milieu approach to teaching language. In R. L. Schiefelbusch, (Ed,), *Language Intervention Strategies* (pp. 193–235). Baltimore, MD: University Park Press.

Horner, R. D. (1980). The effects of an environmental "enrichment" program on the behavior of institutionalized profoundly retarded children. *Journal of Applied Behavior Analysis, 13,* 473–491.

Horner, R. D., & Keilitz, I. (1975). Training mentally retarded adolescents to brush their teeth. *Journal of Applied Behavior Analysis, 8,* 301–309.

Hubbell, R. D. (1977). On facilitating spontaneous talking in young children. *Journal of Speech and Hearing Disorders, 42,* 216–231.

Hunt, P., Goetz, L., Alwell, M., & Sailor, W. (1986). Using an interrupted behavior chain strategy to teach generalized communication responses. *The Journal of The Association for Persons with Severe Handicaps, 11,* 196–204.

Kaczmarek, L. A. (1983). Initiating language/communication behaviors: An analysis of current practice. Unpublished manuscript, University of West Virginia, Morgantown, WV.

Kazdin, A. E. (1977). Assessing the clinical or applied significance of behavior change through social validation. *Behavior Modification, 1,* 427–452.

Kent, L. R. (1974). *Language acquisition program for the retarded or multiply impaired.* Champaign, IL: Research Press.

Klein, M. D., Wulz, W. N., Hall, M. K., Waldo, L. K., Carpenter, S. A., Rathan, D. A., Myers, S. P., Fox, F., & Marshall, A. M. (1981). *Comprehensive communication curriculum guide.* Lawrence: Early Childhood Institute, University of Kansas.

MacDonald, J. D. (1978). Environmental language intervention: Programs for establishing initial communication in handicapped children. In F. Withrow and C. Nygren (Eds.), *Language and the handicapped learner: Curricula, programs, and media* (pp. 12–33). Columbus, OH: Merrill Publishing Co.

MacDonald, J. D. (1985). Language through conversation: A model for intervention with language delayed persons. In S. F. Warren, & A. K. Rogers-Warren, (Eds.), *Teaching functional language* (pp. 89–122). Austin, TX: PRO-ED.

Miller, J. F., & Yoder, D. E. (1974). An ontogenetic language teaching strategy for retarded children. In R. L. Schiefelbusch and L. L. Lloyd (Eds.), *Language perspectives: Acquisition, retardation and intervention* (pp. 505–528). Austin, TX: PRO-ED.

Miller, S. J., & Sloan, J. N. (1976). The generalization effects of parent training across stimulus settings. *Journal of Applied Behavior Analysis, 9,* 355–370.

Mittler, P., & Berry, P. (1977). Demanding language. In P. Mittler, (Ed.), *Research to practice in mental retardation: Education and training,* (pp. 245–251) Vol II. International Association for Scientific Study in Mental Deficiency.

Mount, M., & Shea, V. (1982). *How to recognize and assess pre-language skills in the severely handicapped.* Austin, TX: PRO-ED.

Rincover, A., & Koegel, R. (1975). Setting generality and stimulus control in autistic children. *Journal of Applied Behavior Analysis, 8,* 235–246.

Rogers–Warren, A. (1983). Assessing skill prerequisites for incidental language teaching. Unpublished manuscript. Department of Special Education, Peabody College, Vanderbilt University, Nashville, TN. (Available from author).

Rogers–Warren, A. & Warren, S. (1980). Mands for verbalization: Facilitating the display of newly trained language in children. *Behavior Modification, 4,* 361–382.

Schuler, A. L., & Goetz, L. (1981). The assessment of severe language disabilities: Communicative and cognitive considerations. *Analysis and Intervention in Developmental Disabilities 1,* 333–346.

Sosne, J. B., Handleman, J. S., & Harris, S. L. (1979). Teaching spontaneous-functional speech to autistic type children. *Mental Retardation, 17,* 241–245.

Striefel, S. (1974). *Behavior modification: Teaching a child to imitate.* Lawrence, KS: H & H Enterprises, Inc.

Touchette, P. E. (1971). Transfer of stimulus control: Measuring the moment of transfer. *Journal of the Experimental Analysis of Behavior, 15,* 347–354.

Touchette, P. E., & Howard, J. S. (1984). Errorless learning: Reinforcement contingencies and stimulus control transfer in delayed prompting. *Journal of Applied Behavior Analysis, 17,* 175–188.

VanBiervliet, A., Spangler, P. F., & Marshall, A. M. (1981). An ecobehavioral examination of a simple strategy for increasing mealtime language in residential facilities. *Journal of Applied Behavior Analysis, 14,* 295–305.

Warren, S. F., McQuarter, R. M., & Rogers–Warren, A. K. (1984). The effects of mands and models on the speech of unresponsive language-delayed preschool children. *Journal of Speech and Hearing Disorders, 49,* 43–52.

Warren, S. F., Rogers–Warren, A. K., Baer, D. M., & Guess, D. (1980). Assessment and facilitiation of language generalization. In W. Sailor, B. Wilcox, & L. Brown (Eds.), *Methods of instruction for severely handicapped students* (pp. 227–258). Baltimore, MD: Paul Brookes.

Wolf, M. M. (1978). Social validity: The case for subjective measurement or how applied behavior analysis is finding its heart. *Journal of Applied Behavior Analysis, 11,* 203–214.

Woods, T. S. (1984). Generality in the verbal tacting of autistic children as a function of "naturalness" in antecedent control. *Journal of Behavior Therapy and Experimental Psychiatry, 15,* 27–32.

Part IV

Communication Assessment and Intervention Strategies

CHAPTER 8

Adults at the Presymbolic Level

ROBERT E. OWENS
BRENDA S. ROGERSON

*I*magine a crowded cocktail party or any other scene where two people are introduced and exchange greetings.

"How do you do? Pleased to meet you." Then the inevitable, "And what do you do?"

"I'm a speech-language pathologist."

"Oh, hope you haven't noticed any of my speech defects."

"No, actually most of my work is with people who don't talk yet, and many never will. I work with the severely retarded."

Anyone who has been in this situation can predict the response, "Oh . . . You must be a very special person to be able to take the frustration."

"Quite the contrary, it's my clients who are the special ones with the gift of patience because they have to wait for me while I fumble around and try to figure out the optimum manner of communicating with them." One or two gentle comments follow, and they're off to mingle and to play the scene again.

Cocktail party chatter is hardly the fare of textbooks, but within that last response is the essence of where we, as speech–language pathologists, have found ourselves in regard to the presymbolic adult. As a field, we have bumped along slowly, learning as we went. We have taken a little of this and a little of that and added what David Yoder, past president of the American Speech-Language-Hearing Association, calls "A bad case of the hopes" to produce a myriad of intervention approaches with this population of patient presymbolizers. Yet, as Wulz, Hall and Klein (1983) note, there are still problems.

> Nonverbal severely retarded clients have been a tremendous challenge to speech-language pathologists and special educators. Although the past decade has demonstrated that these [clients] ... can acquire language skills with intensive training, these clients often fail to use language responses spontaneously in appropriate situations. (p. 2)

Clearly, we need to target generalization within an overall intervention strategy because "success must ultimately be measured as a function of its use in interactional situations" (Shane, Lipshultz, & Shane, 1982, p. 74).

Our goal in this chapter is to try to bring together the many intervention approaches into a unified whole. We will try to provide an overall rationale for intervention and to present assessment and treatment procedures that naturally flow from the rationale. We will be as specific as possible and present practical therapy techniques where appropriate.

RATIONALE FOR INTERVENTION

An intervention rationale can come from many places. Ours will be a blend of the special needs of the presymbolic adult population, the presymbolic development of nonhandicapped children, and the successful presymbolic intervention programs reported in the professional literature.

The Needs of the Presymbolic Population

Almost exclusively, presymbolic adults are severely to profoundly retarded, and many are multiply handicapped. Seizure activity is also very prevalent. Most of the population with severe to profound retardation resides in institutions or community residences for the retarded and will need some form of supervision for the remainder of their lives. Here the similarities within the population with severe to profound retardation end. The population with severe to profound retardation is a heterogeneous group of individuals, as varied as the general population that it mirrors.

It may be difficult, therefore, to characterize the communication needs of this group. As with the nonretarded, the interactional patterns of individuals with retardation with others in their environment are important for their development of communication. The nature of these environmental influences has been well documented (Conroy, Efthimiou, & Lemanowicz, 1982). Extended institutionalization results in general deterioration of language abilities, such as decreased initiation of communication (Phillips & Balthazar, 1979).

As a general rule of thumb, one can assume that "The greater the number of disabled people residing in one setting, the greater the likelihood of less communication interaction among the residents" (Shane et al., 1982, p. 74). Certain aspects of language seem to be directly affected (McNutt & Leri, 1979; Montague, Hutchinson, & Matson, 1975). For example, the physical arrangement of furniture in rows may preclude natural communicative interaction. Physical barriers, combined with multiple physical disabilities, may severely reduce the range of communication experience.

In addition, there may be a lack of appropriate verbal interactions between staff and residents. Most staff verbal behavior is comprised of directives that are unlikely to evoke or enhance client communicative behaviors (Tizard, Cooperman, Joseph, & Tizard, 1973). Teaching staff may also violate interactional patterns by frequent interruptions and by unannounced physical directives, such as movement of clients (McNerney, 1980). Directives, in turn, evoke few verbal responses by clients. In contrast, the least-frequent staff behavior — initiated conversation — evokes the most client verbal responses (Prior, Minnes, Coyne, Golding, Hendy, & McGillivray, 1979). Client verbalizations, when they do occur, are generally ignored or receive a staff head nod.

In part, the lack of staff responsiveness reflects their not understanding many clients' idiosyncratic communication systems. For example, we observed one 18-year-old repeatedly going to the center of the classroom. Each time, he was escorted back to his seat and told "Joey, sit." On the fifth cycle, Joey became self-abusive. As outside observers, we did not interpret his centering behavior as purposely distruptive but instead as a signal for attention. No one responded to these behaviors appropriately.

In institutional, vocational, and occupational settings, daily activities can easily become predictable routines. There is little need to make decisions, to ask questions, to comment. In short, there is little need to use language or develop more appropriate communication.

One dilemma, then, is one in which the client's low level of cognitive functioning and various environmental factors combine to mitigate against the development of language. The result is often an individual who initiates very little communication or who exhibits idiosyncratic communication patterns. Briefly, the needs of presymbolic adults are as follows:

□ A responsive communication environment,
□ An initial communication system for reliably expressing individual intentions,

□ A generalizable communication system suited for the communication environment of each individual, and

□ A more conventional sign or symbol system.

Use of Symbols by Nonretarded Children

The one-year-old nonretarded child has experienced 12 months of learning, which becomes evident in the things she talks about and in her uses of language. From the time of her birth, she has been treated as a communication partner by her caregivers. She is asked questions and given turns, even though she can not respond verbally. Chance responses are interpreted as appropriate and meaningful by her caregivers. Gradually, through these "proto-conversations" and early game playing and routines, the child learns the patterns of conversational exchange.

At first, the child's communication is idiosyncratic beyond a general pattern of drawing attention to herself. By the time she is 8 months old, the child's communication has been conventionalized into a recognizable system of gestures. These gestures are far more important than a few physical movements might suggest because the child has demonstrated a definite intention to communicate with a partner. After securing her partner's attention, she gestures and vocalizes. The sequence may be reversed, but the important point is that the child demonstrates her desire to transmit a message. Soon, she is able to request, signal notice, ask questions, and offer objects.

First words or symbols develop to fill these communicative functions within an interactive context between the child and the caregiver. First words may include "mama," "dada," "doggie," "ball," "shoe," "no," and "more." In general, the child talks about what she knows. Her early meanings relate to object appearance, disappearance, and reappearance, to actions, locations, and descriptors. She talks about entities within her world, often entities that she can manipulate, entities that are here and now. In other words, she *maps* her cognitive knowledge onto language. She has spent the first year learning about object functions and about the physical constancy of objects, about object permanance and disappearance and reappearance. More important, she has learned that one object can be used to attain another and that a person can serve the same function. A gesture or a word can summon aid from an observant caregiver. Finally, the child has learned that there are some sounds, such as "doggie," that go with each entity and, for the child, are a characteristic of the entity, just as overall size is a characteristic. These sounds or words and most of the child's cognitive knowledge are acquired within the conversational context of the child and caregivers.

We have already discussed the manner in which the conversational context of the presymbolic adult may be distorted. In addition, many clients may be well below 12 months of age developmentally. Clients functioning below their developmental level within a nonresponsive communication environment may not develop useful communication systems. Without communication to provide the motivation, there is little impetus for learning symbols.

Similarly, it is important for adults with severe and profound retardation to learn to communicate what they know. The building of an initial communication base is essential for learning language later.

Successfully Meeting Client Needs

Several variables affect the quality of programming for the population with severe and profound retardation. Among these are the age of the client, length of institutionalization, degree of impairment, willingness of the environment to cooperate with and to be integrated into intervention, and content and techniques chosen for intervention. In general, programming is more successful with younger clients with no history or a short history of institutionalization. All individuals, retarded or nonretarded, have a developmental pattern that changes fairly rapidly until early adulthood when it begins to slow. Obviously, we can expect to affect change most in the younger years. With institutionalization, we find that the more extended the stay, the more deteriorated are the client's language abilities (Phillips & Balthazar, 1979). In addition, as a group, retarded individuals with higher overall intellectual ability and fewer associated disorders can be expected to achieve more, especially if the environment is an integral part of the intervention and if the content and techniques come from and reflect the communication needs of the client (MacDonald, Blott, Gordon, Spiegal, & Hartmann, 1974; Owens, Bigler–Burke, & Lepre–Clark, 1985). The latter variables of training content and intervention techniques are directly related to two larger intervention issues: the overall intervention strategy and the degree of generalization. Before trying to sketch an optimum approach, we would like to explore each issue briefly.

Intervention Strategy

Traditionally, communication training programs for the institutionalized population with mental retardation have reflected two general intervention strategies. In one approach, the client is taught presymbolic skills prior to introducing symbolic communication (Bricker & Bricker, 1974; MacDonald et al., 1974). In general, this approach has been most successful with young children or the population with mild to moderate retardation. A second approach begins with symbolic communication (Guess, Sailor, & Baer, 1976; Kent, 1974). In recent years, this approach has become a communication-first approach, emphasizing the establishment of an initial communication system and expansion of this system toward symbol use (Keogh & Reichle, 1985; Sternberg, Pegnatore, & Hill, 1983; Yoder, 1985). This approach, in part, reflects behaviorist frustration with the developmental model, which has been characterized as a wait-until-the-client-is-ready approach. In part, the communication-first approach also reflects the frustration of many speech–language clinicians with their clients' slow rate of progress in acquiring these prerequisite skills. This communication-first approach also reflects the realization that clients already communicate prior to professional intervention and an acceptance of the reality that some clients may never reach a symbolic level of communicating. Arguments on both sides of this issue are very strong.

Prerequisite skills training usually includes cognitive, perceptual, social, and/or communicative behaviors that have been found to be significant in nonhandicapped children's acquisition of symbol use. The specific behaviors selected for training vary in number, kind, and scope. For example, Horstmeier and MacDonald (1978) recommended training seven presymbolic sensorimotor cognitive skills, mostly Piagetian in nature, whereas Owens (1982) included 33 cognitive, perceptual, social, and communicative behaviors. The increased number of training targets reflects an attempt to design broader yet small or incremental training steps for the more severely language impaired clients.

According to Haring and Bricker (1976), there are three tenets of the normative developmental model:

1. Development or change follows a developmental hierarchy,
2. Behavior change goes from simple to complex, and,
3. Complex behavior results from coordination or modification of simpler responses.

The speech-language clinician, however, can not assume that every behavior of the normally developing child is an appropriate training target for the severely to profoundly retarded adult. Unfortunately, there is only minimal guidance on this point in the literature. For example, studies with presymbolic institutionalized adults have demonstrated that they attain higher language skills when trained first on prerequisite cognitive behaviors, such as means–ends and object permanence, rather than on language alone (Kahn, 1982). It is difficult for the clinician to know if other behaviors are also important or even more important. Therefore, each speech–language professional must ask him- or herself "which developmental behaviors and what sequences of mastery" (Switzy, Rotatori, Miller, & Freagon, 1979, p. 169). In addition, Wulz et al., (1983) raise the possibility that "The long list of prerequisites required to teach language to [clients with severe to profound retardation] ... may prevent them from learning to communicate" (p. 8). Nor does the dilemma stop here because additional nonnormative training targets (e.g., compensation for physical disabilities or learning of attending skills) may also be needed for a client or clients to learn a skill. Each clinician must determine his/her own theoretical position, as we will do in the following pages, as a basis for corresponding intervention strategies.

At some point in the therapy process, it may become apparent that a client is not capable of further progress and that clinician time is better spent with other clients. Clinicians should consider terminating therapy if the client's skills are so severely limited that he/she is not responding to treatment and/or if the client has plateaued. Clients may plateau for a number of reasons, including environment, physical health, psychological well-being, motivation, and age. (See the section on dismissal criteria at the end of this chapter.)

The communication-first approach attempts to establish an early signal system that can enhance the client's opportunities for interaction. For example, Sternberg et al. (1983) employed a rocking technique between the client and clinician, called "resonance" training, to set up a low-level signal from the client for the activity to continue. Within this procedure and other interrupted chain strategies, such as those of Goetz, Gee, and Sailor (1985), continuation of a pleasurable activity provides the motivation for the client to learn the signal. At a more discriminative level of learning, Reichle, Rogers, and Barrett (1984) were able to train the illocutionary functions of requesting, rejecting, and commenting to an adolescent with severe retardation through the use of the signs "want" and "no" and four object names. The client learned to control acquisition and refusal of entities with the signs. The benefit of such communication-first approaches is that communication becomes more purposeful and is reinforced by natural maintaining contingencies rather than by learned reinforcers.

Generalization

The notion of natural contingencies, raised in the preceding section, is central to the issue of generalization. "The problem," according to Spradlin and Siegel (1982), "is how to incorporate procedures into the initial training that will actively induce generalization" (p. 3). Again, the developmental literature is important because several child development specialists have noted that language develops within the context of caregiver–child conversational interactions. If this is so, it is reasoned that the caregiver–client interaction is also important for adult language development, and that this interaction is a natural one in which language should be acquired.

According to Looney (1980), "Language is an integral part of any interpersonal communication and is best learned in the natural context of those daily interactions" (p. 31). Theoretically, if language is learned within the environment where it will be used, the client should have little difficulty with generalization. The application of an environmental approach affects decisions on the content, place, and manner of training and on who should do the training. Content, according to this model, should reflect the client's environment and the entities the client knows and/or may desire. In addition, training should occur within this environment rather than in a segregated environment, such as a clinic or therapy room. The environmental model presupposes intervention within natural environments throughout the day, in the living unit, classroom, and work area, as well as in the clinical setting.

Language training should be functional. In other words, the language trained should work for the client. For example, several studies have demonstrated that clients with severe to profound retardation learn symbols taught within the context of requests more rapidly than those taught as labels (Litt & Schreibman, 1982; Reichle et al., 1984; Saunders & Sailor, 1979; Stafford, Sundberg, & Braam, 1978).

Finally, the trainers are crucial to the environmental approach. A number of programs for initial language training employ caregiver-trainers as the primary agents of change (Horstmeier & McDonald, 1978; Manolson, 1983; Owens, 1982). Initial success has been accomplished through the use of parents, although institutional staff and even other less severely retarded institutionalized adults can act as language facilitators (Baker, 1976; Briggs & Klein, 1985; MacDonald et al., 1974; Owens et al., 1985; Snell, 1979).

It has been argued that a variety of settings and trainers further retards rather than facilitates language acquisition and generalization for severely to profoundly retarded adults. It is reasoned that if severely to profoundly retarded individuals have difficulty learning, the learning tasks should be as uniform as possible to facilitate generalization. Most language training programs, therefore, follow a more traditional model of individual or group therapy within a clinical setting. Contrary to this reasoning, however, data from child studies indicate that severely retarded children more successfully generalize conversational skills when systematically trained across a variety of different settings and different trainers (Garcia, 1974).

Summary

The individual with severe to profound retardation has truly unique communication needs that are being met by a variety of intervention methodologies. Issues relative to training raise questions about the overall intervention model to be employed with this population. In turn, the overall model affects more procedural questions such as the selection of content and the method of presenting and consequating training behaviors.

AN INTEGRATED INTERVENTION MODEL

A number of successful techniques have been taken and blended together into an integrated whole. Traditional speech–language clinical services for the population with severe to profound retardation rely primarily on isolated therapy within a segregrated climate (Sternat, Nietupski, Messina, Lyon, & Brown, 1977). More appropriate than such "episodic intervention" (Brown, Nietupski, & Hamre–Nietupski, 1976) is a service deivery model that includes sustained longitudinal intervention (Graham, 1976; Kopchick & Lloyd, 1976). Such an intervention model provides for services within the natural environment throughout the day with a variety of clients' caregivers, their natural interactional partners.

Profound retardation implies a slow rate of learning accompanied by a rapid rate of forgetting. Therefore, frequent communication training on a daily basis is essential. The need for consistency of training requires the involvement of caregivers along with the speech–language clinician.

The speech–language clinician, as one of many communication partners, interacts clinically with the client but also instructs others within the classroom, unit, home, or community residence to act as language facilitators. The role of the speech–language clinician becomes that of consultant as well as direct-care service provider. He/she is the chief architect of the individual communication intervention plan and is responsible for all communication-related decisions within the overall intervention team. In addition, he/she is responsible for in-service training of the professional and paraprofessional staff, demonstrations and direct instruction with each client–caregiver dyad, and the maintenance of progress records.

The key to an integrated intervention model is the caregivers who interact most frequently with the client. In institutional settings, this consists primarily of nonprofessional aides, unit staff, and volunteers, as well as teachers, workshop staff, and other professionals. Often these personnel do not see the training of communicative competency as a part of their job.

Ideally, instruction for the presymbolic adult would employ a two-prong approach incorporating both an initial communication system and prerequisite skills instruction. Arguments relative to the benefits of either method are more philosophical than actual. Moreover, the two are not mutually exclusive. An initial signal system can be designed and continually modified for each client simultaneously with teaching the prerequisite skills necessary in order to modify the communication system toward more conventional symbols. Although not every client will ultimately be able to use symbols — whether words, manual signs, pictures, or the like — we believe that all clients should be given the opportunity to achieve their maximum communication potential. Thus, social and cognitive skills are taught while clients' accompanying communication skills continue to improve.

Because the activities within each client's environments form the basis for communication, these activities are the basis for instruction as well. It is this aspect of instruction that is most difficult for caregivers to comprehend because formal training is minimized (Salzburg & Villani, 1983). Communication and language instruction occur at natural junctures within the ongoing activities of each client. Such intervention is often misconstrued to mean formal teaching disguised as fun. This type of hidden teaching, such as language used in preschool action songs, can be just as irrelevant to the context and to the client's communication as formal instruction.

In summary, we are recommending an intervention approach in which instruction occurs within natural conversational contexts in everyday activities. Instruction concentrates on introducing a communication system and on facilitating the acquisition of presymbolic skills. Caregivers fulfill the role of language facilitators under the guidance of the speech–language clinician who is responsible for overall program design. Naturally, it is as important to modify caregiver behaviors as it is those of the client. The critical variable for change is the quality of the client–caregiver interaction.

Instituting an Integrated Intervention Model

There may be resistance to implementating an integrated approach to communication training from other professonals and nonprofessionals who serve individuals who are severely or profoundly retarded. Often such resistance reflects a lack of understanding of the importance of the client's conversational partners in the change process; a lack of knowledge of the importance of communication for language acquisition; a fear that too much will be required of the caregiver for which he/she is not trained; and/or a reluctance, especially among other professionals, to allow the speech–language clinician to prescribe intervention techniques within other clinical settings, such as physical or occupational therapy or the classroom. Generally, all of these hurdles can be overcome through a combination of quiet lobbying, in-service training, and demonstrable success. It is best to begin with a few clients in one setting, such as a classroom. Aides and foster grandparents have functioned effectively as language facilitators in classrooms in large institutional settings (Owens et al., 1985).

Nothing is as persuasive as demonstrated success. Initial efforts should be limited. Caregivers, especially those unfamiliar with their new role as language facilitators, will be incapable of performing all the required teaching immediately. The wise speech–language clinician will target only a few client and caregiver behaviors for initial instruction, those behaviors most likely to result in success. After there have been a few successes, the motivation for the client, caregivers, and speech-language clinician to continue will grow.

Assessment: Initial and Ongoing Process

Each individual program begins with an assessment of the client's current communication skills. Assessment is a process of discovery conducted by each clinician on his/her clients. Although scientific and systematic procedures are used in the gathering of data, the speech-language clinician must rely on his/her creative or artistic skills to synthesize this information into a useful whole and to design relevant intervention procedures.

It is important to recall that assessment is an ongoing process, especially within the integrated model proposed. The speech–language clinician must be constantly aware of the client's skills, content trained, and levels of expertise of the various caregivers.

Several variables should be considered when assessing a client for communicative competency (i.e., the ability to successfully communicate within one's natural environment). These variables, shown in Figure 8–1, relate to both the client and the communication context. Naturally, a variety of methods — including direct observation, caregiver interviews and questionaires, behavior scaling and rating, and direct testing —must be employed to attain an accurate description of each client's unique communicative competencies.

Client-Related Variables

The data on client communication are derived from a number of sources. The speech–language clinician is primarily interested in two aspects of

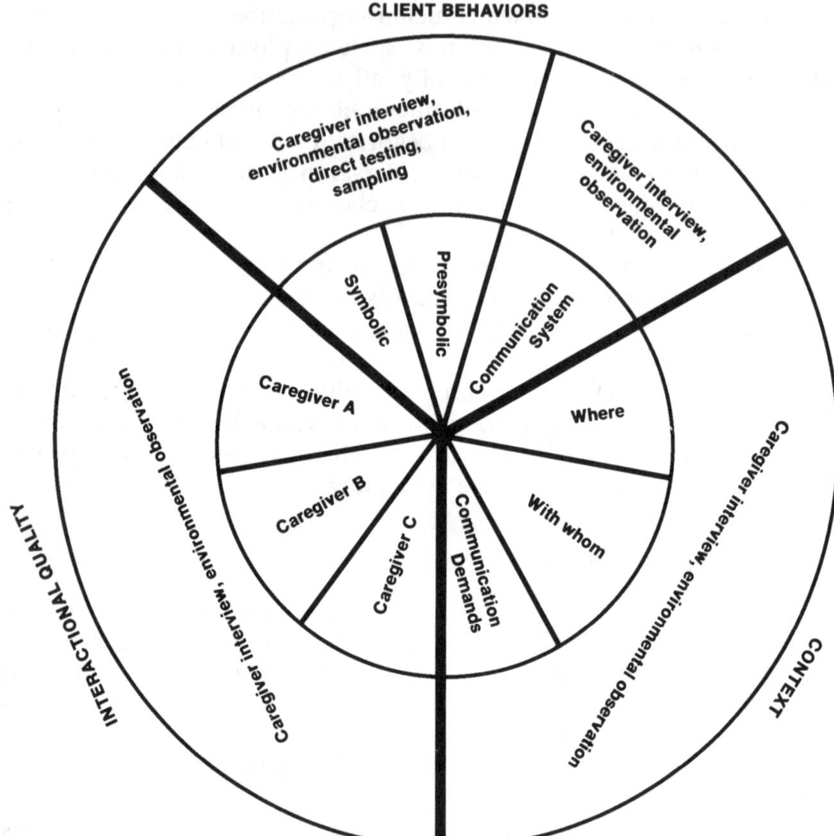

Figure 8-1. *Assessment variables and methods.*

the client's behavior: the current communication system of the client and the level of presymbolic and/or symbolic functioning. A wholistic description of the client's communication system requires a variety of data collection methods. The clinician is interested in the manner and content of both the client's intentional and unintentional commuication.

Not all behaviors are communicative, although each client has at least some communicative behaviors. In general, communicative behaviors are consistent, easily identifiable behaviors that are associated with environmental events or with the client's state. These behaviors may be located at any point along a continuum from appropriate to aberrant. The client who turns away when addressed is communicating. Likewise, the client who becomes self-abusive or increases self-stimulation when he approaches his residence is communicating. It is the relationship between the behavior and the context, not the behavior itself, that indicates communication.

Some communicative behaviors may be message-specific in that each communicates a single message. Each time this behavior is performed, the message is the same, such as the client who consistently taps her mouth when she wants something to drink. Other behaviors may be used to communicate a variety of messages, such as the client who produces a consistent sound pattern for attention, and for needs and pleasure expression. (Iwata, Dorsey, Slifer, Bauman, & Richman, 1982; Schuler & Goetz, 1981).

Intentional and unintentional communication differ primarily with respect to whether the listener is taken into consideration. Typically, intentional communication is addressed to and possibly modified for the audience. The client may establish eye contact, await a turn, respond, interrupt, and/or move toward the listener or to a conspicuous position. The adolescent described earlier who repeatedly walked to the center of the classroom was engaging in a purposeful behavior for his audience, thus demonstrating intentional communication. Carr, Newson, and Binkhoff (1980) found self-injurious behavior to be motivated by a desire to escape and inferred a meaning of "Leave me alone; I don't want to do this!" Unintentional communication does not consider the audience, such as gesturing when no one is present. Situational responses, such as a pucker following a sour taste, would also be unintentional communication unless the client interacted in some way with the audience.

Finally, noncommunicative behaviors may be random or stereotypic behaviors that do not seem to be related to environmental events or to the client's state, such as incessant spinning. We should caution that occasionally behaviors that seem noncommunicative are so only in the eye of the receiver. We have failed as listeners when we can not interpret certain behaviors as communicative. Some professionals contend that regardless of the behavior, it has some functional message value (Schuler & Goetz, 1981). Stated another way, "No matter how we may try, one cannot *not* communicate." (Watzlawick, Beavin, & Jackson, 1967, p. 49).

The manner and content of the client's communication can be assessed via a caregiver questionaire and/or an interview, and by clinician and caregiver observation. The input of all caregivers is important even if these data are very disparate. Reports of extremely high or low communication skills may provide valuable information on caregiver expectations, important data in assessing interactional variables. Calculator's Communication Repertoire Summary (see Chapter 12 of this volume) provides a means of systematically examining and evaluating clients' communicative competencies across a variety of natural settings.

It is important to recognize the communication potential inherent in most behaviors, whether appropriate or aberrant. In the past, intervention has begun with the elimination of inappropriate or aberrant behavior. Such approaches have ignored the communication potential of these behaviors and their role in the limited communication repertoires of many clients with severe to profound retardation. More productive is a strategy of expanding this limited repertoire through gradual modification or the introduction of more appropriate alternative behaviors. Several studies have demonstrated a reduction in aberrant or inappropriate behavior with an increase in more conventional communication (Carr, 1979; Durand, 1982; Horner & Budd, 1983). One important aspect of assessment is analyzing the communicative intention of these behaviors. Donnellan, Mirenda, Mesaros, and Fassbender (1984) presented an assessment protocol for this purpose, reproduced in Figure 8-2. Behaviors are listed across the top, and communicative functions or intentions on the left. The functional categories are derived from a number of taxonomies of the intentions of nonhandicapped children. Initial hypotheses regarding intentions can be formed through observation, but confirmation requires systematic manipulation of antecedent and/or consequential events. Changes in the frequency of a behavior should indicate some relationship between the behavior and these events.

The final step in assessing the client's communication system is direct testing to determine the optimum input and output modes for communication. The three primary expressive and receptive modes of communication are manual–gestural–visual, including gestures, signs, body movement, and/or visual contact or pointing; vocal–verbal–auditory, including intonation, speech sounds, phonetically consistent forms, and/or words; and tactile, including touch and/or physical manipulation, such as moving the listener's hand to a desired object. A skillful communicator uses a combination of all three. Adults with severe to profound retardation may rely on one mode primarily or on different input and output modes. For example, a client may use the auditory mode receptively, understanding single words or short phrases, but rely on a gestural form for expressive communication. Many deaf–blind clients rely on a tactile mode.

Higher functioning presymbolic adults may already have a well-developed communication system of gestures and/or vocalizations. The speech–language clinician should attempt to attain as accurate a description of this system as possible. For very low-functioning clients, on the other hand, the speech–language clinician should assess each of the three modes for startle and notice, focused or directed behavior, and consistent responding. Our experience suggests that close physical proximity, touching, and a gentle, pleasant manner are helpful. For example, with one client, a 22-year-old male with profound retardation, severe scoliosis, and severe mixed cerebral palsy, one author sat next to him, talked quietly, and stroked his cheek. He responded with eye contact and vocalization. Within two hours we had a primitive communication system in which he would look at a spoon, upon a verbal directive, in order to signal "Feed me."

Sternberg et al. (1983) successfully established an initial communication system using physical rocking, an activity that places the client and the clinician in close physical proximity and moving in the same rhythm. Called "resonance" movement, this seemingly pleasurable activity is used by the clinician to assess notice by the client and then to build a responding behavior. Within the assessment phase, the client can be trained to signal the clinician for the behavior to continue. In subsequent instruction, the signal is expanded and modified into a more viable communication behavior. Initially, the client may not respond well to touching or to close proximity. Therefore, initial assessment and teaching may need to focus on toleration and desensitization. This procedure often has dramatic results. With one adolescent, reported to be a "noncommunicator," one author was able to establish an initial signal system in less than a minute. Naturally, expansion and modification of the system took much longer.

After an initial communication system is assessed, the clinician can begin to explore the second aspect of client behavior, which involves presymbolic and/or symbolic functioning. The goal(s) of such assessment is(are) to establish a functional level and/or to describe the client's communication behaviors. The behaviors targeted by each clinician will differ. Table 8–1 presents a list of those presymbolic behaviors considered important for assessment and training by a number of intervention specialists and programs; references are given in the right column. The sequential order represents a developmental hierarchy, modified so that similar behaviors are grouped together and those most easily trained occur first. Table 8–1 is not exhaustive nor exclusive, and the knowledgeable clinician should feel free to add or delete presymbolic behaviors.

Symbolic assessment should include more than a list of the symbols used by the client. MacDonald (1978a) suggested assessing eight semantic–syntactic combinations, whereas Owens (1982b) assessed 11 semantic and 8 illocutionary functions. Other intervention taxonomies stress primarily illocutionary functions (Page, 1982; Wexler, Blau, Dore, & Leslie, 1982).

Again, assessment should begin with observation and caregiver interviews. There is a variety of protocols, listed in Table 8–2, which can be used alone or in combination to determine a client's levels of presymbolic and symbolic functioning. The use of these assessment tools enhances the validity of later testing and encourages caregivers to

Student: ______ Date: ______ Time: ______

Activity: ______

BEHAVIORS

Behavior column headings (left to right):

- •
- •
- •
- PICTURE / WRITTEN WORD
- ONE WORD SPEECH / APPROX.
- ONE WORD SIGN / APPROX.
- COMPLEX SPEECH / APPROX.
- COMPLEX SIGN / APPROX.
- WHINNING / CRYING
- VERBAL / PHYSICAL THREATS
- SWEARING
- SCREAM / YELL
- LAUGHING / GIGGLING
- IMMEDIATE ECHOLALIA
- DELAYED ECHOLALIA
- TOUCHING
- RUNNING
- REACHING / GRABBING
- PUSHING / PULLING
- PROXIMITY POSITIONING
- OBJECT MANIPULATION
- MASTURBATION
- HUGGING / KISSING
- GESTURING / POINTING
- GAZE / STARING
- GAZE AVERSION
- FACIAL EXPRESSION
- TANTRUM
- SELF STIMULATION
- SELF-INJURIOUS BEHAVIOR
- PERSEVERATIVE RITUALS
- INAPP. ORAL / ANAL BEHAVIOR
- BIZARRE VERBALIZATIONS
- AGGRESSION

FUNCTIONS

I. INTERACTIVE

A. REQUESTS FOR
- Attention
- Social Interaction
- Play Interactions
- Affection
- Permission to Engage in an Activity
- Action by Receiver
- Assistance
- Information/Clarification
- Objects
- Food

B. NEGATIONS
- Protest
- Refusal
- Cessation

C. DECLARATIONS/COMMENTS About Events/Actions																																					
About Objects/Persons																																					
About Errors/Mistakes																																					
Affirmation																																					
Greeting																																					
Humor																																					
D. DECLARATIONS ABOUT FEELINGS Anticipation																																					
Boredom																																					
Confusion																																					
Fear																																					
Frustration																																					
Hurt Feelings																																					
Pain																																					
Pleasure																																					
II. NON-INTERACTIVE																																					
A. SELF-REGULATION																																					
B. REHEARSAL																																					
C. HABITUAL																																					
D. RELAXATION/TENSION RELEASE																																					

Figure 8–2. An observational tool for analyzing the communicative functions of behavior. From Donnellan, A., Mirenda, P., Mesaros, R., & Fassbender, L. (1984). Analyzing the communicative functions of aberrant behavior. Journal of the Association for Persons with Severe Handicaps, 9, 201–212. With permission.

TABLE 8–1.
Possible Presymbolic Training Targets

Behavior	Description	Rationale	References
Responding	Ability to respond, in at least one mode, shortly following a caregiver behavior	☐ Important for establishing early interaction through eye gaze, physical movement, etc.	McCormick & Schiefelbusch (1984); Owens (1982a); Page & Goossens (1980); Reichle & Yoder (1980); Waldo (1979)
Motor imitation	Ability to respond with a close approximation of the caregiver's preceding physical behavior	☐ Social concept of following other's model ☐ Cognitive skill of re-presenting a model, especially symbolic skill found in deferred imitation ☐ Skill needed for further training	Baer, Peterson & Sherman (1967); Bricker & Bricker (1974); Horstmeier & MacDonald (1978); Kozloff (1973); Manolson (1983); Owens (1982a); Raymore & McLean (1972); Reichle & Yoder (1979); Swope & Liebergott (1980); Tawney (1979)
Object permanence	Ability to recognize a hidden object when uncovered and to search for hidden objects	☐ Cognitive ability to recongize the object requires storing the object mentally for retrieval ☐ Semantic characteristics established	Bricker & Bricker (1974); Dunst (1980); Horstmeier & MacDonald (1978); McLean & Snyder-McLean (1978); Owens (1982a); Swope & Liebergott (1980); Tawney (1979)
Turn-taking	Ability to respond with a specific behavior shortly following a caregiver model	☐ Social concept of following a model without a directive ☐ Important early interactive skill	McCormick & Schiefelbusch (1984); Owens (1982a)
Functional use of objects	Ability to use common objects for their intended purpose	☐ Semantic characteristics established	Horstmeier & MacDonald (1978); Manolson (1983); Owens (1982a); Swope & Liebergott (1980)

Means–ends	Ability to visualize the means for achieving desired ends through objects and people	☐ Cognitive concept closley correlated with the development of gestures ☐ Symbolic skill of representing the problem	Bricker & Bricker (1974); McCormick & Schiefelbusch (1984); Owens (1982a); Snell (1983); Swope & Liebergott (1980); Tapajna & Finn–Scardine (1981)
Communicative gestures	Ability to convey notions, such as request, notice, give, and show by hand and body movements	☐ Communication concept of expressing intentions ☐ Early illocutionary functions established in which symbols will later be trained	McCormick & Schiefelbusch (1984); Owens (1982a); Reichle & Yoder (1979); Ricke, Lynch & Soltman (1977)
Receptive language	Ability to recognize environmental noises or other input and object names	☐ Linguistic precursor of expressive symbol use	Bricker & Bricker (1974); Horstmeier & MacDonald (1978); Manolson (1983); McCormick & Schiefelbusch (1984); Owens (1982a); Reichle & Yoder (1979); Ricke, Lynch & Soltman (1977); Tawney (1979)
Sound imitation	Ability to vocalize, and to take turns with and imitate vocalizations	☐ Communication precursor to speech production, if the verbal mode is feasible ☐ Complement to augmentative communication	Bricker & Bricker (1974); Horstmeier & MacDonald (1978); Manolson (1983); McCormick & Schiefelbusch (1984); Owens (1982a); Reichle & Yoder (1979); Snell (1983); Swope & Liebergott (1980); Tawney (1979)

TABLE 8–2.
Presymbolic and Symbolic Assessment Protocols

Assessment Tool	Type of Assessment
Hanna, Lippert, & Harris (1982): *Developmental Communication Curriculum Inventory.*	Caregiver questionaire and direct assessment tool.
Horstmeier & MacDonald (1978b): *Environmental Prelanguage Battery.*	Direct assessment tool used in a play format assisted by caregivers. Assesses attending, object permanence, functional use, imitation, and receptive language plus one- and two-word production.
MacDonald (1978); *Environmental Language Inventory.*	Direct assessment tool that assesses early semantic categories in two-, three-, and four-word utterances in three modes of imitation, conversation, and play.
Owens (1982a): *Caregiver Interview & Environmental Observation.*	Interview and observation tool used to establish approximate functioning level, the manner and location of communication, and the communication partners.
Owens (1982b): *Developmental Assessment Tool (DAT).*	Direct assessment tool used to determine level of functioning in auditory and visual attending, imitation, turn-taking, object permanence, means, gestures, receptive language, sound production, and semantic and illocutionary behaviors.
Owens (1982c): *Diagnostic Interactional Survey (DIS).*	Observational tool used to rate the quality of a 10-minute client–caregiver interaction.
Stillman (1978): *The Callier–Azusa Scale.*	Direct assessment tool designed for deaf-blind individuals.
Uzgiris & Hunt (1975): *Assessment in Infancy: Ordinal Scales of Intellectual Development.*	Direct assessment tool based on Piagetian model using play format.

become involved early in the intervention process. In addition, this information can be used to establish an approximate functional level at which to begin more systematic assessment. The "Oliver," a caregiver questionnaire on client behavior (MacDonald, 1978b), instructs caregivers to actually engage in some test exercises with the client and to report the results. Occasionally, a client will not perform for the speech–language clinician in formal testing, and this caregiver data may be a valuable aid.

Although most questionnaires or scales are designed to be used with children, they can be adapted for adults. There is reason to believe that presymbolic and preverbal behaviors of adults with severe to profound retardation follow a sequence of development similar to that of nonhandicapped infants (Owings, 1985). It is important to be mindful, however, that the client is an adult and that some questions may need to be reworded to be more appropriate. At present, there are no communication assessment instruments designed specifically for the adult presymbolic population.

In general, questionnaires or scales are of two types: those that attempt to establish a developmental age and those that are concerned with functioning level. The first, represented by Bzoch and League (1971) and by Sacks and Young (1982), usually ask several questions probing skills corresponding to various age levels to determine the client's receptive and expressive language age. Although many communication and related behaviors are explored, such tools generally do not weigh these behaviors in terms of their importance for later development. Nevertheless, such developmental measures can be helpful, especially when governmental agencies require normative age equivalencies.

Direct testing of age-related communication can be accomplished through the use of infant intellectual, communicative, or development measures (Bayley, 1969; Boyd, Stauber, & Bluma, 1977; Griffith & Sanford, 1975; Rogers, D'Eugenio, Brown, Donovan, & Lynch, 1978). At best, these instruments provide a gross estimate of the client's functional age equivalency. Necessary modifications in testing procedures preclude the outright use of a test's age norms with presymbolic adults with multiple handicaps and mental retardation.

Unfortunately, age-normed development scales and tests used alone often provide only minimal information with which to make intervention decisions for the client. A second measure, scales of functional or behavior level, is more useful. Theoretically, successful performance at each level is a necessary prerequisite to success at the next higher level. Usually, such questionnaires or scales comprise a portion of a published language intervention program and therefore reflect the biases of the overall intervention model (Hanna, Lippert, & Harris, 1982; MacDonald, 1978b; Owens, 1982a). Use is not the same as adoption, however, and these scales can be modified to conform to the clinician's model of initial language training. Both questionnaire and interview formats have been successfully used in the assessment of functioning level.

After the speech–language clinician has an estimate of the client's presymbolic and early symbolic behavior, he/she should attempt to measure this behavior through direct testing. There are a number of commerically available assessment instruments with varying numbers of presymbolic behaviors considered essential to the development of symbol use (Hanna et al., 1982; MacDonald & Horstmeier, 1978; Owens, 1982b). It is helpful if caregivers attend, assist with the assessment, and provide test stimuli from the clients' environments, such as combs or cups. The presence of both the caregiver and familiar objects may enhance the validity of the results and/or the level of client performance. In general, behavioral assessment tools are used to establish the presence or absence of a general class of behavior, such as motor imitation, rather than a specific behavior, such as hand clapping. The clinician attempts to ascertain whether the client has the overall concept, which, in our example, would be using others as models. Even stereotypic or perseverative behavior can be used. In this case, the clinician is interested in the client's performance of the behavior within a few seconds of his/her model. Naturally, these assessment tools need to be adapted for the specific physical limitations of each client. The Callier–Azusa Scale (Stillman, 1978) is designed specifically for the deaf-blind client based on a Piagetian model of early cognitive development. Uzgiris and Hunt (1975) have devised a similar, but more stage-oriented, assessment tool. Because these tools are based on a hierarchical model of development, the results describe general cognitive functioning and suggest goals for further training. The knowledgeable clinician can choose those subtests that he/she feels are most directly related to presymbolic development.

At a symbolic level, the clinician should attempt to assess the depth and breadth of the client's use of symbols. Of interest are the number of symbols in the client's lexicon and the variety of language functions. MacDonald (1978a) provides a format for assessing semantic function in two-, three-, and four-word utterances. Utterances are collected in three contexts: imitation, conversation, and play. A less formal but potentially more useful assessment is a conversational free sample, such as that used by Owens (1982b), in which each utterance is rated for the semantic and illocutionary functions of early child language. Functional category definitions are provided in Appendix A. Although these categories, designed for retarded and nonretarded children, may not be totally appropriate for use with retarded adults, they do suggest a breadth of functions from which to begin (Leonard, Steckol, & Panther, 1983). Neither MacDonald (1978a) nor Owens (1982b) prescribe normative distributions for these functions. Such values are usually situationally related.

Each utterance, whether verbal, manual, or visual, can be recorded and then rated for semantic and illocutionary function. The length of each utterance in symbols and the total number of utterances within each function can be used to compute the mean length of utterance of each function. In general, the data may suggest the following training targets:

- ☐ Teach nonexistent functions.
- ☐ Provide opportunities for the client to use low-frequency functions.
- ☐ Expand the length of shorter functions.
- ☐ Reduce or modify stereotypic, perseverative, or echolalic utterances.
- ☐ Increase the vocabulary available for symbol-specific functions. For example, if the client's only negative is "No way" used as an all-purpose negation, the clinician can train other words in combination with "no."

Obviously, this evaluation process is very extensive. One-hour, one-shot assessments are inappropriate for those presymbolic and early symbolic adults who may exhibit a low incidence of communicative behavior, use inappropriate and unconventional signal systems, and/or have multiple handicaps. Nor is the presymbolic adult the clinician's sole concern in evaluation.

Context-Related Variables

Given the effect of the linguistic and nonlinguistic context on communication and the detrimental effect of the environment upon the communicative behaviors of institutionalized adults, it is imperative that the speech–language clinician evaluate the communication potential of the client's natural environment (for further discussion, see Halle, Chapter 7 in this volume). The clinician is interested in describing the environment and identifying high communication contexts. This information is usually gathered through interviews with caregivers and by observation. The following questions are of interest:

- ☐ What situations are high-communication contexts? Any specific activities? Specific locations? Describe the client's communication behavior in each.
- ☐ What activities or items seem to be of high interest to the client?
- ☐ Which caregivers seem to evoke the most client responses and initiations? Why? Describe the behaviors of these caregivers.
- ☐ Do the communication demands on the client differ relative to context? If so, how? How do these demands relate to the frequency of client communication?

Yoder (1985) recommended a four-step assessment process, first outlined by Brown, Branston, Hamre–Nietupski, Pumpian, Certo, and Gruenewald (1979), that he referred to as an ecological inventory of communication needs and uses. In the first step, the clinician delineates the most relevant and functionally least-restrictive current and subsequent communication environments. These environments may include but not be limited to domestic, vocational, recreational or leisure, educational, and social or communal. These environments are analyzed by subenvironments in Step 2; the clinician is to delineate some of the most relevant and functional activities in each. In Step 3, the clinician determines the skills needed to participate in each activity. In addition, the clinician describes possible adaptations in that activity and/or environment that would allow or enhance the client's participation. From these data, the clinician designs intervention programs to teach the skills necessary for participation. In addition, subsequent changes in the environment are also designed. Although client and context variables are important in themselves, they are most meaningful in an integrated approach when we consider the effect of the client on his/her environment or context and of the environment on the client.

Interactional Variables

If the client's caregivers are to become language facilitators, the quality of the interaction between each caregiver and client must be evaluated initially and throughout intervention. The speech–language clinician must be aware of both client and caregiver behaviors and of the effect of each on the other. As coordinator, the speech–language clinician can then suggest modifications to the caregiver that will, in turn, change the client's communicative behavior. For example, the caregiver who continually directs the client, giving little opportunity for response, might be instructed to refrain from giving instructions, await client requests for assistance, and pause for client turns. The caregiver who responds to client communication initiations primarily with head nods might be trained in verbal turn-taking skills.

Russo and Owens (1982) used a 10-minute observational sample of the client with each primary caregiver. Within this period, the clinician rates the caregivers' uses of natural reinforcement, physical proximity, imitation of client behaviors, expansion, reply and extension, and content appropriate to the client's environment and functioning level. The client is rated for attending to the interaction, referencing or signaling notice, physical proximity, and vocal or verbal responding. The presence of these 10 characteristics has been associated with subjective judgments of good-quality interactions. Dubbed the Diagnostic Interactional Survey

(Owens, 1982c), this tool is used primarily for counseling and as a check on the qualitative changes within the client–caregiver interaction.

Wilcox and Campbell (1983) proposed a more descriptive scale. Client strategies for engagement, termination, and re-engagement are noted, along with the primary modes of signaling, including vocalization and body posture and movement.

A more promising observational tool is *ECO II*, devised by Mac-Donald and Gillette (1982) for assessing, prescribing, and monitoring the communication system between two persons. Four scales, called ECOmaps, cover interaction and conversation, mode, content, and use; they are further divided into four related event classes of client perform-ance, significant-other performance, significant-other teaching strate-gies, and potential problems. The first two classes of client and signif-icant-other performance are rated as an approximate percentage of the time that each interactant engages in the specific behaviors listed. This scaling allows for an estimate of communication match. Severe inequi-ties in scoring signal a potential mismatch for that behavior. For exam-ple, if the significant-other is rated 9 on "initiates contact" while the client receives a 1, this inequity signals an area in need of intervention. In general, a progressive match is desired in which the significant-other is watching the client's performance and modeling slightly above that level. The Teaching Strategies ECOmap, which summarizes clinical and research findings on natural communication events and strategies necessary for the client to produce a higher level of communication per-formance, rates the significant-other's use of these events and strategies. Finally, the Problems ECOmap provides for the identification of specific interactional problems.

Summary

A thorough evaluation of the client's communication system prior to the initiation of therapy is essential. Such an evaluation requires assessment of the client's present communication system and potential for mod-ification and of the client's presymbolic or early symbolic level of functioning. Also of interest are the communication characteristics of the client's environment and of the client–caregiver interaction, includ-ing a description of the communication behaviors of all primary care-givers. A variety of data-collection procedures is needed to attain an adequate description of the client's communication behaviors and con-texts. These variables should be monitored throughout intervention and periodically thereafter to ensure that the client is performing at the optimum communication level.

Systematic Intervention

After the data have been assembled, the clinician devises the client's intervention plan in consultation with other members of the intervention team. All three areas assessed — client-related behavior, context-related situations, and interactions — should be addressed within the integrated model. In this section, we will present an overall model of intervention and discuss the strategies and techniques applicable to each of the three variables of client, context, and interaction.

Overall Integrated Model

The integrated model of intervention that we have proposed targets clients' present communication systems and their presymbolic and early symbolic behaviors, along with the communication behaviors of their primary caregivers. Our goal is to establish communicative environments for clients that target their specific needs.

All primary caregivers should be enlisted as agents of change. As language facilitators, their behaviors will also be targeted for change by the speech–language clinician. It is advisable to begin with a few caregivers, such as one instructor and an aide. Behaviors can be modified through in-service training and modeling. Initial progress may be slow because the speech–language clinician is attempting to modify interactional patterns that have evolved over a period of time, possibly lengthy, to meet the supposed needs and abilities of each interactional participant.

Ideally, the speech–language clinician should see the client on a daily or tri-weekly basis in individual or group therapy sessions. A caregiver should attend with the client at least once per week. When this attendance is not possible, the clinician can observe the caregiver in the natural environment and make suggestions for improving the client–caregiver interaction. Training of caregivers can be done at in-service sessions or following brief observation and data review in the natural environment. Each caregiver should be encouraged to maintain a record of all formal training periods. The speech–language clinician might set aside one day or portion of a day each week to review these records along with his/her own to make decisions on the level, manner, and content of training.

Intervention Techniques

We have found three intervention techniques to be helpful: incidental teaching, stimulation, and formal teaching.

INCIDENTAL TEACHING. As we have used it, *incidental teaching* is an interactional teaching strategy that arises naturally within the daily activities of the client and caregiver or in unstructured situations, and is used by caregivers to modify or strengthen the client's communication behavior. Wherever possible, the client is allowed to control the focus of the interaction by signaling interest in an activity. The goal is to train or strengthen presymbolic or early symbolic behaviors while enhancing naturally occurring communication interactions. In other words, the behavior being targeted is emphasized and trained within daily activities of the client in which it would naturally appear. For example, the client learning about object permanence could encounter natural teaching situations in the bath using nonfloating soap or at the table using misplaced silverware. The caregiver's task it to be aware of the learning potential within each situation and to structure events to enhance learning. In unstructured activities, such as freetime in the unit, the client's expressed interest is the key. Observant caregivers learn to follow the client's lead and to incorporate training into the client's interests. Other examples of possible incidental teaching situations are listed in Table 8–3.

TABLE 8–3.
Examples of Possible Incidental Teaching Situations

Context	Level of Training	Example
Workshop	Motor imitation	Caregiver uses tool and cues client to imitate
	Turn-taking	Client and caregiver take turns assembling an item
	Means–ends	Caregiver has client retrieve tool on a cord or pull the cord to start a piece of equipment
Eating	Motor imitation	Caregiver eats with different tableware and with fingers and cues client to imitate
	Means–ends	Caregiver places self between client and serving bowls so that client must signal "Pass the food"
Dressing	Turn-taking	Caregiver and client hand clothes back and forth sorting them
	Communicative gestures	Caregiver places desired clothing out of client's reach and awaits gesture or cues with "What (do you) want?"
	Receptive language	Caregiver uses clothing item names to cue client to pick them up
Shopping	Object permanence	Client finds items on shelf after seeing an example

Adapted from Owens, R. (1982). *Program for the Acquisition of Language with the Severely Impaired (PALS)*. San Antonio, TX: Psychological Corporation.

A number of studies have reported success, albeit limited, in the use of incidental techniques. Halle, Marshall, and Spradlin (1979) reported an increase in verbal initiations among institutionalized adolescents using a time-delay procedure at meals. In addition, they found that teachers began to use the procedures in other settings. Likewise, Oliver and Halle (1982) reported an increase in initiations with signing for an adolescent child with mental retardation trained in the use of sign. Nor is all the success in expressive communication. McGee, Krantz, Mason, and McClannahan (1983) successfully taught receptive labels to autistic adolescents in a lunch preparation activity in a kitchen area. Although Salzburg and Villani (1983) found that caregivers experienced difficulty generalizing from formal training methods to more incidental techniques, Alpert and Rogers–Warren (1984) claimed success in directly teaching these behaviors to caregivers. Following their review of incidental teaching research, Warren and Kaiser (1986) concluded:

> It is clear from existing literature that incidental teaching (a) teaches target skills effectively in the natural environment; (b) typically results in generalization of those skills across settings, time, and persons; and (c) results in gains in the formal and functional aspects of language. Because research with mentally retarded children is limited in both quantity and scope, the extent to which incidental teaching can remediate serious communication deficits in this population is less clear. (p. 296)

For this reason, we do not recommend sole reliance on this method of training. We have found incidental teaching to be very helpful for generalization and relevancy of training and as an aid against rapid forgetting by clients. Without such techniques, the 24-hour-a-day approach so needed by presymbolic adults is not possible. Most caregivers balk at suggestions of incorporating formalized training into their other responsibilities. In other words, incidental teaching is a practical response to a need for more client instruction and more useful client–caregiver interaction without radical changes in the responsibilities of caregivers.

STIMULATION. The second intervention technique or teaching strategy is *stimulation*, the manner in which the caregivers interact with the client. Ideally, the level of complexity of caregivers' communication behaviors should be slightly above that of the client to serve as a model. According to the *minimal discrepancy principle*, clients will learn best if the model is not so close to their competency level that they are bored and not so far above that they are frustrated (Hunt, 1961).

The use of stimulation techniques may require caregivers to change their expectations of the clients. Caregivers need to expect communication. After this occurs, caregivers can provide appropriate models, structure situations to encourage communication, and allow the client to make choices within the environment that can affect change (Owens, 1982a; Page 1982; Tapajna & Finn–Scardine, 1981).

Our best guide for the selection of appropriate stimulation techniques is the communication behaviors of the mothers of nonhandicapped infants. These behaviors suggest some of the stimulation techniques included in Appendix B. At present, we do not know which behaviors are the most effective, so we would encourage use of all of those that are practical. It is best if caregivers change their own behavior slowly, possibly incorporating one or two changes at a time until comfortable. Clinicians and caregivers should remind themselves that adult clients may not need all of the attention-getting devices used with young children, such as higher pitch and exaggerated intonation. A more adult tonal quality is more appropriate with adult clients.

FORMAL TEACHING. The third intervention technique, *formal teaching*, should occur a few brief times daily and be monitored closely by the speech–language clinician for content, procedures, and client progress. Each skill to be taught should be analyzed in terms of antecedent and consequent events and the steps needed for successful completion. With adults who are severely to profoundly retarded, it is essential that instructional sequences include small increments of change. For example, it is often too difficult for clients to go from verbal imitation, as in response to "Say 'cookie'," to verbal responding, as in answer to "What's this?" The task suggests a training sequence such as the following:

Caregiver	*Client*
"Say 'cookie'."	"Cookie."
"Cookie." (Nod toward client)	"Cookie."
"What's this? Cookie." (Nod)	"Cookie."
"Cookie. What's this?"	"Cookie."
"Cookie." (Delay) "What's this?"	"Cookie."
Gradually lengthen delay and decrease prompt.	
"Cookie. What's this?"	"Cookie."
"What's this?"	"Cookie."

In general, the speech–language clinician needs to design individualized programs that reflect each client's different style and sequence of learning, different cues necessary, reinforcers, success criteria, and content.

Generalization is also affected by the content, manner, and sequence of formal instruction. As mentioned previously, content or instructional items should come from the client's natural environment. In this light, "Cookie," used in the preceding example, should be analyzed to see whether there are natural opportunities for this item to occur. The speech–

language clinician should inquire as to how often the client is asked to identify a cookie or to request one. Incidental techniques can be used to enhance such generalization.

Responses such as "good talking" occur infrequently in the client's daily interactions. Conversational responding by the clinician, such as "um-hm, try some cookie," is more appropriate. Data from child development studies indicate the reinforcing power, not to mention the teaching potential, of expanded or extended responses. In a similar fashion, the reinforcement schedule should also reflect the reinforcement in the environment where the communication will occur in order to aid generalization.

Client Training

As with assessment, client instruction should have the dual focus of the client's communication system and presymbolic or early symbolic skills. In general, the communication system can be expanded and moved toward more symbolic communication. The initial signal system can be modified to include environmental signs and gestures. At this "sign" stage, the client is able to use a related object to signify an event. For example, a washcloth can represent "bath" and a spoon "eat." Sternberg (1984) uses "anticipation shelves" in which the day's activities are represented in sequence by related objects in boxes on a shelf. As the client begins each activity, he removes the object "sign" from its box. The "sign" is never actually used in the activity, although a similar one may be. When the activity is completed, the "sign" goes into a "done" box. Gradually, the client learns to associate the "sign" with the event and to anticipate events. We have found that in the initial stages of training, in contrast to Sternberg (1984), it is helpful for associational learning to actually use the "sign" in the activity and then gradually to distance the two.

In reality, the client is using an initial augmentative system based on environmental signs. The nonambulatory adult, in similar fashion, might look at a television or a record to request television viewing or music, respectively. Although this training may seem easy, it requires sensorimotor learning of at least Stage III, four to eight months of age (Sternberg, 1984). Truly functional symbolic communication using pictures, drawings, Blissymbolics, sign language, and/or words will require even higher cognitive abilities.

Use of the client's communication system should be encouraged whenever possible through incidental and stimulation techniques. The speech–language clinician should reinforce not only the client but also the caregivers for "sign" usage. The more signs are used, the more they can be generalized.

Presymbolic teaching might progress as previously depicted in Table 8–1. Even within this presymbolic instruction, several communication skills, such as turn-taking and gaze-coupling, can be targeted. In addition, newly taught skills can be placed in a turn-taking or an interactive framework.

These newly taught behaviors will have to be continually reviewed within the three teaching strategies of incidental teaching, stimulation, and formal teaching for instruction to be optimal. Suggested methods for training presymbolic skills are included in Appendix C. In addition, several programs are available that provide extensive descriptions of intervention techniques (Bricker & Bricker, 1974; Horstmeier & Mac-Donald, 1978; Manolson, 1983; Owens, 1982a).

Symbolic instruction is best if superimposed on a gestural–vocal base previously taught. It is at the symbolic level that the dual instruction in communication and prerequisite skills join. First taught by imitation in response to cues such as "Say _______," "Sign, _______," "Point to _______," and so forth, symbols can be quickly transferred to a visual cue, such as a nod, and then trained to fulfill a variety of semantic and illocutionary functions. Rather than teaching a large number of single symbols, the speech–language clinician can modify intonation and gestures that accompany a single symbol to express a variety of functions. For example, "cup" when said while pushing it away and turning from it might indicate a negative semantic function and a suggestion-CDR (command-demand-request) or request-for-action illocutionary function. (See Appendix A for category definitions.) A response "cup" after the cup has been drained by the client might represent semantic recurrence and suggestion-CDR again. It is possible, therefore, to train a variety of functions with a few single symbols.

Most of the training procedures and sequences mentioned are equally applicable to clients who will use a combination of speech and augmentative communication. Receptive training with augmentative systems, particularly environmental sign systems, can begin at a relatively low level of presymbolic functioning. This fact does not preclude presymbolic instruction, however, because the more abstract symbol systems, such as Blissymbolics, require a level of symbolic functioning at least as high as that for verbal symbols. A number of effective tools are available for use in selecting the most appropriate augmentative system for a particular client (House & Rogerson, 1984; Owens & House, 1984; Shane & Bashir, 1980).

Obviously, this instruction will occasionally be tedious. The speech–language clinician will need to maintain updated records and to monitor the environment continually to ensure optimum communication for the client.

Modification of Communication Context

The client's communication context can be modified in several ways to enhance communication and teaching. A thorough analysis of the communication demands placed on the client will aid the speech–language clinician in identifying high and low communication contexts. High communication contexts can be encouraged while low ones are modified or eliminated. For example, the arrangement of furnishings or routines can be changed so that the client is placed in more communication situations.

High communication contexts often offer ideal opportunities for incidental teaching. Because the client is already communicating at a high level, the speech-language clinician only needs to change the manner of that communication.

Interactional Changes

The effective use of caregivers as agents of change is well documented (Baker, 1976; Heifetz, 1980; Owens et al., 1985). According to Clark, Baker, and Heifetz (1982), socioeconomic status, pretraining skills, and experience positively correlate with short-term learning success. Even minimum instruction and knowledge of the direction in which training should proceed seems sufficient to enable some caregivers to spontaneously adopt suitable teaching strategies (Cheseldine & McConkey, 1979). Of critical importance, however, is the feedback that caregivers receive from the speech–language clinician regarding their application of their newly acquired teaching skills (Polk, Schilmoeller, Emboy, Holman, & Baer, 1976; Salzburg & Villani, 1983).

The stimulation behaviors discussed previously can be a helpful guide for caregiver interactional behaviors. Wulz et al. (1983) have also reported successful use of their *Instructional Communication Strategy* in which the professional teaches the client responses and the caregivers elicit these responses within the home. The main components of this model are teaching and environmental manipulation. Within the teaching phase, the client is taught to respond to *need-to-communicate* situations. The purpose of the instruction is to expand the client's communication repertoire and to stimulate responding. Within environmental manipulation, the caregiver restructures needs-meeting situations so that the client's needs are not anticipated but are dependent on the client's communication behavior.

Horstmeier and MacDonald (1978) rely on *environmental rules* to restructure client–caregiver interactions. For example, after the client has learned a skill, he/she is required to perform that skill in the natural environment to attain desired entities or privileges. For example, if he/she can sign "eat," he/she is required to do so to get a snack. Previously accepted behaviors are unacceptable; thus, environmental rules affect both client and caregiver behaviors.

Additional suggestions for structuring interactions are offered by MacDonald and Gillette (1982). Some of these that are related to turn-taking are as follows:

- □ Structure the activity for give-and-take.
- □ Follow the client's lead.
- □ Imitate the client.
- □ Wait for the client to take a turn.
- □ Signal the client to take a turn.
- □ Chain responses by the use of turnabouts in which a turn includes both a response to the client's turn as well as a cue for him/her to take another turn.

MacDonald and Gillette's ECOmaps also offer a guide for modifying interactions.

In general, the caregiver is expected to work under the guidance of the speech–language clinician so that incidental teaching occurs within daily activities and routines. He/she is also to be mindful of the stimulation value of his/her communication behaviors and to provide appropriate modeling and feedback. If he/she builds an expectation of communication, he/she is more likely to get it and to recognize it when he/she gets it.

Summary

The client should be seen several times per week by the speech–language clinician. At other times, communication training is administered by caregivers under the direction of the speech–language clinician. The three intervention techniques of incidental teaching, stimulation, and formal training are used simultaneously to modify client behavior, environmental factors, and the client–caregiver interaction.

Dismissal Criteria

Obviously, the speech–language clinician needs to make decisions about the amount and type of service provided and about termination of service. Several variables affect program modification and performance and are critical to decisions of dismissal. The overall design of the intervention program is an integral part of the decision process. Dismissal variables include the client's level of functioning and rate of change, environmental factors, and overall client behavior. The level of client functioning relative to communication adequacy varies with each client and is dependent on the other factors. In short, the speech–language clinician must try to determine performance levels adequate for each client, given his/her overall developmental level and rate of learning curve. Because the overall developmental age of the client may be lowered by perceptual, sensory, neurological, and physical deficits, the rate of learning or evidence of plateauing in the learning curve may be a better criteria for dismissal or for reassessment of the current intervention technique. Overall, however, we can expect a slower rate of change from an adult client who is severely impaired than from a child client who is. A lack of change may require scrutiny of the environmental factors that can be altered, intervention procedures, or the possibility of dismissal.

Environmental variables relate to the client's present and future living, educational, and employment environments. Present and future placement is important not only for program design and for selection of communication mode but also for determining the level of communication competency adequate for these environments. In institutional settings, the signaling of basic needs might be adequate for some clients. To admit this fact is not to admit defeat but to recognize the realities of the client's life.

The last variable is client behavior. One of the first aspects of therapy with many presymbolic adults is the elimination of self-injurious behaviors. Some clients may return to these former behaviors as conditions in the environment change. If this occurs, to the detriment of the therapy situation, dismissal should be considered. Other clients will exhibit what we call the "terminal blahs": nothing seems to awaken a response; in this situation, the clinician who has "given it his/her best shot" should consider dismissal.

One final issue deserves mention: the legal issues involved in dismissal. Public law and government regulations often require that services be maintained for severely communicatively impaired clients. With this and the variables of level of functioning, rate of change, environment, and client behavior in mind, we prefer to consider dismissal as relative to *levels of clinical commitment* (Figure 8–3).

Initial involvement, especially while establishing the client's conventional communication system and beginning instruction, will of necessity involve maximum professional involvement. The speech–language clinician should provide direct service almost on a daily basis. The speech–language clinician's expertise is especially critical at the initial stage of evaluation and design. This level of commitment should shift rapidly to the clinician-directed approach discussed in this chapter. At this level, the clinician is responsible for the overall directing of

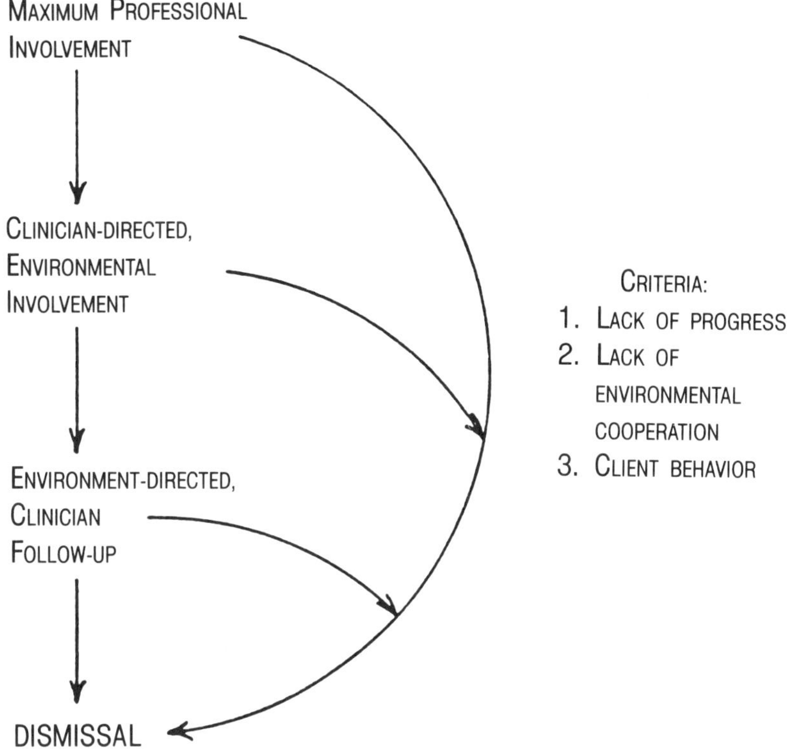

Figure 8–3. Levels of clinical commitment.

therapy and for caregiver instruction and monitoring as outlined. Generally, the client can move to this level of involvement when he/she has some conventional communication system in place, self-injurious behaviors are in control, and presymbolic or symbolic teaching has begun. As the caregiver becomes more adept at planning and monitoring instruction, the clinician's direct intervention services may eventually be replaced with periodic evaluation and followup. The clinician's role becomes increasingly one of a consultant.

Finally, the client may be dismissed when functioning at a developmentally appropriate level or at a level that is adequate for the present- and future-use environments. Natually, the client will need to be reevaluated periodically to ensure that the gains have been maintained.

A realistic view of presymbolic adults may convince the clinician that a particular client is not appropriate for therapy at this time with this clinician using this approach. The speech–language clinician should appraise these three areas of timeliness, appropriateness of the clinician, and appropriateness of the program. If he/she can determine that these three factors are not negatively affecting the client then he/she should attempt to make a decision of dismissal based on client variables. If the client has a long intervention history of failure and has continually failed to make progress despite the use of different clinicians and clinical approaches, we recommend dismissal. If the client's environment will not cooperate and progress has stalled, even with adjustment for clinician and program, we recommend dismissal. Finally, if the client's behavior deteriorates and the intervention sessions deteriorate with it, we recommend dismissal. Our only reluctance about dismissal would be with the client in the initial stages of establishing a conventional communication system. Even rudimentary systems, such as touching someone to continue rocking, can be designed for most clients. We would rather not dismiss a client without this small victory.

One problematic dismissal is that of the client whose communication *seems* adequate for the environment in which it will be used. It is often difficult to determine environmental adequacy. Each clinician must determine what is adequate for the client's setting. He/she can begin by noting the major activities of the client and the intentions that must be expressed by the client within each activity. A thorough analysis of these data should allow the speech–language clinician to deduce some minimal communication competencies needed by the client. To keep therapy focused, it might be best to determine these competencies at the onset of therapy, after the initial evaluation. The outgrowth would be more objective criteria for dismissal of clients who continue to make slow progress and do not injure themselves but are a long way from ever communicating at their developmental level.

Dismissal will be difficult if the clinician has not prepared those in the client's environment to continue the intervention process. Dismissal for reasons such as lack of progress, lack of environmental support, behavioral deterioration, or communication adequacy for the use environment, will require more objective critieria than are currently available.

SUMMARY

The special communication needs of the presymbolic adult reflect the client's skill level and the use environment. Large institutional settings can actually retard communication development. Only an overall integrated intervention program that targets both the client and the environment can hope to effectively change the client's current level of performance. We have presented a model of intervention that targets both client and caregiver behaviors and incorporates instruction into the client's environment with a minimal disruption to the routines and activities in those environments.

REFERENCES

Alpert, C., & Rogers-Warren, A. (1984). *Mothers as incidental language trainers of their language-disordered children.* Unpublished manuscript, University of Kansas, Lawrence.

Baer, D., Peterson, R., & Sherman, J. (1967). The development of imitation by reinforcing behavior similarity to a model. *Journal of Experimental Analysis of Behavior, 10,* 405–416.

Baker, B. (1976). Parent involvement in programming for the developmentally disabled child. In L. Lloyd (Ed.), *Communication assessment and intervention* (pp. 691–733). Baltimore, MD: University Park Press.

Bayley, N. (1979). *The Bayley Scales of Infant Development.* San Antonio, TX: Psychological Corporation, Harcourt Brace Jovanovich.

Boyd, R., Stauber, K., & Bluma, S. (1977). *The portage parent program: Instructor's manual.* Portage, WI: Cooperation Educational Service Agency 12.

Bricker, W., & Bricker, D. (1974). An early language training strategy. In R. Schiefelbusch & L. Lloyd (Eds.), *Language perspectives – acquisition, retardation, and intervention* (pp. 431–468). Austin, TX: PRO-ED.

Briggs, M., & Klein, M. (1985, November). *Training communication interactions in mothers of high risk infants.* Paper presented at the American Speech-Language-Hearing Association Annual Convention, Washington, DC.

Brown, L., Branston, M., Hamre-Nietupski, S., Pumpian, I., Certo, N., & Gruenewald, L. (1979). A strategy for developing chronological age appropriate and functional curricular content for severely handicapped adolescents and young adults. *Journal of Special Education, 13,* 81–90.

Brown, L., Nietupski, J., & Hamre-Nietupski, S. (1976). Criterion of ultimate functioning. In M. Thomas (Ed.), *Hey, don't forget about me! Education's investment in the severely, profoundly, and multiply handicapped* (pp. 16–35). Reston, VA: Division of Mental Retardation, The Council for Exceptional Children.

Bzoch, K., & League, R. (1971). *Assessing language skills in infancy.* Austin, TX: PRO-ED.

Carr, E. (1979). Teaching autistic children to use sign language: Some research issues. *Journal of Autism and Developmental Disorders, 9,* 345–359.

Carr, E., Newson, C., & Binkhoff, J. (1980). Escape as a factor in the aggressive behavior of two retarded children. *Journal of Applied Behavior Analysis, 13,* 101–117.

Cheseldine, S., & McConkey, R. (1979). Parental speech to young Down's syndrome children: An intervention study. *American Journal on Mental Deficiency, 83,* 612–620.

Clark, D., Baker, B., & Heifetz, L. (1982). Behavioral training for parents of mentally retarded children: Prediction of outcome. *American Journal of Mental Deficiency, 87,* 14–19.

Conroy, J., Efthimiou, J., & Lemanowicz, J. (1982). A matched comparison of the developmental growth of institutionalized and deinstitutionalized mentally retarded clients. *American Journal of Mental Deficiency, 86,* 581–587.

Donellan, A., Mirenda, P., Mesaros, R., & Fassbender, L. (1984). Analyzing the communicative functions of aberrant behavior. *Journal of the Association for Persons with Severe Handicaps, 9,* 210–212.

Dunst, C. (1980). *A clinical and educational manual for use with the Uzgiris and Hunt Scales of Infant Psychological Development.* Austin, TX: PRO-ED.

Durand, J. (1982). Analysis of intervention of self-injurious behavior. *Journal of the Association for Persons with Severe Handicaps, 7,* 44–53.

Garcia, E. (1974). The training generalization of conversational speech form in nonverbal retardates. *Journal of Applied Behavior Analysis, 7,* 137–149.

Goetz, L., Gee, K., & Sailor, W. (1985). Using a behavior chain interruption strategy to teach communication skills to students with severe disabilities. *Journal of the Association for Persons with Severe Handicaps, 10,* 21–30.

Graham, L. (1976). Language programming and intervention. In L. Lloyd (Ed.), *Communication assessment and intervention strategies* (pp. 371–422). Baltimore, MD: University Park Press.

Griffith, P., & Sanford, A. (1975). *Learning Accomplishment Profile for Infants.* Winston–Salem, NC: Kaplan School Supply Corp.

Guess, D., Sailor, W., & Baer, D. (1976). *Functional speech and language training for the severely handicapped.* Austin, TX: PRO-ED.

Halle, J., Marshall, A., & Spradlin, J. (1979). Time delay: A technique to increase language use and facilitate generalization in retarded children. *Journal of Applied Behavior Analysis, 12,* 431–440.

Hanna, R., Lippert, E., & Harris, A. (1982). *Developmental Communication Curriculum Inventory.* San Antonio, TX: Psychological Corporation.

Haring, N., & Bricker, D. (1976). Overview of comprehensive services for the severely/profoundly handicapped. In N. Haring & L. Brown (Eds.), *Teaching the severely handicapped* (pp. 17–32). New York: Grune & Stratton.

Heifetz, L. (1980). From consumer to middleman: Emerging roles for parents in the network of services for retarded children. In R. Abidin (Ed.), *Parent education and intervention handbook.* Springfield, IL: Charles Thomas.

Horner, R., & Budd, C. (1983). *Teaching manual sign language to a nonverbal student: Generalization of sign use and collateral reduction of maladaptive behavior.* Eugene: University of Oregon Center on Human Development.

Horstmeier, D., & MacDonald, J. (1978a). *Ready, Set, Go — Talk to Me.* San Antonio, TX: Psychological Corporation.

Horstmeier, D., & MacDonald, J. (1978b). *Environmental pre-language battery.* San Antonio, TX: Psychological Corporation.

House, L., & Rogerson, B. (1984). *Comprehensive screening tool for determining the optimal communication mode.* East Aurora, NY: United Educational Services, Inc.

Hunt, J. (1961). *Intelligence and experience.* New York: Ronald Press.

Iwata, B., Dorsey, M., Slifer, K., Bauman, K., & Richman, G. (1982). Toward a functional analysis of self-injury. *Analysis and Intervention in Developmental Disabilities, 2,* 3–20.

Kahn, J. (1982, May). *Cognitive training and its relationship to language of profoundly retarded children.* Paper presented at the American Association on Mental Deficiency Annual Convention, Boston, MA.

Kent, L. (1974). *Language acquisition program for the retarded or multiply impaired.* Champaign, IL: Research Press.

Keogh, W. J., & Reichle, J. (1985). Communication intervention for the "difficult-to-teach" severely handicapped. In S. Warren and A. Rogers-Warren (Eds.), *Teaching functional language: Generalization and maintenance of language skills* (pp. 157–194). Austin, TX: PRO-ED.

Kopchick, G., & Lloyd, L. (1976). Total communication for the severely language impaired: A 24-hour approach. In L. Lloyd (Ed.), *Communication assessment and intervention strategies* (pp. 501–521). Baltimore, MD: University Park Press.

Kozloff, M. (1973). *Reaching the autistic child: a parent training program.* Champaign, IL: Research Press.

Leonard, L., Steckol, D., & Panther, K. (1983). Returning meaning to semantic relations: Some clinical implications. *Journal of Speech and Hearing Disorders, 48,* 25–35.

Litt, M., & Schreibman, L. (1982). Stimulus specific reinforcement in the acquisition of receptive labels by autisitic children. *Analysis and Intervention in Developmental Disabilities, 1,* 171–186.

Looney, P. (1980). Instructional intervention with language-disordered learners. *Directive Teacher, 2,* 30–31.

MacDonald, J. (1978a). *Environmental Language Inventory.* San Antonio, TX: Psychological Corporation.

MacDonald, J. (1978b). *OLIVER: Parent-administered communication inventory.* San Antonio, TX: Psychological Corporation.

MacDonald, J., Blott, J., Gordon, K., Spiegal, B., & Hartmann, M. (1974). An experimental parent-assisted treatment program for preschool language-delayed children. *Journal of Speech and Hearing Disorders, 39,* 295–315.

MacDonald, J., & Gillette, Y. (1982). *ECO II: Ecological communication system.* Columbus, OH: Nisonger Center, The Ohio State University.

Manolson, A. (1983). *It takes two to talk.* Toronto, Canada: Hanen Early Language Resource Center.

McCormick, L., & Schiefelbusch, R. (1984). *Early language intervention.* Columbus, OH: Merrill Publishing Co.

McGee, G., Krantz, P., Mason, D., & McClannahan, L. (1983). A modified incidental-teaching procedure for autistic youth: Acquisition and generalization of receptive object labels. *Journal of Applied Behavior Analysis, 16,* 329–338.

McNerney, C. (1980). Patterns of nonverbal interaction in teachers of the severely handicapped: Toward an increased awareness of nonverbal communication. *Dissertation Abstracts International, 42,* 4401A–4402A.

McNutt, J., & Leri, S. (1979). Language differences between institutionalized and non-institutionalized retarded children. *American Journal of Mental Deficiency, 83,* 339–345.

Montague, J., Hutchinson, E., & Matson, E. (1975). Comparative computer content analysis of the verbal behavior of institutionalized and noninstitutionalized retarded children. *Journal of Speech and Hearing Disorders, 18,* 43–57.

Oliver, C., & Halle, J. (1982). Language training in the everyday environment: Teaching functional sign use to a retarded child. *Journal of the Association for Persons with Severe Handicaps, 8,* 50–62.

Owens, R. (1982a). Caregiver Interview and Environmental Observation, *Program for the acquisition of language in the severely impaired.* San Antonio, TX: Psychological Corporation.

Owens, R. (1982b). Developmental Assessment Tool, *Program for the Acquisition of language in the severely impaired.* San Antonio, TX: Psychological Corporation.

Owens, R. (1982c). *Diagnostic interactional survey (DIS).* San Antonio, TX: Psychological Corporation.

Owens, R., Bigler–Burke, L, & Lepre–Clark, C. (1985, November). *It can't happen here: Language facilitators with residential retarded populations.* Paper presented at the American Speech–Language–Hearing Association Annual Convention, Washington, DC.

Owens, R., & House, L. (1984). Decision-making processes in augmentative communication. *Journal of Speech and Hearing Disorders, 49,* 18–25.

Owings, N. (1985, May). *Communication and the mentally retarded.* Paper presented at Conference on Communication and the Developmentally Disabled: The State of the Art in 1985, Buffalo, NY.

Page, J. (1982, May). *The communication game: Pragmatics and early communication training for severely/profoundly retarded individuals.* Paper presented at the American Association on Mental Deficiency Annual Convention, Boston, MA.

Page, J., & Goossens, C. (1980, November). *Application of pragmatics to communication intervention with the severely/profoundly retarded.* Paper presented at the American Speech–Language–Hearing Association Annual Convention, Detroit, MI.

Phillips, J., & Balthazar, E. (1979). Some correlates of language deterioration in severely and profoundly retarded long-term institutionalized residents. *American Journal of Mental Deficiency, 83,* 402–408.

Polk, X., Schilmoeller, G., Emboy, L., Holman, J., & Baer, D. (1976, May). *Prompted generalization through experimenters' instructions: A parent training study.* Paper presented at the annual meeting of the Midwestern Association of Behavior Analysis, Chicago, IL.

Prior, H., Minnes, P., Coyne, T., Golding, B., Hendy, J., & McGillivray, J. (1979). Verbal interactions between staff and residents in an institution for the young mentally retarded. *Mental Retardation, 17,* 65–70.

Raymore, S., & McLean, J. (1972). A clinical program for carryover of articulation therapy with retarded children. In J. McLean, D. Yoder, & R. Schiefelbusch (Eds.), *Language intervention with the retarded.* Baltimore, MD: University Park Press.

Reichle, J., Rogers, N., & Barrett, C. (1984). Establishing pragmatic discriminations among the communicative functions of requesting, rejecting, and commenting in an adolescent. *Journal of the Association for Persons with Severe Handicaps, 9,* 31–36.

Reichle, J., & Yoder, D. (1979). Communication behavior of the severely and profoundly mentally retarded: Assessment and early stimulation strategies. In R.

York & E. Edger (Eds.), *Teaching the severely handicapped* (Vol. IV). Columbus, OH: Special Press.

Reidlich, C., & Herzfeld, M. (1983). *0 to 3 Years: An Early Language Curriculum.* Moline, IL: Linguisystems.

Ricke, J., Lynch, L., & Soltman, S. (1977). *Teaching strategies for language development.* New York: Grune & Stratton.

Rogers, S., D'Eugenio, D., Brown, S., Donovan, C., & Lynch, E. (1978). *Early Intervention Developmental Profile.* Ann Arbor, MI: University of Michigan Press.

Russo, J., & Owens, R. (1982). Development of an objective observation tool for parent-child interaction. *Journal of Speech and Hearing Disorders, 47,* 165–173.

Sacks, J., & Young, E. (1982). Infant Scale of Communication Intent. *Pediatrics Update, 7,* 1–5.

Salzburg, C., & Villani, T. (1983). Speech training by parents of Down Syndrome toddlers: Generalization across settings and instructional contexts. *American Journal of Mental Deficiency, 87,* 403–413.

Saunders, R., & Sailor, W. (1979). A comparison of three strategies of reinforcement on two-choice learning problems with severely retarded children. *Journal of the Association for Persons with Severe Handicaps* (Formerly AAESPH Review), *4,* 323–333.

Schuler, A., & Goetz, C. (1981). The assessment of severe language disabilities: Communicative and cognitive considerations. *Analysis and Intervention in Developmental Disabilities, 1,* 333–346.

Shane, H., & Bashir, A. (1980). Election criteria for the adoption of an augmentative communication system: Preliminary considerations. *Journal of Speech and Hearing Disorders, 45,* 408–414.

Shane, H., Lipshultz, R., & Shane, C. (1982). Facilitating the communicative interaction of nonspeaking persons in large residential settings. *Topics in Language Disorders, 2,* 73–84.

Snell, M. (1979). Higher functioning residents as language trainers of the mentally retarded. *Education and Training of the Mentally Retarded, 14,* 77–84.

Snell, M. (Ed.). (1983). *Systematic instruction of the moderately and severely handicapped* Columbus, OH: Merrill Publishing Company.

Spradlin, J., & Siegal, G. (1982). Language training in natural and clinical environments. *Journal of Speech and Hearing Disorders, 47,* 2–6.

Stafford, M., Sundberg, M., & Braam, S. (1978, May). *An experimental analysis of mands and tacts.* Paper presented at the Fourth Annual Conference of the Midwestern Association of Behavior Analysis, Chicago, IL.

Sternat, J., Nietupski, J., Messina, R., Lyon, S., & Brown, L. (1977). Occupational and physical therapy services for severely handicapped students: Towards a naturalized public school service delivery model. In E. Sontag, J. Smith, & N. Certo (Eds.), *Educational programming for the severely and profoundly handicapped* (pp. 263–278). Reston, VA: Division on Mental Retardation. The Council for Exceptional Children.

Sternberg, L. (1984). *Prelanguage communication programming techniques. Work-*shop at State University of New York at Geneseo.

Sternberg, L., Pegnatore, L., & Hill, C. (1983). Establishing interactive communication behaviors with profoundly mentally handicapped students. *Jour-*

nal of the Association for Persons with Severe Handicaps, 8, 39–46.

Stillman, R. (1978). *The Callier–Azuza Scale.* Dallas, TX: Callier Center for Communication Disorders, The University of Texas at Dallas.

Switzy, H., Rotatori, A., Miller, T., & Freagon, S. (1979). The developmental model and its implications for assessment and instruction for the severely/profoundly handicapped. *Mental Retardation, 17,* 167–170.

Swope, S., & Libergott, J. (1980). *What is the use of talking: The preschool language impaired child.* Workshop presented at the Al Sigl Center, Rochester, NY.

Tapajna, M., & Finn–Scardine, L. (1981, November). *Comprehensive program planning for non-speech communication.* Paper presented at American Speech–Language–Hearing Association Annual Convention, Los Angeles.

Tawney, J. (1979) *Programmed Environments Curriculum.* San Antonio, TX: Psychological Corporation.

Tizard, B., Cooperman, D., Joseph, A., & Tizard, J. (1973). Environmental effects on language development: A study of young children in long stay residential nurseries. *Annual Progress in Child Psychiatry and Child Development,* 705–728.

Uzgiris, I., & Hunt, J. (1975). *Assessment in infancy: Ordinal scales of intellectual development.* Urbana: University of Illinois Press.

Waldo, L. (1977). *Functional communication board training for the severely multihandicapped.* Paper presented at the American Speech and Hearing Association Annual Convention, Chicago.

Warren, S., & Kaiser, A. (1986). Incidental language teaching: A critical review. *Journal of Speech and Hearing Disorders, 51,* 291–298.

Watzlawick, P., Beavin, J., & Jackson, D. (1967). *Pragmatics of human communication.* New York: W. W. Norton & Co.

Wexler, K., Blau, A., Dore, J., & Leslie, S. (1982, April). *A pragmatic view of how nonverbal and vocal persons communicate.* Paper presented at New York State Speech–Language–Hearing Association Annual Convention, West Liberty, NY.

Wilcox, M., & Campbell, P. (1983, November). *Assessing communication in low-functioning multihandicapped children.* Paper presented at the American Speech–Language–Hearing Annual Convention, Cincinnati, OH.

Wulz, S., Hall, M., & Klein, M. (1983). A home-centered instructional communication strategy for severely handicapped children. *Journal of Speech and Hearing Disorders, 48,* 2–10.

Yoder, D. (1985, May). *Communication and the severely-profoundly retarded.* Paper presented at Conference on Communication and the Developmentally Disabled: The State of the Art in 1985, Buffalo, NY.

☐ *Functional Category Definitions*

Function	Examples

Semantics

Nomination: Naming a person or object using a single-or multiword name or a demonstrative plus a name.

Coffee, Shoe, This spoon
(Demonstrative + Nominative)

Location: Marking spatial relationships. Utterances may contain single location words or two-utterances containing an agent, action, or object plus a location word. The function can be demonstrated in response to "where" questions.

Partner: Where's hat?
Client: Chair.

Ball–table, Dog–chair, Throw me, Throw here (X + Locative)

Negation: Marking of nonexistence, rejection, and denial using single negative words or a negative followed by another word. Rejection generally develops first and marks an attempt to prevent or to stop an event. Nonexistence marks the absence of an object once present. This object has disappeared or is not present as expected. Denial marks rejection of a proposition.

No, Gone, No eat, No cookie
(Negative + X)

Partner: Time for medication.
Client: No (or No take).

Stop it, No want
(pushes object away)
Gone, Away, No,
No soda (Client drank it),
No ride (Ride is over)

Partner: See the cake?
Client: No cake.

Modification

Possession: Appreciating that an object belongs to or is frequently associated with someone. Single-word utterances signal the owner's name. In two-word utterances, the owner and the object are mentioned with stress on the owner.

Mine, Jane, My sock, Joe, Coffee
(Possessor + Possessed)

Soda (Client clutches soda tightly)

Function	Examples
Attribution: Using descriptors for properties not inherently part of an object.	Big, Little, Hot stove, Big shoe (Attribute + Attributed)
Recurrence: Understanding that an object can reappear or an event can be reenacted.	More, More run, More juice (Recurrence + Recurrer)
Notice: Signaling that an object has appeared or an event has happened, or that the communication partner's attention is sought.	Hi Tom, Bye, Look Jim (Introducer + X)
Action: Marking an activity by naming the actor (agent), action, or recipient of the action (object). Two-word utterances consist of combinations of these categories.	(While observing John throw a ball): John (Agent), Throw (Action), Ball (Object), John throw (Agent + Action), Throw ball (Action + Object)

Illocutionary

Function	Examples
Answer: Client responds to questions. The questioner's behaviors are a cue for the client's response; the response probably would not be produced without this cue. The client's responses are cognitively related to the question, although they need not be correct.	*Partner:* What's this? *Client:* Hammer. *Partner:* Is this a mirror? *Client:* No. (An answer whether correct or incorrect.)
Question: Client asks for information or verification by addressing the other person. The client's behavior is a stimulus and indicates that he expects an answer. The client may ask himself questions when engaged in egocentric play.	What's this?, That?, What?, Soda?
Reply: Client makes a meaningful response to the content of the other speaker's previous utterance, a verbal cue external to the client. The client may continue to build on the content and ignore the form of the utterance, such as responding to a question without answering it. In many cases, the client will build on the content *and* respond with an appropriate form. This category does not include mere repetition.	*Partner:* John, bring me the scissors. *Client:* Okay (or No). *Partner:* This is a nice room. *Client:* My room. *Partner:* Do you want a soda? *Client:* I love soda. (Not an answer, but a reply to the content.)
Elicitation: Client self-repeats in response to a request for clarification or in response to "Say 'X'." Elicitation is a form of reply.	*Client:* Eat ice cream. *Partner:* What? *Client:* Eat ice cream. *Partner:* Say "comb." *Client:* Comb.

Function	Examples
Continuant: Client signals that he is listening and wants to continue the interchange or that he missed what was said. Continuant is a form of reply.	Uh-huh, Okay, What?, Huh?
Declaration: Client makes a statement that is situationally related and for communication but is not in response to another speaker. The utterance is similar to a commentary. Cues are internal or situational not conversational. This category also includes situationally related phonemic exclamations.	Uh-oh, Car go (while watching out window). *Partner:* This is a nice room. *Client:* My room. (Reply) Big bed. (Declaration)
Practice: Client repeats or imitates in part or whole what he or another person says with little change in the intonation that would indicate a change of intent. In addition, internal replay without added, new information is considered *practice.* This category also includes counting, singing, babbling, or rhyming behaviors in which the client seems to be experimenting or rehearsing. Perseverative responses, even if the other person interjects an utterance between them, are considered *practice* as long as they do not mark discrete events or objects.	*Partner:* Shoe. *Client:* Shoe. *Partner:* I have a big cake. *Client:* Big cake. (Practice) Big, big, big. (Practice) *Partner:* Throw the ball. *Client:* Throw ball. (Throws) (Practice) Throw ball (Throws) (Declaration) *Partner:* Throw the ball. *Client:* Throw ball. (Throws) (Practice) Throw ball. (No action) (Practice) Throw ball. (No action) (Practice)
Name: Client labels an object or event that is present, but the label is not in response to a question. This behavior is usually accomplished by pointing or nodding.	Dress, That dress, This hat.
Suggestion, command, demand, request: The primary function of the client's utterance is to influence another person's behavior by getting that person to do something or to give the client permission. The form may vary but the function is the same.	Want comb, Stop that, Coffee, Help. *Client:* Throw ball. (Partner throws) Throw ball. (Partner throws) Throw ball. (Partner throws)

Adapted from Owens, R. (1982). *Program for the Acquisition of Language with the Severely Impaired (PALS).* San Antonio, TX: Psychological Corporation.

☐ *Stimulation Techniques*

☐ Speak in short, clear sentences. Words should be one or two syllables, and sentence length should be approximately three to five words.

☐ Use a small, core vocabulary that includes objects, actions, and people in the client's environment.

☐ Repeat sentences to the client, varying the form only slightly.
   Example: "See the dog? John, see dog?"

☐ Speak slowly and clearly. Pause between clauses and after content words. Content words should also be stressed and meaning interpretation aided by exaggerated intonation.

☐ Talk about objects and activities in which the client shows an interest. This procedure will help to map early semantic functions. Items should be discussed in a redundant manner that fosters semantic conceptualization.
   Example: "John want coffee? Coffee hot. Hot touch. Coffee burn. John, careful with coffee."

☐ Discuss your actions with the client.
   Example: "Mary (I am) putting mix in bowl. Now, Mary, crack egg. Put egg in bowl. Stir. Next, Mary add . . ."

☐ Gesture or use simple signs *when it helps* message interpretation.

☐ Be sure to allow an opportunity for the client to answer, even if it is very limited. Responding in turn is a valuable pragmatic skill. Do not dominate the interaction.

☐ Occasionally imitate the client's behavior, both vocal and nonvocal. Such imitation conveys caring to the client and also teaches a valuable social skill.

☐ Get the client's attention before any interaction. During the interaction, the client may need to be gently returned to the interaction.

☐ Try to display a genuine interest in client-based activities. This feeling can be fostered by care-givers who participate at the same physical level as the client.

☐ ☐ ☐

Additional general stimulation procedures for the *symbolic training levels:*

☐ Make sure that the client understands the words before being cued to use them expressively. With multiword phrases; assess to ensure that the client is not cuing to just one word.

☐ Reinforce all spontaneous utterances; they represent generalization.

☐ Expand or extend client words and phrases. Expansion is an immediate same-word-order response to a client utterance that makes that utterance more correct by adding a few other words or sounds. Extension is an immediate reply to a client utterance that uses pronouns and/or synonyms to extend the meaning into new contexts.

□ Do not ask too many questions because they may discourage the client from communicating.

Reprinted from Owens, R. (1982a). *The Program for the Acquisition of Language with the Severely Impaired (PALS)*. San Antonio, TX: Psychological Corporation.

☐ *Suggested Methods for Training Presymbolic Skills*

Level	Suggestions
Responding or turn-taking	☐ Use resonance training or behavior chain interruption variations. ☐ Use the client's most reliable input and output modes. ☐ Imitate the client. ☐ Engage in appropriate behavior such as tossing a ball, throwing horseshoes, or other such recreation or leisure activities. ☐ Build chains of attending–nonattending.
Motor imitation	☐ Progress from limb or trunk to head and then to the face and mouth for clients who will probably develop speech or an oral component to communication. ☐ Work on memory skills by first pairing similar movements, then dissimilar ones. Dissimilar pairings may require verbal, partial physical, or physical prompts for the client to produce the correct sequence. ☐ Reduce physical prompts quickly to forestall client reliance. Fade prompts rather than using an all-or-none pattern. ☐ Train deferred imitation toward the end of this level because this behavior requires the highest level of cognitive skills. ☐ Accept approximations from clients with motor problems because no specific behavior will lead to symbol use. Of interest is training the general notion of following your partner's model. ☐ Imitation with meaningful environmental objects can be trained shortly after limb imitation and will encourage exploration and problem solving. Name behaviors and objects for the client to aid concept development.
Object permanence	☐ Progress from finding an object hidden while the client is watching to one hidden while the client was absent or not watching.

Level	**Suggestions**

Object permanence *(continued)*

- ☐ Use many of the natural daily situations when we must search for missing items.
- ☐ First place the uncovered object within the client's reach and cue him/her to touch it. Progress to a partially covered object, then fully covered. A cloth over an object suggests its shape; a hard cover does not. Begin with cloth covers.
- ☐ Verbalize, sign, etc. "No," "All gone," "More," and object names for the client so that he/she gains the semantic concepts of negation (disappearance), recurrence, and appearance and reappearance. Use names of the hiding places to facilitate the semantic concept of location. Avoid use of "here" and "there"; these terms are too abstract.
- ☐ Visually impaired clients can use tactile methods.
- ☐ Watch for recognition of success in the client's facial expression initially.

Turn-taking

- ☐ Build small chains of turns using the behaviors previously trained.
- ☐ Go from turn-taking with objects or actions to eye contact. The goal is a brief coupling followed by a break, recoupling; and so on. Earlier visual attending training should focus on this later training and not try to develop client stares.

Functional use of objects

- ☐ Use familiar, environmental, functional objects.
- ☐ Remember that an object may have many functions that will foster development of a "definition" of that object.
- ☐ Demonstrate functions for severely motorically impaired clients. Provide opportunities for them to participate as much and in as many varied ways as possible.
- ☐ Train items that can form the basis of the client's early lexicon.

Means–ends

- ☐ Train objects as means first, then progress to people.
- ☐ Use two trainers when teaching client to signal another person. One trainer prompts the client while the other acts as the recipient of the client's signal. Remember that we are not yet at the level of gesturing. The recipient should be within touching range of the client.

Communicative gestures

- ☐ Train through imitation.
- ☐ Requesting is the easiest to train. Consequate naturally. Do not cue the client to request an item you can not or will not give or the behavior has no function.
- ☐ Remember when training pointing that the goal is not name discrimination. Do not offer the client a choice of items. Pointing can occur naturally very often in the environment.
- ☐ Cue each gesture in a distinctly different manner to aid the client's performance and to foster the development of intentions.

Level	Suggestions
Communicative gestures *(continued)*	☐ Initially accept the gesture alone but later require that the client gain his/her audience's attention.
Receptive language	☐ Train auditory memory for sound sequences, auditory recognition of environmental sounds, and word and/or sign recognition. ☐ Use objects for training that the client has used in the past, particularly in functional-use training. ☐ Use locational (correct object closer to the client) and physical prompts to aid learning of object names. Clients can signal name–referent pairing by pointing with hands, feet, head pointers, and so on, by signaling yes or no, by eye contact, electronically, and so on. Be creative. One client laughed when the wrong item was touched by the clinician.
Sound imitation	☐ Get spontaneous production under your control by reinforcing only those sounds that occur within a short period following the model. A response cannot be modified unless it is under the caregiver's control. ☐ Progress from any response to turn-taking to imitiation of specific sounds through shaping. Use sounds the client has produced spontaneously before or labial sounds that are easier to shape. ☐ Pair vocalizations and motor imitations initially, such as "whee-e-e," "m-m-m," "uh-oh," "bye," "pfb-b-b-b" (engine sound), sighs, yawns, and lip smacking.

CHAPTER 9

Optimizing Functional Communication for Persons with Severe Handicaps

JOE REICHLE, LAURA PICHÉ-CRAGOE,
JEFF SIGAFOOS, AND SCOTT DOSS

nthusiasm is growing for language intervention procedures designed to meet the needs of persons with severe handicaps. This enthusiasm has been the result of a number of advances, including:

- [ ] Recognition that there may be fewer prerequisites for beginning language intervention than previously believed (Reichle and Yoder, 1985; Rice, 1983);
- [ ] Demonstrations of successful implementation of pragmatically based graphic and gestural mode programs (Carr & Durand, 1985; Horner & Budd, 1985; Keogh & Reichle, 1985; and numerous others); and
- [ ] Increased opportunities for communicative emissions that occur as a result of instruction in more normalized environments.

Even though tremendous advances have been made, several important variables related to the functional use of communicative behavior are only beginning to be explored.

Preparation of this work was supported in part by Contract No. 300–82–0363 awarded to the University of Minnesota from the Division of Innovation and Development, Special Education Programs, U.S. Department of Education. The opinions expressed herein do not necessarily reflect the position or policy of the U.S. Department of Education, and no official endorsement should be inferred.

Many of these variables are outgrowths of the same advances that led to our current effectiveness in teaching persons with severe handicaps to communicate. The focus of this chapter is to address a number of issues that currently challenge those working with persons who exhibit severe handicaps in their attempts to determine when to begin communication intervention programs, and how best to implement these programs to ensure the optimal use of skills that are taught. Seven specific topics will be addressed in this chapter:

1. Determining when to implement communication intervention;
2. Selecting communicative functions that should be targeted in initial intervention;
3. Selecting the form of behavior to use in initial communicative intervention;
4. Ensuring valid use of established communicative repertoires;
5. Addressing variables that are likely to result in the use of communicative behavior in natural contexts;
6. Implementing communication intervention in an effort to replace socially unacceptable communicative methods;
7. Ensuring that a learner does not become overly dependent in using newly established communicative behavior in situations in which it is inappropriate and considering criteria to use in selecting particular augmentative mode(s).

DETERMINING WHEN TO IMPLEMENT COMMUNICATION INTERVENTION (ARE THERE COMMUNICATIVE PREREQUISITES?)

Keogh and Reichle (1985) pointed out that even though from birth to about 8 months of age infants are unable to carry out "goal-oriented actions," they do exercise a significant amount of control over their environment — whether intentionally or incidentally. For example, most infants cry at birth. Cries often produce contingent results (e.g., attention, food, relief from discomfort). Ample evidence exists to support the view that the frequency of vocalizing is influenced by its antecedents and consequences (Rheingold, Gerwitz, & Ross, 1959; Weisberg, 1963). Whether the increased frequency is "intentional" or not, the message interpreted by the caregiver or listener is that the child wants or needs something. Some persons with severe handicaps get no further than the cry. However, we do know that vocal behavior that is reinforced may, at some point, become an operant response class, under the control of the prevailing reinforcement contingencies. Because the intervention strategies that are successful in establishing requesting behavior require only that the learner emit some socially acceptable motor or vocal behavior, we believe that intervention can proceed with few prerequisites other than the identification of persons, objects, or events that are likely to reinforce the selection of a socially acceptable discrete voluntary behavior that will ultimately serve as the communicative emission.

Attempts to establish initial communicative skills often become stymied because of a number of cognitive prerequisites (in the areas of means–end, cause and effect, and imitation) that are not currently part of the learner's repertoire.

Reichle and Karlan (1985), as well as Reichle and Keogh (1986) reviewed the relationship between cognitive prerequisites and the establishment of early communicative behavior and concluded that

1. The relationship between behavior and its consequences can be taught. Consequently, to require the development of certain cognitive classes prior to instituting communication training, as some have suggested, may not be warranted.
2. In part, the value of imitative behavior in initial language intervention rests on its use as a response prompt. In the verbal mode, it is very difficult to prompt a response unless the learner's vocal behavior is under imitative control. However, a variety of prompts other than imitative models (e.g., physical guidance, gestures) may be used to establish graphic and gestural mode communicative behavior.

Reichle and Keogh (1986) have suggested that if a learner produced discrete voluntary behavior and several positive reinforcers can be identified, intervention to establish a generalized requesting repertoire may be initiated. Further, if no positive reinforcers can be identified, but situations and/or objects that the learner actively dislikes (i.e., negative reinforcers) are identified, a generalized rejecting response may be taught.

The conclusion that certain cognitive skills may facilitate the acquisition of communicative behavior seems reasonable. At the same time, available data do not support the lack of certain cognitive prerequisites as sufficient evidence to exclude learners with severe handicaps from communicative intervention (Rice, 1983). The important predictors of success in early communication intervention efforts are the identification of positive and/or negative reinforcers. When this is accomplished, generalized communicative symbols and gestures for requesting, rejecting and other functions may be taught.

SELECTING COMMUNICATIVE FUNCTIONS THAT SHOULD BE TARGETED IN INITIAL INTERVENTION

There is a growing body of literature describing intervention procedures for establishing communicative repertoires in persons with severe handicaps. In addition, there is growing emphasis on considering pragmatic functions to organize early intervention efforts. Keogh and Reichle (1985), for example, suggested teaching one response (e.g., "want") as a generalized request, another response (e.g., "no") as a generalized rejection, and other responses (e.g., "book," "pop," "cracker") for providing information. Consequently, at the single-symbol level, the use of "want" paired with reaching toward a bottle of pop would be interpreted as a request. The production of the "pop" symbol in isolation would be treated as an example of providing information and would be reinforced with something other than pop (e.g., "That's right!"). Producing a "no" symbol when pop was offered would be interpreted as a reject and the pop would be removed. At the two-symbol level, "want + pop" would be interpreted as a specific request, and "drink + pop" would be interpreted as a comment or provision of information, with the reinforcer again being something other than pop. Several recent investigations have successfully implemented intervention protocols addressing the intervention logic delineated by Keogh and Reichle to teach persons with severe handicaps an initial repertoire of communication behavior (Piché-Cragoe, Reichle, & Sigafoos, 1986; Reichle & Brown, 1986; Reichle, Rogers, & Barrett, 1984; Reichle & Sigafoos, 1986).

The rationale for making initial vocabulary correspond to a specific pragmatic function is supported by the findings of LaMarre and Holland (1985), who found that nonhandicapped preschoolers had difficulty generalizing the use of identical verbal response topographies across requesting (mand) and providing information (tact) functions. Calculator and Delaney (1985) have corroborated this finding with a developmentally disabled population who failed to utilize newly acquired vocabulary across multiple communicative functions.

Several arguments also support the selection of generalized requesting as the initial communicative function to teach. First, generalized request responses are likely to allow learners to access a wide variety of reinforcers in natural environments with little intervention. In addition, establishing a generalized requesting response allows the acquisition of a functional response class without having to focus simultaneously on the acquisition of a discrimination among different symbols [that is, a learner may be taught to touch a single symbol in the absence of any others as an initial requesting strategy (see Keogh and Reichle, 1985)].

Teaching rejecting as an initial communicative topography also offers several advantages. Again, numerous opportunities to use a generalized reject symbol may exist in the learner's natural environment (particularly with learners who emit high rates of excess behavior to escape or avoid scheduled activities). For some learners, the use of a generalized reject symbol may serve to decelerate existing excess behaviors by producing a socially acceptable yet functionally equivalent replacement behavior (Carr & Durand, 1985; Mirenda & Donnellan, 1986). However, the disadvantage that results from teaching a generalized reject as the initial topography may be that it establishes the interventionist as a person who delivers aversive objects or events, rather than the presenter of positive reinforcers. To offset this potential problem, Reichle and Keogh (1986) have suggested the implementation of concurrent intervention procedures to teach both generalized requesting and generalized rejecting early in language intervention.

A third communicative function often targeted for initial intervention involves social exchanges that are tied solely to generalized reinforcers. For example, numerous investigators (MacDonald, 1985; Murphy & Messer, 1977; Ratner & Bruner, 1978; and others) have reported that nonhandicapped children engage in turn-taking events that involve both gestural and vocal behavior. Piaget, for example, reported instances in which children participated in child-initiated sequences of vocal imitation in which each child systematically took turns vocalizing. At later points in development, investigators have described instances in which children show and point (Murphy & Messer, 1977) to objects and events with the only consequence being the social reaction obtained from another person (Reichle & Yoder, 1979). Many of the behaviors are emitted while the communicative partner is already attending to the learner. Consequently, it is difficult to argue that the behaviors are maintained by attention per se.

Several language interventionists have written about the importance of including these social exchanges as initial targets for communicative intervention (MacDonald, 1985; McLean & Snyder–McLean, 1978). Although these early interpersonal exchanges are important, many individuals who have severe handicaps may not be reinforced by such purely social exchanges. The prospect for conversationally based communication intervention strategies may therefore be less straightforward with such individuals.

Three general communicative functions (rejecting, requesting, and social exchange) have been described as potential initial communication intervention targets. With most individuals, instructional objectives representing each of these classes of communication can be implemented concurrently. However, some individuals may have so few obvious dislikes that it may be difficult to implement a "rejection" intervention. Similarly, there may be learners for whom the identification of positive reinforcers is very difficult. If such is the case, the interventionist may wish to initially implement only the program (requesting or rejecting) for which instructional stimuli have been identified.

SELECTING THE FORM OF BEHAVIOR TO BE USED IN COMMUNICATION INTERVENTION

Persons exhibiting severe handicaps may have idiosyncratic methods for requesting, rejecting, or commenting, which have previously been or are currently effective, such as learners who request permission to leave an activity to go to the bathroom by holding their crotch, or request cookies by rubbing their stomach. Sometimes (as in our former example), the communicative form represents socially unacceptable behavior. In other instances, the communicative gestures may be effective only if others have learned how to interpret the response [e.g., producing loud vocalization (da) when hungry.] The dilemma for the interventionist is whether to maintain a communicative behavior that is already part of the learner's repertoire but marginally acceptable socially or to maintain a communicative behavior that is not readily understood by the general community but is produced accurately. The alternative is to teach a new behavior that is socially acceptable. Maintaining a current yet socially questionable behavior may result in quicker generalized use (as the focus of the intervention is designed to increase the frequency of an existing behavior rather than to establish a new one). However, the speed of initial generalized use must be weighed carefully against the social validity of the behavior established. If listeners in community settings do not readily comprehend the learner's communicative repertoire, the interventionist is placed in the awkward position of being forced to establish an augmentative system to supplement the learner's original method of communicating. If such a supplement is necessary, any intervention time saved as a result of selecting an existing behavior may be neutralized. Furthermore, the graphic symbol or gesture targeted to supplement the original idiosyncratic response form might create an additional set of awkward alternatives for the interventionist.

One solution to this dilemma involves establishing a new and readily understandable response form, while at the same time extinguishing the use of the original symbol. Unfortunately, this solution may result in learners emitting emotional outbursts (e.g., aggression) when a formerly acceptable communicative emission no longer produces a reinforcer. These outbursts may also result in erratic performance during the early phases of intervention. A second solution involves teaching a discrimination between contexts that reinforce the use of the original symbol from contexts that reinforce the use of the newly established form.

In general, the application of the following set of criteria will result in a decision that is in the learner's best interest. If a behavior already part of the learner's behavioral repertoire is to be established as an acceptable communicative behavior: (1) it must not be part of an existing repertoire of excess behavior (i.e., although shaking ones head to indicate "no" may be a socially acceptable behavior, some learners may emit high rates of stereotypic back and forth head bobbing); (2) the general public must be able to guess its meaning; and (3) its emission must not call undue negative attention to the user (the topography used is socially acceptable). Even though some existing gestures used by the learner may be targeted as communication goals, there is a need to determine a long-term empirically driven strategy to plan augmentative communication systems that will serve the learner over time. Next, decision-making strategies used to accomplish this goal will be examined.

SELECTING AUGMENTATIVE MODES

Because there may be a tendency to plan only for the learner's current rather than long-term needs in selecting communicative topographies to supplement vocal or verbal communicative production, it becomes important to consider objective methods for selecting augmentative modes that serve the learner's current as well as future needs. Reichle and Karlan (1985) suggested that traditional augmentative decision rules tend to advocate a two-tiered decision-making process in which the learner's candidacy for *some* system is followed by a second set of criteria to determine *which* augmentative system might be the most appropriate. An alternative to a two-tiered decision-making process is the simultaneous consideration of a learner's candidacy for some system and also the specific type of system(s) best suited for that learner. This decision-making process is based on the difficulty in determining the "best" communication system for a particular learner in the absence of empirical data.

Alpert (1980) identified a training and assessment procedure for determining the optimal nonspeech mode to use with autistic children after the decision has been made to consider speech alternatives. Basically, this procedure involves teaching specific language responses in two *successively* taught nonspeech modes. This strategy might be considered to be a process for generating "performance baselines" in learning alternative language skills (i.e., signing and graphics). By comparing the respective acquisition rates between baselines, the interventionist may be able to identify empirically a single modality for long-term intervention.

In addition, Alpert (1980) pointed out some of the risks in using decision rule strategies such as those proposed by Chapman and Miller (1980), and Shane (1980), especially with individuals who have normal hearing and the physiologic capacity for producing speech. According to Alpert (1980), for such individuals,

> Alternative nonspeech intervention will be attempted only after
> the child has persistently failed to learn functional vocal behavior.
> This is unfortunate, for not only does the child remain without a
> means of communicating during the entire training period, but as
> the child gets older, the probability that he will acquire functional
> communication skills may be reduced. (p. 401)

Alpert's (1980) selection strategy suggests that decisions regarding
the need for and best type of augmentative system follow a preventive
logic. That is, rather than specifying an arbitrarily imposed failure
criterion, Alpert suggests utilizing learner-generated data to stimulate
the decision-making process. As such, there is no need in Alpert's decision process to set a specific selection criterion (i.e., the learner must perform at "x" level of accuracy to select a specific system). Outcomes from
Alpert's system would result in either the selection of a superior
augmentative mode or no clear evidence to support the selection of a
single mode.

Although useful, there may be potential disadvantages in Alpert's
approach. The use of a sequential selection strategy (implementing only
one mode at a time) may delay the learner's acquisition of meaningful
communicative skills if, for example, the mode to be sampled second
proves to be the most effective. To accept the necessity of sequentially
sampling modes, it would be vital to determine the disadvantages, if
any, in implementing concurrent intervention in two separate augmentative modes. If a concurrent sampling of learner performance in two or
more modes could be achieved, the superiority of one augmentative system over another might become obvious at an earlier point. In addition,
although learner performance is critical, other criteria may be important
to consider (e.g., communicative demands of the learner's environments
such as whether the learner's environment includes persons familiar
with sign language). Additional considerations beyond learner's performance are detailed in Shane (1986). Alternatives for the implementation of concurrent modality sampling are detailed in Reichle and
Karlan (1985).

In general, a strategy of establishing performance baselines in the
selection of augmentative systems has great appeal in that it is an
empirically based decision rule model sensitive to individual differences. Also, it leads interventionists to engage in preventative practices
regarding communicative deficits.

ENSURING VALID USE OF ESTABLISHED COMMUNICATIVE REPERTOIRES

Traditionally, explicit requesting has been taught without requiring the
learner to match his/her verbal request to the object selected (Guess,

Sailor, & Baer, 1974; Kent, 1974). That is, the object requested by the learner is selected dutifully by the interventionist and given to the learner. In effect, the learner need not attend to the response emitted because any response in his/her repertoire is likely to be reinforced.

Tetlie and Reichle (1986) reported that among persons with severe handicaps, the form of the requests emitted often did not correspond to the object selected, even though learners had acquired and were maintaining signs and/or graphic symbols of the objects available. During each of 40 probes, two objects were made available to the learner. Initially, objects were offered nonverbally. If this failed to evoke a response, the experimenter verbally prompted the learner to select an object (e.g., "What do you want?"). Following emission of a request, learners were allowed to select one of the available objects. Results suggested that, for the most part, learner's requests did not match their reinforcer selections at levels above those predicted by chance.

The finding that young learners frequently lack a correspondence between verbal and nonverbal behavior is well documented in the literature (Baer, Williams, Osnes, & Stokes, 1984; Guevremont, Osnes, & Stokes, 1986a, 1986b; Israel & Brown, 1977; Risley & Hart, 1968). However, most often, as in the preceding investigations, the phenomena has been examined in describing or commenting rather than requesting functions. During describing exchanges there may often be no differential consequences for corresponding versus noncorresponding emissions. For example, an adult comes home after spending 2 hours at a nightclub and is greeted by a spouse querying, "Where have you been?" The response "Late at work again!" may well be greeted with a reinforcing statement ("You work too hard") because the spouse doesn't realize that the statement was less than truthful.

Requests, on the other hand, are subject to differential reinforcement. If you ask for a soft drink at a restaurant thinking that you had requested a beer, you will undoubtedly be disappointed when the soft drink arrives at the table and will, no doubt, take steps to ensure that the same error does not occur in the future.

Because the initial repertoire of a person with severe handicaps may consist largely of response forms that produce a variety of reinforcers and because the effort to produce a request specific to the object(s) available may represent a discrimination not part of the learner's repertoire, the learner may adopt a strategy that involves touching some symbol indiscriminatively because, by and large, the result will be fairly acceptable. That is, any reinforcer may be better than nothing at all.

Piché-Cragoe et al. (1986) described a procedure used to establish valid requesting with learners who were severely intellectually delayed. An array of two objects were presented to the learner; one for which the learner had acquired an object label and the other for which the learner had no label but could access by emitting a generalized request "want." During intervention opportunities, the behaviors of emitting a correct sign or symbol (i.e., either "want" or "want + object label") and selection of the corresponding object were treated as a two-component chain of behaviors. To increase the probability of a correct selection response, some stimulus arrays consisted of a preferred object, for which the learner had an object label, paired with an object that had little reinforcement value. During other opportunities, a reinforcer for which the learner had no object label was paired with an object that had little reinforcement value. For example, a learner might be presented with one array consisting of a ball (reinforcer for which an object label had been taught) and an eraser (a nonreinforcing object). The teacher displayed the array and asked, "What do you want?" and then prompted the learner to produce " want + ball." After producing "want + ball," the learner was allowed to select an object. If the learner signed "want + ball" but attempted to select eraser, the array was removed before he/she touched an object. Results obtained with five persons with severe handicaps suggested that the procedure was successful in establishing valid requests, that is, learners would select the object that corresponded to their previous request.

Intuitively, the truthfulness of communicative behavior is accepted unless there is good reason to believe otherwise. However, the existing data suggest that unless some component of the intervention requires the learner to chain his/her verbal and nonverbal behavior, correspondence between the two repertoires may not emerge. A lack of correspondence may represent a significant although inconspicuous reason why established communicative behavior does not appear to be used functionally. At the very least, *occasional* probes that require the learner to emit a request and chain to that request the selection of the matching object should be implemented. Although such probes require additional preparation, the information obtained may result in the identification of a subtle yet significant communicative deficiency.

ADDRESSING VARIABLES THAT ARE LIKELY TO RESULT IN THE USE OF COMMUNICATIVE BEHAVIOR IN NATURAL CONTEXTS

Halle (1982) stated that teaching language in the natural environment requires that the learner initiate communication in the absence of explicit instructional stimuli (e.g., verbal cues, gestural prompts). However, as Warren and Rogers–Warren (1980) noted, most intervention strategies teach children to respond to just such stimuli rather than to initiate communicative behavior in their absence. Most individuals who serve persons with severe handicaps agree that their clients are not particularly good at using their communicative repertoire in a self-initiated fashion.

The complexity of addressing variables involved in establishing self-initiated (spontaneous) communicative behavior begins with the difficulty in attempting to define spontaneity (see Halle, Chapter 7 of this volume). For many, the definition of spontaneity is rooted in the absence of verbal cues as the discriminative stimulus for language use. Stokes and Baer (1977) suggested a variety of variables that influence the generalized use of behavior (i.e., train sufficient examplars, teach common stimuli), which suggest that the spontaneous emission of behavior, for some learners, may result from less rigid or explicit instructional paradigms.

One method suggested by Stokes and Baer (1977), — teaching common stimuli — may minimize the generalization demands on the learner. This can be accomplished by including within treatment the social and physical stimuli that are salient and functional in the learner's natural environment. Some examples of teaching common stimuli include targeting objects for intervention that the learner is likely to encounter outside of the training environment, or utilizing persons in the learner's natural environment (e.g., teachers, aides) to carry out the intervention. Among the stimuli that may control communicative emissions are the presence of others, the proximity of those present, the attentiveness of those present, and whether a potential listener is producing behavior that calls attention to him/herself. Additional variables involve the presence of objects or events about which to speak. These include the proximity of referents to the learner, visibility of the referents, and sounds or smells of the referents. In addition, the learner's immediate prior history with the referent may influence the probability that he/she will produce communicative behavior. For example, if a learner has just eaten a cookie but is not satiated, the fact that he/she has sampled a reinforcer may result in a spontaneous request controlled by this prior experience even though no cookie is present.

To date, intervention literature addressing spontaneous communicative use among persons with severe handicaps is sparse. Halle, Baer and Spradlin (1979) taught several persons with severe handicaps to request their meal in a cafeteria by using a time–delay procedure to fade a controlling verbal prompt. Gobbi, Cipani, Hudson, and Lapenta-Neudeck (1986) used a time–delay procedure to transfer control of requests from modeled or vocal prompts to the presence of reinforcers in two children with severe retardation. Charhop, Schreibmann, and Thebodeau (1985) also described the use of a time–delay procedure to increase the frequency of nonprompted speech in seven children with autism. Carr and Kologinsky (1983) established the presence of an interventionist as the controlling stimulus to establish a spontaneous requesting repertoire in several persons with autism. None of the preceding investigators, however, attempted to determine directly whether learners came to their respective requesting tasks with an existing strategy for recruiting their listeners' attention as part of the requesting episode. Each of the preceding investigators made the assumption that when a learner emitted a request, his or her listener would be attending.

Traditionally, the ability to recruit the attention of potential communicative partners is viewed as an important prerequisite skill for spontaneous communicative behavior. Of course, in the vocal mode, whenever an utterance is produced it has the potential of recruiting the listener's attention. Unfortunately, some augmentative systems do not have this capability. In gestural and graphic modes, the speaker must create a sound or position him or herself to be seen or engage in other attention-getting behaviors if listeners are not already attending. Regardless of the topography of the attention-getting device, recruiting an audience necessitates the emission of a chain of at least two discrete behaviors (attention getting + intended utterance) before the communicative response can have its desired effect.

However, attention signals are laborious to establish during the early phases of augmentative communication intervention (Sobsey & Reichle, 1986). To teach an attention-getting response, a response approximation must be emitted prior to the delivery of the instructor's attention. If the teacher delivers a response prompt, attention may not serve as a reinforcer for the call (because the teacher is already attending). However, teaching attention-getting responses and establishing a repertoire of signs or graphic symbols or spoken vocabulary, represent concurrent intervention objectives. For example, let us assume that the learner is being taught to use a communication board. Further, let us assume that the learner has insufficient oral motor control to emit vocal speech. At the completion of an interactive episode (centered around an activity that was reinforcing for the learner), the interventionist might begin to depart. If the behavior selected to represent "attention getting" was emitted, the interventionist would reappear and continue the interaction. During other daily activities in which *object reinforcers were offered* by the interventionist, the learner could be taught (1) to use either a generalized requesting strategy "want" to request or an explicit request strategy "want + object name" and (2) to refrain from using the "attention-getting" response.

After an attention-getting response has been established, procedures can be implemented to ensure that attention-getting responses are emitted only in those situations in which an audience must be recruited. During the implementation of this procedure, objects used during requesting intervention would be placed in locations that were near and available to the learner but could not be readily accessed by him/her. For example, if a can of soda represented a frequently requested item, the learner might be assigned some task near a vending machine (which the learner had not yet been taught to use). On some occasions, the interventionist would remain near the learner and continue to focus attention on him/her. During this condition, the learner should request soda by producing "want + soda." On other occasions, the interventionist might be further away and not attending to the learner. This latter condition would require the attention signal followed by "want + soda" after the interventionist had appeared.

Although reasonable, the preceding strategy assumes that attention signals originally taught to obtain social interaction will generalize to situations in which an attention signal is used as part of a chain of behaviors leading to a request for objects. If such generalization does not readily occur, or, if the learner is not reinforced by social interaction, a different approach to the establishment of an attention-getting signal may be warranted.

One alternative, which avoids the necessity of teaching the learner to discriminate between situations in which it is necessary to produce an attention-getting signal from those in which the learner already has the listener's attention, is to teach the learner to chain an attention-getting response to all requests. The attention signal could, in effect, be used as the generalized request. However, one disadvantage of this strategy would be the frequent disruptions that could occur from the noise of the attention-getting signal being used in situations in which it was not necessary (i.e., when the learner already had the listener's attention).

Thus far our discussion of communicating in natural contexts has focused on initiating interactions. Another critical area of concern with respect to contextually acceptable communication involves the ability to continue to exchange (maintain) communicative behavior in the context of a conversation (MacDonald, 1985). The inability to respond rapidly to previous communicative behavior and to switch easily from being a speaker to being a listener and then back to being a speaker is highly contributory to atypical conversational patterns reported among communication aid users (Beukelman et al., 1985; Farrier, Yorkston, Marriner, & Beukelman, 1985; Light, Collier, & Parnes, 1985). Those who have investigated the use of communication aids are in unanimous agreement that the use of such aids results in a very slow response rate when compared with the response rate of vocal speech (Yoder & Kraat, 1984).

Although much of the interactional deficiencies may be attributed to the augmentative aid user, speaking partners may contribute significantly to the deficiency. To compensate for the slow output of the non-vocal speaker, the speaking member of a dyad frequently falls into a "yes–no" probe strategy. In this interactional technique, the verbal communicative partner steers the interaction by asking a high proportion of questions that demand only a head nod or some other easy-to-produce signal from the nonvocal partner. This technique avoids long pauses in the conversational exchange that might otherwise occur while the communication aid user is selecting a message. Other speaking individuals appear to rely less on "yes–no" probes and more on initiating two topics of conversation (one that requires a response from the nonspeaking listener and one that does not). For example, the speaking member of the dyad may ask "Where are we going today?" While the nonspeaking individual is formulating a message, the verbal member of the dyad may initiate the second topic, "Boy, I forgot to put the cat outside." During subsequent exchanges the speaking member of the dyad may continue to pursue both topics. The difficulty for the communication aid user is obvious. He/she must emit a response relevant to the first topic and at the same time listen to a different topic. This task is analogous to one in which the listener might try to write a letter while carrying on a conversation. In the double-topic conversational strategy just described, it is likely that the communication aid user will pursue the topic that requires the most obligatory responses, as it has become generally accepted that communication aid users have a tendency to engage in communicative emissions primarily when they are obligated to do so.

At first glance it would appear that communication aid users engage in atypical interactional strategies. In fact, it appears that their verbal speaking partners also engage in atypical interactional styles. There may be several implications relative to intervention, none of which have, for the most part, been empirically scrutinized.

Few interventionists have emphasized implementing instructional procedures aimed at increasing the speed of communicative behavior. However, speed of emission is easily quantified and lends itself well to a changing criterion design in which reinforcement is contingent on increasingly quicker emissions of a target message. Vocabulary selected for this type of intervention might be those items that are used fairly often in obligatory daily routines. A second strategy may involve allowing the augmentative system user to rely on mixed-mode communication. For example, headshake gestures to represent "yes" and "no" are socially acceptable and may be much quicker to emit than touching the symbols "yes" and "no." When asked "What do you want?" in the presence of a desired object, it may be quicker to point to the actual object than to find the appropriate symbol (depending on the method of symbol display). Finally, educating the speaking communicative partner in the use of time-saving interactive strategies that do not intrude on the learner's communicative intent can assist in speeding up the interaction. For example, in spoken conversation, it is considered impolite to interrupt in order to guess the content of a message prior to its completion. Although in nonspeaking–speaking dyads, interruption may be very helpful as a method of compensating for the augmentative system user's slow rate of communicative production, it may result in a loss of communicative control by the nonspeaking person (see Bedrosian, Chapter 10 of this volume).

Frequently, parents and professionals assume that an augmentative system user's lack of spontaneity would be solved if the individual could access an electronic aid that produces synthesized speech. Although electronic communication aids represent marvelous inventions, serious limitations must be considered in their use.

One example lies in the area of synthesized speech output. Recent studies examining the intelligibility of synthetic speech (Hoover, Reichle, Van Tassel, & Cole, in press; Logan, Pisoni, & Green, 1985) have found that inexpensive text-to-speech synthesizers such as Votrax and Echo II were significantly less intelligible than natural speech. Consequently it may not be reasonable to expect that an individual, after being fit with a speech producing electronic aid, will automatically be better understood.

In spite of intelligibility difficulty, improvement in the recognition of synthetic speech as a result of practice has been reported (Greenspan, Nusbaum, & Pisoni, 1985; Hoover et al., in press; Schwab, Nusbaum, & Pisoni, 1983). Although practice may be of benefit to those who interact frequently with a communication aid user, it does not address the need for highly intelligible messages in a variety of community settings where there will be little opportunity for a practice effect to influence intelligibility.

Hoover et al. (in press) suggested that highly redundant and long utterances helped improve the intelligibility of the final word of an utterance (e.g., I'm hungry, let's *eat*). With Echo II or Votrax, an intellectually normal college student typically recognizes about 20 percent of the single-syllable speech-synthesized words such as "eat". When placed in a redundant context such as "I'm hungry, let's *eat*" the intelligibility of the final word increases to about 70 percent. Logically, one might conclude that longer redundant messages should be "programmed" behind symbol spaces. Although doing this will improve the intelligibility of synthesized speech for an intellectually normal adult listener, the effects on a person with intellectual and/or communicative handicaps are difficult to predict.

Being able to communicate quickly is an aspect of interactional efficiency taken for granted in the verbal mode. Speed of communication represents a viable intervention target that cannot automatically be resolved with electronic technology. Further increasing the speed with which communicative exchanges occur is not the sole responsibility of the augmentative system user. Speaking individuals can alter their interactional styles to allow the nonverbal participant an opportunity to gain experience in becoming faster in emitting messages.

IMPLEMENTING COMMUNICATION INTERVENTION IN AN EFFORT TO REPLACE SOCIALLY UNACCEPTABLE COMMUNICATION METHODS

A substantial amount of excess behavior (i.e., self-injury, tantrums, aggression) may be socially motivated, falling into two broad classes: escape behavior controlled by negative reinforcement, and attention-seeking behavior controlled by positive reinforcement (Carr & Durand, 1985). Many behavior problems may also be accurately conceptualized as a primitive form of nonverbal communicative behavior.

Evidence that excess behavior may be functionally controlled by escape from or avoidance of aversive stimulation has been empirically demonstrated with respect to aggressive behavior (Carr, Newsom, & Binkoff, 1980), tantrums (Carr & Newsom, in press), and self-stimulatory behavior (Durand & Carr, 1983). Other investigators (Weeks & Gaylord-Ross, 1981) successfully manipulated task demands (easy versus hard) and obtained corresponding changes in excess behavior. In addition, evidence is overwhelming that excess behaviors are maintained by positive reinforcement contingent on the emission of these behaviors (see Carr & Durand, 1985).

Carr and Lovaas (1982) speculated that to the degree that establishing a socially acceptable escape or attention-getting response provides consistent access to reinforcement (positive for attention getting; negative for escape or avoidance), one would expect the alternative response to gradually replace the problem behavior provided that the problem behavior is less consistently reinforced. Several independent investigaions appear to provide corroborative evidence for Carr and Lovaas's speculation. Ainsworth & Bell (1977) reported that learners who cried least often had the greatest number of alternative behaviors to recruit attention and escape or avoid presentation of undesired events. Schodell and Reiter (1968) observed that autistic learners who displayed socially acceptable communicative behavior emitted fewer instances of self-injurious behavior. Finally, Talkington, Hall, and Altman (1971) reported that noncommunicating persons with intellectual delays emitted a higher frequency of aggressive behavior than communicating persons with intellectual delays.

The notion that excess behavior may serve communication functions for some learners with severe handicaps is intriguing for several reasons. First, one of the defining characteristics of severely handicapped learners is the presence of very limited behavioral repertoires, in particular, the absence or relative deficit of "normal" communication skills. Severely handicapped learners, like the rest of us, need to communicate their needs and preferences to others and they will use the behavioral tactics at their disposal that reliably produce desired outcomes. If excess behaviors that are reinforced in social contexts satisfy this need, the individual has already demonstrated his/her ability to communicate. Second, the viewpoint that much excess behavior may have communicative intent is intrinsically educative in orientation because it suggests ways of reducing excess behavior by replacing it with more socially acceptable means of producing desired outcomes rather than simply suppressing the excess behavior (Meyer & Evans, 1986). In other words, if the communicative intent of an excess behavior for a particular learner can be identified via a functional analysis (or at least if a good working hypothesis can be generated about the function that the excess behavior is serving for the person), the interventionist should be able to use this information to select appropriate forms of communication to teach to the person. By identifying the communication function of the excess behavior, the interventionist has also, by definition, identified an important instructional goal for the learner.

When considering the communicative intent of excess behavior among learners with severe handicaps, it is necessary to establish that communicative alternatives exist at very rudimentary levels. In normal development, Wolff (1969) presented evidence that infants display socially oriented crying in a number of different situations. By the third week of life, mothers were capable of differentiating between cries of distress and cries that were produced simply because of the attention that they produce. By the age of 3 months, infants also cried when certain favorite toys were removed.

Ainsworth and Bell (1977) in a longitudinal study of infant crying from birth to the age of 1 year, showed that crying became socially oriented as the infant grew older. Over the course of the year, the infant cried less when the mother was not near and more when she was near, implying some stimulus control over the crying. The predictable effect on maternal behavior was to pick the infant up when he or she was crying. There was a substantial negative correlation between infant crying and infant communication involving facial expression, gesturing, and noncrying vocalization. That is, the development of communication skills appeared to be related to a decreased tendency to cry.

The common theme of the research describing communicative phenomena in normal development is that crying or other nonvocal behavior appeared to serve important communication functions for very young children. Further, as more socially acceptable forms of communication skills developed, behaviors such as crying and aggression were used less frequently (e.g., Brownlee & Bakeman, 1981). The implication of this for a population which, for the most part, does not develop as rapidly or as far is clear. If new communication skills are not acquired, skills presently in the person's repertoire must suffice to communicate needs and desires.

Although this correlational research is provocative and consistent with a social–communicative hypothesis of excess behavior (Carr & Durand, 1985), it cannot demonstrate in a useful, applied way the relationship between excess behavior and communication function.

Horner and Budd (1985) reported a study in which a nonverbal, autistic 11-year-old boy displayed yelling and "grabbing" of objects. A functional assessment demonstrated that the student engaged in these behaviors to obtain particular objects. The student was taught signs representing objects to request them in training situations and subsequently was taught to use these signs in the regular classroom environment to request needs and desires (generalization training). Substantial reductions in the behavioral excesses were noted as an effect of the communication training.

Carr and Durand (1985) demonstrated that behavioral excesses of developmentally disabled children could be reduced by replacing the excess behaviors with a functionally equivalent communicative response. First, a behavioral assessment was implemented to determine the function of the behavioral excesses. Attention, for example, was delivered either rarely or frequently and the task the child was asked to perform was either easy or difficult. As a result, two variables — the frequency of adult attention delivered and difficulty of tasks — were explored systematically. After it was determined in which of the four situations the child predictably engaged in excess behavior (i.e., rare-easy, frequent-easy, rare-difficult, frequent-difficult), hypotheses were generated about what function the excess behavior served for the child. For example, it was hypothesized that a child who engaged in the problem behavior when adult attention was delivered rarely did it for attention.

When a child's excess behavior was shown to occur in the presence of difficult task demands, teaching the child to solicit assistance reliably decreased the level of the excess behavior; when the excess behavior was shown to occur during low levels of adult attention, teaching the child to solicit praise (but not assistance) decreased the level of the excess behavior. Teaching irrelevant phrases to the child (asking for assistance when the functional assessment suggested an attention-seeking function for the excess behavior) did not result in a decrease in the level of the excess behavior. Durand and Kishi (1986) have also shown that teaching the appropriate use of *request* and *reject* devices to developmentally disabled persons with dual sensory impairments who displayed behavioral excesses resulted in decreases in excess behaviors.

Socially motivated excess behavior can be decreased through the acquisition of functional communication signs, graphic symbols, or verbalizations. Interventionists considering the use of such an approach for reducing problem behaviors need to bear the following factors in mind if they are to be successful. First, because communicative intent is presumed to underlie the display of excess behavior in many cases, a functional behavior assessment must be conducted prior to the implementation of communicative intervention to a) verify that the excess behavior is socially motivated, and b) match the correct communicative topography to the communicative purpose served by the excess.

Second, some commitment must be made by staff regarding the stimuli selected for use in generalized requesting and generalized rejecting intervention programs. For example, the items selected as targets for rejecting intervention must be objects or events that recruit excess behavior. Some undesired items, such as medications, should not be used initially as the focus of generalized rejecting intervention, because it would be impossible to consistently allow the learner to avoid medication.

Third, an effort must be made to develop a system to prompt the desired communicative behavior prior to the emission of an excess behavior. Delivering a response prompt for a generalized request or generalized reject gesture after the emission of an excess behavior may only serve to reinforce a chain of behaviors that involve the excess behavior. It is inevitable that during the initial stages of an intervention program designed to teach generalized rejecting, a substantial number of teaching opportunities will be less than efficient. If possible, it is important that during these occasions the learner not be allowed to immediately avoid the target event.

Finally, we carefully caution that not all excess behavior is "communicative–social" in nature. It is possible that some individuals hit other people because hitting people is fun and not because they obtain attention or escape or avoid any person or event. If no clear communicative intent can be determined, it is unclear that communicative intervention necessarily would have a significant impact on the excess behavior.

After a socially acceptable communicative behavior has replaced an excess topography, the degree to which the newly established communicative behavior will replace excess behaviors in contexts outside the stimulus conditions present during intervention is unclear. Our experiience suggests that if a generalized rejecting response is taught in the presence of undesired events, there is relatively little generalization of its use to situations in which the learner has become satiated on a reinforcer and wants no more of it. For example, if a learner readily accepts "coffee" (a known reinforcer), we have rarely observed the use of a generalized reject sign or graphic symbol when the learner has become satiated with coffee.

The prospect that communication intervention can play a role in the reduction of socially unacceptable behaviors represents an exciting avenue for future research. This area also represents an important need for the integration of procedures used to systematically analyze the function of excess behavior into communication intervention curricula[1].

ENSURING THAT A LEARNER DOES NOT BECOME OVERLY DEPENDENT IN USING NEWLY ESTABLISHED COMMUNICATIVE BEHAVIOR IN SITUATIONS IN WHICH IT IS INAPPROPRIATE

Even though a learner may initiate generalized requests, precautions may need to be taken to ensure that he/she is capable of discriminating between situations that require requests and those situations that do not require the mediation of another individual. Guess, Benson, and Siegel-Causey (1985) emphasized the importance of teaching persons with severe handicaps to exert some degree of control over their environment. Failure to do so may result in a phenomenon described by Seligman (1975) as "learned helplessness." Teaching persons with severe handicaps to discriminatively use a generalized requesting gesture, symbol, or vocalization represents one strategy that may help avoid the acquisition of learned helplessness. Unfortunately, some learners are not given opportunities to discriminate between situations requiring a request and those requiring learner action during acquisition. Consequently, they may overgeneralize the use of requests to situations in which they should be able to act independently. Reichle and Barrett (1986) described a learner who frequently "overgeneralized" the use of a generalized request response to situations that did not require a request (e.g., serving oneself from a plate within reach while eating family style).

Reichle, et al. (1986) successfully taught an adult with autism to use a generalized request symbol discriminately during the implementation of a food-preparation task. Specifically, during the implementation of a sandwich-making task, removing a "twist-tie" from the bread wrapper

---

[1]Editor's Note: Applications of child-based findings to adults with mental retardation must be pursued cautiously in light of the absence of data supporting such generalizations.

served as the major obstacle for the learner. During intervention opportunities, the instructor positioned herself near the learner as he began the sandwich-making task. Upon reaching the point where the learner had difficulty, the interventionist asked "Do you need help?" During some intervention opportunities, the "twist tie" was nearly off the bread wrapper and could be removed easily. On other occasions, the twist tie was wrapped tightly around the bread (so that the learner could not remove it without assistance). Next, the learner was prompted to the twist tie. If the twist tie was loose, the learner was reinforced only if he removed the twist tie and continued preparing the sandwich. If the learner spent several seconds attempting to open the tight twist tie but was unsuccessful, the instructor pointed to a communication wallet (a prompt that controlled the learner's selection of a request for assistance symbol, i.e., "Help"). During successive teaching opportunities, the teacher faded systematically and simultaneously the magnitude of the verbal prompt and pointing prompt. Eventually the learner came to use the "help" symbol only when he actually needed help and not when the twist tie could be removed easily.

Some learners may begin using their generalized request or reject symbol at times, or in situations in which the interventionist cannot honor the learner's communicative request or rejection. (For example, the learner who makes numerous requests for a cookie right before lunchtime, or the learner who indicates a desire to leave a required work activity by using his generalized reject.) A solution to this dilemma is to establish discriminative stimuli in situations in which use of the learner's generalized request or reject utterance is acceptable and reinforce its use in that context. At the same time the interventionist could select situations in which use of the learner's request or reject symbol is clearly not acceptable and put requests or rejects that occur in those situations on extinction.

SUMMARY

For the most part, the issues that face the communication interventionists of the 1980s focus on more complicated and subtle aspects of communicative use. It has been demonstrated that persons with severe handicaps can be taught communicative repertoires. In question is how the interventionist can best structure the intervention procedures to maximize the functional use of communicative behavior.

Establishing functional use of communicative behavior requires a synthesis of intervention objectives that traditionally have been viewed as separable. No longer can the interventionist think of decelerating a socially motivated unacceptable behavior without first contemplating its replacement with a socially acceptable alternative. No longer can the interventionist consider teaching a particular communicative intent without considering the steps that must be taken to ensure that it is socially valid and to ensure its generalization (and minimize the possibility of overuse).

In the area of selecting an augmentative mode, interventionists rarely have specified how the graphic symbols or gesture signs would be used to augment speech. Care must be taken by the interventionist to match the communicative context to the communicative topography that will be accepted. No longer is the interventionist's job one of selecting an augmentative system or systems. Instead, the conditional use of each of several communicative modes must be considered, depending on the demands of the environment.

The future holds great promise for individuals with communicative deficits — but so does the present. A number of areas are raised in this chapter that if *systematically* addressed would lead to more normalized communicative behavior for some persons with severe handicaps. Most of these areas do not require sophisticated equipment or additional staff. Instead, very systematic and well-documented implementation are required. Hopefully, the scientific rigor that resulted in the demonstrations of communicative acquisitions in the 1970s and 1980s will be able to focus on the subtle issues confronting the communication interventionist today.

REFERENCES

Ainsworth, M., & Bell, S. (1977). Infant crying and maternal responsiveness. *Child Development, 48,* 1200–1207.

Alpert, C. (1980). Procedures for determining the optimal nonspeech mode with autistic children. In R. L. Schiefelbusch (Ed.), *Nonspeech language and communication analysis and intervention* (pp. 389–420). Baltimore, MD: University Park Press.

Baer, R., Williams, J., Osnes, P., & Stokes, T. (1984). Delayed reinforcement as an indiscriminable contingency in verbal/nonverbal correspondence training. *Journal of Applied Behavior Analysis, 17,* 29–44.

Brownlee, J., & Bakeman, R. (1981). Hitting in toddler–peer interaction. *Child Development, 52,* 1076–1079.

Calculator, S., & Delaney, D. (1986). Comparison of nonspeaking and speaking mentally retarded adults clarification strategies. *Journal of Speech and Hearing Disorders, 51,* 252–259.

Carr, E. (1977). The motivation of self-injurious behavior: A review of some hypotheses. *Psychological Bulletin, 84,* 800–816.

Carr, E., & Durand, V. (1985). Reducing behavior problems through functional communication training. *Journal of Applied Behavior Analysis, 18,* 111–126.

Carr, E., & Kologinsky, E. (1983). Acquisition of sign language by autistic children II. Spontaneity and generalization. *Journal of Applied Behavior Analysis, 16,* 297–314.

Carr, E., & Lovaas, O. (1982). Contingent electric shock as a treatment for severe behavior problems. In S. Axelrod & J. Apsche (Eds.), *Punishment: Its effects on human behavior* (pp. 221–245). New York: Academic Press.

Carr, E., & McDowell, J. (1980). Social control of self-injurious behavior of organic etiology. *Behavior Therapy, 11,* 402–409.

Carr, E., & Newsome, C. (in press). Demand-related tantrums: conceptualization and treatment. *Behavior Modification.*

Carr, E., Newsome, C., & Binkoff, J. (1980). Escape as a factor in the aggressive behavior of two retarded children. *Journal of Applied Behavior Analysis, 13,* 101–117.

Chapman, R., & Miller, J. (1980). Analyzing language and communication in the child. In R. Schiefelbusch (Ed.), *Nonspeech language intervention strategies.* Baltimore: University Park Press.

Charhop, M., Schreibman, L., & Thebodeau, M. (1985). Increasing spontaneous verbal responding in autistic children using time delay. *Journal of Applied Behavior Analysis, 18,* 155–166.

Durand, V., & Carr, E. (May, 1983). *The functional significance of self-stimulatory behavior.* Paper presented at the meeting of the American Psychological Association, Anaheim, CA.

Durand, V., & Kishi, G. (1986). Reducing severe behavior problems among persons with dual sensory impairments: An evaluation of a technical assistance model. Unpublished manuscript, State University of New York at Albany.

Farrier, L., Yorkston, K., Marriner, N., & Beukelman, D. (1985). Conversational control in norm paired speakers using an augmentative communication system. *Augmentative and Alternative Communication, 1,* 65–73.

Gobbi, L., Cipani, E., Hudson, C., & Lapenta–Neudeck, R. (1986). Developing spontaneous requesting among children with severe mental retardation. *Mental Retardation, 24,* 357–364.

Greenspan, S., Nusbaum, H., & Pisoni, D. (1985). Generalization of training with synthetic words and sentences. *Research on speech perception (Progress Report #11).* Bloomington, IN: Indiana University.

Guess, D., Benson, H., & Siegel–Causey, E. (1985). Concepts and issues related to choice making and autonomy among persons with severe disabilities. *The Journal of the Association for Persons with Severe Handicaps, 10,* 79–86.

Guess, D., Sailor, W., & Baer, D. (1974). To teach language to retarded children. In R. L. Schiefelbusch & L. L. Lloyd (Eds.), *Language perspectives: Acquisition, retardation and intervention* (pp. 529–564). Austin, TX: PRO-ED.

Guevremont, D., Osnes, R., & Stokes, T. (1986a). Preparation for effective self-regulation: The development of generalized verbal control. *Journal of Applied Behavior Analysis, 19,* 99–104.

Guevremont, D., Osnes, R., & Stokes, T. (1986b). Programming maintenance after correspondence training interventions with children. *Journal of Applied

Behavior Analysis, 19, 215–219.

Halle, J. (1982). Teaching functional language to handicapped: An integrative model of naturalistic environmental teaching techniques. *The Journal of the Association for Persons with Severe Handicaps, 7,* 29–37.

Halle, J., Baer, D., & Spadlin, J. (1979). Time delay: A technique to increase language use and facilitate generalization in retarded children. *Journal of Applied Behavior Analysis, 12,* 431–439.

Hoover, J., Reichle, J., Van Tasell, D., & Cole, D. (in press). The intelligibility of synthesized speech: Echo II vs. Votrax. *Journal of Speech and Hearing Research.*

Horner, R., & Budd, C. (1985, March). Acquisition of manual sign use: Collateral reduction of maladaptive behavior, and factors limiting generalization. *Education and Training of the Mentally Retarded,* 39–47.

Hulbut, B. Iwata, B., & Green, J. (1982). Nonvocal language acquisition in adolescents with severe physical disabilities: Blissymbols versus iconic stimulus formats. *Journal of Applied Behavior Analysis, 15,* 241–258.

Israel, A., & Brown, M. (1977). Correspondence training, prior verbal training and control of nonverbal behavior via control of verbal behavior. *Journal of Applied Behavior Analysis, 10,* 333–338.

Kent, L. (1984). *Language intervention procedures for the severely retarded.* Champaign, IL: Research Press.

Keogh, W., & Reichle, J. (1985). Communication intervention for the "difficult to teach" severely handicapped. In S. Warren & A. Rogers–Warren (Eds.), *Functional Language Intervention* (pp. 157–196). Baltimore, MD: University Park Press.

LaMarre, J., & Holland, J. (1985). The functional independence of mands and tacts. *Journal of the Experimental Analysis of Behavior, 43,* 5–19.

Light, J., Coller, B., & Parnes, P. (1985). Communication interaction between young nonspeaking physically disabled children and their primary caregivers: Part 1 — Discourse patterns. *Augmentative and Alternative Communication, 1,* 74–83.

Logan, J., Pisoni, D., & Greene, B. (1985). Measuring the sequential intelligibility of synthetic speech using a sentence verification task. *Research on speech perception (Progress Report #10).* Bloomington, IN: Indiana University.

Lovaas, O. I., Berberich, J. P., Perloff, B., & Schaeffer, B. (1966). Acquisition of imitative speech in schizophrenic children. *Science, 151,* 705–707.

MacDonald, J. (1985) Language through conversation: A model for intervention with language delayed persons. In S. Warren & A. Rogers-Warren (Eds.), *Teaching Functional Language* (pp. 89–122). Austin, TX: PRO-ED.

McLean, J., & Snyder-McLean, L. (1978). *Transactional approach to early language training.* Columbus, OH: Merrill.

Meyer, L., & Evans, I. (1986). Modification of excess behavior: An adaptive and functional approach for educational and community settings. In R. Horner, L. Meyer, & H. D. Fredericks (Eds.), *Education of Learners with Severe Handicaps* (pp. 315–350). Baltimore, MD: Brooks.

Murphey, C., & Messer, D. (1977). Mothers, infants, and pointing: A study of gesture. In H. R. Shaffer (Ed.), *Studies in mother-infant interaction.* New York: Academic Press.

Piche'-Cragoe, L., Reichle, J., & Sigafoos, J. (1986). Requesting validity intervention. Unpublished manuscript, University of Minnesota, Minneapolis.

Ratner, N., & Bruner, J. (1978). Games, social exchange and the acquisition of language. *Journal of Child Language, 5,* 391–402.

Reichle, J., Anderson, H., & Schermer, G. (1986). Establishing the discrimination between requesting objects, requesting assistance and "helping yourself." Unpublished manuscript, University of Minnesota, Minneapolis.

Reichle, J., & Barrett, C. (1986). The bounds of generalization for requesting and rejecting behavior in a person with severe handicaps. Unpublished manuscript, University of Minnesota, Minneapolis.

Reichle, J., & Brown, L. (1986). Teaching the use of a multipage direct selection communication board to an adult with autism. *Journal of the Association for Persons with Severe Handicaps, 11,* 68–72.

Reichle, J., & Karlan, G. (1985). The selection of an augmentative system in communication intervention: A critique of decision rules. *Journal of the Association for Persons with Severe Handicaps, 10,* 146–156.

Reichle, J., & Karlan, G. (in press). Selecting augmentative communication interventions: A critique of candidacy criteria and a proposed alternative. In L. Lloyd & R. L. Schiefelbusch (Eds.), *Language Perspectives II.* Austin, TX: Pro-Ed.

Reichle, J., & Keogh, W. (1986). Communication instruction for learners with severe handicaps. Some unresolved issues. In R. Horner, L., Meyer, & H. D. Bud Fredericks (Eds.), *Education of Learners with Severe Handicaps* (pp. 189–220). Baltimore, MD: Brooks.

Reichle, J., Rogers, N., & Barrett, C. (1984). Establishing pragmatic distinctions among the communicative functions of requesting, rejecting and commenting in a severely retarded adolescent. *The Journal for the Association for Persons with Severe Handicaps, 9,* 31–36.

Reichle, J., & Sigafoos, J. (1986). Teaching discriminative use of generalized and explicit requests to a person with severe handicaps. Unpublished manuscript, University of Minnesota, Minneapolis.

Reichle, J., & Yoder, D. (1979). Assessment and early stimulation of communication in the severely and profoundly mentally retarded. In R. York & E. Edgar (Eds.), *Teaching Children with Severe Handicaps,* (Vol. IV, pp. 176–192). Columbus, OH: Merrill.

Reichle, J., & Yoder, D. (1985). Communication board use in severely handicapped learners. *Language, Speech, and Hearing Services in Schools, 16,* 58–63.

Rheingold, H., Gerwitz, J., & Ross, H. (1959). Social conditioning of vocalizations in the infant. *Journal of Comparative Psychology, 52,* 68–73.

Rice, M. (1983). Contemporary accounts of the cognition/language relationship: Implications for speech–language clinicians. *Journal of Speech and Hearing Disorders, 48,* 347–359.

Risley, T., & Hart, B. (1968). Developing a correspondence between the nonverbal and verbal behavior of preschool children. *Journal of Applied Behavior Analysis, 1,* 267–281.

Rogers–Warren, A., & Warren, S. (1980). Pragmatics and generalization. In R. L. Schiefelbusch (Ed.), *Communicative competence: Assessment and intervention* (pp. 157–201). Baltimore, MD: University Park Press.

Savage–Rumbaugh, S. (1984). Verbal behavior at a procedural level in a chimpanzee. *Journal of the Experimental Analysis of Behavior, 41,* 223–250.

Schwab, E., Nusbaum, H., & Pisoni, D. (1983). *Some effects of training on the perception (progress report #10).* Bloomington, IN: Indiana University.

Seligman, M. (1975). *Helplessness: On depression, development and death.* San Francisco, CA: W. H. Freeman.

Shane, H. (1980). Approaches to assessing the communication of nonoral persons. In R. L. Schiefelbusch (Ed.), *Nonspeech language and communication analysis and intervention* (pp. 197–224). Baltimore, MD: University Park Press.

Shodell, M., & Reiter, H. (1968). Self-mutilative behavior in verbal and nonverbal schizophrenic children. *Archives of General Psychiatry, 19,* 453–455.

Sobsey, D., & Reichle, J. (1986). Components of reinforcement for attention signal switch activation. Unpublished manuscript, University of Minnesota, Minneapolis.

Stokes, T., & Baer, D. (1977). An implicit technology of generalization. *Journal of Applied Behavior Analysis, 10,* 349–367.

Talkington, L., Hall, S., & Altman, R. (1971). Communication deficits and aggression in the mentally retarded. *American Journal of Mental Deficiency, 76,* 235–237.

Tetlie, R., & Reichle, J. (1986). The match between signed request and object selection in four learners with severe handicaps. Unpublished manuscript, University of Minnesota, Minneapolis.

Warren, S., & Rogers–Warren, A. (1980). Current perspectives in language remediation: A special monograph. *Education and Treatment of Children, 5,* 133–153.

Weeks, M., & Gaylord–Ross, R. (1981). Task difficulty and aberrant behavior in severely handicapped students. *Journal of Applied Behavior Analysis, 14,* 449–463.

Weisberg, P. (1963). Social and nonsocial conditioning of infant vocalizations. *Child Development, 39,* 377–388.

Wolff, P. (1969). The natural history of crying and other vocalizations in early infancy. In B. Foss (Ed.), *Determinants of Infant Behavior, 4* (pp. 81–109). London: Methvein.

Yoder, D., & Kraat, A. (1984). Intervention issues in nonspeech communication. In J. Miller, D. Yoder, & R. Schiefelbusch (Eds.), *Contemporary issues in language intervention. ASHA Reports, 12.*

CHAPTER 10

Adults Who Are Mildly to Moderately Mentally Retarded: Communicative Performance, Assessment and Intervention

JAN L. BEDROSIAN

Setting: Therapy room in an adult activity center.

Participants: Rob, a 24-year-old adult with moderate mental retardation, and a speech–language clinician.

Intervention goal: Production of locatives in complete sentences in response to picture cards.

CLINICIAN. Rob, where's the car? [*holds up first picture card*].

ROB. The car is *in* the garage.

CLINICIAN. All right. Very nice. Now where's the car? [*holds up second picture card*].

ROB. The car in front of the garage.

CLINICIAN. OK, can you say the car *is* in front of the garage? Say the whole thing.

ROB. The car *is* in front of a car.

CLINICIAN. The garage.

ROB. Garage.

CLINICIAN. OK, where's the spoon? [*holds up third picture card*].

ROB. The spoon is on top. Oh, the spoon is *in* the cup.

CLINICIAN. All right, let's say that again so you don't forget.

ROB. Yeah. The spoon is in the cup.

CLINICIAN. Good. You corrected yourself. That's really good. You realized you said it wrong at first.

ROB. Where's your husband?

CLINICIAN. Where's my husband? Where do you think? Where do you think he is? Can you guess?

ROB. Working.

CLINICIAN. He's working. That's right. Where's the cat, Rob? [*holds up fourth picture card*].

ROB. The cat is on the chair.

CLINICIAN. Very good. Now, where's the....

*T*raditionally, language programs for adults who are mildly to moderately mentally retarded have focused primarily on phonologic, syntactic, or semantic performance without considering pragmatic–communicative performance, that is, how one uses language in social interactions. Attempts have been made to correct the distortion of sounds, omission of auxiliary verbs, and use of inappropriate vocabulary. These attempts, however, have often excluded the context of communication involving "the linguistic and nonlinguistic elements that make up the communicative setting of language performance" (Spinelli & Terrell, 1984, p. 31). As a result, language goals for this population have rarely been functional. Functional communication skills involve those that are useful to the adult in terms of meeting his/her environmental and communication demands. Owings and Guyette (1982) stated that "it is more useful for an adult client to be able to order a hamburger or ask directions home with a single- or two-word utterance than to know the specific semantic–syntactic aspects of plural /s/ morpheme use" (p. 188). Moreover, these programs have often been so structured and controlled by the clinician that they no longer resemble normal adult conversational interaction.

The transcript presented at the opening of this chapter illustrates such a program. The speech–language clinician selected a remediation goal emphasizing semantic performance. It may have been that the correct production of locatives was a functional goal for this adult with mental retardation, depending on the communicative demands placed on him at home and at the work activity center that he attended. However, teaching this language behavior in response to picture cards in a stimulus–response paradigm may not have been the best approach for achieving functional communication skills or the generalization of those skills. In the course of normal conversational interaction, an individual is not required to respond to picture cards to demonstrate his/her knowledge of correct locative forms. Likewise, an individual is also not required to "say the whole thing" (Prutting, Bagshaw, Goldstein, Juskowitz, & Umen, 1978). If an intervention program ignores context while teaching locative forms (or any other language behavior), the client is placed in a position of not knowing when to use these forms, where to use them, how to use them, with whom to use them, and why to use them (Chapman, 1976b).

Another problem illustrated in this transcript, although a common characteristic of clinical discourse, is that of clinician control (Bedrosian & Prutting, 1978; Prutting et al., 1978). The clinician exhibited at least two types of conversational control. One type of control was expressed through questioning, which involved chaining (i.e., the use of successive questions across turns by a single participant) and arching (i.e., responding to a question with a question) (Mishler, 1975). Chaining was exhibited throughout the transcript, most notably in the first two conversational turns of the clinician in which she sought known information about the location of objects depicted. Arching occurred in response to the client's only question, which involved the location of the clinician's husband. As a result of these types of questioning used by the clinician, the client was forced to assume a passive responding role in the conversation.

Another type of control demonstrated by the clinician involved the topic of conversation. All but one of the conversational topics were initiated by the clinician. When the client attempted to initiate a topic regarding the clinician's husband, the clinician responded by arching his question and subsequently changing the topic to get him back on task. Again, the client was placed in a passive conversational role. Each type of clinician control prevented the client from taking a lead in the interaction, resulting in a conversation that no longer resembled competent adult discourse (Weimann, 1977). It would appear that language programs for adults who are mentally retarded typified by this type of structure would not foster the ultimate goal of achieving communicative competence (Hymes, 1974), important for independent community living skills and job employability. A competent communicator can be defined as one who:

- □ Has implicit knowledge of the social rules that guide the use of language in various social settings and interactions.
- □ Is able to communicate, both verbally and nonverbally, an intentional message in such a way that it is accurately sent and accurately received by the listener.
- □ Is able to repair a conversation if a breakdown in the communication occurs.
- □ Has access to a variety of means for expressing the same communicative intention.
- □ Is an active listener capable of providing feedback and support, and maintaining the flow of a conversation.

□ Is able to exhibit some control in a conversation.
□ Can deal effectively with others in terms of establishing positive relationships.

The purpose of this chapter is to present clinical procedures for teaching functional and competent communication skills to adults who are mildly to moderately mentally retarded in order to avoid the problems encountered in the language program just described. Initially, a review of the literature describing the communicative performance of this population will be presented. This will be followed by a discussion of procedures for the following:

1. Assessing the adult's communication skills in a variety of settings and participant interactions.
2. Categorizing communication skills.
3. Selecting appropriate intervention goals.
4. Facilitating or teaching communication skills in a variety of settings and participant interactions.
5. Measuring the effectiveness of intervention as exemplified through a case study.

Although the speech–language clinician would assume the primary responsibility for assessing and categorizing communication skills and selecting intervention goals, the teaching procedures can be administered by other professional staff with minimal consultation from the speech–language clinician.

COMMUNICATIVE PERFORMANCE

Relatively few studies have examined the communicative performance of adults who are mildly to moderately mentally retarded. Together, these studies do consider a broad range of conversational and discourse behaviors, including communication functions, topic, repair (e.g., requests for clarification), turn-taking, control, and narrative or story-telling skills. As these six behaviors are discussed, the reader is encouraged to consider the results as representing general communication characteristics of the population of adults with mental retardation. We are dealing with a heterogeneous population (Abbeduto & Rosenberg, 1980; Bedrosian & Prutting, 1978) in which individual differences must be recognized for purposes of communication assessment and intervention.

Communication Functions

The first conversational behavior of interest involves that of communication intentions or functions: "the reasons why people talk" (Chapman, 1981, p. 112). A few studies have examined communication function usage of adults who are mildly to moderately mentally retarded in a variety of conversational settings. Owings and McManus (1980) examined the types of communication functions expressed by a 28.4-year-old adult who was moderately mentally retarded in monologues and in interactions with peers and a counselor. The following communication functions were studied: question, information-giving, information-giving to self, command, criticism, praise, description, imitation, and repetition. Results indicated that the adult with mental retardation used all of the communication functions examined, and that the frequency of usage of each varied as a function of the speaking situation. Specifically, the most frequently occurring communication function expressed in monologues involved information-giving to self. When interacting with peers, questions and imitation occurred most frequently compared with questions and information-giving exhibited with the counselor. The investigators suggested that the subject had "some realization of the social consequences of speech acts" (Owings & McManus, 1980, p. 314).

In a subsequent study involving the same communication functions, Owings and McManus (1982) observed communication function use by nine adults who were moderately mentally retarded interacting with their program counselor in three living environments. The environments, each varying in the degree of independence allowed for the residents, consisted of a group home, an apartment cluster, and a semi-independent living situation. Across all living situations, the most frequently occurring communication functions were questions and information-giving. Of interest was the finding that the living environments that fostered greater independence were associated with fewer communication functions being exhibited by the adults with mental retardation. For example, more questions were expressed by adults living in the group home than in the other two more independent living situations. The investigators suggested that there might be less reason or opportunity for asking questions in the more independent living situations than in the group home. Nevertheless, both studies demonstrated that the communicative intents of these adults varied as a function of the conversational setting. Similar findings regarding the language performance of normal language-learning children with comparable cognitive levels have also been reported (Wilkinson, Heibert, & Rembold, 1981).

Communication functions specifically constituting adjacency pairs (i.e., those pairs of turns in which the second turn is in response to the first) have also been examined (Abbeduto & Rosenberg, 1980). Examples of adjacency pairs include question–answer and request–compliance. The investigators observed the communicative performance of seven adults who were mildly mentally retarded engaged in triadic interactions with each other during mealtime conversation. With respect to communication functions, results indicated that most adjacency pairs were initiated by assertions and questions as opposed to requests, commissives (i.e., statements in which the speaker commits her/himself to performing a future action), and expressives (i.e., statements involving the expression of feelings, opinions). The low percentage of occurrence of the latter two communication functions did, however, indicate that the adults "were capable of encoding fairly abstract content in their utterances" (Abbeduto & Rosenberg, 1980, p. 417). The majority of adjacency pairs were completed by acknowledgments, agreement–disagreements, and requests for either clarification or more information. A further analysis of the adjacency pairs indicated that most were direct rather than indirect speech acts (i.e., sentences in which the communicative intent does not match the linguistic structure). These findings resembled those reported by Owings and McManus (1980, 1982) in that the adults with mental retardation were capable of using a variety of communication functions.

Only one study, to my knowledge, has investigated the abilities of adults with mental retardation to comprehend communication functions, as evidenced by their nonverbal responses. (Another study involving comprehension of contingent queries as evidenced by verbal responses is reviewed in the discussion of conversational repair abilities). In their study, Paul and Cohen (1985) focused specifically on comprehension of indirect requests. The subjects, eight adults with autistic behaviors and eight IQ-matched adults with mild mental retardation, were tested with similar stimulus sentences in both a structured condition and an unstructured conversational condition. Each condition involved a coloring task. The subjects with mental retardation were found to perform better (i.e., they comprehended more indirect request forms) than the subjects with autistic behaviors in both conditions, with performance consistent between conditions. In addition, the performances of both groups of subjects were similar to those of normal 4- to 6-year-old children. An investigation of this same ability using a more age-appropriate task is warranted for both of these adult populations.

Communication functions of adults who are mildly to moderately mentally retarded have also been examined within the framework of topic and conversational repair. These aspects of communication functions are addressed in the sections that follow.

Topic

Topic, the proposition or set of propositions or subject matter about which the speaker is either providing or requesting new information (Ervin–Tripp, 1973; Keenan & Schieffelin, 1976), is one of the basic components of communication (Hymes, 1962). Not only is topic a means through which a person can coordinate his/her conversations and actions with others, but it is also part of what regulates or sequences a conversation (Bedrosian, 1985). Individuals who are competent in the area of topic are capable of clearly initiating and establishing their topics on the conversational floor, maintaining their own topics as well as those initiated by others, and introducing new topics with appropriate topic-changing devices (e.g., "Oh by the way…").

A few studies have examined the topic performance of adults who are mildly to moderately mentally retarded during natural, unstructured discourse. Abbeduto and Rosenberg (1980), in the investigation described previously in this section, examined the ability of their subjects to engage in cooperative conversations. The majority of conversational turns of the adults who were mildly mentally retarded occurred in adjacency pairs. In addition, more than 50 percent of the adjacency pairs were initiated by nonobligating turns [i.e., turns that "do not obligate the listener to respond," (Abbeduto & Rosenberg, 1980, p. 412)]. These findings suggested that the adults were actively involved in a coordinated exchange of information even though they were not always obligated to do so. A further examination of topic involved an analysis of the average number of turns maintained per topic. Across the three groups studied, the average number of turns per topic ranged from 7 to 21. The investigators stated that the topic-maintenance abilities of these adults did not appear to be impaired.

A more extensive analysis of topic performance was conducted by Bedrosian (1979). Two adults who were moderately to severely mentally retarded participated in conversational interactions involving peers, parents, and a normal young child. The type of subject matter and communicative intent of topic initiations, as well as the nature of continuous (i.e., topic-maintenance turns) and discontinuous (i.e., topic-initiation turns) discourse turns (Keenan & Schieffelin, 1976) were examined. It was found that both the subject matter and communicative intent of topic initiations varied as a function of the conversational setting. Some of the subject matters (e.g., fantasy and name-calling) initiated with peers were not initiated with parents, reflecting the appropriate adherence to discourse rules employed by "normal" speakers (Ervin–Tripp, 1973). Overall, the majority of topic initiations involved discussions of the here and now. The communicative intent of topic initiations consisted primarily of informatives as opposed to various forms of requests, although more requests were used to initiate topics with peers and the child than with parents.

Most continuous discourse turns for both of the adults with mental retardation in the analysis involved acknowledgments and responses to questions, in contrast to the more difficult use of topic incorporating by their parents. These less sophisticated topic-maintenance devices, similar to the use of repetitions reported by Owings and McManus (1982), may function for these adults as a compensatory strategy (Kirchner & Skarakis–Doyle, 1983) for participating in a conversation. For example, a speaker's use of acknowledgments allows her/him to stay actively involved in a conversation even though she/he may not be comprehending the information presented. Discontinuous discourse turns consisted primarily of new topic initiations and reintroductions, with the latter functioning as a strategy for reinitiating unsuccessful topic initiations or for maintaining a conversation. Bedrosian concluded that these adults, although somewhat unsophisticated in their manner of interaction, were capable of following basic discourse rules related to topic.

In both of these studies, then, the topic performance of adults with mental retardation was examined in the context of natural discourse. Only one study, to my knowledge, has involved a more controlled investigation of topic, specifically involving topic maintenance. Warne and Bedrosian (1986) studied the topic-maintenance abilities of four adults who were moderately mentally retarded in a popcorn-popping activity. These abilities were examined under three conditions in which the referent was either present or absent, related or unrelated to the ongoing activity (Retherford, 1980). Five stimulus statements were constructed for each of the three conditions. Verbal and nonverbal turns following stimulus statements were transcribed and coded for the type of topic relationship involved. Results indicated that three of the four subjects exhibited continuous discourse, primarily involving the use of acknowledgments, across conditions even when the referent was absent and unrelated. These findings were similar to those regarding normal preschool children (Retherford, 1980). Again, the use of acknowledgments could have functioned as a compensatory strategy for staying in a conversation even when the referent was not related to the ongoing activity. Continued investigation of the topic performance of adults who are mildly to moderately mentally retarded is warranted.

Conversational Repair

Conversational repair includes the ability to both signal and respond to misunderstandings or breakdowns in communication as they relate to the referent (Garvey, 1975, 1977; Keenan & Schieffelin, 1976) or appropriateness of topic (Retherford, 1980). In studies of the conversational repair abilities of adults with mild to moderate mental retardation engaged in natural unstructured discourse, results have indicated that these adults are capable of signaling communicative distress through the use of requests for repetition, clarification, and more information (Abbeduto & Rosenberg, 1980; Bedrosian & Prutting, 1978). In addition, evidence of responding to these types of requests has been reported (Abbeduto & Rosenberg, 1980).

Studies involving investigations of conversational repair abilities in controlled situations have also been conducted. Warne & Bedrosian (1986) examined the referent repair mechanisms (e.g., request for repetition, questioning of referent, question regarding appropriateness of topic) used by four adults who were moderately mentally retarded under the three referent conditions previously described. Three of the four subjects were found to exhibit repair, with the primary device involving requests for confirmation. Repair of referent was used more frequently when the referent was absent and unrelated than when the referent was absent and related. This finding was opposite that reported for normal preschool children (Retherford, 1980), who appeared less sophisticated in the use of referent repair mechanisms than the adults with mental retardation. None of the adults questioned the appropriateness of topic changes when the referent was absent and unrelated to the ongoing activity. The investigators speculated that this finding might have been attributed to the adults' unawareness of the conversational rules governing the marking of topic changes (Keenan & Schieffelin, 1976), or that their low social status prevented them from questioning the conversational performance of an authority figure.

In a study comparing the communicative performance of adults with autistic behaviors and IQ-matched adults with moderate mental retardation, Paul and Cohen (1984) analyzed various responses to requests for repair or contingent queries (i.e., requests for confirmation, neutral requests for repetition, requests for specific constituent repetition). Each adult was engaged in a short conversation with an investigator who interjected four examples of each of the three types of contingent queries listed previously. Although difficulties were exhibited by both groups of subjects, results indicated that the adults with mental retardation were more competent in responding appropriately to the different types of contingent queries than were the adults with autistic behaviors. Therefore, the adults with moderate mental retardation studied in these investigations were capable of signaling and responding to communicative distress under controlled conditions.

Turn-Taking

According to Sacks, Schegloff, and Jefferson (1974), turn-taking is a "basic form of organization for conversation" (p. 700). *Turn-taking* involves a system of rules describing how participants construct and exchange turns in conversation, as well as how they repair violations in the distribution of conversational turns. Relatively few studies have examined the turn-taking abilities of adults who are mildly to moderately mentally retarded.

Abbeduto and Rosenberg (1980), in the investigation previously described, also examined the turn-taking performance of their subjects while conversing with one another. Across triads, relatively few turn-taking errors (i.e., interruptions or overlap) were exhibited, although individual differences were reported. The investigators concluded that the adults in their study used the same turn-taking mechanisms as normal speaking adults and that "the turn-taking system used in retarded adults' conversation is as efficient as that of nonretarded adults" (p. 422).

Only one study has investigated the ability of adults with mental retardation to repair violations of turn-taking. In the previously described controlled conditions studied by Warne and Bedrosian (1986), two of the five stimulus statements for each condition were planned interruptions that were designed to examine the adults' strategies (e.g., discontinuation of talking, reintroduction of interrupted utterance) for repairing turn-taking violations. Results indicated that each adult exhibited at least one type of repair strategy. Although the primary repair device involved discontinuation of talking upon interruption, other repair devices involving reintroductions were employed. These findings were similar to those regarding strategies of "normal" adults for repairing turn-taking violations (Sacks et al., 1974). The adults with mental retardation in these two studies were, therefore, capable of following normal discourse rules for turn-taking.

Conversational Control

Conversational control involves the abililty to manage discourse in such a way that one's own interpersonal goals are accomplished. It has been validated that two of the dimensions along which participants seek to define the nature of their relationship are that of control and dominance–submission (J. Capella, personal communication, 1980). Bedrosian and Prutting (1978) conducted an investigation of these dimensions in the communicative interactions of four adults who were moderately to severely mentally retarded across various conversational settings. These settings involved interactions with a speech–language clinician, peers, parents, and a normal young child. Relational communication coding schemes involving the analysis of questions and subsequent responses (Folger & Puck, 1976; Mishler, 1975) were applied to the data. Although not always able to hold a dominant position in a conversation (even when conversing with a young child), the adults with mental retardation were found capable of expressing the same types of control (e.g., the use of arching) as normal speaking adults. The types of control expressed by each adult with mental retardation varied as a function of the conversational setting. In addition, differences existed in the types and frequencies of control expressed by the four adults. Clearly there is a need to examine other types of control (e.g., topic control) not investigated in this study.

Narratives

A *narrative* involves "the telling of a story" whereby a conversational participant relates "a series of events that happened in the past" (Kernan & Sabsay, 1983, p. 3). To date, only one study has investigated the narrative skills of adults with mild mental retardation (Kernan & Sabsay, 1983). In this study, various levels of the semantic structure of the narratives produced by these adults (number was not specified) were examined in the context of a counseling group in a sheltered workshop. The adults were found to exhibit problems related to the semantics of the sentence (e.g., the selection of incorrect vocabulary), the cohesion between sentences (e.g., misuse of articles and pronouns), and segments of the narrative (e.g., absent or ill-formed summary statements, incorrect temporal sequence of events related to the story). The investigators stated that these problems were similar to those exhibited by normal speakers, but differences existed in terms of the frequency and multiplicity with which these problems occurred in the narratives of the speakers with mental retardation. Kernan and Sabsay concluded that "the frequency and multiplicity of these problems have a cumulative effect that accounts for much of the impression that 'something is wrong' with the speech of these individuals" (p. 33). Further investigation of the narrative skills of this population under controlled conditions is warranted.

Summary of Communicative Performance

The communicative performance of adults with mild to moderate mental retardation can be briefly summarized as follows. These adults, in spite of their lingusitic deficiencies, are capable of following several rules of normal discourse. However, conversational difficulties are still exhibited. These difficulties are often dealt with through the use of compensatory strategies that allow them to remain participants in conversation. Again, individual differences exist reflecting the heterogeneity of the population. Therefore, it is the responsibility of the speech–language clinician in conjunction with other professional team members to identify individual communicative strengths, weaknesses, and compensatory strategies to provide functional and competent communication skill programming. In the remaining sections of this chapter, a communication assessment and intervention program is discussed. This material represents a revision of material presented previously (Bedrosian, 1982).

CRITERIA FOR CLIENT SELECTION

Specification of Criteria

The communication assessment and intervention program that follows applies only to those adults with mental retardation who meet specific criteria. The criteria for selection are that the individual

- ☐ Be capable of communicating verbally through speech as opposed to relying on only nonspeaking (e.g., gestures, sign, communication board) means for expressing communicative intentions.
- ☐ Have intelligible speech performance.
- ☐ Be functioning at least in Piaget's preoperational period (two to seven years) of cognitive development (Ginsburg & Opper, 1969).
- ☐ Have a language comprehension level no lower than 2½ to 3 years of age.
- ☐ Have a language production level no lower than 2 to 3 years of age.

Rationale for Criteria

Although the program was designed for and conducted with speaking adults with mental retardation, the teaching procedures can be modified for nonspeaking adults using various augmentative communication systems. Calculator (see Chapter 11 of this volume) presents special considerations for communication skill programming with nonspeaking adults. In regard to the second criterion listed in the preceding section, intelligible speech performance implies that despite any existing articulation difficulties, the adult can be understood in most communicative situations.

Information regarding an adult's developmental levels of cognition, language production, and comprehension is necessary for selecting appropriate communication goals, grading the procedures and instructions used in teaching a specific communication skill, and determining the acceptability of a communicative initiation or response. For example, in terms of cognitive information, a communication goal involving the use of indirect request forms would not be selected for adults who were functioning in the early preoperational stage. This particular communication skill appears to be related to higher levels of cognitive development according to the literature regarding language acquisition by normal children (Bates, 1976). Based on experiential data, adults functioning in the early preoperational stage have rarely been able to spontaneously use indirect request forms without a direct imitation model. Likewise, in terms of language production information, procedures for teaching requests for repetition to adults functioning in the early stages of syntactic production would not include the use of requests in the form of "Could you say that again?". Instead, requests involving "What?" or "Huh?" would be more appropriate. Again, based on experiential data, adults functioning in these early linguistic stages have rarely been able to spontaneously use more advanced syntactic forms without a direct imitation model. The specific language behaviors taught in the program do follow a developmental model, contrary to the recommendations of Brown, Shiraga, Rogan, York, Zanella, Albright McCarthy, Loomis, and VanDeventer (see Chapter 6 of this volume). However, the actual communication goals and teaching procedures are reflective of normalization principles in that they are adult-oriented rather than child-oriented.

Adaptive procedures for formally assessing adults with mental retardation are presented by Morse (see Chapter 5, of this volume). For information related to informal Piagetian procedures for assessing cognitive performance, the reader is referred to Gill (1979), and Wetherby and Gaines (1982). Specific methods for assessing the language production and comprehension skills of the adult population can be found in the discussion by Owings and Guyette (1982).

COMMUNICATION ASSESSMENT PROCEDURES

Data Collection

Procedures for assessing communication skills initially involve the collection of data in a variety of settings and participant interactions. The communicative interactions selected for assessment may vary for each adult who is mentally retarded, depending on his/her daily living and vocational and educational experiences. For example, the communicative interactions encountered in a large institutional setting may be different from those encountered in a group home setting. Nevertheless, it is desirable to assess the adult's communicative performance in an interaction with a peer, a "significant other" adult (whether that adult be a parent, group home supervisor, case manager, or a vocational skill trainer), and a speech-language clinician. The actual data collection procedures involve a 10-minute audiotaped or, when possible, a video-taped recording of the adult in at least three of the following types of interactions.

Adult–Peer Interaction

The adult–peer interaction can be recorded in a variety of situations, including mealtime, leisure, and recreational activities. If the interaction occurs in a clinical setting, the clinician encourages the adults with mental retardation to sit down but does not instruct them to talk. Instead, the following instructions to be given by the clinician are recommended: "Excuse me, I forgot something. I'll be right back." These instructions are effective in evoking conversation between adults who are mentally retarded. The adult and his/her peer should be the only individuals present during the recording.

Adult–'Significant-Other'–Adult Interaction

This particular interaction can also occur in a variety of situations, depending on the significant other adult involved. For example, if the significant other involves a primary caregiver in a private or group home setting, the following conversational situations are suggested: before or after work, at mealtime, while preparing meals, at bedtime, or while discussing chores (Bedrosian & Prutting, 1978). If the significant other adult involves a sheltered workshop supervisor, a conversational situation involving instruction in a work-related activity is recommended. In each case, the significant other adult should be instructed to interact as normally as possible with the adult who is mentally retarded.

Adult-Peer-Clinician Interactions

This triadic interaction is desired for purposes of assessing the communication skills of the adult who is mentally retarded in a group in which there is usually an unequal number of speaking turns across participants. Of interest is whether the adult takes fewer or more turns than his/her peer (Abbeduto & Rosenberg, 1980). For this interaction, a clinical setting involving living room furniture rather than the traditional table and chair setup is recommended to promote conversation.

Adult–Clinician Interaction

Another interaction with the clinician, in the clinical setting just described, is suggested for the clinician to evoke specific conversational skills from the adult with mental retardation. These procedures are "warranted when specific aspects of language are to be analyzed, when frequency of occurrence in naturalistic settings is limited, or if the usual situations do not afford detailed analysis of a specific language behavior" (Miller, 1981, p. 139). By violating normal rules of discourse or expected styles of interaction, the clinician can address one or more of the following questions as they relate to the adult:

1. What strategies does the adult with mental retardation use to repair planned turn-taking violations involving interruptions? For cxample, will he/she discontinue talking, reintroduce his/her interrupted utterance, or reintroduce the topic of his/her interrupted utterance (Warne & Bedrosian, 1986)?
2. Will the adult use requests for repair, involving requests for repetition or clarification, in response to utterances that are deliberately produced unintelligibly?
3. What strategies does the adult use to respond to various types of planned requests for repair? For example, will he/she confirm, repeat, or revise his/her utterance? Or, will he/she not provide any response (Paul & Cohen, 1984)?
4. Will the adult attain the attention of a listener who deliberately exhibits verbal and/or nonverbal behaviors of disinterest? For example, will he/she continue to talk even though the listener removes eye contact? Also, what strategies does the adult use to obtain the attention of an inattentive listener? For example, will he/she tap the listener's shoulder or use the listener's name?
5. Will the adult initiate topics following planned periods of silence?
6. Can the adult maintain topics initiated by the use of informative statements as opposed to various types of requests characteristic of clinical discourse?
7. Will the adult question the appropriateness of topics that are deliberately initiated "out of the blue" (Warne & Bedrosian, 1986)?

Data Analysis

After the various participant interactions, either a detailed system of conversational analysis or, if working under time constraints, a communication skills checklist (see Appendix A) is applied to the data. Communication behaviors incorporated in the checklist include topic, repair, turn-taking, control, politeness, and various nonverbal behaviors. The intervention procedures that follow incorporate these same communicative areas.

A separate checklist is used for each of the participant interactions assessed. A place for including descriptive information about the nature of each interaction is provided at the beginning of the checklist. The clinician is instructed to check the appropriate descriptor for each skill. A column for recording frequency data, if described, is also provided.

Categorization of Communication Skills

Based on the results of the communication skills checklist, the communicative performance of each adult who is mentally retarded is categorized into general styles of interaction along dimensions of dominance or submission. Operationally defined, a *dominant* individual is one who initiates a greater number of topics than his/her peer or significant other across the interactions assessed, expresses at least one type of control, and exhibits consistent performance in his/her group intervention placement. The categorization of communication skills is necessary for purposes of grouping adults and selecting intervention goals.

COMMUNICATION INTERVENTION PROCEDURES

Intervention Agents and Settings

A variety of agents and settings is incorporated into the communication intervention program to facilitate code-switching abilities (i.e., the ability to modify one's style of interaction according to listener characteristics) and generalization. Group rather than individualized programming is also recommended to facilitate code switching and generalization. The initial intervention agents include the clinician and a peer group in the clinical setting previously described. The adults in each group are selected according to their styles of interaction. Each group consists of no more than three adults, composed of both dominant and submissive individuals (i.e., two dominant adults and one submissive adult, or two submissive adults and one dominant adult). The rationale for mixing styles of interaction in each group is that it creates a dynamic atmosphere for intervention. Sex, cognitive level, and language production and comprehension levels can vary within each group as long as special teaching considerations are made.

As the program progresses, other intervention agents and corresponding settings are included. These agents will vary according to the major setting in which the clinical intervention takes place. For example, in a sheltered workshop, other intervention agents can include administrative and secretarial staff in the context of office settings, and vocational supervisors on the work floor. In an institutional setting, direct care staff can also participate in the program. If community transportation is available, intervention agents and settings can include waiters in restaurants, clerks in stores, and drivers on buses.

Intervention Design

Several single-subject experimental designs for measuring changes in communicative behavior as a result of intervention are available (Hersen & Barlow, 1976). For purposes of this program, however, a multiple-baseline design across behaviors is recommended. For each adult, the independent (i.e., treatment) variable is applied sequentially to at least two separate communication target behaviors. While both or all behaviors are being measured simultaneously, only one is treated at a time. As soon as the criterion is met for the first behavior, the treatment variable is then applied to the next behavior or dependent variable.

Structure of Intervention Sessions

A minimum of two weekly 30-minute intervention sessions is suggested. The first 5 minutes of each session are devoted to probe and baseline measurements in which the natural frequency of occurrence of all communication target behaviors selected for each adult is recorded. During this time, the clinician refrains from initiating topics and from giving teaching instructions or feedback, but does respond to topics initiated by the adults. Intervention procedures are applied during the remaining 25 minutes of each session.

A sample data sheet for recording simultaneous communication behaviors across adults in a group is presented in Figure 10–1. Probe and baseline date (i.e., frequency of spontaneous communication target behaviors occurring during the first 5 minutes of a session) are recorded in the first two rows of each grid. Treatment data (i.e., frequency of evoked, instructed, and spontaneous communication target behaviors occurring during the remaining 25 minutes of a session) are recorded in the last three rows of each grid.

Long-Term Intervention Goal

Throughout this book, the need for developing *functional* and *competent* communication skills in the population of adults with mental retardation has been stressed. To achieve functional skills, the short-term intervention goals focus directly on pragmatic behaviors within the communicative context, rather than the more traditional goals focusing on articulation, syntactic, and semantic behaviors in isolation. This should not imply, however, that these latter three behaviors are not incorporated into the program. In fact, the criteria for client selection specified earlier are partly based on these speech and language areas. However, a primary difference between this program and the traditional language programs is that articulation, syntactic, and semantic skills in

Name: _______________________   Target Behavior(s): _______________________

Date: _______________________   Task/Procedure: _______________________

Baseline
Evoked
Instruction
Spontaneous
Notes:

Name: _______________________   Target Behavior(s): _______________________

Date: _______________________   Task/Procedure: _______________________

Baseline
Evoked
Instruction
Spontaneous
Notes:

Figure 10–1. Sample data sheet.

this program are facilitated indirectly within a communicative context. For example, precise articulation may be emphasized when a communicative breakdown results from a lack of intelligibility, rather than training articulation (i.e., through drills) as an isolated skill. Likewise, syntactic skills appropriate for one's developmental level of functioning may be emphasized in the context of issuing meaningful requests. The adult with mental retardation should be taught how to use his/her long-established speech and language behaviors more effectively for broader communicative purposes.

To achieve competent communication skills, the short-term intervention goals also attempt to teach active rather than passive communication behaviors characteristic of traditional program goals. For example, the adults are taught how to initiate topics through the use of requests for information. Adults with mental retardation have been placed in a responding role far too long. The development of both functional and competent communication skills in this population is therefore warranted.

Short-Term Intervention Goals

The initial selection of short-term intervention goals primarily involves an increase in the frequency of topic initiations for submissive adults and a decrease in the frequency of topic initiations for dominant adults. The rationale for selecting these goals was derived from the findings of Weimann (1977), which demonstrate that speakers in dyadic interactions were judged as more socially competent when both participants initiated an equal number of topics than when one participant initiated the majority of topics. Input from parents and guardians and professional team members is always considered in the actual selection of intervention goals. Other short-term goals are outlined in the discussion of specific teaching procedures.

The criterion for skill attainment requires three consecutive baseline measures in which the targeted communication behaviors are emitted at a desired level. For example, for increasing topic initiation, the criterion involves a greater or equal number of topics initiated by the submissive adult in relation to the other group participants for three consecutive baselines.

General Teaching Procedures

Communication is facilitated through instruction, modeling, role-playing, and feedback regarding performance. The latter takes several forms, including further instruction for incorrect performance; audiotaped feedback to allow judgment of one's own performance; and peer judgment of performance. These techniques have been effective with adults who are mentally retarded (Gibson, Lawrence, & Nelson, 1976).

Procedures for teaching a specific communication skill often vary across adults, depending on their developmental levels of functioning. Generally, the first procedure employed for teaching a communication skill is that of instruction involving a definition of the skill and a discussion of its use. Adults functioning at a comprehension level of 2 to 3 years of age may not be capable of understanding the varied uses of a skill. In this case, the desired communication skill is modeled.

The next teaching procedure involves an explanation of a role-playing task to practice the communication skill. For example, for teaching a topic initiation involving a departure, the clinician would state: "Let's pretend that you were going to be leaving me. What would you say to me? Now let's practice doing it." Adults functioning primarily in early preoperations may not be capable of responding to a role-playing task (Flavell, 1977). Therefore, in this case, the actual situation and skill are modeled either by the clinician or a higher functioning peer in the group.

The final teaching procedure involves practice using the communication skill in a variety of participant interactions and settings. Again, depending on their levels of cognitive development, the adults are also encouraged to solve problems, identify the behaviors involved in a new communication skill, and think of alternative ways of expressing the same communicative intent. Unlike other communication-skill training programs for adults who are mildly to moderately mentally retarded (e.g., Roessler & Lewis, 1984; Rusch, Karlan, Riva, & Rusch, 1984; Rychtarik & Bornstein, 1979), this intervention program considers developmental levels of cognition and language production and comprehension, as well as the interrelationships between these domains.

Specific Teaching Procedures

Specific teaching procedures employed for various communication goals have been reported by Bedrosian (1982, 1985). The communication goals and specific teaching procedures that follow have been modified from the previously cited references in that they are more thorough and apply directly to the adult population. A summary of these goals and procedures is presented in Table 10–1.

Increasing the Frequency of Topic Initiations

To increase the frequency of topic initiations, teaching procedures involve various communicative functions and discourse rules. (Note that

TABLE 10-1.

An Outline of Communication Goals and Teaching Procedures

Communication Goal	Teaching Procedure
Increasing the frequency of topic initiations	1. Departures 2. Greetings 3. Attention-getting devices 4. Introductions of new people 5. Expression of needs 6. Initiation of requests for information 7. Initiation of request for repetition 8. Expression of ideas and opinions
Decreasing the frequency of topic initiations	1. Turn-taking 2. Listening skills 3. Decreasing interruptions
Increasing the frequency of other-oriented topic initiations	1. Rationale 2. Greetings and requests for information 3. Acknowledgments 4. Describing appearances
Increasing the frequency of self-oriented topic initiations	1. Rationale 2. Expression of ideas and opinions 3. Description of appearance 4. Expression of feelings 5. Questions of self-interest
Decreasing commanding styles of interaction	1. Definition 2. Modifying a command 3. Evoking polite or indirect request forms 4. Nonverbal language and paralinguistic features 5. Role-playing judgment tasks 6. Monitoring performance
Increasing the frequency of topic maintenance turns	1. Acknowledgments 2. Topic incorporation 3. Topic-changing devices 4. Monitoring performance
Increasing the frequency of eye contact when initiating a topic in a group	1. Describing facial features 2. Imitating nonverbal behaviors 3. Giving instructions 4. Structured game 5. Use of other nonverbal behaviors 6. Monitoring performance

Note: Adapted from Bedrosian, J. L. (1985). An approach to developing conversational competence. In D. N. Ripich & F. M. Spinelli (Eds.), *School discourse problems* (pp. 231–255). San Diego, CA: College–Hill Press.

in the following presentation, "adult" is used to refer to the adult with mental retardation being discussed.)

1. *Departures.*
   A. Departures are defined to the adults as: "Goodbye"; "Bye"; "Bye-bye"; "So long"; "See you later"; "Take care"; "Wait just a minute"; "I'll be right back"; or "I'll talk to you later."
   B. Situations in which departures are appropriate are discussed: when leaving one or more people with whom one has been interacting for any period of time. For example, when leaving for the day; when leaving for only a few minutes to do another task or join another conversation; when leaving for several hours; and when ending a telephone conversation. The adults are asked to contribute their ideas about appropriate uses of departures.
   C. Role-playing procedures are used to set up the situations just specified. For example, the adult is asked how he/she would express a departure when leaving his/her primary caregiver for the day. In instances in which the adult does not spontaneously initiate a departure, the clinician either models the desired communication behavior or uses the phrase: "What do you say when you leave someone?" to evoke the departure.
   D. Situations in which departures are not appropriate (e.g., when starting a conversation, in the middle of a conversation, and when not leaving one or more persons with whom one has been interacting) are also discussed. The adults are again asked to make suggestions about the inappropriate use of departures.
   E. Role-playing judgment tasks are used by having the adult judge whether a departure had been used appropriately in the various situations presented.
   F. The adults are supervised in their uses of departures with other participants. For example, in a sheltered workshop setting, individuals from the group are instructed to borrow an object from a secretary. Upon leaving the secretary, the use of departures is monitored.
2. *Greetings.* Procedures for teaching greetings (e.g., "Hi"; "Hello"; "How are you?"; "Good morning"; "How are things going?") are similar to those for teaching the use of departures.
3. *Attention-getting devices.* Keenan and Schieffelin (1976) stated that to initiate a topic, the speaker must first get the attention of the intended listener.
   A. Ways of getting the listener's attention are discussed: "saying the listener's name; tapping the listener on the shoulder; moving within the visual field of the listener; using a louder voice; leaning

forward in the direction of the listener; and using eye contact with the intended listener when in a group of participants" (Bedrosian, 1985, p. 244).

B. To evoke attention-getting devices, role-playing procedures are employed. For example, the adult is instructed to give an object to the clinician. The clinician then "plays hard to get" by ignoring the adult's attempts to deliver the object. If the adult does not spontaneously use an attention-getting device, the desired communication behavior is modeled, or the clinician instructs: "Tell/show me what you can do to get me to look at you" in order to evoke an attention-getting device.

C. The adults are supervised in their use of attention-getting devices with other participants. For example, in a group home setting, the adult is instructed to give a message to his/her primary caregiver while the caregiver is engaged in a conversation with another person. The use of attention-getting devices upon entering the conversation is monitored.

4. *Introductions of new people.*

A. Four steps in making an introduction are discussed:

a. The initial greeting, often accompanied by a handshake;

b. Requesting the name of the other, or stating one's own name;

c. Stating one's own name, or requesting the name of the other; and

d. An acknowledgment of the exchange (e.g., "It's nice to meet you").

B. Role-playing procedures are used for purposes of practicing the four steps of an introduction. The adults, when capable, are instructed to identify each step of the introduction.

C. Situations in which introductions are not always appropriate are also discussed, for example, when interacting with a store clerk or bus driver.

D. For additional practice of introductions, strangers are occasionally invited to a group and instructed not to initiate any greeting or introduction. The clinician records the amount of time it takes before an adult initiates an introduction.

5. *Expression of needs.* Because a speaker must often have a need to communicate to initiate a topic, these needs are created in several ways.

A. Tasks are structured such that each dominant adult in the group has the materials necessary to perform or complete the tasks. The submissive adult is not given the necessary task materials in order to evoke the initiation for expression of needs. These tasks can include cooking or putting together a jigsaw puzzle.

B. Each dominant adult in the group is given his/her work compensation for buying a favorite food item (e.g., soda pop) during the day. The submissive adult is not given any money in order to evoke the initiation for expression of needs.

C. When possible, groups are taken to a restaurant, a social setting that requires everyone to order his/her food from restaurant personnel in order to eat.

D. For each situation specified above, a three-step procedure is used if the adult does not initiate his/her needs:

a. The adult is asked if he/she has everything needed for the task or situation.

b. The adult is then asked what he/she needs.

c. If no initiation occurs, the adult is then questioned directly: "Do you need (*name of object needed*)?".

6. *Initiation of requests for information.*

A. To account for differences in comprehension levels across adults in a group, the instruction "ask a question" is not employed for evoking requests for information because some adults might instead answer (Chomsky, 1969). Instead, to evoke a question about one's weekend activities or feelings about a particular situation, for example, the following instructions are given: "What did (*name of a group participant*) do over the weekend? How does (*name of group participant*) feel about (*specification of topic*)? How can you find out?" (Bedrosian, 1985, p. 245). A question is modeled for the adult if he/she does not respond following the instruction. Any question form corresponding to the adult's syntactic level of development is accepted as long as the request is directed to the topic being discussed.

B. After the adults are able to initiate requests for information in the clinical setting, they are then supervised in the initiation of these requests in other settings. For example, during lunchtime the adults are instructed to use requests for information with other peers.

7. *Initiation of requests for repetition.*

A. To evoke a request for repetition (e.g., "What?"), the clinician will occasionally whisper or deliberately mumble nonsense syllables. If the adult does not spontaneously initiate a request for repetition, the following steps are taken:

a. The adult is asked: "What did I just say? How can you find out what I just said?"

b. If there is still no initiation of repair, a request form corresponding to the adult's syntactic level of development is modeled. For example, the request form "Say again, please" is modeled for adults functioning between Structural Stages I and II (Miller, 1981), as opposed to "Can you say that again?" for adults functioning between Structural Stages IV and V. These

structural stages are based on data regarding the developmental progression of syntactic skills in normal language learning children (Miller, 1981).
   B. Similar procedures are used if an adult has not been listening to his/her peers conversing in the group.
8. *Expression of ideas and opinions.*
   A. Various issues (e.g., friendship, dating, marriage, being alone, responsibilities, jobs, getting fired from a job) are raised. The adult is asked to express his/her own ideas and opinions about each issue, as well as to request information regarding the ideas and opinions of others.

Decreasing the Frequency of Topic Initiations

The teaching procedures for decreasing the frequency of topic initiations are designed under the assumption that as the submissive adults initiate more topics, there is less conversational floor time for topic initiations by the dominant adults. The procedures focus on turn-taking and listening activities, as well as on decreasing the frequency of interruptions.

1. *Turn-taking.*
   A. One procedure for facilitating turn-taking skills involves the use of a structured game (e.g., the board game Parchesi) whereby each adult can talk only when it is his/her turn in the game. At the beginning of each game, the order of turns among participants is established. Following a turn, the dominant adult is sometimes asked to identify the group participant who has the next turn.
   B. During conversation, the clinician frequently designates turns among participants when implementing procedures for increasing the frequency of topic initiations. The importance of taking turns in conversation is stressed.
   C. Submissive adults are occasionally instructed in procedures for gaining the conversational floor from the dominant adults. For example, they are taught to use verbal and nonverbal attention getting devices, or to use speaking volumes louder than that of the dominant adults (Meltzer, Morris, & Hayes, 1971).
2. *Listening skills.*
   A. To facilitate listening skills, the adult is instructed to repeat what the previous speaker has said before he/she can initiate a topic.
   B. Another procedure involves questioning the adult about the content of the immediate speaker's turn: "What did (*name of speaker*) just say?" Procedures for evoking a request for repetition are implemented if the adult cannot respond.

C. Referential communication tasks (Longhurst & Reichle, 1975) can also be used. For example, the adult is seated at a table across from another participant with a wooden partition separating the two. Identical everyday objects are placed in front of each participant. The listener is required to point to the object that matches the functional description given by the speaker.

D. The body language of a listener is also discussed, using the judgment task. The adults are required to determine the difference between an interested listener versus a bored listener, as well as role play each type of listener in reponse to a participant talking. An interested listener is defined as one who "looks at the speaker; uses verbal and/or nonverbal acknowledgments; and/or sits with his/her body facing the speaker" (Bedrosian, 1985, p. 247). In contrast, a bored listener is defined as one who "engages in another activity, not looking at the speaker; does not use verbal or nonverbal acknowledgments; talks while the speaker is talking; turns away from the speaker; and/or walks out of the room during the conversation" (Bedrosian, 1985, p. 247).

3. *Decreasing the frequency of interruptions.* Decreasing the frequency of interruptions could be implemented as a separate goal, although a tentative relationship between interruptions and topic initiations has been reported (Bedrosian, 1982). Therefore, for purposes of this chapter, decreasing interruptions will be considered as a procedure for decreasing topic initiations. The procedures are as follows:

A. The adults are given a definition of interruption: "Interruption means talking when someone else is already talking."

B. Each adult is asked to immediately identify his/her interruption during the course of a conversation by using the following line of questions:

a. "Who was talking just now?";

b. "What did you just do?", in order to evoke the response, "Interrupt";

c. "What do you need to do?", in order to evoke the response "Wait" or "Wait until he/she stops talking" (Bedrosian, 1985, p. 247).

C. Following an interruption, the adult is also instructed as to what to say to repair it (e.g., "Excuse me," "I'm sorry I interrupted").

D. A task requiring the adult to judge when a speaker has stopped talking is used in a variety of settings and participant interactions. Specifically, the adult is given a message to deliver to a person engaged in a conversation with another. The adult is instructed to wait and to deliver the message only when the person stops talking or acknowledges his/her presence. The same line of questioning specified in 3B is used if the adult interrupts the person talking.

E. Appropriate uses of interruptions are also discussed (e.g., in case of an emergency). In these cases, appropriate interrupting devices are taught. For example, for those adults capable of using complex sentences involving coordinating conjunctions, the phrase "Sorry to interrupt, but..." is used.

F. If an adult is functioning at least in middle preoperations with comparable levels of language production and comprehension, more sophisticated instructions about turn-taking cues (Weiman & Knapp, 1975) are given. The adult is asked to watch for the following cues used by a speaker to indicate that he/she is not ready to give up the conversational floor:

   a. Use of coordinating conjuctions (e.g., "and", "but") either followed by a pause or prolonged;

   b. Prolongation of words;

   c. Use of expressions like "Ahm" followed by a pause; and

   d. Use of eye contact by looking up at the ceiling to indicate thinking (Bedrosian, 1985, p. 248).

   The adult is instructed to deliver a message to the clinician who uses these cues while talking, and to wait until the clinician is done with his/her turn.

G. Submissive adults are occasionally taught how to respond when interrupted. These responses involve the use of various turn-taking repair mechanisms (Warne & Bedrosian, 1986). For example, following an interruption, the submissive adult is instructed to repeat his/her interrupted utterance: "What did you say? Tell us again."

Increasing the Frequency of Other-Oriented Topic Initiations

Some adults with mental retardation primarily initiate topics about themselves (Bedrosian, 1982). For these adults, establishing positive relationships with others is often difficult. The criterion for this goal involves an equal or greater number of other-oriented topic initiations as opposed to self-oriented topic initiations for three consecutive baselines. The teaching procedures are as follows:

1. The reason for initiating topics about the other is discussed: "It is important to show the other person that you are interested in him/her so the he/she will want to be your friend. So you must learn to focus on the other person by remembering to greet him/her and to find out different things about that person, instead of always just talking about yourself" (Bedrosian, 1985, p. 248).

2. The procedures described previously for teaching greetings and requests for information are used for this goal. The adult is instructed to go up to a variety of individuals and use a greeting followed by a request for information before he/she can begin to talk about him/herself. If the adult exhibits difficulty in thinking of topics about which he can request other-oriented information, appropriate topics (e.g., favorite sport, hobbies, likes and dislikes) are suggested.

3. If necessary, the adult is later taught to acknowledge the response to his/her request for information prior to talking about him/herself. The acknowledgment can be either verbal (e.g., "Uh-huh") or nonverbal (e.g., a head nod). Such a procedure facilitates smoother topic changes (Bedrosian, 1979).

4. To encourage focusing on the other person, the adult is instructed to describe the appearance (e.g., color and texture of clothes, height, weight, color of hair and eyes) of another participant in the group.

Increasing the Frequency of Self-Oriented Topic Initiations

Some adults who are mentally retarded seek information about others but appear shy in offering information about themselves unless questioned directly (Bedrosian, 1979). For these adults, procedures for teaching self-oriented topic initiations are employed. The criterion for this goal involves achieving an equal or greater number of self-oriented topic initiations as opposed to other-oriented topic initiations over three consecutive baselines.

1. The reason for initiating topics about oneself is discussed: "We would like to get to know you better. What you think and feel are important to us. You have a lot to offer."

2. The procedures described previously for teaching expression of one's own ideas and opinions are employed. If the adult's first intervention goal involved an increase in the frequency of topic initiations, these procedures would not have been used in the group at that time in order to meet the requirements of using a multiple baseline design across behaviors.

3. To encourage focusing on oneself, the adult is instructed to describe his/her own appearance.

4. The adult is encouraged to express his/her feelings about experienced or anticipated events (e.g., losing a parent, helping a friend).

5. One way to start a conversation about oneself is to ask someone a question related to one's own interests. For example, if Person A likes photography and wants to talk about it, he/she could ask Person B the following question: "Do you like photography?". After Person B's response, whether positive or negative, Person A could then discuss his/her own interests in photography. This sequence of questioning and sharing information about oneself is discussed with the adults and practiced in various participant interactions and settings.

Decreasing Commanding Styles of Interaction

Adults who initiate topics primarily through the use of commands may be signaling potential interpersonal conflicts. Procedures for decreasing the frequency of command styles of interactions are as follows.

1. Commands are described to the adults as being bossy.
2. If the adult makes a command, he/she is immediately asked to try another way of saying the same thing: "How else can you say that?" If a command form is again given, the clinician models a polite or indirect request form corresponding to the adult's level of syntactic development.
3. Situations are arranged to evoke polite or indirect request forms from the adult. For example, the adult is instructed to make various requests of another participant: "In a nice way, how can you get (*name of participant*) to (*name of action*)?". In this situation, the adult is required to use a polite or indirect request form corresponding to his/her level of syntactic development. For example, adults operating between Structural Stages I and II (Miller, 1981) are instructed to use the command form with a politeness marker: "Open the window, please." Adults operating between Structural Stages III and IV are instructed to use "can" in forming an indirect request: "Can you open the window, please?". Adults operating in Structural Stage V are instructed to use "could" in forming the request: "Could you open the window, please?". If the adult uses a command form, procedures for modifying the command are employed.
4. Nonverbal language and paralinguistic features are also included in the instructions for making a polite request. The adults are instructed to
   A. Smile or have a pleasant look on their faces while requesting, rather than looking angry;
   B. Sit with their arms relaxed to the side rather than sitting with arms crossed;
   C. Put their feet on the floor rather than crossing legs;
   D. Use rising inflection at the end of their request.
5. Role-playing judgment tasks are employed by having the adult judge if another group participant has made a nice request or a bossy request in various situations.
6. The adult's use of polite or indirect request forms is monitored in various settings (e.g., on the work floor, at mealtime).

Increasing the Frequency of Topic-Maintenance Turns

For those adults who exhibit difficulties in maintaining topics, the following procedures are employed.

1. The use of a verbal or nonverbal acknowledgment in a question–response–acknowledgment sequence is taught. For example, the adult is instructed to produce a request for information, listen to the response, and use an acknowledgment. The adult is then questioned about the content of the response to determine if he/she was indeed listening. This procedure involves minimal topic-maintenance skills.
2. Another way to keep a topic going involves the use of topic incorporation (i.e., adding new but related information) (Keenan & Schieffelin, 1976). The adults are asked to describe various aspects of a single object or issue: "What else can we say about this?".
3. For those adults functioning at least in late preoperations, topic-changing devices (e.g., "Oh, by the way..." or "Not to change the topic but...") can be taught. The adults are instructed to use such devices only after they have initially maintained the topic of the previous speaker's turn.
4. The adult's topic-maintenance abilities are monitored in various settings.

Increasing the Frequency of Eye Contact When Initiating a Topic in a Group

Using eye contact when initiating topics in a group setting can be considered either as a procedure for increasing the frequency of topic initiations or as a separate goal. Findings reported by Bedrosian (1982) indicated a possible relationship between these two communicative behaviors. This relationship and the corresponding clinical implications are discussed in the case study that follows. Although eye contact is not necessary for initiating topics in a dyadic interaction (Kendon, 1965), it can serve as a useful attention-getting device for initiating topics in a group interaction. The criterion for this goal involves the use of eye contact on all topic initiations for three consecutive baseline–probe measures. The teaching procedures are as follows.

1. The adults are instructed to describe various facial features (e.g., color of eyes and hair, length of hair, size of nose, freckles) of the participants in the group.
2. Each adult participates in a mirror-image exercise in which he/she imitates the nonverbal behaviors of another participant.
3. The adult is asked to give an instruction to a particular member of the group using eye contact: "Tell/ask (*name of participant*) to get the

(*name of object*) or to do (*name of action*). Remember to look at him/her to get his/her attention" (Bedrosian, 1985, p. 249).
4. If the adult exhibits difficulty in using eye contact the following branch steps are employed:
    A. The adult is instructed to turn his/her body toward the intended listener.
    B. He/she is instructed to say the name of the intended listener.
    C. He/she is asked to look at the forehead or the top of the intended listener's head.
    D. He/she is instructed to lean toward the intended listener.
    E. He/she is instructed to tap the shoulder of the intended listener.
5. The adult's use of eye contact is monitored in other settings.

CASE STUDY

Data demonstrating the effectiveness of the communication intervention program just described have been reported by Bedrosian (1982). A case study illustrating some of the intervention procedures is presented here to demonstrate the use of a multiple-baseline design across behaviors.

Client Description

Linda, 25.8 years of age, had a primary diagnosis of mild mental retardation with some autistic-like behaviors. Her hearing was reported to be within normal limits. Linda resided at home with her family and was attending a sheltered workshop in which the communication assessment and intervention program was conducted.

In terms of her cognitive performance, Linda has a reported full-scale IQ of 55 as measured with the *Leiter International Performance Scale* (Leiter & Arthur, 1969). Results of an informal Piagetian cognitive assessment (Gill, 1979) indicated that she had variable performance across tasks: early to middle preoperations for seriation and dichotomies; middle to late preoperations for free sorting; and late preoperations for drawing. Conservation and transitivity tasks were not mastered.

A variety of informal and standardized procedures were used for assessing Linda's comprehension of language. She comprehended question types acquired by normal language-learning children from 2.6 to 4.0 years of age (Chapman, 1976a). Her comprehension of locatives was similar to that of a 3.4 year old (Hodun, 1975). Finally, Linda exhibited a mental age of 6.6 years on the Oral Commissions subtest of the Detroit Tests of Learning Aptitude (Baker & Leland, 1959).

In terms of language production, Linda had a mean length of utterance (MLU) in morphemes of 1.95, corresponding to Brown's Late Stage I (Miller, 1981). This MLU was influenced by a high frequency of one-word acknowledgments. Results of a structural-stage analysis (Miller, 1981) indicated that she was functioning between Structural Stages II and III for syntactic development.

Communication Assessment Results

By using the communication skills checklist, frequency data were recorded for each of the three participant interactions (i.e., peer, group, clinician) assessed. Linda only initiated topics in the group interaction. In this interaction, her two topic initiations were fewer than those initiated by the other participants. Neither initiation was accompanied by eye contact. Her eyes were directed primarily at the floor. A staff report corroborated these findings. The subject matter of these two topic initiations involved referents in the present. The communicative intent of her topic initiations consisted of requests for information and attention. In terms of participant-oriented topics, both of Linda's topic initiations related to the other participants.

The majority of Linda's topic-maintenance turns consisted of responses to questions and acknowledgments. Topic incorporating was rarely employed. Turns that did not maintain the topic involved either new topic initiations or evasion of questions. Control was expressed by the use of multi-uttered questions and chaining.

Based on the results of the assessment, particularly those involving the infrequency of the topic initiations, Linda's communication skills were categorized as submissive. She was initially grouped with two dominant peers. Because of some scheduling problems, she was later regrouped with one dominant peer and one submissive peer.

Intervention Goals

Two intervention goals were selected: first, to increase the frequency of topic initiations; and second, to increase the frequency of eye contact when initiating topics. The intervention program was conducted over a 13-month period.

Communication Intervention Results and Interpretation

The intervention results are summarized in Figure 10–2. Each of the first three data points represents a 5-minute average of the frequency of communication target behaviors emitted during a 10-minute assessment

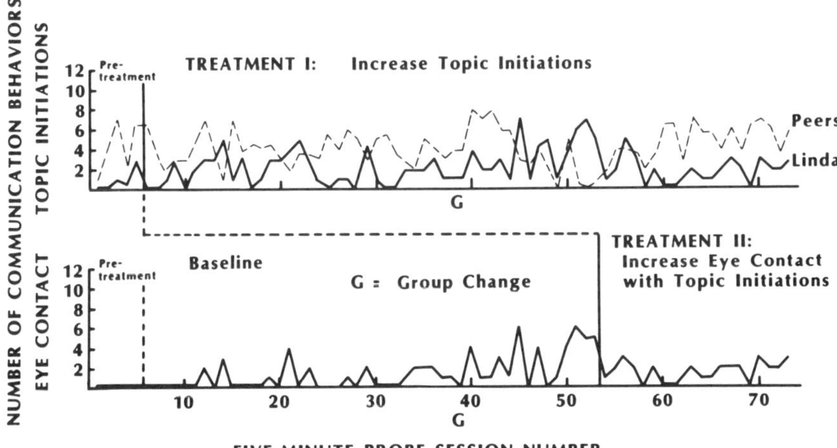

Figure 10–2. *Number of total topic initiations and topic initiations accompanied with eye contact in 5-minute probe sessions across program phases for Linda.*

interaction. The fourth and fifth data points represent the frequency of communication target behaviors emitted by Linda during her initial placement with the peer assigned to her intervention group. The average number of topics initiated by her peers is also plotted to determine whether the criterion for increasing topic initiations was met.

Pretreatment

During the pretreatment phase, the adult initiated fewer topics than the other participants across all sessions. None of her topic initiations was accompanied by eye contact.

Treatment I

During Treatment I, Linda increased the frequency of her topic initiations. She met the criterion for this goal by the 53rd session when she had initiated a greater number of topics than her peers for three consecutive probe sessions. Although the frequency of her initiations was not that different from baseline, she was assuming a more dominant position in the group, as demonstrated by examining her data relative to those of other group members. It should be noted that criterion was met within 10 sessions after the group change. This change may have influenced the adult's performance. Based on our knowledge of discourse rules alone, one's communicative performance does change as a factor of the other participants involved. During this phase, Linda also exhibited an increase in her use of eye contact with topic initiations, although eye contact was not being directly taught.

Treatment II

Upon the initiation of Treatment II, Linda met the criterion for the second intervention goal relatively quickly. By the 64th session, she had used eye contact with all topic initiations for three consecutive probe sessions, and did so again as evidenced by sessions 70 through 74. During this phase, she also exhibited a decrease in the frequency of the topic initiations compared with her topic performance in Treatment I. It is possible to at least speculate, therefore, that the intervention procedures for increasing topic initiations were effective in bringing about the changes desired observed in the first treatment phase. Moreover, staff at the sheltered workshop commented on Linda's increased frequency of interacting with peers after the intervention program.

The findings regarding the changes observed in the frequency of eye contact during Treatment I as well as the relative speed with which the criterion was met in Treatment II may imply a possible relationship between topic initiations and eye contact (i.e., as the frequency of topic initiations increase, so does the frequency of eye contact). The assumptions of using a multiple-baseline design across behaviors may have been violated in this case because the two communication behaviors targeted appeared to be related rather than independent. A benefit of using such a design, however, is that we are able to obtain more information regarding the complex relationship between communication behaviors. This information has important clinical implications in that larger units of communication behaviors could be treated in future intervention programs (e.g., the use of eye contact could be a procedure employed when teaching topic initiation).

COMMUNICATION EXIT CRITERIA: FINAL COMMENTS

How competent do these adults have to be as communicators to be dismissed from the communication program? It may not be realistic to expect "normal" communicative competence from these individuals. Yet the communication exit criteria must consider independent living and employment needs of each individual. Indeed, many of the communication target behaviors outlined in this chapter have been found to be critical in the abilities of these adults to successfully interview for (Elias, Sigelman, & Danker–Brown, 1980) and maintain (Malgady, Barcher, Towner, & Davis, 1979) a job. Continued direct clinical services may be needed until these communication goals have been met to ensure successful community living.

Based on clinical experience, these newly learned communication skills will most likely have to be monitored (e.g., through consultative services) for a while, and for some adults, indefinitely. This latter statement is not meant to discourage educators, but simply to remind us that we are dealing with a unique population and a very complex process called communication.

In closing, I would like to add that many of the higher cognitively functioning adults enrolled in the communication program became so good at adhering to normal rules of discourse that they actually began to expect the same communicative performance from vocational staff. If we as educators are going to take on the challenge of teaching communicative competence, we are also going to have to be willing to look closely at our own styles of communication.

REFERENCES

Abbeduto, L., & Rosenberg, S. (1980). The communicative competence of mildly retarded adults. *Applied Psycholinguistics, 1,* 405–426.

Baker, H. J., & Leland, B. (1959). *Detroit test for learning aptitude.* Indianapolis, IN: The Bobbs–Merrill Co., Inc.

Bates, E. (1976). *Language in context: The acquisition of pragmatics.* New York: Academic Press.

Bedrosian, J. L. (1979, May). *Communicative performance of mentally retarded adults — A topic analysis.* Paper presented at the American Association on Mental Deficiency Convention, Miami Beach, FL.

Bedrosian, J. L. (1982). A sociolinguistic approach to communication skills: Assessment and treatment methodology for mentally retarded adults. *Dissertation Abstracts International, 42,* 4338A.

Bedrosian, J. L. (1985). An approach to developing conversational competence. In D. N. Ripich & F. M. Spinelli (Eds.), *School discourse problems* (pp. 231–255). San Diego, CA: College–Hill Press.

Bedrosian, J. L., & Prutting, C. A. (1978). Communicative performance of mentally retarded adults in four conversational settings. *Journal of Speech and Hearing Research, 21,* 79–95.

Chapman, R. (1976a). Eliciting answers to questions: The development of question comprehension in preschool children. In J. Miller (Ed.), *A developmental approach toward assessing communicative behavior in children.* Unpublished manuscript, University of Wisconsin, Madison.

Chapman, R. (1976b, April). *Pragmatics.* Paper presented at the Wisconsin Speech and Hearing Association Convention, Madison, WI.

Chapman, R. S. (1981). Computing child's mean length of utterance in morphemes. In J. F. Miller (Ed.), *Assessing language production in children: Ex-*

perimental procedures (pp. 22–25). Austin, TX: PRO-ED.

Chomsky, C. S. (1969). *The acquisition of syntax in children from 5 to 10.* Cambridge, MA: M. I. T. Press.

Elias, S. F., Sigelman, C. K., & Danker-Brown, P. (1980). Interview behavior of and impressions made by mentally retarded adults. *American Journal of Mental Deficiency, 85,* 53–60.

Ervin-Tripp, S. M. (1973). *Language acquisition and communicative choice.* Stanford, CA: Stanford University Press.

Flavell, J. H. (1977). *Cognitive development.* Englewood Cliffs, NJ: Prentice-Hall, Inc.

Folger, J., & Puck, S. (1976, October). *Coding relational communication: A question approach.* Paper presented at the International Communication Association Convention, Portland, OR.

Garvey, C. (1975). Requests and responses in children's speech. *Journal of Child Language, 2,* 41–63.

Gibson, F. W., Lawrence, P. S., & Nelson, R. D. (1976). Comparison of three training procedures for treating social responses to developmentally disabled adults. *American Journal of Mental Deficiency, 81,* 376–387.

Gill, G. (1979). Piagetian cognitive assessment — Procedures from a variety of sources arranged for convenient clinical use. Unpublished manuscript, University of Wisconsin, Madison.

Ginsburg, H., & Opper, S. (1969). *Piaget's theory of intellectual development: An introduction.* Englewood Cliffs, NJ: Prentice-Hall, Inc.

Hersen, M., & Barlow, D. H. (1976). *Single case experimental designs: Strategies for studying behavior change.* New York: Pergamon Press.

Hodun, A. (1975). *Comprehension and the development of spatial and temporal sequence terms.* Unpublished doctoral dissertation, University of Wisconsin, Madison.

Hymes, D. (1962). The ethnography of speaking. In T. Gladwin & W. Sturtevant (Eds.), *Anthropology and human behavior* (pp. 15–53). Washington, DC: Anthropological Society of Washington.

Hymes, D. (1974). On communicative competence. In J. B. Pride & J. Holmes (Eds.), *Sociolinguistics* (pp. 269–293). Baltimore, MD: Penguin Education.

Keenan, E. D., & Schieffelin, B. B. (1976). Topic as a discourse notion: A study of topic in the conversation of children and adults. In C. N. Li (Ed.), *Subject and topic* (pp. 335–384). New York: Academic Press.

Kendon, A. (1965). Some functions of gaze direction in social interaction. Unpublished report to Science Research Council.

Kernan, K. T., & Sabsay, S. (1983). *Semantic deficiencies in the narratives of mildly retarded speakers.* Unpublished manuscript, University of California, Los Angeles.

Kirchner, D., & Skarakis-Doyle, E. (1983). Developmental language disorders: A theoretical perspective. In T. M. Gallagher & C. A. Prutting (Eds.), *Pragmatic assessment and intervention issues in language (pp. 215–246).* Austin, TX: PRO-ED.

Leiter, R., & Arthur, G. (1969). *Leiter International Performance Scale.* Chicago, IL: C. H. Stoelting Co.

Longhurst, T. M., & Reichle, J. E. (1975). The applied communication game: A comment on Muma's "Communication game: Dump and play." *Journal of Speech and Hearing Disorders, 40,* 315–319.

Malgady, R. G., Barcher, P. R., Towner, G., & Davis, J. (1979). Language factors in vocational evaluation of mentally retarded workers. *American Journal of Mental Deficiency, 83,* 432–438.

Meltzer, L., Morris, W. N., & Hayes, D. P. (1971). Interruption outcomes and vocal amplitude: Explorations in social psychophysics. *Journal of Personality and Social Psychology, 18,* 392–402.

Miller, J. F. (1981). *Assessing children's language production: Experimental procedures.* Baltimore, MD: University Park Press.

Mishler, E. (1975). Studies in dialogue and discourse: II. Types of discourse initiated by and sustained through questioning. *Journal of Psycholinguistic Research, 4,* 99–121.

Owings, N. O., & Guyette, T. W. (1982). Communication behavior assessment and treatment with the adult retarded: An approach. In N. J. Lass (Ed.), *Speech and language: Advances in basic research and practice* (Vol. 7, pp. 185–216). New York: Academic Press.

Owings, N. O., & McManus, M. D. (1980). An analysis of communication functions in the speech of a deinstitutionalized mentally retarded client. *Mental Retardation, 18,* 309–314.

Owings, N., & McManus, M. (1982). *Analysis of communication function use by adult mentally retarded clients in three residential settings.* Paper presented at the 106th annual meeting of the American Association on Mental Deficiency, Boston, MA.

Paul, R., & Cohen, D. J. (1984). Responses to contingent queries in adults with mental retardation and pervasive developmental disorders. *Applied Psycholinguistics, 5,* 349–357.

Paul, R., & Cohen, D. J. (1985). Comprehension of indirect requests in adults with autistic disorders and mental retardation. *Journal of Speech and Hearing Research, 28,* 475–479.

Prutting, C., Bagshaw, N., Goldstein, H., Juskowitz, S., & Umen, I. (1978). Clinician–child discourse: Some preliminary questions. *Journal of Speech and Hearing Disorders, 43,* 123–139.

Retherford, L. (1980). *Three-, four-, and five-year-old children's ability to maintain topic under three conditions.* Unpublished doctoral dissertation, University of Wisconsin, Madison.

Roessler, R. T., & Lewis, F. D. (1984). Conversation skill training with mentally retarded and learning disabled sheltered workshop clients. *Rehabilitation Counseling Bulletin, 27,* 161–171.

Rusch, J. C., Karlan, G. R., Riva, M. T., & Rusch, F. R. (1984). *Teaching mentally retarded adults conversational skills in employment settings.* Unpublished manuscript, University of Illinois, Urbana–Champaign.

Rychtarik, R. G., & Bornstein, P. H. (1979). Training conversational skills in mentally retarded adults: A multiple baseline analysis. *Mental Retardation, 17,* 289–293.

Sacks, H., Schegloff, E. A., & Jefferson, G. (1974). A simplest systematics for the organization of turn-taking for conversation. *Language, 50,* 696–735.

Spinelli, F. M., & Terrell, B. Y. (1984). Remediation in context. *Topics in Language Disorders, 5,* 29–40.

Warne, D., & Bedrosian, J. L. (1986). *Turn-taking and topic maintenance abilities of mentally retarded adults.* Unpublished manuscript, Kansas State University, Manhattan.

Weimann, J. M. (1977). Explication and test of a model of communicative competence. *Human Communication Research, 3,* 195–313.

Weimann, J. M., & Knapp, M. L. (1975). Turn-taking in conversations. *Journal of Communication, Spring,* 75–92.

Wetherby, A. M., & Gaines, B. H. (1982). Cognition and language development in autism. *Journal of Speech and Hearing Disorders, 47,* 63–70.

Wilkinson, L., Heibert, E., & Rembold, K. (1981). Parents' and peers' communication to toddlers. *Journal of Speech and Hearing Research, 24,* 383–388.

☐ *Communication Skills Checklist*

Name of client: _______________________________

Date of interaction: _______________________________

Type of participant interactions: _______________________________

Type of setting: _______________________________

Length of interaction: _______________________________

Instructions: Check the appropriate skill descriptor that follows:

I. Topic Initiations

    A. Frequency of client's topic initiations in comparison to the other participant(s):

        1. None ☐

        2. Less than ☐

        3. Approximately equal to ☐

        4. More than ☐

	Yes	No	Sometimes	Not applicable	Frequency
B. Subject matter of topic initiations					
1. Talks about referents in the past	☐	☐	☐	☐	☐
2. Talks about referents in the future	☐	☐	☐	☐	☐
3. Talks about referents in the present	☐	☐	☐	☐	☐
4. Talks about fantasy-related referents	☐	☐	☐	☐	☐

	Yes	No	Sometimes	Not applicable	Frequency
5. Calls people names	□	□	□	□	□
6. Uses noise/sound-word play in appropriate situations	□	□	□	□	□
7. Repeats old topics on a daily basis	□	□	□	□	□
8. Initiates new topics on a daily basis	□	□	□	□	□

C. Communicative intent of topic initiations

	Yes	No	Sometimes	Not applicable	Frequency
1. Able to get attention of listener	□	□	□	□	□
2. Able to greet others	□	□	□	□	□
3. Able to express departures when leaving	□	□	□	□	□
4. Able to make introductions	□	□	□	□	□
5. Able to initiate needs	□	□	□	□	□
6. Able to initiate questions	□	□	□	□	□
a. Requests for information	□	□	□	□	□
b. Requests for repetition or clarification	□	□	□	□	□
c. Requests for action	□	□	□	□	□
d. Requests for permission	□	□	□	□	□
e. Requests for attention	□	□	□	□	□
7. Able to give information	□	□	□	□	□
8. Uses commands	□	□	□	□	□

D. Participant orientation of topic initiations

	Yes	No	Sometimes	Not applicable	Frequency
1. Talks mostly about self	□	□	□	□	□
2. Talks about the other, as well as self	□	□	□	□	□
3. Talks mostly about other	□	□	□	□	□

II. Maintaining topics

A. Able to keep topic going

	Yes	No	Sometimes	Not applicable	Frequency
1. Responds to questions	□	□	□	□	□
2. Acknowledges topic (e.g., "Uh-huh")	□	□	□	□	□
3. Offers new information that is related	□	□	□	□	□
4. Requests more information about a topic	□	□	□	□	□
5. Able to ask requests for repetition/clarification if message is not clear	□	□	□	□	□
6. Repeats what another has said	□	□	□	□	□

	Yes	No	Sometimes	Not applicable	Frequency
7. Agrees with others	□	□	□	□	□
8. Disagrees with others	□	□	□	□	□

B. Not able to keep a topic going

	Yes	No	Sometimes	Not applicable	Frequency
1. Intentionally evades/ignores a question	□	□	□	□	□
2. Initiates a topic immediately following a topic initiation by a prior speaker	□	□	□	□	□
3. Engages in monologues	□	□	□	□	□
4. Initiates two or more consecutive topics within the same speaking turn	□	□	□	□	□
5. Uses topic changing devices (e.g., "Oh, by the way...")	□	□	□	□	□

III. Conversational Repair of the Referent

A. Able to respond to requests for repair

	Yes	No	Sometimes	Not applicable	Frequency
1. Confirms utterance	□	□	□	□	□
2. Repeats utterance	□	□	□	□	□
3. Revises utterance	□	□	□	□	□
4. Does not respond	□	□	□	□	□

B. Able to use requests for repair

	Yes	No	Sometimes	Not applicable	Frequency
1. Requests for repetition	□	□	□	□	□
2. Requests for clarification	□	□	□	□	□
3. Requests for confirmation	□	□	□	□	□
4. Questions appropriateness of topic	□	□	□	□	□
5. Expresses lack of understanding	□	□	□	□	□

IV. Turn-taking

	Yes	No	Sometimes	Not applicable	Frequency
A. Is easily interrupted	□	□	□	□	□
B. Interrupts others	□	□	□	□	□
C. Answers questions for others	□	□	□	□	□
D. Has long speaking turns	□	□	□	□	□
E. Designates turns for others in a group	□	□	□	□	□
F. Sensitive to listener cues (e.g., can tell if listener is interested or bored)	□	□	□	□	□

	Yes	No	Sometimes	Not applicable	Frequency
G. Excuses self when interrupting	□	□	□	□	□
H. Repairs turn-taking violations					
1. Discontinues talking	□	□	□	□	□
2. Reintroduces interrupted utterance	□	□	□	□	□
3. Reintroduces topic of interrupted utterance	□	□	□	□	□

V. Control

	Yes	No	Sometimes	Not applicable	Frequency
A. Chains questions	□	□	□	□	□
B. Arches questions	□	□	□	□	□
C. Uses multi-uttered questions within the same speaking turn	□	□	□	□	□
D. Uses multi-uttered commands within the same speaking turn	□	□	□	□	□
E. Is successful in interrupting others	□	□	□	□	□

VI. Politeness

	Yes	No	Sometimes	Not applicable	Frequency
A. Able to make indirect requests	□	□	□	□	□
B. Uses commands	□	□	□	□	□
C. Use politeness markers of "please," "Thank you," "excuse me"	□	□	□	□	□

VII. Observation of nonverbal behaviors

	Yes	No	Sometimes	Not applicable	Frequency
A. Stands/sits too close to others when talking	□	□	□	□	□
B. Stands/sits too far away from others when talking	□	□	□	□	□
C. Stands/sits at appropriate social distances when talking	□	□	□	□	□
D. Uses nonverbal head nods to acknowledge	□	□	□	□	□
E. Uses nonverbal means of getting attention to initiate topic (e.g., taps on shoulder, points)	□	□	□	□	□

	Yes	No	Sometimes	Not applicable	Frequency
F. Use of eye contact					
1. Able to use eye contact to designate a listener in a group when initiating a topic	□	□	□	□	□
2. Uses eye contact while listening	□	□	□	□	□

Note: Adapted from Bedrosian (1985), Bedrosian & Prutting (1978), Paul & Cohen (1984), and Warne & Bedrosian (1986).

Teaching Functional Communication Skills to Nonspeaking Adults with Mental Retardation

STEPHEN N. CALCULATOR

As a speech–language pathologist employed in a residential setting that served adults who were multiply handicapped, I frequently shared the frustrations of residents and staff for whom communication breakdowns were normal occurrences. It was the early 1970s, a time when speech and communication were viewed synonymously. The client without speech was perceived to be one without communication and, worse yet, one with nothing to say. It was a time when communication training consisted of techniques designed to improve the articulation and comprehension abilities of clients. The clinician's task was simply identifying where on the continuum of normal speech–language development the client had faltered, then attempting to accelerate the latter's progress through this revered sequence. Such was the course of treatment, irrespective of the client's age and previous therapy history.

Clients who failed to progress despite having received therapy of sufficient duration were viewed as presenting poor prognoses for communication growth. They were then relegated to a corner of the caseload in which the clinician could annually reconfirm their lack of progress, further reinforcing the belief that such clients would not benefit from speech therapy. In the meantime, clinicians were not spared the troublesome observations of caregivers, who noted that despite the "significant" communicative gains (e.g., abilities to produce increasingly larger numbers of sounds and words in imitation and in response to picture cues) displayed by some persons receiving therapy, they saw no evidence of these same individuals reaping any corresponding benefits while in their residences. Communication breakdowns and the mutual frustrations accompanying them were no less frequent than prior to training.

Unable to communicate functionally through speech, these residents consistently left their oral skills with their clinicians back in the clinic room upon returning to their residences, where they continued to rely on various gestural and other nonverbal means of communicating their wants and needs. Nonspeakers who were fortunate enough to interact with staff capable of deriving meaning from these nonverbal exchanges, and willing to spend the time necessary to sort out their intentions, maintained a desire to communicate. For others, the passage of time was accompanied by a growing stockpile of episodes of communication failure, each progressively eroding their desire to communicate. Communicative attempts diminished and a passive style of communication became common. Astute observers noted that it was as though these individuals failed to understand the meaning of communication as a tool for manipulating their environments.

BACK TO THE FUTURE

Contemporary descriptions of the communication abilities of adults who are mentally retarded repeatedly point out the submissive interaction styles of these persons [see chapters by Calculator (Chapter 4); Bedrosian (Chapter 10); Owens and Rogerson (Chapter 7); and Haney, Wilson, and Halle (Chapter 3)]. Despite a shifting orientation from speech to communication, from clinic-based to more naturalistic (i.e., ethnographic) intervention, from preoccupations with language form and content to encouraging purposeful uses of communication, clinicians and others continue to find many of these adults unmotivated to communicate their most basic wants, needs, feelings, and ideas. This has necessitated expanding the scope of intervention beyond the clients to include others coming into regular contact with them. Yoder and Calculator (1981) stated that the principle goal of intervention should be maximizing individuals' abilities and opportunities to interact with a broad range of listeners while minimizing the extent to which they are dependent on these same listeners for deriving the intended meaning of their messages.

Emergence of Augmentative Devices

To approach this goal of improved interactional skills, several problem areas had to be addressed. Clients unable to communicate through speech alone also required supplementary (i.e., *augmentative*) forms of communication. This was addressed by introducing *aided* (communication prostheses such as language boards, communication notebooks, computers, electronic communication devices) and unaided (gestural and signing systems) modes of communication.

In designing alternate communication strategies for nonspeaking adults with mental retardation, a common ideology pervading the implementation of these aided and unaided systems has stressed their uses as augmentative devices. Beukelman, Yorkston, and Dowden (1985) defined *augmentative techniques* as those designed to support, enhance, or augment the communication of nonspeakers (i.e., persons who are not independent verbal communicators in all situations). Intervention begins with a recognition of communicative behaviors (verbal and non-verbal) already in the nonspeaking individual's repertoire.

The augmentative system then serves one of three major roles. First, it could be the primary means of communication, particularly for those clients whose existing repertoires of communicative behaviors limit them to transmitting a severely restricted and highly ambiguous set of messages. Second, the augmentative system could be a supplementary means of communication, particularly for those clients experiencing difficulty being understood (generally, or with respect to specific listeners), and thus in need of a device for clarifying their messages. In this case, existing modes of communication continue to be reinforced and valued by others because they serve a communicative function in particular communicative contexts, whereas the augmentative strategies are prompted in situations requiring their use for more efficient and accurate message exchanges. For example, a pointing gesture might continue to be encouraged in a context in which the nonspeaking adult has been given a cup of black coffee and he points to a picture of cream. Conversely, this same gesture might evoke a listener's requesting that the non-speaker augment his/her message (e.g., through the use of a sign or picture appearing on a communication board) in a situation in which the client points toward the kitchen while watching television, thus confusing the listener as to the intended meaning. Third, the augmentative system could be a facilitative means of communication, particularly for those individuals who rarely initiate communicative exchanges and are described as having no apparent desire to communicate with others. The provision of aided devices has frequently been associated with subsequent corresponding improvements in speaking intelligibility (Kraat,

1985; Silverman, 1980, provide comprehensive reviews of this literature) and increased numbers of message initiations and/or requests (Calculator & D'Altilio–Luchko, 1983; Glennen & Calculator, 1985). Similar benefits have been attributed to the introduction of unaided (e.g., signing) modes of communication (Reichle & Karlan, 1985; Romski, Sevcik, & Joyner, 1984).

Although the provision of an augmentative means of communication can have a significant impact on the abilities of adults with mental retardation to successfully engage in discourse, other factors of equal or greater importance contribute to the eventual outcome of an augmentative instruction program. Several investigators have failed to note significant differences in the frequency, clarity, and overall effectiveness with which nonspeakers communicate after the provision of an augmentative device relative to their pre-instructional reliances on unintelligible vocalizations and indiscriminant gestures (Calculator, 1984; Calculator & Dollaghan, 1982; Harris, 1982; Light, Collier, & Parnes, 1985). A review of published and unpublished research in this area revealed that nonspeaking persons with mental retardation using augmentative aids tend to engage in fewer interactions, have fewer conversational partners, and engage in shorter exchanges than their speaking counterparts (Kraat, 1985). The size, complexity, and cost of an aid, regardless of its impressive appearance, bears no consistent relation to the manner in which it will ultimately be used by the nonspeaker and listeners in the various settings in which interaction occurs. How many times have we seen the nonspeaking adult communicating with a speaking friend through a familiar 20-questions approach (yes/no responses) while seated in front of a microcomputer with voice output capabilities?

In addition to the system itself, augmentative communication programs for adults who are mentally retarded must consider the communicative and related abilities of the nonspeaker as well as his/her listeners. These factors are discussed in the following sections in terms of candidacy criteria influencing the decision of whether to recommend augmentative instruction for a specific client and, given such intervention is deemed to be justified, the directions such instruction might take.

FACTORS TO CONSIDER PRIOR TO INITIATING AUGMENTATIVE INSTRUCTION

Six factors appear to be particularly important when attempting to determine the candidacy of adults with mental retardation for augmentative modes of communication. These factors are cited below and then discussed with respect to how they relate to the intervention process.

1. Cognitive abilities
2. Social skills,
3. Motor skills,
4. Outcomes of previous speech therapy,
5. Age, and
6. Environmental receptivity.

Examining the Notion of Cognitive Prerequisites and Constraints

Hardy (1983) pointed out that the intellectual limitations of nonspeaking persons with mental retardation impose severe constraints on the content of augmentative instruction with such individuals. Generally speaking, as the degree of retardation increases, the long-term prognosis for functional communication diminishes. Similarly, the potential impact of an augmentative system on the size and quality of a client's discourse repertoire is largely determined by the intellectual abilities of the individual (Silverman, 1980).

These comments should not be misconstrued as indicating that there is a pool of persons with mental retardation who are too intellectually handicapped to benefit from augmentative instruction. Given that we adopt a position that all behavior is potentially communicative (e.g., changes in body tone, affect, facial expression, reaching, pointing, crying, grimacing), the role of augmentative modes in supplementing the existing communicative skills of these individuals becomes apparent. Individuals operating at higher intellectual levels are receptive to a broader range of augmentative options [including systems requiring an understanding of the symbolic nature of language, which is prerequisite to the use of signing, Blissymbols, traditional orthography (i.e., the English alphabet), etc.]. These individuals can be expected to use their aids to express a significantly greater number of meanings, conveyed though a broader range of forms, for a greater number of purposes than their lower intellectually functioning peers.

Cognitive Constraints on Aided Forms of Communication

Individuals operating in the mild range of mental retardation are expected to be more capable of using aids that require relatively difficult operating strategies. Whereas *direct selection* (pointing directly to the picture, word, object) may be a viable means of indicating messages across a broad range of levels of intellectual functioning, increasing cognitive abilities are associated with successful uses of *scanning* (where clients wait as potential items on the communication display appear before them and the task is to signal when the desired item is highlighted) and, even more so, encoding systems. In the latter method, nonspeaking persons convey the coordinates (e.g., location on the horizontal and vertical axes) of an item, and the listener then identifies the corresponding item on the communication display.

Cognitive Constraints on Unaided Forms of Communication

Yorkston and Dowden (1984) described three levels of gestures representing ascending levels of symbolic load for their users. At the lowest level are coverbal (paraverbal) gestures, which are useful in conveying emotional states, attitudes, status, and participating in turn-taking within conversations. Referential gestures are the next level of gestures, in which successful transmission of meaning requires the presence of the object or event to which is being referred. Pointing to and showing objects typify gestural behavior at this level. The third level, iconic gestures, is associated with the use of hand shapes and movements that replicate or suggest the form of the object being represented. For example, the gesture for "drink" would replicate this same action.

As we progress from one level to the next in the above system, we would expect the learnability of gestures associated with each level to diminish. Similarly, the learnability of signs is purportedly affected by various factors (Doherty, 1985; Karlan & Lloyd, 1983; Luftig, 1984). For example, functional signs (i.e., those that an individual will have frequent opportunities to use in a variety of natural settings, and that will serve to enhance his/her degree of independence in those settings) are acquired more readily than nonfunctional signs. In addition, the following conventions may be useful in selecting signs to teach to adults who are mentally retarded, given our goals include maximizing these individuals' successes:

1. Teach signs requiring contact with the body prior to those produced away from the body. Doherty (1985) suggested that it might be useful to add bodily contact to signs not calling for such locations to promote learning as long as such modifications are not introduced at the cost of reducing the intelligibility of the sign.
2. Begin with symmetrical signs (i.e., those in which both hands assume identical shapes and reciprocal movements).
3. Begin instruction with highly translucent signs (i.e., those employing hand shapes that mirror or suggest by their appearance the corresponding referent). Mayberry (1976) discusses *molding* as a method of teaching signs to individuals who are mentally retarded. The client's hands are molded around the object being represented (i.e., a "cup"),

thus simultaneously conveying the sign. Nontranslucent signs are taught through a combination of shaping, physical prompting, and modeling.

4. Signs that clients can observe themselves producing are acquired more readily than those that are not visible.

5. Signs referring to concrete referents are easier than those referring to abstract referents.

Augmentative System Usage Relative to Cognitive Stages

Several investigators have suggested that the linguistic abilities of individuals who are mentally retarded are highly correlated with their corresponding levels of cognitive functioning (Calculator, Chapter 4 of this volume; Kamhi & Johnston, 1982; Yoder & Calculator, 1981). These and similar findings have prompted other investigators (Chapman & Miller, 1980; Musselwhite & St. Louis, 1982; Owens & House, 1984; Shane & Bashir, 1980) to specify cognitive prerequisites to the implementation of augmentative systems. Results of these investigations are integrated in the following discussion, with sensorimotor assignments based on the writings of Piaget, as interpreted by Ginsberg and Opper (1967).

Chapman and Miller (1980) likened providing a communication board to an individual functioning below Sensorimotor Stage IV to offering a teething ring to an infant. Such adults are not expected to be capable of recognizing the communicative value underlying their behavior (i.e., there is no intentionality to their actions). At Sensorimotor Stage V (mental age between 12 and 18 months), the individual might be expected to use an augmentative aid to request and comment on persons, objects, and actions in the immediate here-and-now environment. The use of symbols can now be introduced, although such forms remain limited to highly concrete representations such as object miniatures, objects, natural gestures, highly iconic signs, photographs, and some pictures. Messages convey an expanding range of communicative intents as the individual progresses from this stage to the next, with forms moving from one- to multi-word or unit messages.

It is at Sensorimotor Stage 6 (mental age between 18 and 24 months) and beyond that individuals who are mentally retarded are expected to be able to use symbolic forms of communication to refer to objects and events removed from the immediate setting. The complexity of symbols used meaningfully by the client is believed to be determined by corresponding levels of cognitive functioning. Owens and House (1984) proposed the following sequence, from lesser to greater complexity and abstractness, of symbol usage. Non-speech Language Initiation Program (Non-SLIP) (Carrier, 1974) < models or miniatures < pictographs <

pictures < line drawings < Blissymbols < printed words < traditional orthography and numerical encodings. Owens and House do not provide data supporting the clinical usefulness of this hierarchy, nor is this information contained elsewhere. There does not appear to be any justification for witholding symbol instruction at one level until a criterion is met at a preceding level. Similarly there is no rationale for practices in which graphic systems (e.g., line drawings) are abandoned in favor of more abstract forms of representation (e.g., Blissymbols), despite individuals' proven abilities to use the less "sophisticated" systems to meet their daily communication needs. The choice of how to represent items on a communication display can not be guided solely by an individual's capabilities of learning one system or another. Instead, this process of selecting symbol type(s) must also consider the individual's *use* of symbols, across a variety of settings and listeners, each imposing a special set of communication demands.

Symbols representing higher levels of abstraction and complexity are also those permitting access to a potentially unlimited number of meanings. Object boards and, to a lesser extent, photographs and pictures may be restricted to conveying meanings in a 1:1 fashion, with each item depicted representing a single referent. More symbolic forms such as traditional orthography and Blissymbols can be combined and sequenced to result in an infinite number of messages, depending upon the nonspeaking individuals' capabilities and use of these symbols in actual conversational exchanges.

Clark (1984) advised against introducing symbol systems in which the underlying logic is beyond the nonspeaking individual's grasp. Otherwise, the use of such systems may represent nothing more than clients' rotely responding to meaningless visual configurations. Many of us have observed clients using picture, word, and similar communication displays, clients who can point to these various configurations on command and in response to various visual and auditory cues, and are yet unable to recognize these same representations when encountered in other contexts, performing as though they are suddenly confronted with a completely novel stimulus.

Summary

In conclusion, although there appears to be a relationship between cognitive ability and corresponding communication skills, the precise nature of this relationship remains unknown. There appears to be little if any empirical support for the practice of witholding augmentative instruction from clients until they demonstrate a specific level of cognitive functioning, for example, 12 to 18 months (Reichle & Karlan, 1985).

Instead, a more feasible approach might consist of tempering the form and content of such instruction based on the cognitive and associated abilities of the client. As individuals gain increasing experience and success in communicating, we might expect concurrent changes in their understanding of communication and motivation to communicate.

Social Skills

Another factor important to consider before initiating augmentative instruction involves social skills. Three social skills have been found to be predictive of success in implementing augmentative instruction (Chapman & Miller, 1980; Musselwhite & St. Louis, 1982; Owens & House, 1984):

1. An understanding of turn-taking,
2. Ability to establish and maintain eye contact with listeners,
3. Ability to maintain joint attention with a listener to a common object or event.

Matas, Mathy–Laiko, Beukelman, and Legresley (1985) required their clients to be capable of establishing and maintaining eye contact for a minimum of 3 seconds and to attend to tasks for approximately 3 minutes in order to be considered candidates for augmentative training.

Adults with mental retardation may present several unique social obstacles to augmentative instruction. The effects of long-term institutionalization and regimenting of routines on diminishing the need and motivation to communicate have been discussed by Calculator (1985). We must also consider whether the client has listeners he/she is sufficiently interested in communicating with, or whether he/she is equally content being alone. The client who demonstrates a lack of interest in others, rarely initiates interactions despite opportunities to do so, sees little value in communication as a means of manipulating what appears to be an inflexible environment cannot be expected to suddenly communicate upon being provided with a "means" to do so. Unless these social obstacles are addressed prior to or concurrently with communication instruction, we cannot expect the effects of intervention to be immediately beneficial or endurable.

Motor Skills

Behaviors cited in this category have included a persistence of primitive oral reflexes (e.g., biting, gag, rooting, sucking) and additional evidence suggesting a lack of speech motor control (Shane & Bashir, 1980). Unlike the young child who is mentally retarded, the adult is not expected to resolve these problems through maturation and instruction. There is no evidence to suggest that activities designed to inhibit these reflexes, or to increase speech motor control through various *pre-articulatory* exercises designed to increase the strength, coordination, or range of movement of particulator articulators, can result in changes in the speech of these individuals.

Results of Prior Speech Therapy

Again, a different set of criteria should be applied when examining this factor in children who are mentally retarded compared with adults who are mentally retarded. Although a period of speech therapy (1 year is often recommended, but this varies) is often advised for children prior to initiating augmentative intervention (e.g., Owens & House, 1984), a different tact should be used for adults. Given that our ultimate goal is to maximize functional communication skills as soon as possible, any supporting modes of communication introduced to the client that will facilitate progress toward this goal should be attempted. The evidence described earlier suggesting that the introduction of augmentative instruction has no deleterious effects on speech production and may, instead, facilitate speech and overall communication development further contradicts the practice of refraining from augmentative training contingent upon the results of speech instruction.

Age

Beukelman and Yorkston (1982) cited several differences between nonspeaking children and adults (intellectually normal) with respect to their corresponding needs for augmentative aids. The authors' comments are equally applicable to persons functioning in the mild range of mental retardation who were raised in noninstitutional settings. Compared with children, adults have greater needs for independence (e.g., directing the activities of their personal care attendants), increasing exposure to persons who are unfamiliar with them and/or their idiosyncratic modes of communication, and greater language skills resulting from experience and instruction. Each of these factors enhance the adult's likelihood of benefitting from augmentative intervention.

However, Beukelman and Yorkston (1982) noted that adults are generally less tolerant than children of the communicative restrictions (e.g., limited vocabulary) imposed on them when using these devices, and are thus more likely to abandon them and revert back to their original means of expressing their wants and needs. For those individuals who are intellectually handicapped, and those having experienced lengthy periods of institutionalization, aging is associated with an increasingly distorted understanding of the nature of communication and a lack of motivation to communicate.

Environmental Receptivity

In evaluating nonspeaking adults' candidacy for augmentative intervention, and then determining the particular system(s) to pursue with them, the effect such aids will have on their listeners' styles of interaction must be considered. Which listeners will be responsive to the aid and which will be resistant (e.g., by subsequently avoiding interacting with the client)? Given that listener instruction (e.g., learning a repertoire of signs or how to care for an electronic communication device) is necessary prior to effectively communicating with the nonspeaking individual, which listeners will be receptive to such instruction? Unless accepting responses await or can be easily established among their listeners, nonspeakers' enthusiasm toward using the best-conceived augmentative systems is quickly extinguished.

Enhancing Listener Responsiveness

Romski et al. (1984) discussed three types of conversational partners for nonspeakers: (1) those familiar with the individual as well as his/her communicative mode(s); (2) those familiar with the individual but not his/her means of communication; and (3) those unfamiliar with the client and his/her methods of communicating. We cannot assume that the mere fact that a client is well-liked will result in an ability to evoke similar feelings toward the way in which he/she communicates. To the contrary, a common rationale offered by familiar listeners to explain their resistance to augmenting a client's existing communication repertoire is their fear of its interfering with their already unencumbered means of interacting with him/her. Such comments should not be dismissed as representing laziness and/or selfishness on the part of these listeners. It should be impressed upon them that existing means of interacting with the client that have proven successful should continue to be reinforced. The augmentative system simply represents a potential means of avoiding and/or resolving situations that previously resulted in communication breakdowns and inefficient message transactions.

These same listeners (those familiar with the client but not his/her augmented means of communication) can serve a valuable role in teaching unfamiliar listeners to recognize and respond optimally to the adult's existing means of communicating. A *Communication Repertoire Summary* (see Appendix A) can be administered to a variety of listeners to identify and evaluate the effectiveness of modes of communication presently used by the nonspeaker and his/her respective listeners, along with the messages coded through each corresponding mode. The summary can also be used to promote consistency of responses across listeners.

SELECTING COMMUNICATION MODES

Competent communicators, irrespective of whether they are mentally retarded and nonspeaking, possess a variety of communication modes and the intuitive skills that enable them to determine which mode to use in a given conversational setting. Depending on the situation (e.g., our listener's status, language, cognitive abilities, and age; objects and events occurring at the time the message is sent; the verbal context), the competent communicator selects a combination of aided (e.g., designating pictures and objects) and unaided (e.g., speech, gestures, facial expressions for conveying message content. It would thus appear counterproductive to preface augmentative intervention by first identifying *the* mode by which a client is to be instructed to communicate. This contradicts the practice of evaluating a nonspeaking client's candidacy for unaided instruction (signing), then pursuing this track without considering aided modes (Owens & House, 1984; Shane & Bashir, 1980). These decision-making matrices depict aided forms of communication such as communication boards and computers as last-resort measures, which should not be taken until a client is determined to be a poor candidate for unaided instruction.

It should thus come as no surprise that surveys of augmentative system usage among children and adults who are mentally retarded consistently find that these nonspeakers rely primarily on signs and gestures (Fristoe & Lloyd, 1978; Matas et al., 1985). The findings of the Matas et al. survey are summarized in Table 11-1.

TABLE 11-1

Distribution of Augmentative Communication System Usage by Nonspeaking Persons with Mental Retardation (%).

	Signing	Gestures/Emotion	Language Boards	Electronic
Mildly/moderately mentally retarded	47.9	33.6	14.3	2.5
Severely/profoundly mentally retarded	47.4	32.0	20.1	0.0

Note: Data are from survey by Matas et al. (1985).

Despite the continuing popularity of unaided approaches with those who are mentally retarded, Clark (1984) predicted that aided systems will grow increasingly more popular for use with this population. According to Clark, graphic symbols facilitate nonspeaking individuals' abilities to become integrated within the community because of their intelligibility to naive listeners. Conversely, signs are not a generally understood mode of communication and may thus necessitate access to an interpreter to permit conversations with naive listeners. Furthermore, Romski et al. (1984) pointed out that graphic systems may be easier to learn than signs, requiring simple recognition of items depicted rather than the noncued type of recall associated with gestural or signing systems.

If we could only continue to remember *why* we decided to introduce augmentative instruction to a client to begin with, as such intervention then proceeds, we might then be able to avoid instructional strategies that promote single-mode transmission across all prospective listeners and situations at the expense of communication. Each time we reject a nonspeaker's clearly interpretable use of a gesture, and instead redirect him/her to a clinician-preferred mode of communication to convey the same meaning, we are discouraging communication. Communication is similarly discouraged by refusals to acknowledge or comply with communication-board-transmitted messages judged by a clinician to be of insufficient length and complexity (despite their clarity), and the ensuing tug-of-wars in which the nonspeaking adult is prodded to revise the form of the message only serve to discourage communication.

Rather than providing training in one mode of communication to the exclusion of all others, we might better serve the needs of these adults by exposing them to a variety of expressive modes. Reichle and Karlan (1985) indicated that nonspeaking adults may be more likely to successfully convey their communicative needs when they have access to mixed modes of production. They provide the example of a client being taught to use a communication board to convey the majority of his messages while signs are introduced as a means of encoding meanings that are difficult to depict graphically (e.g., "walk," "drink," "think").

NEEDS ASSESSMENT

The decision to augment an adult's existing communication repertoire can only be made after a systematic analysis of the client's present abilities to meet the communicative demands being imposed on him/her is completed. The client should be observed in a variety of settings, with a variety of familiar and unfamiliar listeners. The observer identifies those communicative skills that are essential for independent functioning in each respective setting (e.g., the types of requests, refusals, comments, informal exchanges). Next, the client's present and projected (with training incorporating existing modes of communication in his/her repertoire) capabilities to meet each of these demands is judged. Given that a sufficient discrepancy is noted between the client's communicative needs and capabilities offered by his/her existing communicative repertoire, the introduction of an augmentative means to meet these same needs should be considered.

INSTRUCTIONAL VARIABLES INFLUENCING LIKELIHOOD OF PROGRAM SUCCESS

As a practicing speech–language consultant, I have witnessed too many unsuccessful outcomes of "successful" augmentative intervention programs. Perhaps most upsetting, because they involve avoidable circumstances, are instances in which adults who are mentally retarded can demonstrate particular linguistic skills (signing or graphic vocabulary, forms, intents) in therapy, yet fail to use these behaviors spontaneously in other settings. Although many factors contribute to this outcome, some of the more common culprits I have encountered are discussed below.

Method of Instruction

It has become increasingly clear with the mentally retarded population that the way in which a skill is taught will greatly influence the way in which it is subsequently performed. Where signs, pictures, Blissymbols, sight words, and so forth are taught exclusively through a series of vocabulary drills in which targeted responses (particular signs or designations of particular graphic symbols) are evoked on cue, we should not expect to see the recipients of such instruction using these same symbols for purposes beyond rotely responding to their listeners requesting already known information. Several investigators have commented on the inabilities of children who are mentally retarded to generalize vocabulary use beyond those same functions taught (Glennen & Calculator, 1985; Reichle & Yoder, 1985). Children taught to label do not subsequently use these same symbols to request objects, comment, state, clarify, or request information. These findings suggest the need to provide adults with multiple opportunities to use their newly acquired communicative behaviors to convey a variety of communicative intents across a variety of listeners and situations as early in treatment as is practical.

Environmental Response

As Kraat (1985) pointed out, conversing with a nonspeaker who uses an aided system requires systematically violating many rules governing speaker-to-speaker interaction. If the aid is not equipped to produce output independently (e.g., through a speech synthesizer, printer or liquid crystal display), the listener may be expected to repeat each word as it is conveyed by the nonspeaker. This necessitates positioning oneself in close enough proximity to the nonspeaker to interpret his/her messages. The speaker must often assume a dominant role in the conversation, setting topics, phrasing questions and remarks in ways that will permit the nonspeaker to respond within the contraints (e.g., limited vocabulary) of the aid. Communication through these aids is generally slow, proceeding at rates of between 2 (for scanning aids) and 30 (for direct selection) words per minute. This is a drastic difference from the 175-to-220 words-per-minute rate associated with speech (Foulds, 1980; Vanderheiden, 1984). It once again becomes the listener's responsibility to initiate topics and set up client responses of limited length and content for conversation to flow smoothly.

As was discussed earlier, not all listeners are able or willing to make these types of adjustments when interacting with nonspeakers. This necessitates concurrent listener instruction as well as flexible mode usage on the part of the client.

Need for Listener Instruction

Calculator and D'Altilio-Luchko (1983) reported on the case of a 24-year-old nonspeaking woman (post head trauma) who resided in a nursing home and used a communication board to augment her limited vocal and gestural repertoire. Data were recorded to measure sequential changes in her communicative behavior as a factor of (1) modifying the content and organization of the board; (2) teaching her to functionally use her revised system (e.g., to comment, request information of others, complement staff, vary the form of her messages relative to the urgency of her messages and degree of imposition on her listeners, and clarify messages); and (3) listener instruction. This latter phase consisted of providing an experimental group of staff with an overview of augmentative communication, specific interaction strategies they could employ to facilitate interactions with the client, opportunities to role play with the board, and so forth.

Calculator and D'Altilio-Luchko (1983) then compared this group of listeners with those who did not receive instruction. Unlike their counterparts, instructed listeners were subsequently found to provide the client with more opportunities to communicate. They positioned themselves close enough to her to make board communication possible, particularly when asking open-ended questions. When out of her proximity, these listeners limited their messages to permit the client to resort to her vocal and gestural repertoire. Conversely, listeners who did not receive instruction continued to constrain the nature of her responses when in proximity while phrasing open-ended questions at a distance that precluded her ability to respond via the communication board, and thus inhibited her likelihood of responding at all.

Several other counterproductive patterns have been ascribed to uninformed listeners when engaged in discourse with nonspeaking individuals (Goosens & Kraat, 1985; Shane & Cohen, 1981):

- ☐ Talking around the nonspeaker, not expecting the latter to participate in the conversation
- ☐ Answering their own questions (i.e., talking for the nonspeaker)
- ☐ Using language which underestimates the nonspeaker's language competence
- ☐ Frequently interrupting the nonspeaker and abruptly changing topics.
- ☐ Anticipating communication needs and thus preempting the nonspeaker's need to communicate
- ☐ Faking comprehension
- ☐ Increasing their volume

Strategies for Listener Instruction

Vicker (1985) provided suggestions for group home staff regarding ways of recognizing and enhancing the communication skills of adults with mental retardation. According to Vicker, all persons possess methods of communicating, some more efficient and conventional than others. To successfully interact with such persons, it is thus imperative that staff be aware of their clients' present means of communication (which might include behaviors such as biting, turning away, rocking, etc.), and the meanings associated with these behaviors. Cirrin and Rowland (1985) cited the following eight nonverbal behaviors as enabling them to exhaustively describe the communicative attempts of 10 youths between the ages of 10 and 18 who were severely mentally retarded (1) signing, (2) pointing; (3) nodding (to affirm or negate); (4) extending or offering objects; (5) opening palm of extended hand as a receiving gesture; (6) physical contact such as touching and physically manipulating the listener; (7) pushing away or moving away from an object; and (8) idiosyncratic, consisting of nonconventional gestures such as hand clapping and table banging. Behaviors were determined intentional based on the direction of behavior (gaze and body orientation), listener proximity, joint focus (alternating gaze between listener and desired referent), substitution of means (upon being precluded from acquiring objects on their own), and the persistence of the behavior towards the listener.

This process of recognizing and interpreting communication behavior can be further enhanced by instruments such as the Communication Repertoire Summary (provided in Appendix A) as described earlier. A second observational tool that is particularly useful for assessing the communicative potential of aberrant behavior is presented by Donnellan, Mirenda, Mesaros, and Fassbender (1984), and is summarized by Owens and Rogerson in Chapter 8 of this volume.

In conclusion, it is apparent that *nonspeaking* individuals who are mentally retarded are, none the less, communicating individuals who frequently must rely on their listeners' interpretational skills to communicate effectively. This is not only the case for individuals relying exclusively on ambiguous gestural and vocal repertoires but also those using augmentative devices. I have previously used the term *prototypic interactant* (Calculator, 1984) to refer to listeners who are ideally attuned to the unique interactional behaviors of their presymbolic clients. Such listeners are particularly adept at interpreting their clients' behaviors while concurrently providing them with an ideal mix of verbal and nonverbal stimulation. As with clients operating at higher levels of intellectual and communicative ability, the behaviors of their listeners exert significant influences on these individuals' motivation, opportunities, and styles of communication.

Replacing One Idiosyncratic Mode With Another

Two primary reasons for introducing augmentative systems (aided and unaided) are to expand the range of unambiguous messages available to the client and to increase his/her pool of potential conversational partners. It is thus surprising to find graduates of such instruction who now communicate through signs and or graphic systems and yet are no more intelligible to listeners than they were prior to intervention. Each time a distorted form of a sign is introduced or accepted, or an indiscriminant point to a communication board is responded to in the instructional setting, a future opportunity for conversational breakdown is born. Clients using such systems often revert back to their original forms of communication, which were less effortful and no less ambiguous than these purportedly more sophisticated techniques.

Before modifying signs or pointing techniques, the anticipated effect such changes will have on message transmission must be examined. Field testing these changes on naive listeners before introducing them to the client can eliminate the need to teach and then later "un-teach" these behaviors. Bornstein and Jordan (1984) provided empirical data describing the intelligibility of 330 signs to highly sophisticated signers when one or a combination of features (i.e., handshape, location, movement) was distorted. Information was also presented regarding signs and meanings with which these distorted forms were frequently confused. Communication success can be maximized, by modifying clients' uses of aided and unaided systems so that they gain greater access to the system in use, while being certain such changes do not sacrifice the interpretability of their messages.

Mistaken Focus

When introducing augmentative communication instruction to adults, it is essential that communication take precedence over language. Interactions such as the following should be avoided:

INSTRUCTOR: How are you feeling today? [*Client has entered room and sat down*].

CLIENT: Good [*signing*]

INSTRUCTOR: No. Watch me. I am good today. [*Models expanded form of client's utterance*].

CLIENT: I good [*signed*]

INSTRUCTOR: Well, let's come back to that one again later!

Rather than accepting the client's initial response to her request, which although elliptic was an appropriate form in this context, the instructor shifted the focus of this exchange from a sincere information request to a laborious linguistic exercise. In addition to sanctioning the client for providing an appropriate response, the instructor has modeled an alternative reply that, under natural circumstances, would certainly call attention to her client. Imagine the following interaction with a client who has succumbed to her clinician's wishes for grammatic completeness.

LISTENER: Where are you going tonight?

ADULT: I am going to a movie [*conveyed on her communication board*]

LISTENER: How are you going to get there?

ADULT: I am going to get there by car [*conveyed on her board*]

LISTENER: Oh. Is Roger driving you over?

ADULT: Yes. Roger is driving me over [*Again conveyed on board*]

Mode Devaluation

As was indicated earlier, communicatively competent adults who are not mentally retarded possess broad repertoires of modes, any one or combination of which may be called on at a given time. Whereas a simple point or facial expression might be sufficient under certain circumstances, other circumstances might call for the use of accompanying gestures, words, and visual aids (e.g., books or diagrams). It would thus appear to be worthwhile to also encourage more flexible mode selection in adults who are mentally retarded, rather than sanctioning their contextually appropriate use of modes other than the particular one being taught, as in the following dialogue.

INSTRUCTOR. Okay, we're all done for today. Where would you like to go now?

ADULT. [*points towards window*].

INSTRUCTOR: No. Show me on your communication board.

ADULT. [*gestures a modified form of the sign "go"*].

INSTRUCTOR. Show me [*as she directs her client's attention to the communication board*].

ADULT. [*slouches in her chair, obviously upset*].

INSTRUCTOR. [*takes client's hand and directs it to the picture connoting "outside"*]. There. Outside. You want to go outside. Show me where you want to go.

A similar situation arises when a family member who contends she has no difficulty understanding her nonspeaking sister's speech is chastised for failing to require consistent use of her communication board at home. A more realistic expectation might be to reserve home use of the communication board to those situations in which conversational breakdowns occur and clarification is needed. At the same time, this adult should continue to be encouraged to rely on her aid as a primary means of communication with other less familiar listeners who are not as adept at interpreting her speech.

If we are to maximize the likelihood that our clients will be able to meet the changing communication demands imposed on them by listeners who differ with respect to their own mode preferences, we must incorporate instruction in code switching into our programs. Similarly, opportunities should be provided for these adults to hone their skills using their augmentative and pre-existing communicative skills with familiar and nonfamiliar adults.

Institutional/Environmental Constraints

Adults residing in residential settings may be confronted with several additional factors that may limit their successful uses of augmentative systems (Shane, Lipschultz, & Shane, 1982). The high rates of staff turnover characterizing these settings result in a constantly fluctuating level of familiarity with these adults and their methods of communication. In situations in which staff-to-client ratios are particularly poor, routines may have been established for the sake of efficiency, presenting little opportunity for residents to communicate choices, initiate communication, or manipulate listeners' behaviors toward them. Wants and needs may be systematically met on a pre-set schedule with no room for the spontaneity upon which augmentative sytems are contingent. Finally, adults residing in such settings may be limited with respect to the range of experiences and novel events transpiring from one day to the next, resulting in their frequently lacking any new information or experiences to share with others.

In addition to gearing intervention in such settings toward optimizing the quality of interaction between these adults and with staff, instruction should target anticipated communication needs in community settings. Many of the communicative behaviors and rules pertinent to institutional living have little correspondence to events outside this setting (Calculator, 1985).

The passive styles of interaction associated with nonspeaking persons with mental retardation are as pervasive beyond the walls of the institution as within. Institution-like routines and the preemptive styles of discourse associated with them are observed in community-based settings as well.

A growing body of evidence suggests that these individuals can be instructed to assume more active roles in interaction. Glennen and Calculator (1985) successfully taught two nonspeaking children to use vocabulary, previously restricted to serving a labeling function, to request objects. The investigators relied on a combination of expectant delays (Halle, 1982) and structured events (Hart & Risely, 1978; Hart & Rogers–Warren, 1978) to shape these skills. Similar successs was reported by Reichle and Yoder, 1985), who taught four preschoolers who were severely mentally retarded to label and then request objects through a combination of delay and prompting procedures. Similar research is warranted for the adult population.

A PARADIGM FOR FACILITATING FUNCTIONAL COMMUNICATION SKILLS

The preceding sections provided a lengthy discussion of client, listener, experiential, and environmental factors that are related to the successful implementation of augmentative intervention programs with adults who are mentally retarded. A systematic needs assessment can be performed to examine the relative impact each of these factors has on the adult's ability to meet present and projected communicative demands. This same assessment serves as a basis for determining a client's candidacy for augmentative instruction and the directions such instruction should take.

The outcomes of such intervention should be reflected in observable gains in *adaptive behavior,* defined by Grossman (1983) in terms of the effectiveness or degree to which individuals meet the standards of personal independence and social responsibility expected of them, considering their age and cultural group. A successful augmentative intervention program is one that enhances the client's vocational prospects, independence in the community, social functioning, and ability to comply with community standards.

Brown, Nietupski, and Hamre–Nietupski's (1976) *Criterion of Ultimate Functioning* provides a yardstick for evaluating whether particular program objectives are consistent with this broader theme of improved adaptive behavior. Objectives should target skills that are necessary for these individuals to function as productively and independently as possible in the various social, vocational, and residential settings in which they live. Applications of this ideology to the area of augmentative intervention might take the following forms:

1. Opportunities should be available for these adults to interact with persons who are nonhandicapped outside their immediate residences in a variety of social and vocational settings. Shane et al. (1982) observed that as the number of persons with disabilities residing in one setting increases, their likelihood of interacting with one another decreases proportionately. This suggests the need to incorporate peer instruction into all program efforts. For example, methods of depicting symbols on a communication board should not be based solely on the nonspeaking adult's capabilities. Instead, a single concept might be presented as a word (for interaction with intellectually normal listeners), while also providing a line drawing to facilitate interactions with nonreading conversational peers.

2. Instruction should encourage these individuals to use their aids spontaneously in response to natural antecedents. The work of Glennen and Calculator (1985) and Cirrin and Rowland (1985), discussed previously, incorporated clinical situations that simulated interactions their clients might be confronted with outside of therapy. Desired objects were placed out of reach or taken away, unfair situations were set up in which clients were deprived of materials already offered to peers, and so forth.

3. When possible, instruction should be carried out in those same settings in which clients will eventually be expected to use their aids. This will facilitate generalization while also providing opportunities to model appropriate interaction strategies for other listeners in these

respective settings. We can also be more assured that our program content is addressing realistic needs, and our targeted behaviors are situationally relevant.

4. A variety of instructional arrangements should be used to prepare clients to use their aids in a variety of speaking contexts. When limiting instruction to one-on-one teaching, adults are not confronted with situations in which they must secure the attention and maintain the interest of their listeners, repair conversational breakdowns, censor interruptions, and so forth. Bedrosian (Chapter 10 in this volume) provides a comprehensive curriculum for teaching discourse skills in group settings that, although intended for speaking adults, could easily be applied to nonspeakers.

5. Program content should address age-appropriate skills. Teaching a client to use her communication board to request that a waitress bring cream with her coffee would be more beneficial than teaching her to indicate "baby" in response to the instructor's holding up a doll and asking, "What's this? Show me on your board!"

6. Program failures should be attributed to inappropriate content (e.g., unmotivating, developmentally inappropriate, nonfunctional) and technique (nongeneralizable) and not to client ineptness. Hopefully the days of "could not test" and "does not benefit from instruction" will be replaced by instructional techniques that seek to maximize individuals' functional communication repertoires to the greatest extent possible given their own limitations and strengths, and those of their listeners.

7. If the focus of augmentative intervention is to improve clients' interaction skills across a variety of settings and listeners, it is essential to involve as many persons as possible in the program at every step in the process. We have accomplished little when a client's communicative effectiveness is reserved for a restricted set of listeners in a finite number of environments. Similarly, program gains must be measured in terms of actual changes in clients' interactional skills across listeners and settings.

FINAL COMMENTS

Future work in the area of augmentative communication intervention must continue to shift away from a fascination with the growing number and sophistication of system options available, to a critical appraisal of how such modes can be used to augment the existing communicative skills of adults with mental retardation. The introduction of these systems should arise from situations in which clients' communicative abilities are insufficient for meeting their present and projected communicative needs. Our goal is to arrive at the optimal system, representing a variety of listener and setting-dependent modes, rather than identifying clients who are candidates for prefabricated aids.

REFERENCES

Beukelman, D., & Yorkston, K. (1982). Communication interaction of adult communication augmentation system use. *Topics in Language Disorders, 2*, 39–53.

Beukelman, D., Yorkston, K., & Dowden, P. (1985). *Communication augmentation: A casebook of clinical management.* Austin, TX: PRO-ED.

Bornstein, H., & Jordan, I. (1984). *Functional signs.* Austin, TX: PRO-ED.

Brown, L., Nietupski, J., & Hamre–Nietupski, S. (1976). Criterion of ultimate functioning. In M. Thomas (Ed.), *Hey, don't forget about me! Education's investment in the severely, profoundly, and multiply handicapped* (pp. 2–17). Reston, VA: Division of Mental Retardation.

Calculator, S. (1984). Prelinguistic development. In W. Perkins (Ed.), *Language handicaps in children* (pp. 63–71). New York: Thieme–Stratton.

Calculator, S. (1985). Describing and treating discourse problems in mentally retarded children: The myth of mental retardese. In D. Ripich & F. Spinelli (Eds.), *School discourse problems* (pp. 125–147). San Diego, CA: College-Hill Press.

Calculator, S., & D'Altilio–Luchko, C. (1983). Evaluating the effectiveness of a communication board training program. *Journal of Speech and Hearing Disorders, 48,* 185–192.

Calculator, S., & Dollaghan, C. (1982). The use of communication boards in a residential setting. *Journal of Speech and Hearing Disorders, 14,* 281–287.

Carrier, J. (1976). Application of a nonspeech language system with the severely handicapped. In L. Lloyd (Ed.), *Communication assessment and intervention strategies* (pp. 523–547). Baltimore, MD: University Park Press.

Chapman, R., & Miller, J. (1980). Analyzing language and communication in the child. In R. Schiefelbusch (Ed.), *Nonspeech language and communication: Analysis and intervention* (pp. 159–196). Baltimore, MD: University Park Press.

Cirrin, F., & Rowland, C. (1985). Communication assessment of nonverbal youths with severe/profound mental retardion. *Mental Retardation, 23,* 52–62.

Clark, C. (1985). A close look at the Standard Rebus System and Blissymbolics. *The Journal of the Association for Persons with Severe Handicaps, 9,* 37–48.

Doherty, J. (1985). The effects of sign characteristics on sign acquisition and retention: An integrative review of the literature. *Augmentative and Alternative Communication, 1,* 108–121.

Donnellan, A., Miranda, P., Mesaros, R., & Fassbender, L. (1984). Analyzing the communicative functions of aberrant behavior. *The Journal of the Association for Persons with Severe Handicaps, 9,* 201–212.

Foulds, R. (1980). Communication rates for nonspeech expression as a function of manual tasks and linguistic constraints. In D. S. Childress & R. N. Scott (Eds.), *Proceedings of the International Conference on Rehabilitation Engineering* (pp. 83–87). Toronto, Canada: Rehabilitation Engineering Society of North America.

Fristoe, M., & Lloyd, L. (1978). A survey of the use of nonspeech systems with the severely communication impaired. *Mental Retardation, 4,* 99–103.

Ginsburg, H., & Opper, S. (1969). *Piaget's theory of intellectual development.* Englewood Cliffs, NJ: Prentice-Hall.

Glennen, S., & Calculator, S. (1985). Training functional communication board use: A pragmatic approach. *Augmentative and Alternative Communication, 1,* 134–142.

Goosens, C., & Kraat, A. (1985). Technology as a tool for conversation and language learning for the physically disabled. *Topics in Language Disorders, 6,* 56–70.

Grossman, H. (Ed.). (1983). *Classification in mental retardation.* Washington, DC: American Association on Mental Deficiency.

Halle, J. (1982). Teaching functional language to the handicapped: An integrative model of natural environment teaching techniques. *Journal of the Association for the Severely Handicapped, 7,* 29–37.

Hardy, J. (1983). *Cerebral palsy.* Englewood Cliffs, NJ: Prentice-Hall.

Harris, D. (1982). Communication interaction processes involving nonvocal physically handicapped children. *Topics in Language Disorders, 2,* 21–37.

Hart, B., & Risley, T. (1979). Promoting productive language through incidental teaching. *Education and Urban Society, 10,* 407–429.

Hart, B., & Rogers-Warren, A. (1978). A milieu approach to teaching language. In R. Schiefelbusch (Ed.), *Language intervention strategies.* Baltimore, MD: University Park Press.

Kamhi, A., & Johnston, J. (1982). Towards an understanding of retarded childrens' linguistic deficiencies. *Journal of Speech and Hearing Research, 25,* 435–445.

Karlan, G., & Lloyd, L. (1983). Considerations in the planning of communication intervention: Selecting a lexicon. *The Journal of the Association for the Severely Handicapped, 8,* 13–25.

Kraat, A. (1985). *Communication interaction between aided and natural speakers: A state of the art report.* Toronto, Canada: Canadian Rehabilitation Council for the Disabled.

Light, J., Collier, B., & Parnes, P. (1985). Communication interaction between young nonspeaking physically disabled children and their primary caregivers: Part 1 — Discourse patterns. *Augmentative and Alternative Communication, 1,* 74–83.

Luftig, R. (1984). An analysis of initial sign lexicons as a function of eight learnability variables. *The Journal of the Association for Persons with Severe Handicaps, 9,* 193–200.

Matas, J., Mathy-Laiko, P., Beukelman, D., & Legresley, K. (1985). Identifying the nonspeaking population: A demographic study. *Augmentative and Alternative Communication, 1,* 17–31.

Mayberry, R. (1976). If a chimp can learn sign language surely my nonverbal client can too. *Asha, 18,* 223–228.

Musselwhite, C., & St. Louis, K. (1982). *Communication programming for the severely handicapped: Vocal and nonvocal strategies.* Austin, TX: PRO-ED.

Owens, R., & House, L. (1984). Decision-making processes in augmentative communication. *Journal of Speech and Hearing Disorders, 49,* 16–25.

Reichle, J., & Karlan, G. (1985). The selection of an augmentative system in communication intervention: A critique of decision rules. *The Journal of the Association for Persons With Severe Handicaps, 10,* 146–156.

Reichle, J., & Yoder, D. (1985). Communication board use in severely handicapped learners. *Language, Speech and Hearing Services in the Schools, 16,* 146–157.

Romski, M., Sevcik, R., & Joyner, S. (1984). Nonspeech communication systems: Implications for language intervention with mentally retarded children. *Topics in Language Disorders, 5,* 66–81.

Shane, H., & Bashir, A. (1980). Election criteria for the adoption of an augmentative communication system: Preliminary considerations. *Journal of Speech and Hearing Disorders, 45,* 408–414.

Shane, H., Lipschultz, R., & Shane, C. (1982). Facilitating the communicative interaction of nonspeaking persons in large residential settings. *Topics in Language Disorders, 2,* 73–84.

Silverman, F. (1980). *Communication for the speechless.* Englewood Cliffs, NJ: Prentice–Hall.

Vanderheiden, G. (1964). Technology needs of individuals with communication impairments. *Seminars in Speech and Language, 5,* 59–67.

Vicker, B. (1985). *Recognizing and enhancing the communication skills of your group home clients.* Bloomington, IN: Indiana University Developmental Training Center.

Yoder, D., & Calculator, S. (1981). Some perspectives on intervention strategies for persons with developmental disorders. *Journal of Autism and Developmental Disorders, 11,* 107–123.

Yorkston, K., & Dowden, P. (1984). Nonspeech language and communication systems. In A. Holland (Ed.), *Language disorders in adults* (pp. 283–312). Austin, TX: PRO-ED.

☐ *Communication Repertoire Summary*

IDENTIFYING INFORMATION

Name of Client: ____

Date: ___________

Informant/Relationship: ____

How long have you known the client: ______________________________

How well do you know the client? ________________________________

How long have you worked with clients who are developmentally disabled? ____

NATURE OF INTERACTIONS

Three locations and/or settings (e.g., mealtime, bathing, sensory stimulation, pool, cooking, canteen, hygiene) in which you and the client are often in proximity with one another and thus are able to interact with one another:

1. ____

2. ____

3. ____

Client's most effective means of communicating with you (Cite those modes and submodes — listed later in this Summary — that the client uses when communicating with you and that appear to work most effectively for the client in conveying his/her messages cleary and quickly *to you.*

Your most effective means of communicating with the client. (Cite modes and submodes of communication that *you* use, alone or in combination, with this client and find to be most effective when interacting with him/her. Also comment on other aspects of your style of interacting with this client that have proven to be particularly helpful to *you* in interactions with this client.

Estimated intelligibility of messages across all settings (i.e., please circle the statement that most accurately describes how understandable this client is *to you* each time he/she conveys messages in his/her various ways).

1. Almost always understand this client

2. I can usually understand this client as long as I have a general idea of what has been going on at the time of the message (contextual cues).

3. I can occasionally understand this client, but frequently I find myself guessing at his/her meaning.

4. I rarely know what this client is trying to communicate to me.

5. I never know what this client is communicating, nor do I know when he/she is communicating at all.

CLIENT'S COMMUNICATIVE MODE(S)

(Corresponding rates of success and percentages of use.)
Assign *percentages* to each of the following modes and submodes so that the total use of submodes (e.g., conventional signs and adapted signs) across all of the modes (i.e., signs, gestures, aided communication, and vocal/verbal) totals 100 percent.

Signs

Overall intelligibility (refer to ratings described earlier): _________

Usage:	Setting 1	Setting 2	Setting 3
Conventional signs	_________	_________	_________

(Cite name of formal system, if known)

Adapted signs	_________	_________	_________

(Cite name of system, if known)

Total Sign Use:___________%

Gestures

Overall intelligibility (refer to earlier described ratings): _________

Usage:	Setting 1	Setting 2	Setting 3
Natural gestures	_________	_________	_________
Amerind	_________	_________	_________
(American Indian Sign Language)			
Pantomime	_________	_________	_________
Idiosyncratic	_________	_________	_________
Other	_________	_________	_________

(If other, please describe):_______________________________

Total Gesture Use:___________%

Aided Communication

Overall intelligibility (refer to earlier described ratings): _____________

Name of device(s): ____

Type of symbols: ____

> (Indicate source/reference of symbols, if commercially available).

Means of indicating: ______________________________________

> (Method: direct select, scan, encode; and how this action is
>   performed)
> (If using a switch, describe/name it, and cite how it can be obtained
if commercially produced).

Type of outputs: ____

> (e.g. speech synthesis and graphic)

Usage:	Setting 1	Setting 2	Setting 3
	_____________	_____________	_____________

Total Aided Use:_____________%

Vocal/Verbal

Overall intelligibility (refer to earlier ratings): __________________

Usage:	Setting 1	Setting 2	Setting 3
	_____________	_____________	_____________

Total Vocal/Verbal Use:_____________%

Totals by setting:	_____________	_____________	_____________
	100%	100%	100%

Extraneous Behavior

(Please describe behaviors that this client often engages in that do not
appear to you to serve any function, for example, they may be self-
stimulatory in nature: ___________________________________

____

____

Client's Communication with You

Setting 1 (Location, time of day, activity, etc.): _______________

What Was Said (meanings)   *Functions*

(List messages)   (Refer to codes at end of Summary)

(Attach additional pages if necessary)

Setting 2 (Location, time of day, activity, etc.) _______________

What was said? (meanings)   *Functions*

(Attach additional pages if necessary)

Setting 3 (Location, time of day, activity, etc.): _______________

What was said? (Meanings)   *Functions*

(Attach additional pages if necessary)

Codes for Communication Functions

Respond/acknowledge (**R**)   Greet (**G**)
Give information (**I**)   State (**S**)
Request information (**RI**)   Express emotions/feelings (**E**)
Attention seeking (**AS**)   Name/label (**N**)
Request object (**RO**)   Reject (**RJ**)
Request action (**RA**)   Attention directing (**AD**)
Request clarification (**RC**)   Commenting (**C**)

Part V

Summary

CHAPTER 12

Some Conclusions About Programming for Adults With Mental Retardation

STEPHEN N. CALCULATOR
JAN L. BEDROSIAN

*T*he contents of this book demonstrate a significant change from traditional views of the communication needs of adults with mental retardation. Although the contributing authors represent different disciplines, several issues relevant to communication assessment and intervention recur throughout the book. A summary of these issues is presented here, followed by a discussion of future directions in communication programming and research related to adults with mental retardation.

ASSESSMENT

Communication assessment for adults with mental retardation has traditionally involved the administration of child-normed standardized tests (Calculator, Chapter 4). The results from such tests are based on comparisons made between the adults' performance and that of children functioning at similar levels of language and cognitive development. Unfortunately, there has been a misapplication of this normative data, giving us a false license to treat these adults as children. We frequently find ourselves occupying the role of caregivers, providing nurturance for our charges. Likewise, this misapplication has resulted in the continued isolation of these individuals (despite deinstitutionalization efforts) from the rest of the adult population through "special" educational, vocational, and residential placements (Antonak, Chapter 1). If we continue to isolate adults who are mentally retarded and view them as youths, we offer them little opportunity or incentive to take their place among other adults in society. Instead, we promote their continued economic, social, and physical overdependence on others.

The alternative approach to communication assessment for adults who are mentally retarded offered in this book involves an informal examination of their communicative performance in a variety of natural contexts (Halle, Chapter 7). Rather than comparing these adults' communicative performance with that of normal language-learning children, each adult is viewed in terms of his/her own unique communication profile. Questions raised from the assessment revolve around the communication strengths and weaknesses exhibited by adults with mental retardation (Bedrosian, Chapter 10; Calculator, Chapter 11), as well as around the social validity or acceptance of these adults' communicative performance (Haney, Wilson, & Halle, Chapter 3; Reichle, Piche–Cragoe, Sigafoos, & Doss, Chapter 9). Several authors provide protocols and procedures appropriate for assessing the communicative performance of adults with mental retardation in a variety of settings with different listeners (Bedrosian, Chapter 10; Calculator, Chapter 11; Morse, Chapter 5; Owens & Rogerson, Chapter 8; Reichle et al., Chapter 9). No longer can we limit our assessment to the clinical setting.

If one still chooses to administer a standardized communication-cognitive test to an adult who is mentally retarded, care must be taken to ensure valid measures of the adult's performance. Morse, in Chapter 5, discussed methods of modifying testing procedures to delineate not only the learning problems of these individuals, but also their learning strengths and preferences. Results obtained from such test modifications could have an effect on subsequent instruction in that the strengths and preferences identified could be highlighted to promote ultimate communication functioning in various normalized work and residential environments.

INTERVENTION

Communication intervention for adults with mental retardation has traditionally focused on their form of language, without considering their use of language (Falvey, Bishop, Grenot–Scheyer, & Coots, Chapter 2). For example, programming efforts may have been directed toward teaching the correct label and articulation of "hamburger" in response to a picture card in the clinical setting, rather than toward teaching the communication skills necessary for ordering a hamburger in a restaurant. In addition, programming efforts have not always been age appropriate for the adult (Brown, Shiraga, Rogan, York, Zanella Albright McCarthy, Loomis, & Van Deventer, Chapter 6) perhaps stemming again from the misapplication of normative data. As a result, traditional intervention programs have continued to promote the isolation and dependence of these adults. Certainly, the ability to communicate effectively with a variety of listeners in different settings has an impact on the degree of participation and independent functioning attainable in society.

Throughout this book the authors have attempted to lay a foundation for future discussions of what constitute best communication-related practices when working with adults who are mentally retarded. Discrepancies do arise as to the applicability of a developmental model in determining program content and in sequencing instructional objectives for these individuals. Contrast, for example, the recommendations made by Owens and Rogerson (Chapter 8) with those of Brown et al. (Chapter 6), particularly with respect to the justification for teaching cognitive and communicative prerequisites, prior to or concurrent with communication instruction. There is, however, a general consensus of opinion that *all* programs efforts should be directed toward maximizing these adults' opportunities and abilities to participate in normalized settings. For example, Owens and Rogerson's discussions of cognitive training (in the areas of casuality, imitation, and object permanence) stress the integration of such skills into everyday interactions in the natural environment.

Intervention designed to (1) facilitate the onset of less ambiguous methods of communication (Owens & Rogerson, Chapter 8), (2) promote spontaneous uses of communication (Halle, Chapter 7), and (3) expand the range of meanings, modes, and functions of communication attempts (Reichle et al., Chapter 9) must be accompanied by efforts concentrating on the provision of environments that will value and continue to foster the development and use of communication by adults with mental retardation. This requires that all program efforts consider the current and projected milieus in which these adults participate, with intervention targeting those skills that will be immediately useful in enhancing their likelihood of functioning more independently in these settings (Brown et al., Chapter 6; Calculator, Chapter 11; and Falvey et al., Chapter 2).

As Bedrosian (Chapter 10) pointed out, it is also essential that the scope of programming go beyond the individual and promote discourse skills that will enhance the abilities of these individuals to participate in a variety of conversational settings with different listeners. Owens and Rogerson (Chapter 8) shared this perspective — discussing the use of a consultative model in assuring that the introduction of communication skills take place in those same settings and with those same listeners — that the skills themselves are projected to be useful.

FUTURE DIRECTIONS IN PROGRAMMING AND RESEARCH

Several nontraditional approaches to assessing and facilitating the communicative performance of adults with mental retardation have been presented in this book. However, despite the progress we have made, many questions remain unanswered. There is a continued need for documented successes in applying more innovative and realistic service delivery models with this population. Additional data are warranted in the following areas:

1. What factors (e.g., social, cognitive, emotional, physical) can be used to most accurately predict the extent to which adults with mental retardation may benefit from communication instruction; their ultimate levels of communication behavior; and levels beyond which little further progress can be expected to occur? The latter might serve as an objective set of criteria on which to base program termination.
2. What are optimal and appropriate targets for communication instruction for adults displaying different levels of functioning (e.g., communicative, cognitive, social)? How are such objectives conditioned by considerations of the settings and respective listeners with which these adults interact?
3. To what extent should communication instruction target adults with mental retardation relative to current and projected listeners in their various environments? This includes considerations of the role of multimodal (e.g., signs, vocal, verbal, graphic) instruction.
4. What are the communicative needs of elderly adults with mental retardation? How would normalization principles be applied in meeting the unique needs of these adults within their respective living environments?
5. What are the implications for language learning by children receiving input from parents who are mentally retarded? Preliminary findings indicate that the children of mothers who are mentally retarded are "at-risk for developmental delay, particularly in language" (Feldman, Case, Towns, & Betel, 1985, p. 253). Whether we morally agree or disagree with marriage and childbearing among those who are mentally retarded, methods of incorporating communication instruction within the family unit must be addressed.

CONCLUSION

In summary, it is the authors' hope that this book will provide increased impetus to clinicians and other investigators who are ready to pick up the challenge of designing and applying appropriate communication assessment and intervention strategies for adults who are mentally retarded. Such efforts must cross ideologic boundaries (e.g., the ongoing civil war between advocates of developmental versus remedial logic). They must also transcend professional boundaries (i.e., turf constraints). Given that we accept the position that communication instruction for these adults must address functional community-based needs, the role of the speech–language clininian as the sole, or primary, purveyor of communication instruction must be reassessed.

Finally, if these adults are to assume their places in society, it is essential that they be expected to function as adults and not as children. Future clinical and rescarch endeavors, both formal and informal, must consistently reinforce this notion. The communication skills that are taught and addressed must be those valued in adults, not children.

REFERENCES

Feldman, M. A., Case, L., Towns, F., & Betel, J. (1985). Parent education project I: Development and nuturance of children of mentally retarded parents. *American Journal of Mental Deficiency, 90,* 253–258.

Author

Subject

Italic page numbers refer to tables and figures.

Notes

Notes

<u>Notes</u>

<u>Notes</u>

Notes

Notes

Notes

Notes

Notes

Notes